The iPhone Manual – Tips and Hacks

A complete user guide to getting the best out of your iPhone and iOS 14

Wallace Wang

Packt
BIRMINGHAM—MUMBAI

The iPhone Manual – Tips and Hacks

Commissioning Editor: Pavan Ramchandani
Acquisition Editor: Srikanth Varanasi
Senior Editor: Keagan Carneiro
Content Development Editor: Divya Vijayan
Technical Editor: Deepesh Patel
Copy Editor: Safis Editing
Project Coordinator: Kinjal Bari
Proofreader: Safis Editing
Indexer: Rekha Nair
Production Designer: Shankar Kalbhor

First published: November 2020

Production reference: 2061120

Published by Packt Publishing Ltd.
Livery Place
35 Livery Street
Birmingham
B3 2PB, UK.

ISBN 978-1-83864-101-6

www.packt.com

This book is dedicated to anyone who ever bought and used a piece of technology that promised to make their life better but found it only made their life more confusing and complicated. The problem is that technology is often created by tech-savvy people for other tech-savvy people. If you find technology intriguing but intimidating, you'll find that the iPhone may be the perfect smartphone for you. This book is dedicated to those willing to get out of their comfort zone and take a chance to learn something new.

Packt.com

Subscribe to our online digital library for full access to over 7,000 books and videos, as well as industry leading tools to help you plan your personal development and advance your career. For more information, please visit our website.

Why subscribe?

- Spend less time learning and more time coding with practical eBooks and Videos from over 4,000 industry professionals
- Improve your learning with Skill Plans built especially for you
- Get a free eBook or video every month
- Fully searchable for easy access to vital information
- Copy and paste, print, and bookmark content

Did you know that Packt offers eBook versions of every book published, with PDF and ePub files available? You can upgrade to the eBook version at packt.com and as a print book customer, you are entitled to a discount on the eBook copy. Get in touch with us at customercare@packtpub.com for more details.

At www.packt.com, you can also read a collection of free technical articles, sign up for a range of free newsletters, and receive exclusive discounts and offers on Packt books and eBooks.

Contributors

About the author

Wallace Wang has written dozens of computer books over the years, including *Microsoft Office for Dummies* and *Beginning Programming for Dummies*, along with Macintosh and iPhone books such as *macOS Programming for Absolute Beginners*, *Beginning iPhone Development with Swift 5*, *Pro iPhone Development with Swift 5*, and *Beginning ARKit for iPhone and iPad.*

When he's not helping people discover the fascinating world of programming, he performs stand-up comedy and appears on two radio shows on KNSJ in San Diego, called Notes From the Underground and Laugh In Your Face Radio.

In his free time, Wallace also writes a screenwriting blog called The 15 Minute Movie Method and a blog about the latest cat news on the internet called Cat Daily News.

About the reviewer

Rudra S Misra is an Apple Certified Trainer and, since 2009, Rudra has been working on the Apple ecosystem. He conducts training on various aspects of macOS and iOS, such as management, troubleshooting, deployment, and app development for his wide range of clients, from corporates, Apple India channel partners, and Apple solution providers, to educators and individuals. Rudra is actively involved in app development, content creation, R&D with new technology, technical blogging, and technology awareness programs.

Packt is searching for authors like you

If you're interested in becoming an author for Packt, please visit `authors.packtpub.com` and apply today. We have worked with thousands of developers and tech professionals, just like you, to help them share their insight with the global tech community. You can make a general application, apply for a specific hot topic that we are recruiting an author for, or submit your own idea.

Acknowledgements

First, this book would never have been created with out all the hard-working people at Packt who helped put it together: Divij Kotian, Keagan Carneiro, and Divya Vijayan.

I would also like to thank the many people who had nothing to do with this book but still played an influential role in my life in some form or another:

Dane Henderson, Kristen Yoder, and Jody Taylor, who help me co-host a radio show on KNSJ.org called "Notes From the Underground."

Chris (the Zooman) Clobber and Sarah Burford, who help me co-host another radio show on KNSJ.org called "Laugh In Your Face Radio."

Leo (the man, the myth, the legend) Fontaine, Freddie King, and Terry Sanchez at Twin Dragons.

Thanks go to Michael Montijo, who spend nearly two decades pitching his animated TV series to different networks before finally finding success. During much of that time, he'd drive from Phoenix to Los Angeles (five hours one-way) to talk to network executives. If you want to achieve success, a large part is simply commitment, dedication, and lots of hard work.

Final thanks go to Cassandra (my wife) and Jordan (my son). More thanks go to Oscar and Mayer (our cats) for providing my life with lots of interesting tasks that usually involve some form of biological fluid splattering on the floor after being ejected from one end of the cat or the other.

Table of Contents

4

Making Phone Calls

5

Sending Text Messages

6

Using Siri

7

Taking and Sharing Pictures

8

Listening to Music

9

Browsing the Internet with Safari

10

Sending and Receiving Email

11

Using FaceTime

12

Reading eBooks

13

Storing Contact Information

14

Setting Appointments and Reminders

15

Writing Notes and Recording Voice Memos

Preface

When Apple introduced the iPhone in 2007, it redefined the smartphone market. Over a decade later, the iPhone continues advancing smartphone technology with innovations such as biometrics (fingerprint and facial recognition), contactless payment (Apple Pay), voice recognition (Siri), and touchscreen interfaces.

With so many features packed into an iPhone, many people simply use what features they can learn on their own and often overlook additional features that they might find useful if they knew they even existed.

That's the purpose of this book, to explain different features of the iPhone that many people may not be aware of and teach people how and why to use these features to make their iPhone an even more indispensable tool than ever before.

Who this book is for

This book is for anyone who has an iPhone and would like to know more about how to take advantage of its various features. If you're a beginner, intermediate user, or even someone already familiar with using an iPhone, this book can work as a tutorial or a reference to help you get the most out of your iPhone in the shortest amount of time.

What this book covers

Chapter 1, *Learning Basic Touch Gestures*, explains the common touch gestures needed to control the iPhone.

Chapter 2, *Using the New iOS 14 Apps*, describes how to use the latest features in iOS 14.

Chapter 3, *Customizing Sound, Look, and Privacy Settings*, shows how to customize your iPhone so it works exactly the way you want.

Chapter 4, *Making Phone Calls*, explains all the different ways to make and receive phone calls.

Chapter 5, *Sending Text* **Messages**, explains how to send and receive text messages.

Chapter 6, Using Siri, shows how to use Siri in different ways to perform common tasks.

Chapter 7, Taking and Sharing Pictures, explains how to capture video and still images.

Chapter 8, Listening to Music, shows how to store and play audio files.

Chapter 9, Browsing the Internet with Safari, shows how to navigate around web pages using the built-in Safari browser.

Chapter 10, Sending and Receiving Email, shows how to connect to an email account to send and receive messages.

Chapter 11, Using FaceTime, shows how to make video phone calls using FaceTime.

Chapter 12, Reading eBooks, shows how to get eBooks and audiobooks and read different types of eBooks.

Chapter 13, Storing Contact Information, shows how to store, retrieve, and edit the names of important people.

Chapter 14, Storing Appointments and Reminders, explains how to keep track of your appointments and use reminders to help you remember them.

Chapter 15, Writing Notes and Recording Voice Memos, explains how to store ideas as text or audio recordings.

Chapter 16, Getting Directions with Maps, shows how to use the Maps app to find nearby areas along with directions for how to get there.

Chapter 17, Getting Time, Weather, and Stock Information, shows how to use the Clock app to set timers or get time and weather information from different parts of the world. It also explains how to track stocks.

Chapter 18, Using Apple Pay, explains how to set up Apple Pay and send cash electronically to others with an iPhone.

To get the most out of this book

This book is geared toward novices and experienced iPhone users who own a recent iPhone and want to know more about its various features so that they can use them as quickly as possible. After reading this book, readers will have a better idea of what their iPhone can do and which features they might want to start using. More importantly, readers will also learn how to customize their iPhone to make it work exactly the way they prefer.

Download the color images

We also provide a PDF file that has color images of the screenshots/diagrams used in this book. You can download it here: `https://static.packt-cdn.com/downloads/9781838641016_ColorImages.pdf`.

Get in touch

Feedback from our readers is always welcome.

General feedback: If you have questions about any aspect of this book, mention the book title in the subject of your message and email us at `customercare@packtpub.com`.

Errata: Although we have taken every care to ensure the accuracy of our content, mistakes do happen. If you have found a mistake in this book, we would be grateful if you would report this to us. Please visit `www.packtpub.com/support/errata`, selecting your book, clicking on the Errata Submission Form link, and entering the details.

Piracy: If you come across any illegal copies of our works in any form on the Internet, we would be grateful if you would provide us with the location address or website name. Please contact us at `copyright@packt.com` with a link to the material.

If you are interested in becoming an author: If there is a topic that you have expertise in and you are interested in either writing or contributing to a book, please visit `authors.packtpub.com`.

Reviews

Please leave a review. Once you have read and used this book, why not leave a review on the site that you purchased it from? Potential readers can then see and use your unbiased opinion to make purchase decisions, we at Packt can understand what you think about our products, and our authors can see your feedback on their book. Thank you!

For more information about Packt, please visit `packt.com`.

1
Learning Basic Touch Gestures

Before Apple introduced the iPhone in 2007, mobile phones often sported confusing keyboards that flipped open and required you to press multiple keys just to type a single character. Not surprisingly, these early mobile phones were often confusing and clumsy to use.

When Apple introduced the iPhone, they introduced an entirely new way to interact with a mobile phone. Instead of forcing users to type on cramped physical keyboards and squint at information crammed into tiny screens with poor resolution, the iPhone displayed nothing but a blank screen.

This blank screen doubled as both a viewing screen and a virtual interface. Instead of sporting physical buttons, the iPhone could display virtual buttons that could adapt to whether the user wanted to type a text message, an email, or a website address. By adapting to the user, the iPhone screen proved far more versatile than previous mobile phones.

The key to controlling an iPhone lay in its touchscreen, which could interpret touch gestures to perform different commands. Although today's iPhone is vastly different from the first iPhones of 2007, the touchscreen interface remains largely the same. To get the most out of your iPhone, you must learn not only what touch gestures are available, but when and how to use them.

In this chapter, we will cover the uses of these gestures in the following sections:

- Using tap gestures
- Using swipe gestures
- Using long-press gestures
- Using drag gestures
- Using pinch gestures
- Using rotation gestures

Using tap gestures

If you've ever pointed at something in a book or magazine, you've used a tap gesture. Tap gestures consist of pointing at – that is, tapping – something on the iPhone screen, such as an icon or a hyperlink. After tapping the screen briefly with one finger to select that item, you then lift your finger off the screen.

Think of tap gestures as similar to pointing and clicking with a mouse on a traditional PC.

Tap gestures let you tell your iPhone, "See what I'm pointing at? That's what I want." Since tap gestures select items, they represent a common yet simple touch gesture you'll use all the time.

Tap gestures are commonly used to choose commands or select items represented by the following onscreen elements:

- Icons
- Buttons
- Text
- Pictures

Tapping an icon or button to choose a command immediately causes something to happen, giving you visual feedback that you tapped on an item. For example, tapping an app icon from the Home screen loads that app, while tapping a button might dismiss a dialog or open up a different screen, as shown in *Figure 1.1*:

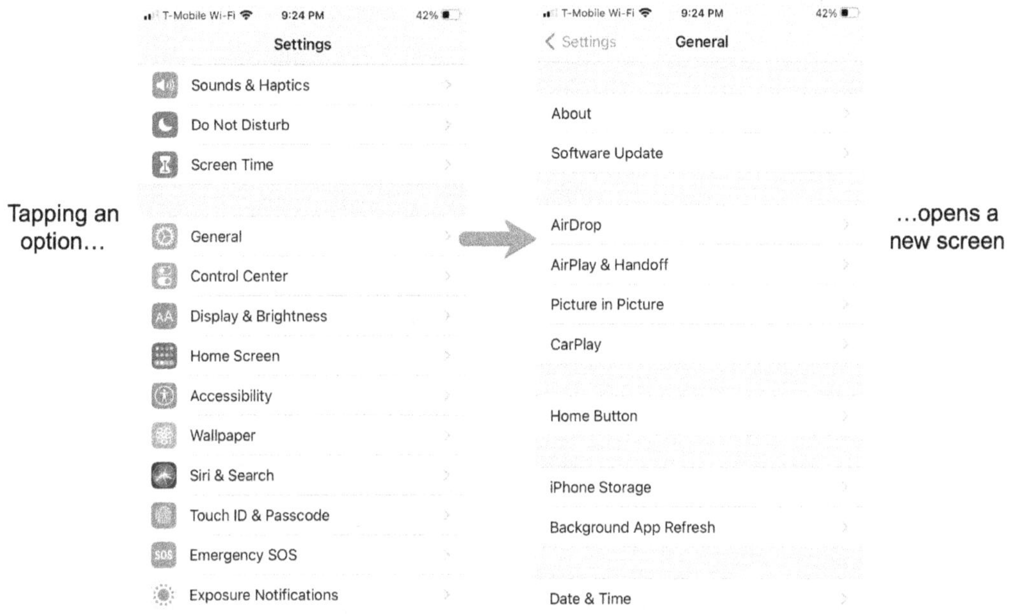

Figure 1.1 – Tapping a button loads another screen

Besides causing an action to occur, the tap gesture can also select items displayed in a list. The Mail and **Messages** apps display a list of email and text messages, respectively. When you want to read a specific message, you scroll through a list of messages and tap on the one you want to view its entire contents.

When you want to move, send, or delete items such as pictures, messages, or files, you need to select one or more items by tapping on them. Tapping typically highlights the selected items in some way, such as displaying a check mark, as shown in *Figure 1.2*. After selecting one or more items, you can then choose a command to move, send, or delete those selected items:

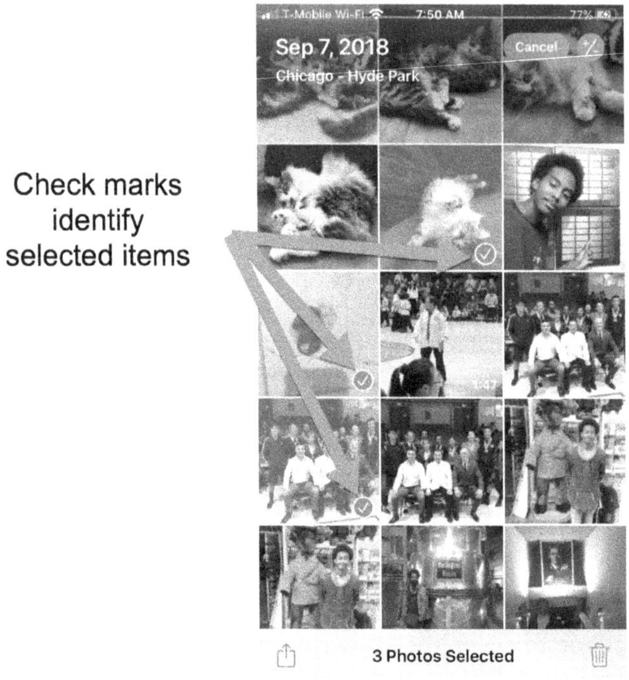

Figure 1.2 – Tapping on pictures selects those items

Since the tap gesture acts as a pointing tool, you can also use the tap gesture to move the cursor when editing text. On a traditional computer, you can move the cursor using a mouse or the cursor keys, but on the touchscreen of an iPhone, you must move the cursor by tapping where you want to place it.

Using swipe gestures

Think of reading a book or magazine. When you're done reading a page, you can put your finger on the far edge of the page and swipe to the left or right to turn to the next (or previous) page. That swiping gesture works exactly the same way on the iPhone.

Swipe gestures are similar to scrolling to view more information on a traditional PC. Such gestures involve placing one fingertip on the edge of the screen, and then sliding your finger in an up, down, left, or right direction, as shown in *Figure 1.3*:

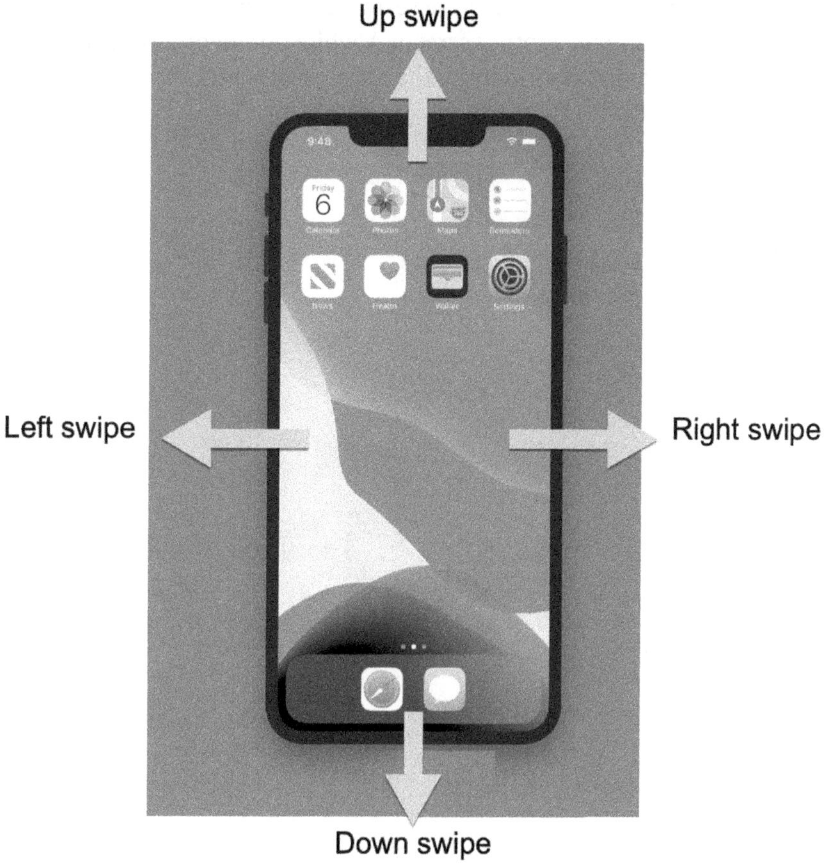

Figure 1.3 – The four directions for a swipe gesture

Swipe gestures are one of the most common gestures used on the iPhone. Whenever you want to see additional options or switch to another screen, try swiping in all four directions. If an app does not support a swipe gesture, you can't damage anything by swiping, since nothing will happen.

Using left- and right-swipe gestures to navigate screens

One common use for swipe gestures is to navigate from one screen to another, just like turning pages in a book. The left- and right-swipe gestures are often used to navigate between multiple screens within a single app.

To show there are multiple screens available, a series of dots appears at the bottom of the screen where each dot represents another screen. A white dot identifies the currently displayed screen while dimmed dots identify the number of screens available if you swipe left or right, as shown in *Figure 1.4*:

Figure 1.4 – Dots identify the number of hidden screens to the left and right

In *Figure 1.4*, there's only one dimmed dot to the right of the white dot, and three dimmed dots to the left. This means there's only one more screen to view if you swipe left, but three available screens to view if you swipe right. Dots identify both how many screens are available to view and how many are hidden to the left and right of the currently displayed screen.

The most common place that these dots can be seen is on the Home screen, but they also appear in other apps that need to display multiple views of nearly identical information, such as the Weather app (see *Figure 1.4*). To get familiar with the left- and right-swipe gestures, follow these steps:

1. Turn on your iPhone.
2. The Home screen should appear. The more apps installed on your iPhone, the more screens the Home screen needs to display them all.

3. Look for the dots at the bottom of the screen to identify how many screens are available.
4. Swipe left.

   Notice that, each time, the Home screen displays a different screen filled with app icons. The last screen will be the App Library screen that organizes apps into common categories, such as **Social** and **Utilities**, as shown in *Figure 1.5*:

Figure 1.5 – The App Library screen appears when you keep swiping left

5. Swipe right.

   Notice that, each time, the Home screen displays the previous screen. When you swipe right on the main Home screen, the iPhone displays a Screen text field along with widgets that display information from different apps such as showing news, weather, stock quotes, or appointments you've scheduled, as shown in *Figure 1.6*. This screen is called the **Today View** and is meant to display a list of useful information you might need that day:

Figure 1.6 – The Today View lists a search text field and widgets

Later in this book, you'll learn how to customize both the Today View and the App Library.

Using left-swipe gestures to delete items in a list

Many apps display information in rows, such as the Mail app, which displays messages, or the Notes app, which displays the names of different notes in a list. Deleting items usually takes two steps:

1. Tap the **Edit** button.
2. Tap the item you want to delete.

As a shortcut, you can also swipe left on list items to display options such as deleting that chosen item:

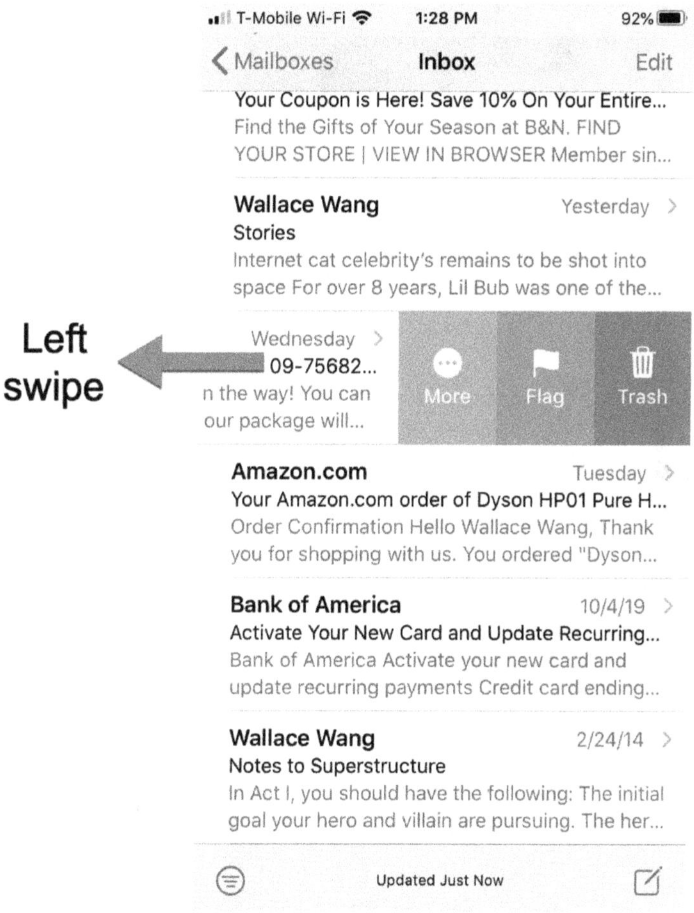

Figure 1.7 – Swiping left displays a list of options for an item in a list

Depending on the app, that list of options may include a Delete, Remove, or Trash option. Other times, you may see several additional options, as shown in *Figure 1.7*.

Using the down-swipe gesture to view Notifications Center

Apps will occasionally display messages called notifications. For example, the News app might display the latest story, while another app might simply display a message from the company that made the app.

While you can view notifications individually, it's often easier to view them all at once in the Notifications Center, which you can access by using a down-swipe gesture. To open the Notifications Center, follow these steps:

1. Place one fingertip at the top of the iPhone screen, as shown in *Figure 1.8*:

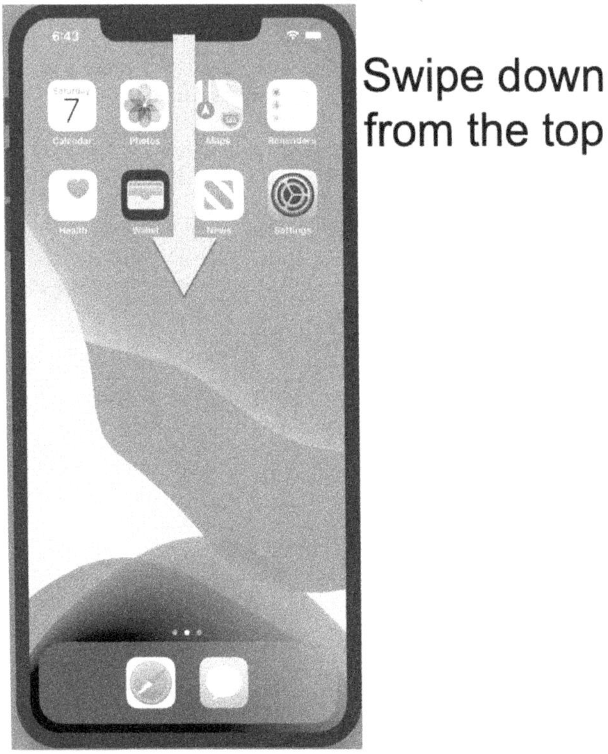

Figure 1.8 – Start the down swipe

2. Swipe down until **Notification Center** appears, as shown in *Figure 1.9*:

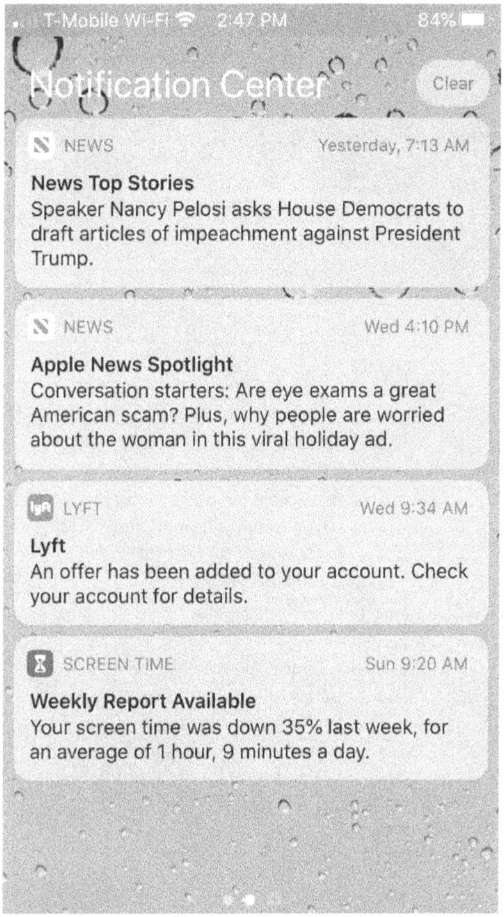

Figure 1.9 – Notification Center

3. Swipe up from the bottom of the screen to return to the Home screen.

Using up- and down-swipe gestures to view more information

Both up- and down-swipe gestures are commonly used to display more information on the screen. The most intuitive use for up- and down-swipe gestures occurs when viewing lists of items, such as text messages or pictures stored in the **Photos** app.

Any time you see a list of items, use the up and down gestures to scroll up and down to view more information that may not fit on the screen, as shown in *Figure 1.10*:

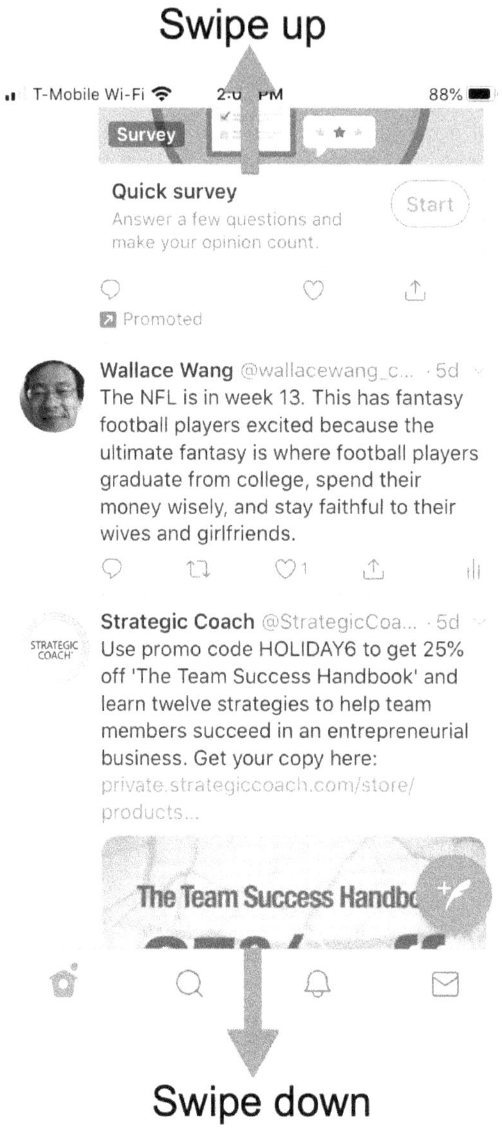

Figure 1.10 – Up and down swipes let you scroll through a list

Any time you see information partially obscured by the top or bottom of the screen, that's a visual clue that you can swipe up or down to view more information. Even if nothing is obscured, try swiping up and down just in case there may be more information hidden out of sight.

Using up - and left/right-swipe gestures to switch apps

You can have multiple apps running at the same time, even though you can only view one app at a time. When you have two or more apps running at once, you can easily switch between apps.

For iPhones without a Home button, place one fingertip at the bottom of the screen and swipe up to the center of the screen as shown in *Figure 1.11*:

Figure 1.11 – Swipe up to the center of the screen

For iPhones with a Home button, press the Home button twice in rapid succession.

In both cases, all open apps appear as multiple windows on the screen, as shown in *Figure 1.12*:

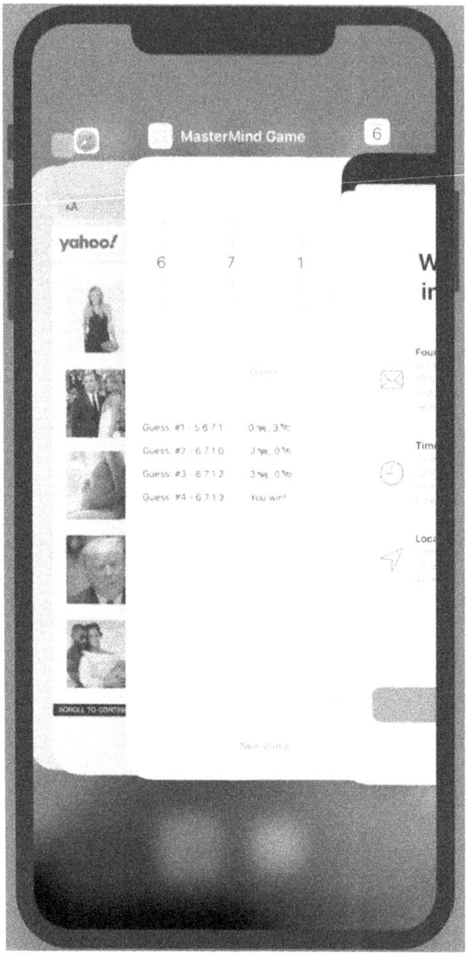

Figure 1.12 – Viewing all open apps at once

By viewing all open apps, you can quickly jump to the one you want to use. If there's an open app you no longer want to use, you can swipe up to shut that particular app down completely.

Using swipe gestures to open Control Center

If you need to access iPhone features such as screen brightness or volume, turn your iPhone into a flashlight, or open common apps such as the Camera or Calculator, you can open Control Center.

To open Control Center, you need to do one of two swipe gestures, depending on whether you do it on an iPhone that has or does not have a Home button:

- On iPhones without a Home button, swipe down starting in the upper-right corner of the iPhone screen as shown in *Figure 1.13* to open Control Center, shown in *Figure 1.14*. Then swipe up from the bottom of the screen to hide Control Center:

Figure 1.13 – A left and down diagonal-swipe gesture

- On iPhones with a Home button, swipe up from the bottom of the screen to display Control Center, as shown in *Figure 1.14*. Then swipe down from the top of the screen to hide Control Center:

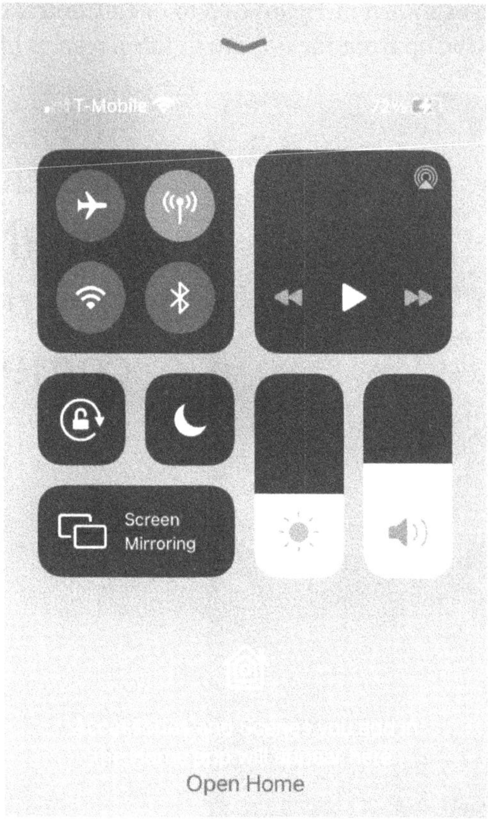

Figure 1.14 –Swiping up from the bottom edge displays the Control Center screen

Just remember that the gesture you use to display Control Center is the opposite of the gesture you use to hide Control Center.

Using long-press gestures

Similar to the tap gesture is the long-press gesture. With the tap gesture, you touch the screen briefly and then lift your finger away. With the long-press gesture (also called tap and hold), you press the screen over an item and hold it until the iPhone responds in some way, typically by displaying one or more options you can choose from.

To make those options go away, just tap anywhere on the screen, away from the list of options that appeared.

Think of long-press gestures as similar to right-clicking with a mouse to view a submenu of options on a traditional PC.

On the Home screen, the long-press gesture can display commonly used commands for a specific app, along with general commands for editing the Home screen. When you long-press the **Camera** and **Maps** icons on the Home screen, the **Camera** app displays shortcuts for taking selfies or videos, while the **Maps** app displays shortcuts for marking locations or searching nearby, as shown in *Figure 1.15*:

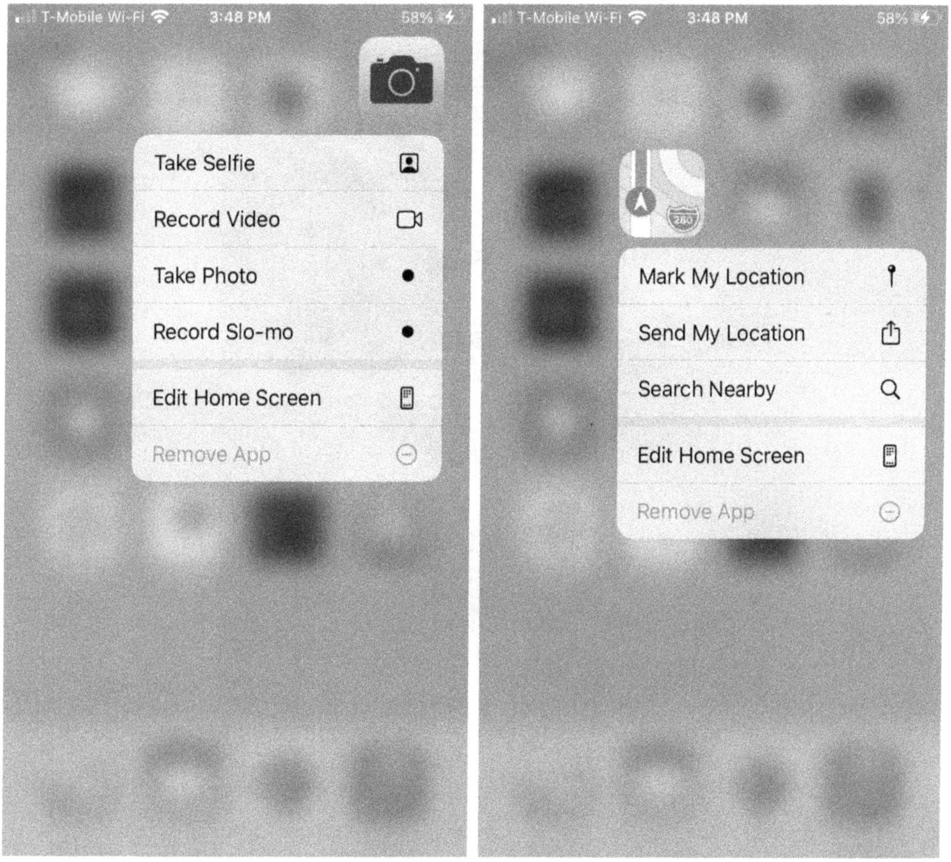

Figure 1.15 – Long-press gestures on a Home screen icon displays shortcuts

Besides displaying options for apps on the Home screen, the long-press gesture can also display options for text and pictures sent as either a text or email message. This can be handy to display options for saving, copying, or sharing a message or image, as shown in *Figure 1.16*:

Figure 1.16 – Long-press gestures on a picture sent as a text message

When working with text, the long-press gesture can select a single word and display additional options, as shown in *Figure 1.17*:

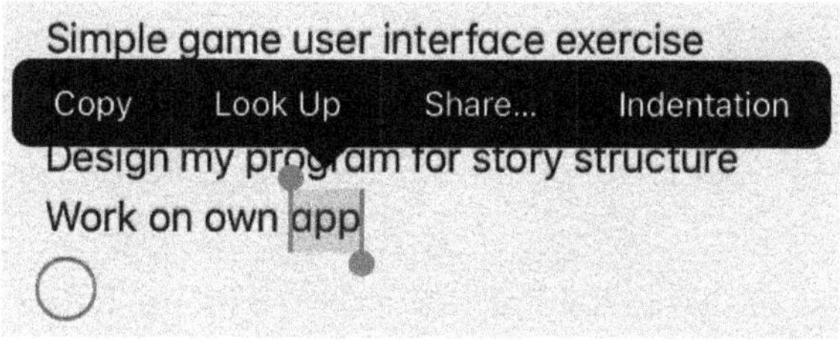

Figure 1.17 – Long-press gestures on text selects a word and displays options

In the Maps app, a long-press gesture places a marker to define a specific location, as shown in *Figure 1.18*. This long-press gesture allows you to mark a specific location rather than just point and scroll on a map:

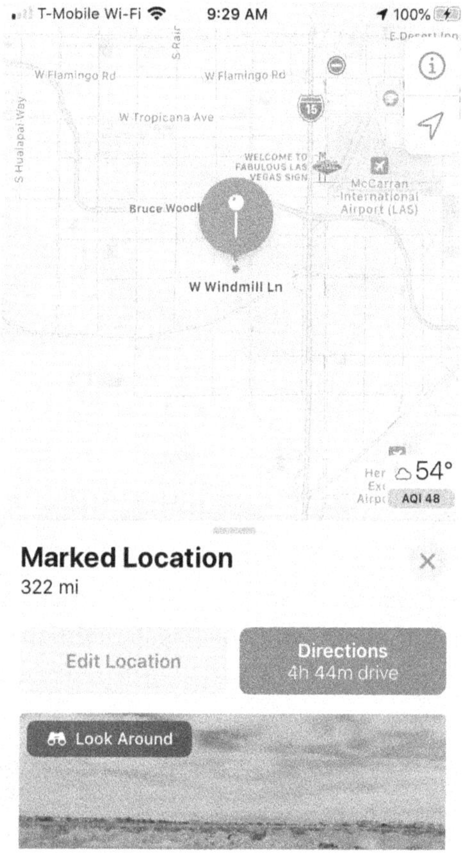

Figure 1.18 – A long-press gesture places a marker in the Maps app

As a general rule, any time you want to get more information, try a long-press gesture on that item. If nothing happens, then you're already seeing all information available.

Using drag gestures

Drag gestures occur when you place a finger over an item on the screen, slide your finger across the screen, then lift your finger off the screen. Drag gestures typically move items, select text, or draw lines.

Think of drag gestures as similar to holding down the left mouse button and moving (or *dragging*) the mouse on a traditional PC.

On the Home screen, the drag gesture is used to move app icons around the Home screen, as shown in *Figure 1.19*. The drag gesture typically works with the long-press gesture as follows:

1. Open the Home Screen and use the long-press gesture to select an item.
2. Drag the item to a new location.
3. Lift your finger off the screen:

Dragging an icon...
...moves that icon to a new location

Figure 1.19 – Dragging lets you move an icon on the Home screen

4. When working with text, the drag gesture is used to select text.
5. First, you use the long-press gesture to select a word.
6. Then you drag the selection handles that appear to the left and right of the selected word. Dragging these selection handles highlights additional text, as shown in *Figure 1.20*:

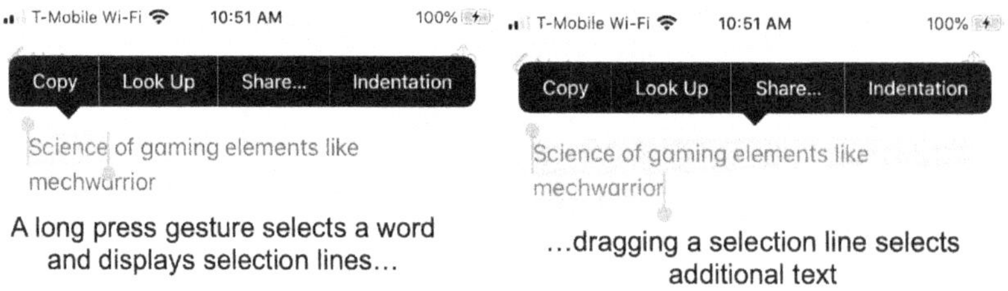

Figure 1.20 – Dragging a selection handle can select more text

With icons and images, drag gestures are most often used to move items. With text, drag gestures are most often used to drag a selection handle to highlight additional text.

Using pinch gestures

Pinch gestures are two-finger gestures where you place two fingertips on the screen and either move them apart or closer together to zoom in and out. Pinch gestures are most commonly used with both text and pictures so you can zoom in to see details and zoom back out again, as shown in *Figure 1.21*:

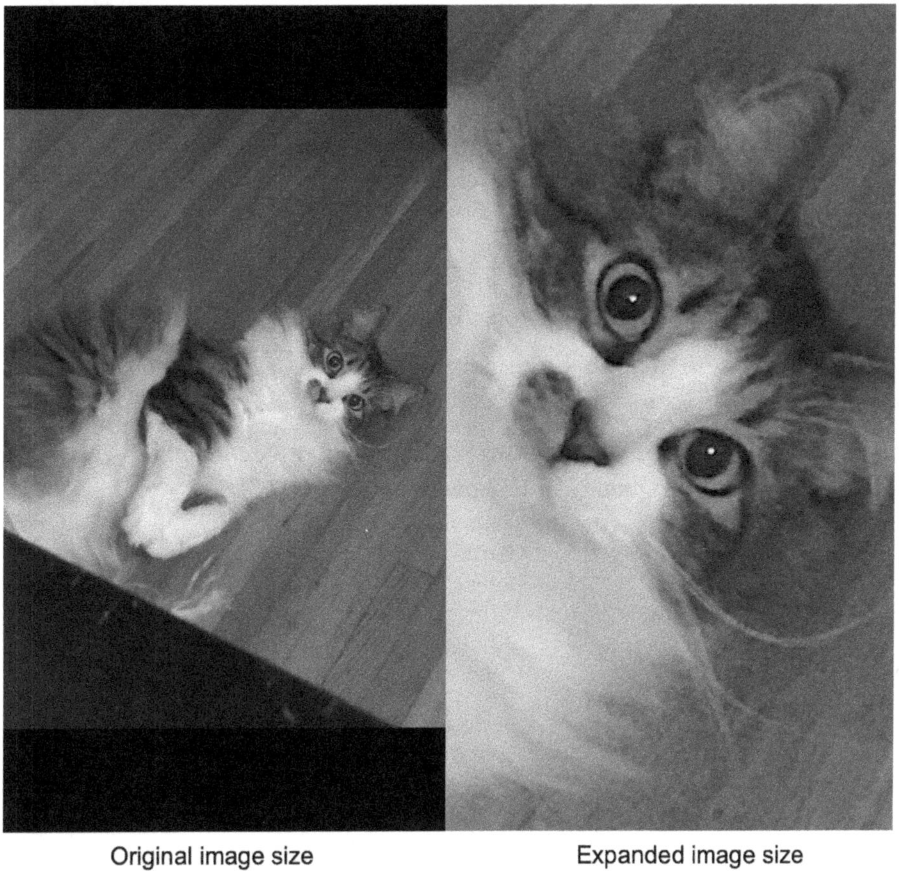

Figure 1.21 – Pinching can expand (and shrink) text and images

Think of pinch gestures as similar to changing the size of an item using the scroll wheel with a mouse on a traditional PC.

Pinch gestures are often used with drag gestures as follows:

1. Use the pinch gesture (moving two fingertips apart) to expand text or an image, as shown in *Figure 1.22*:

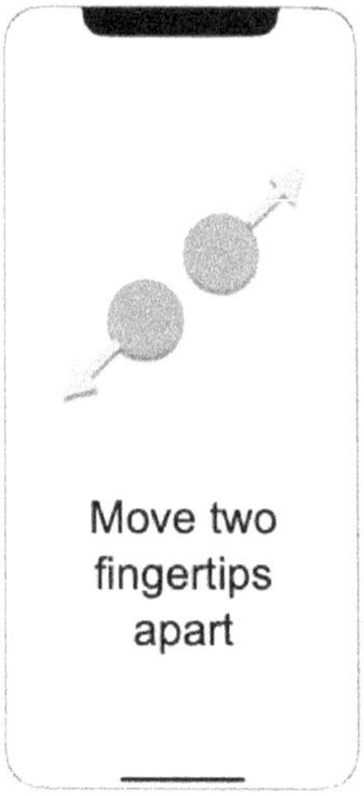

Figure 1.22 – Using the pinch gesture to expand a view

2. Use the drag gesture to position the expanded text or image to display what you want to see.
3. Repeat the pinch gesture (moving two fingertips closer together) to shrink the text or image back to its original size, as shown in *Figure 1.23*:

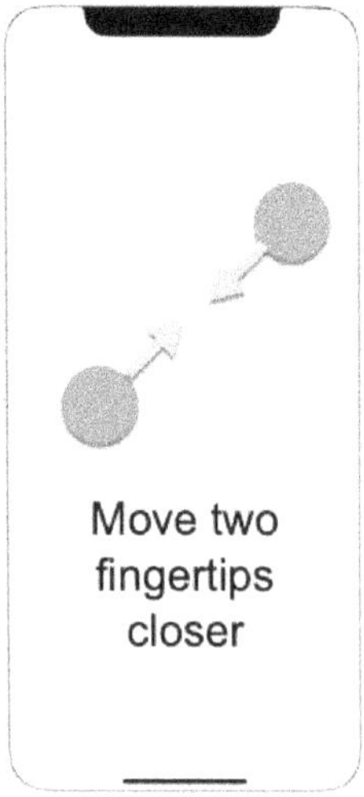

Figure 1.23 – Using the pinch gesture to shrink a view

Remember that when you reach the maximum or minimum size of an image, the pinch gesture will no longer work. This is the iPhone's way of letting you know when you've reached a maximum or minimum size.

Using rotation gestures

Rotation gestures are another two-finger gesture where you place two fingertips on the screen, but then move them in a circular motion, either clockwise or counter-clockwise, as shown in *Figure 1.24*:

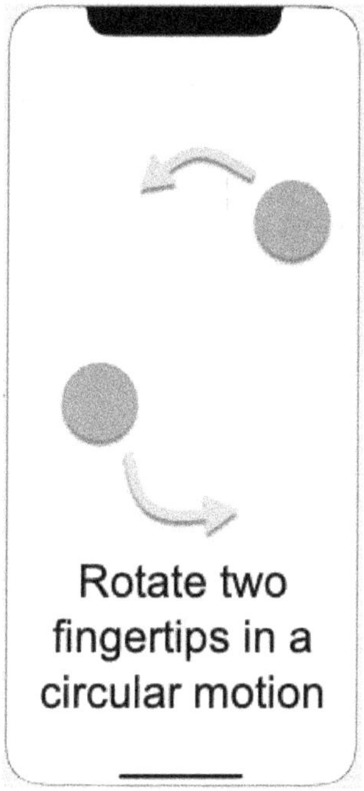

Figure 1.24 – The rotation gesture involves two fingertips moving in a circular motion

Rotation gestures are commonly used to rotate images inside apps, such as rotating an image within the Pages word processor app, as shown in *Figure 1.25*:

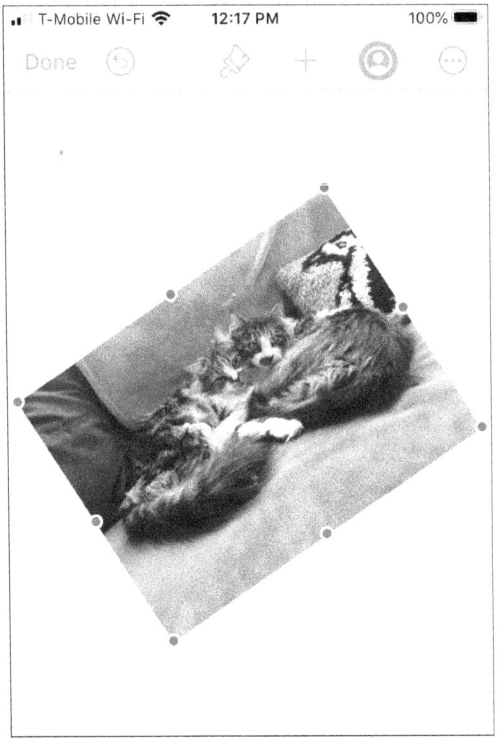

Figure 1.25 – The rotation gesture rotates an image

Think of rotation gestures as similar to moving the rotation handle of an image being edited on a traditional PC.

Summary

Touch gestures let you take complete control of your iPhone, so it's important that you know the basics of all these gestures and the common ways to use them. While not all apps will support every type of touch gesture, most touch gestures can be used interchangeably across different apps. Here is a quick summary of the gestures we went through in this chapter:

- Tap gestures are most often used to select an icon or image, or position the cursor within some text.
- Swipe gestures are most often used to navigate to another screen or slide an item in a list to the left to delete that item.

- Long-press gestures are most often used to display additional information about an icon, image, or word.
- Drag gestures are most often used to move an icon or image, or to select text.
- Pinch gestures are most often used to zoom the screen magnification in or out.
- Rotation gestures are most often used with images to rearrange their orientation.

In many cases, apps won't always give you any visual clues when you might be able to use different touch gestures, so try experimenting with these touch gestures in different parts of every app.

The most common touch gestures are taps and swipes, so try these three touch gestures in every app to see what they might do (if anything).

The second most common touch gestures are long presses and pinches. The long-press gesture typically displays a menu of additional commands, while the pinch gesture expands or shrinks an item to make it larger (and easier to see) or smaller (back to its original size).

By understanding common touch gestures, you'll be able to control your iPhone no matter which app you may use, now or in the future.

Once you understand basic touch gestures, you'll be ready to learn more about common user interface features of iPhone apps in the next chapter. With your knowledge of touch gestures and user interface features, you'll be able to use most almost every type of app you might use on your iPhone.

In the next chapter, we will look at the new iOS 14 apps.

2
Using the New iOS 14 Apps

In 2020, Apple introduced iOS 14, the latest operating system for the iPhone. Besides adding new features, iOS 14 also includeds a **Translate** and a **Magnifier** app. The Translate app lets you convert spoken or written words into another language, while the **Magnifier** app lets you turn your iPhone camera into a magnifying glass to help you read text that may be too small to read comfortably.

By learning how to use these new apps, as well as using the new features of iOS 14, you can get comfortable with using common user interface elements of iPhone apps. Since most apps work in similar ways, the more apps you use, the easier it will be to use your iPhone.

In the last chapter, you learned how to use common finger gestures to control different features of an iPhone. In this chapter, you'll learn the common elements of iOS by experimenting with the latest features of iOS 14:

- The **Magnifier** app
- The **Translate** app
- The **App Library**

Using the Magnifier app

Many people have a hard time reading text up close. This can be due to farsightedness or trying to read small print in low-lighting conditions. If you ever forget or misplace your reading glasses, you can use the **Magnifier** app on your iPhone, which appears as shown in *Figure 2.1*:

Figure 2.1 – The Magnifier app

To start the **Magnifier** app, you need to use two different gestures: swipe and tap. First, you'll need to use the swipe gestures to scroll through the different Home screens on your iPhone until you find the **Magnifier** app icon. Once you find the **Magnifier** app, you can start it by tapping the icon. Once the **Magnifier** user interface appears, you can point your iPhone camera at text or any item you want to see, as shown in *Figure 2.2*:

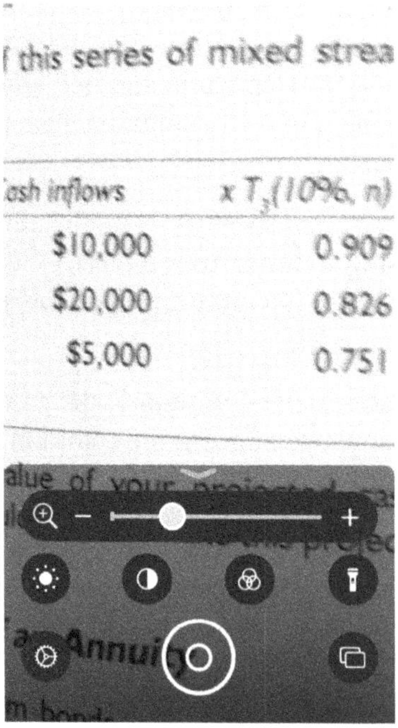

Figure 2.2 – Using the Magnifier app

The **Magnifier** app consists of buttons and sliders. Tapping an icon performs an action, while swiping the slider left or right lets you increase or decrease a value, such as brightness or magnification. Let's begin:

1. To save space, only the zoom slider appears. If you want to display the brightness or contrast sliders, you'll need to tap the **brightness** or **contrast** icons, as shown in *Figure 2.3*:

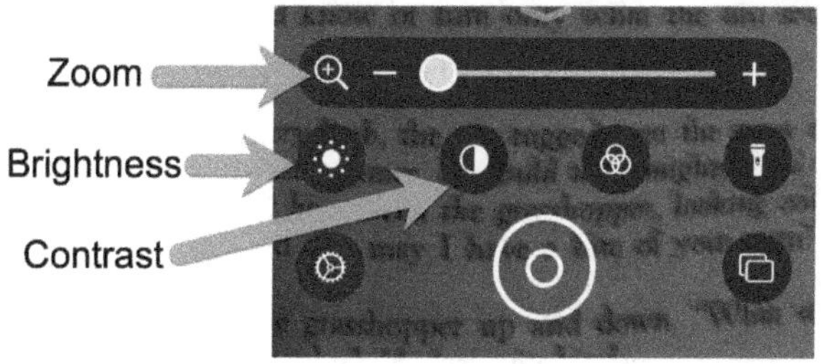

Figure 2.3 – The zoom, brightness, and contrast icons

2. When you tap the **brightness** or **contrast** icons, a slider appears so that you can adjust either the brightness or contrast. Swiping left and right on the slider changes that option, such as zoom, brightness, or contrast.
3. When you no longer want to see the brightness or contrast sliders, tap the **brightness** or **contrast** icons again. (Note that the zoom slider always remains visible by default.)
4. If you tap the **color filter** icon, a list of different color filter options appears, as shown in *Figure 2.4*:

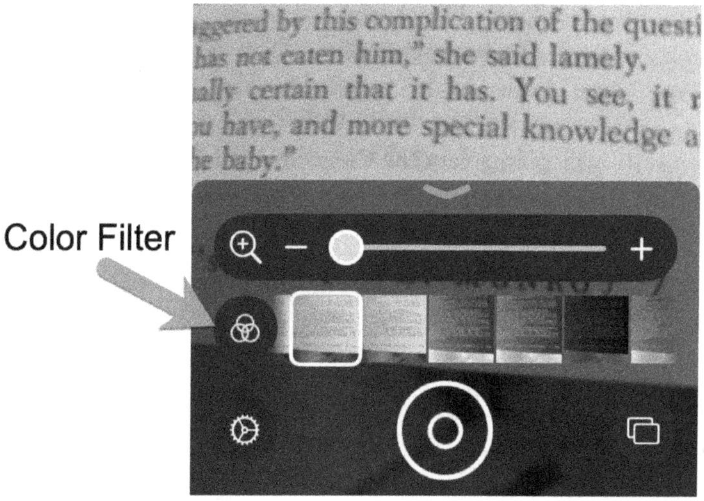

Figure 2.4 – The color filter icon

5. To illuminate an object, tap the **flashlight** icon, as shown in *Figure 2.5*. This **flashlight** icon toggles between turning the flash on or off to illuminate the area in front of your iPhone:

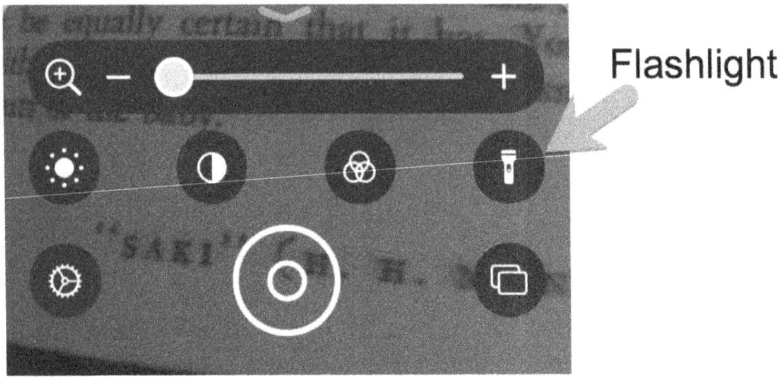

Figure 2.5 – The flashlight icon

6. Most apps offer a way to customize the app, so to do that in the **Magnifier** app, tap the **settings** icon, as shown in *Figure 2.6*:

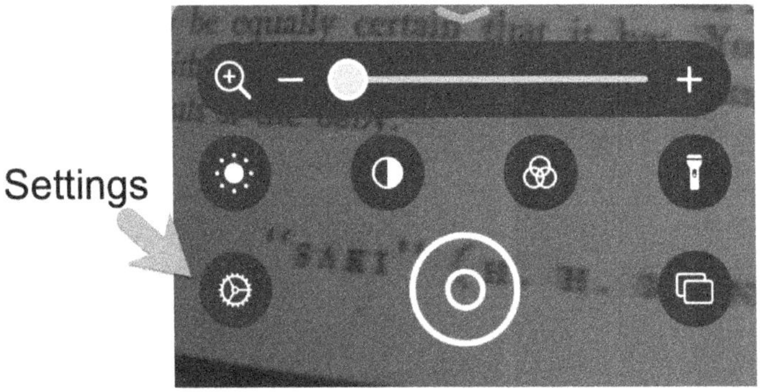

Figure 2.6 – The settings icon

7. Tapping the **settings** icon displays the **Customize Controls** screen, which displays options in a list. Two common features of lists are that they allow you to delete items or move items.
8. To delete items, you can tap the **delete** icon, which looks like a white dash inside a red circle.
9. To move an item, you can swipe up or down on a three-line icon, often called a "hamburger menu" since it looks like the top and bottom of a bun with a patty inside, as shown in *Figure 2.7*:

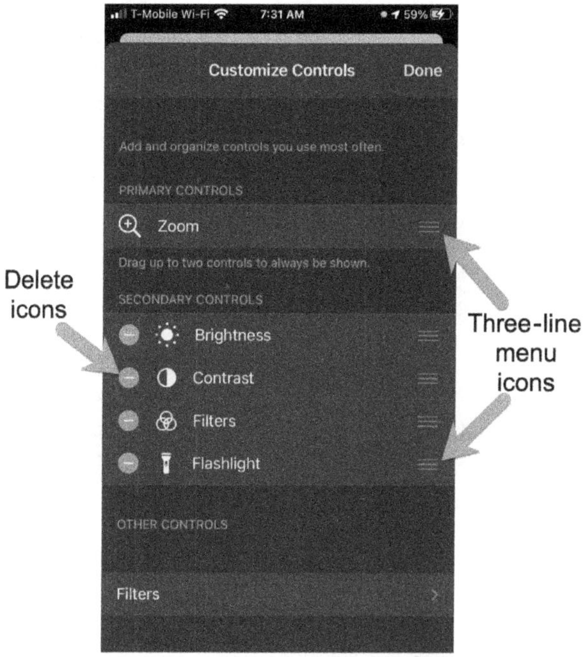

Figure 2.7 – The Customize Controls screen

When you're done with the **Customize Controls** screen, tap the **Done** button in the upper-right corner of the screen. By experimenting with the **Magnifier** app, you can learn the basic gestures and user interface elements, which can help you use nearly any app in no time.

One unique feature of the **Magnifier** app is that it allows you to capture an image to view or share it with others. (However, note that when you capture a picture with the **Magnifier** app, that picture is not saved but stored temporarily.) This lets you capture pictures and view them later at your convenience. The two buttons for capturing and viewing images are shown in *Figure 2.8*:

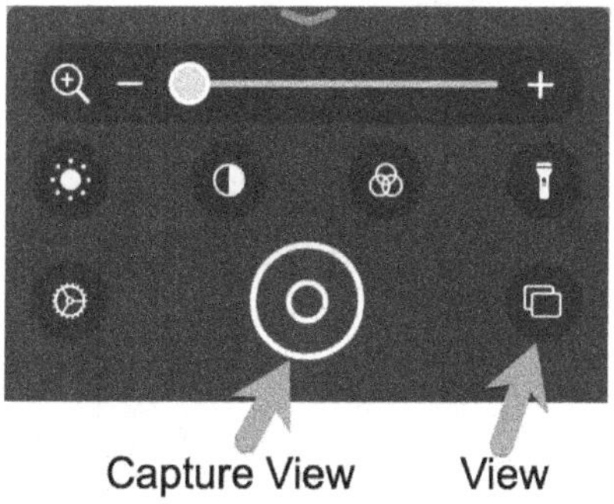

Figure 2.8 – The capture view and view buttons

Tapping the **capture view** button captures a picture of whatever you see through the iPhone camera. Once you've captured an image, you can view the captured image at your leisure without the need to hold your iPhone camera over a page anymore. The **capture view** button turns into a **close** button, so when you no longer want to view the static image you captured, click the **close** button, as shown in *Figure 2.9*:

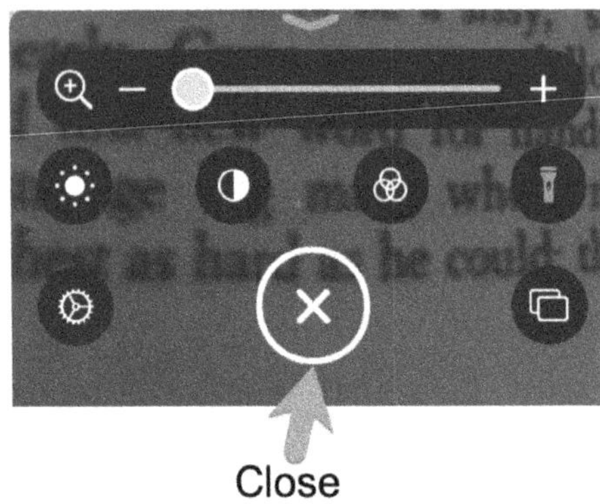

Figure 2.9 – The capture view button turns into a close button

Once you've captured an image, you can tap the close button to dismiss that image. However, if you capture an image and want to temporarily save it, tap the **View** button instead. This turns the **capture view** button into a + button to capture additional images, along with displaying the **View** button with the number of images temporarily stored, as shown in *Figure 2.10*:

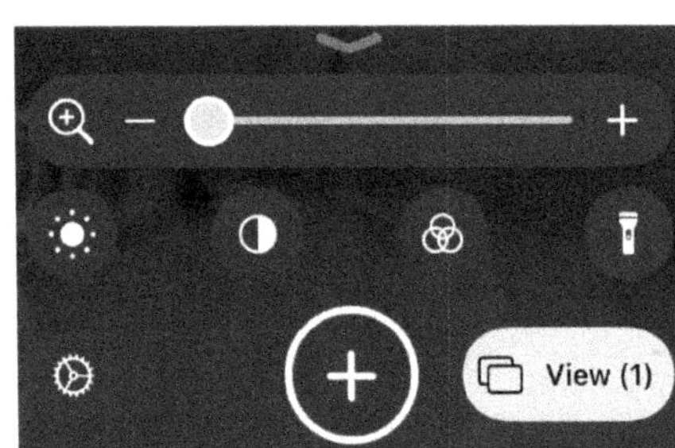

Figure 2.10 – The buttons change slightly when capturing multiple images

If you tap the + button, you can capture additional images. If you tap the **View** button, you can view previously captured images. To dismiss a previously captured image, tap the **End** button in the upper-left corner.

The **Magnifier** app makes it easy to either view images while holding your iPhone or to capture images that you can review later so that you don't have to hold your iPhone over a page.

Like most apps, the **Magnifier** app makes icons and buttons easy to spot. To see how another app works, let's take a look at the new **Translate** app.

Using the Translate app

While some people may be multilingual, most people know their native language well but may not feel comfortable speaking another language fluently. That's why Apple included a new **Translate** app in iOS 14. The purpose of the **Translate** app is to let you either speak or type words in one language and see and hear a translation in another language.

Currently, the **Translate** app can translate to and from the following languages:

- Arabic
- Chinese (Mandarin)
- English (US and UK)
- French
- German
- Italian
- Japanese
- Korean
- Portuguese
- Russian
- Spanish

The **Translate** app appears as shown in *Figure 2.11*:

Figure 2.11 – The Translate app

The **Translate** app displays two different screens depending on whether you are holding your iPhone in portrait or landscape mode. Portrait mode is meant to let you either speak or type text to translate, as shown in *Figure 2.12*:

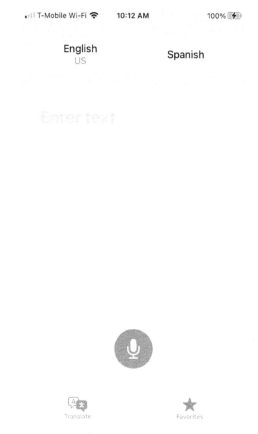

Figure 2.12 – The Translate app in portrait mode

Landscape mode can translate a conversation and let both people comfortably view the screen, as shown in *Figure 2.13*:

Figure 2.13 – The Translate app in landscape mode

To define which languages you want the **Translate** app to use, hold the **Translate** app in portrait mode. Then, tap the two language buttons at the top of the screen. When you tap a language button, a list of supported languages appears, as shown in *Figure 2.14*:

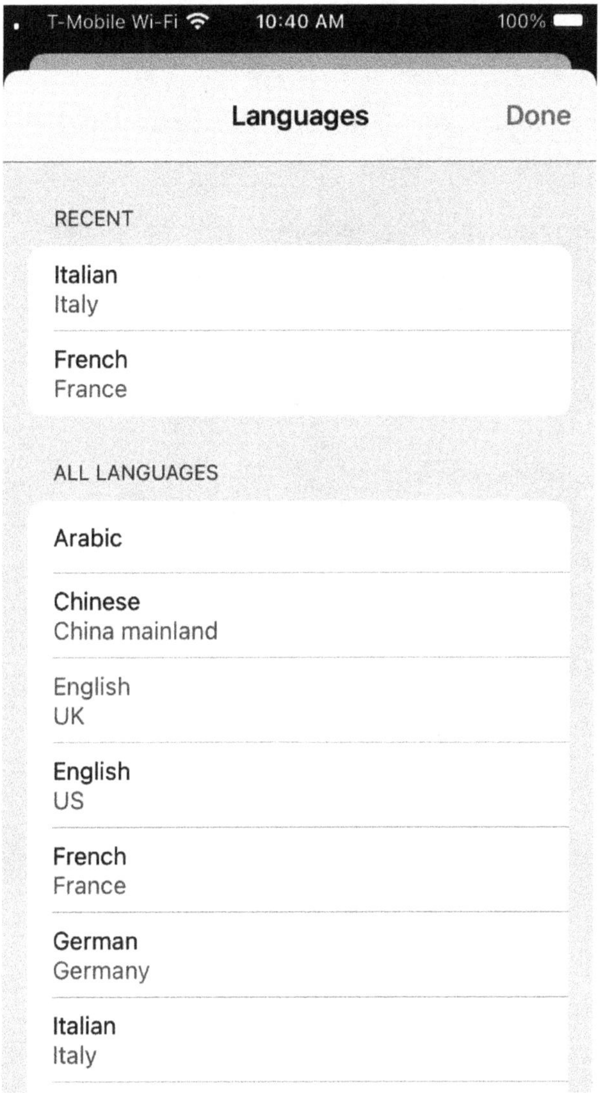

Figure 2.14 – Choosing a language in the Translate app

Tap a language to use, and then tap the **Done** button in the upper-right corner of the screen. By doing this for both the input and output languages, you can translate between multiple languages.

Once you've defined the two languages to use, you can now translate using either text or speech. To translate text:

1. Tap the **Enter text** box to make the virtual keyboard appear.
2. Type your text and tap the **Go** button in the bottom-right corner of the virtual keyboard.
3. The **Translate** app displays your text, along with the translation in your chosen language, as shown in *Figure 2.15*:

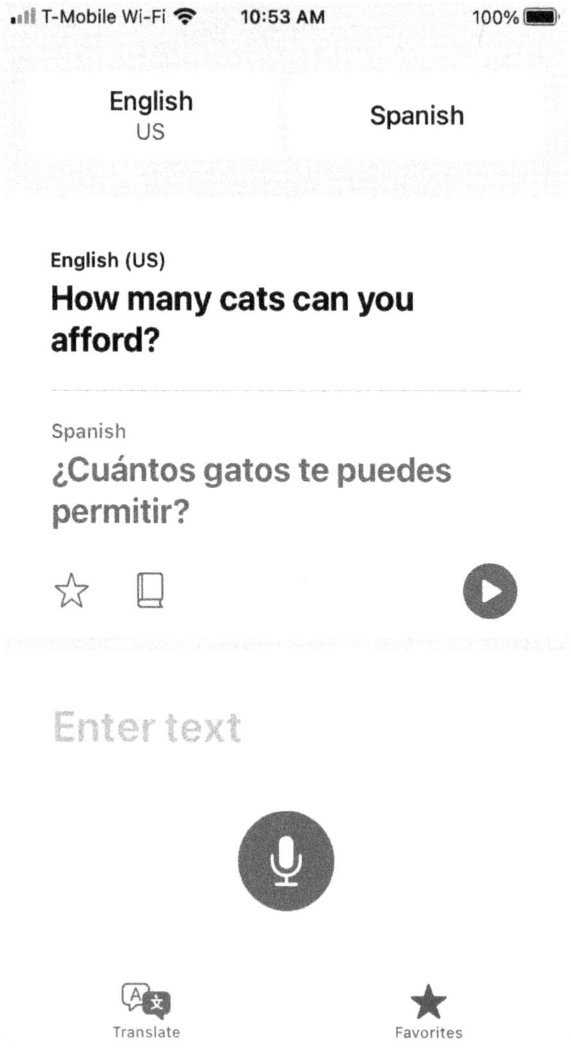

Figure 2.15 – Translating text

To translate speech, tap the **microphone** button. The **Translate** screen displays an audio image, along with text that says **Listening…**, as shown in *Figure 2.16*:

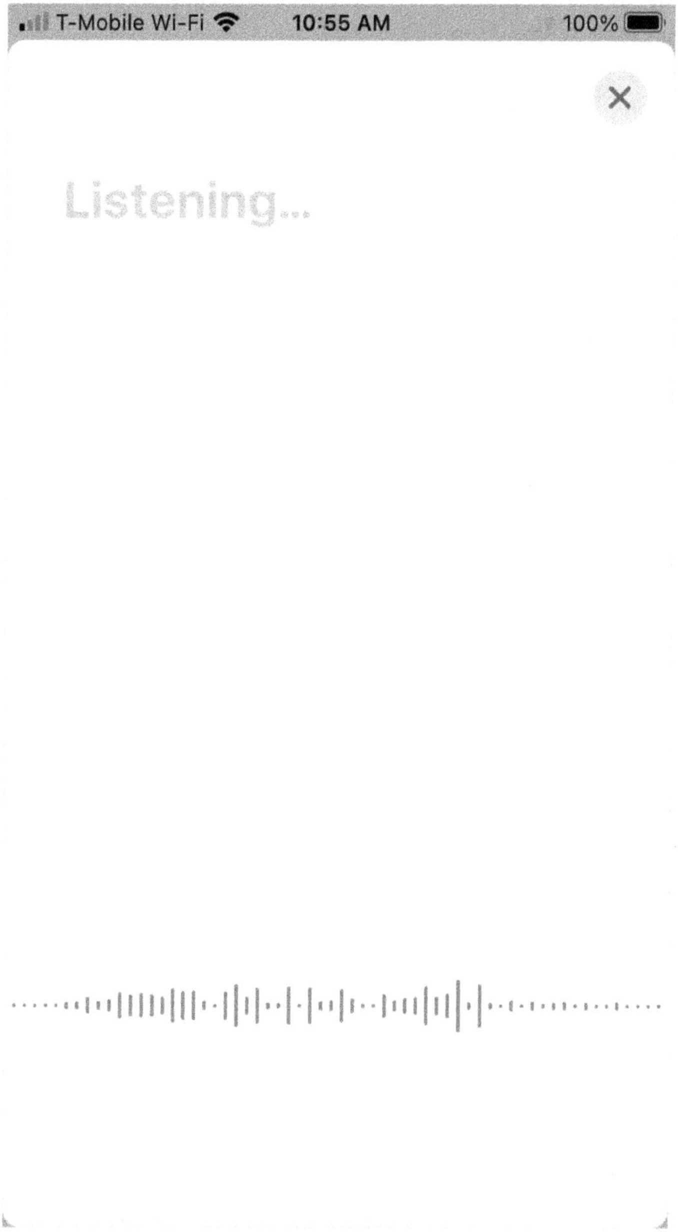

Figure 2.16 – Capturing audio input

Speak the words you want to be translated and then stop when you're done. After a few seconds, the **Translate** app will display the translated text as shown in *Figure 2.15*). The Clear button lets you delete all text inside a text field with one tap. Whether you entered text by typing or through speech, you'll see three icons (**favorites**, **dictionary**, and **play**) under the translated text, as shown in *Figure 2.17*:

Figure 2.17 – The favorites, dictionary, and play icons

Tapping the **Favorites** icon stores the translated text in the **Favorites** category, which you can view at any time by tapping the **Favorites** icon in the bottom-right corner of the screen.

Tapping the **dictionary** icon displays the **Dictionary** pane. Now, you can tap on any word to view its dictionary definition, as shown in *Figure 2.18*:

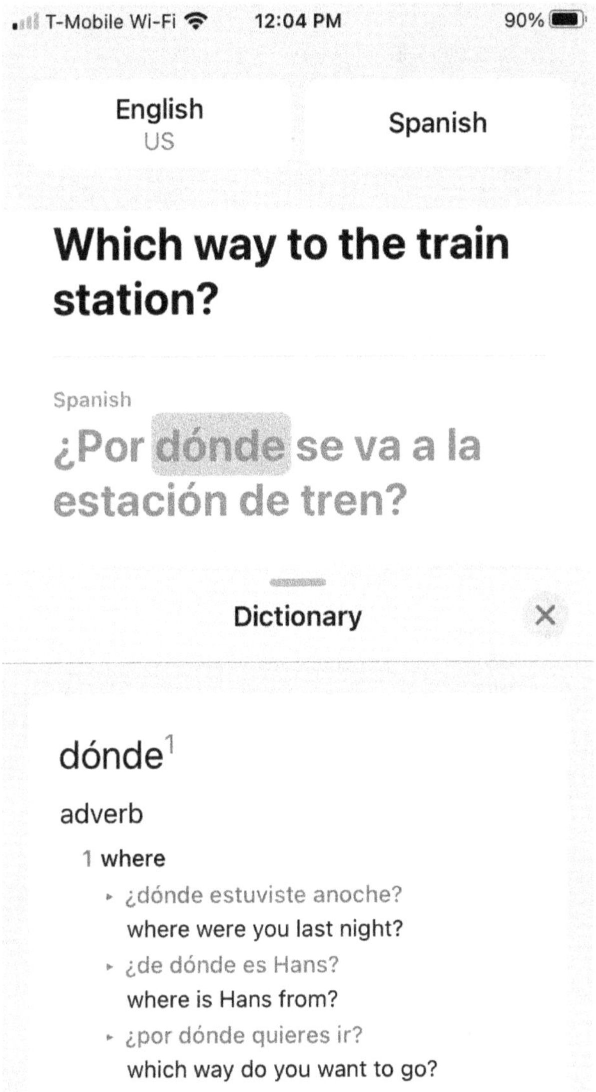

Figure 2.18 – The Dictionary pane lets you identify the meaning of each translated word

When you no longer want to use the dictionary, tap the close icon (**X**) in the upper-right corner of the **Dictionary** pane.

Tapping the **play** icon lets you hear Siri speak the translated text out loud. This can be handy for hearing the correct pronunciation of a translated sentence or for playing the translated text to another person.

If you have stored any translations by tapping the **Favorites** icon, or if you want to view a list of your most recent translations, you can tap the **Favorites** icon in the bottom-right corner of the screen. This opens the **Favorites** list as shown in *Figure 2.19*:

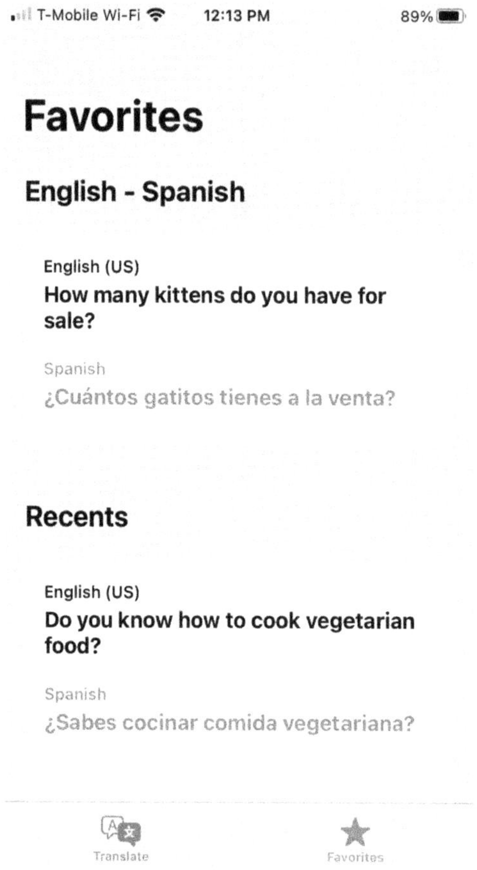

Figure 2.19 – The favorites icon displays all translations marked as favorites plus recent translations

To unmark a translation as a favorite, simply tap on the translation and tap the **favorites** icon to toggle it off and on.

Using the **Translate** app in portrait mode can be handy when you need translations for writing or reading. However, when you want to talk to someone who doesn't speak your language, it's easier to use the **Translate** app in landscape mode (see *Figure 2.13*):

1. Hold your iPhone in portrait orientation, then start the **Translate** app, and tap the language that you speak (in the upper-left corner of the screen).
2. Tap the language that the other person speaks (in the upper-right corner of the screen).

3. Tilt your iPhone to landscape orientation. If necessary, tap the **Translate** button at the bottom of the screen. The screen splits in half to display your spoken words and the translation, as shown in *Figure 2.20*:

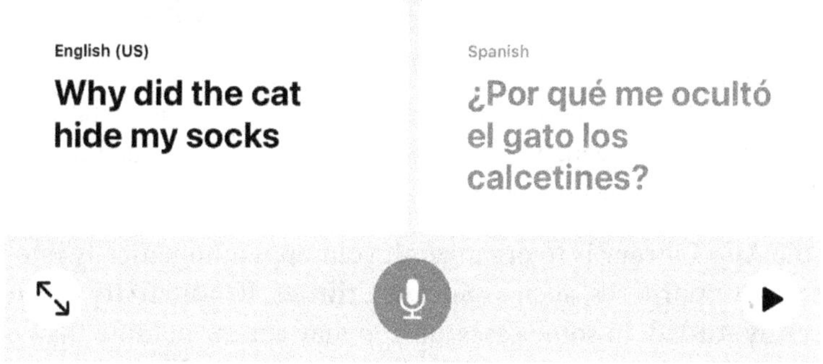

Figure 2.20 – Displaying text and its translation in landscape orientation

4. Tap the button in the bottom-left corner that displays arrows pointing in opposite directions. This displays only your translated text to make it easy for someone to read it, as shown in *Figure 2.21*:

Figure 2.21 – Displaying only translated text

5. Tap the button in the bottom-left corner of the screen (which contains two chat icons) to return back to viewing your original text and the translated text side by side.

As an alternative to showing the translated text to others, you can also tap the **play** button in the bottom-right corner so that Siri can speak the translated text out loud.

By using the **Translate** app, you can communicate with others who may not speak your language. This can help you both get your thoughts across with a minimal amount of frustration, thanks to the iPhone.

If you plan on using the **Translate** app often, you'll probably want to move it to a prominent location on your Home screen. For another way to find apps, consider using the **App Library**, another new feature in iOS 14.

Using the App Library

While you can move and group related app icons around the Home screen, most people don't do that because it's time-consuming. As a result, it's far more common to store apps all over the Home screen and then have a hard time finding exactly which app you want at any given time.

To reduce this problem, iOS 14 offers an **App Library**, which appears when you swipe left multiple times on the Home screen. The number of left swipes you need depends on the number of Home screens your iPhone has.

The purpose of the **App Library** is to organize all your apps automatically into related groups with descriptive purposes, such as **Social**, **Utilities**, **Productivity & Finance**, **Travel**, and **Recently Added**. In some cases, an app may appear in more than one category, such as the **Translate** app appearing in the **Recently Added** and **Information & Reading** groups, as shown in *Figure 2.22*:

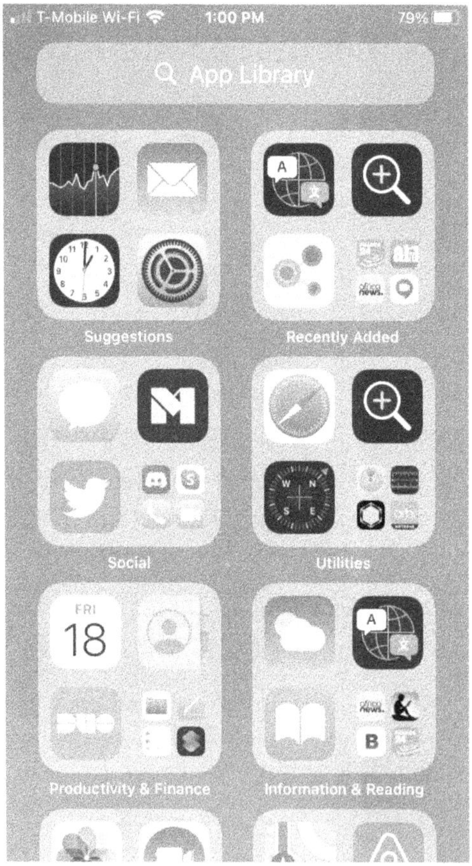

Figure 2.22 – The App Library

By scrolling through the list of **App Library** categories, you can find and tap on the app you want to use, such as the **Translate** or **Magnifier** apps. Since the **App Library** hides your least-used apps, you won't see all available apps in the **App Library**.

If you want an app that doesn't appear in the **App Library**, tap the **App Library** search field at the top of the screen to display an alphabetical list of all the installed apps on your iPhone, as shown in *Figure 2.23*:

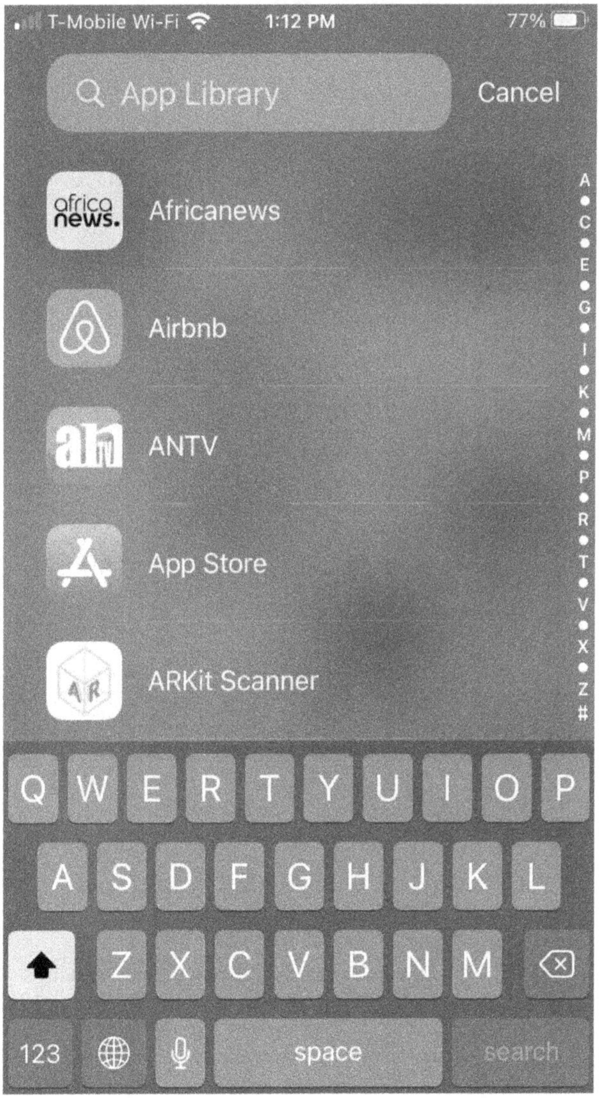

Figure 2.23 – Tapping the App Library search field displays an alphabetical listing of all the installed apps

You can scroll through this alphabetical list of apps and then tap the app name you want to use. As a faster alternative, you can tap on the index that appears on the right. Tapping on an index lets you jump to app names beginning with a certain letter, such as **T** or **R**.

You can also type all or part of an app name in the **App Library** search field. Each time you type another letter, the list of all matching apps narrows, as shown in *Figure 2.24*:

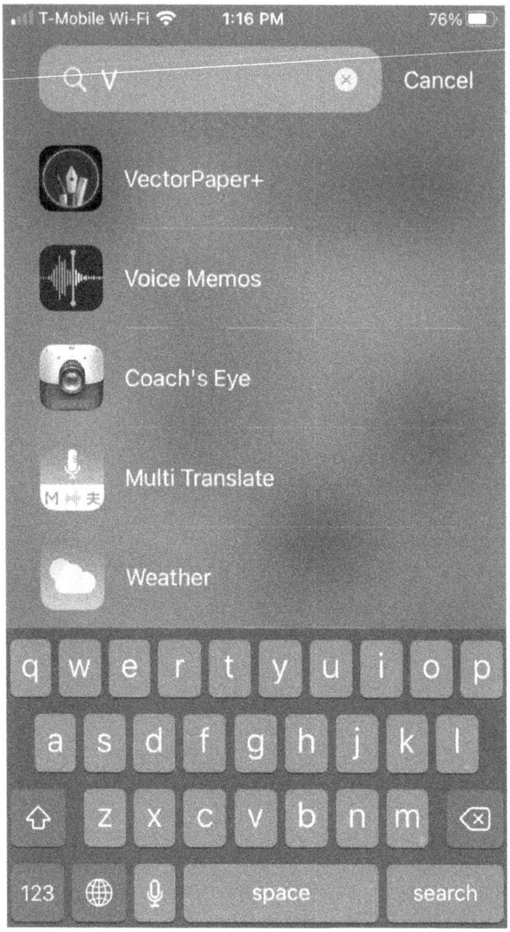

Figure 2.24 – Typing part of an app name helps the App Library display a limited number of apps

When you see the app you want to use, just tap on that app's icon. The **App Library** gives you both a visual and a textual way to find the app you want to use at any given time.

Summary

Three of the latest features in iOS 14 are the **Magnifier** app, the **Translate** app, and the **App Library**. The **Magnifier** app can replace reading glasses or magnifying glasses to help you read small print or examine items closely.

The **Translate** app can help you communicate with someone who may not speak your language. As long as both you and the other person speak and read one of the languages supported by the **Translate** app (such as German, French, Arabic, Russian, or English), you'll be able to chat and write to each other in the language you're most comfortable writing or speaking.

Finally, use the **App Library** to help you find an app you want to use. Over time, you gradually add apps faster than you remove them. The end result is that your Home screen winds up getting cluttered with lots of apps that you don't have the time to organize. That's when you can rely on the **App Library** to organize apps for you automatically or help you find an app by searching for it by name.

For many people, when they get an iPhone, their first task is to customize it by changing background images or choosing different ringtones, and that's what you'll learn how to do in the next chapter.

3

Customizing Sound, Look, and Privacy Settings

Many people are perfectly happy with using their iPhone exactly the way it came out of the box. However, others like the idea of customizing their iPhone to make it more personal. For example, you might want to display a picture of your dog in the background or change the sound your iPhone makes every time you get a call so that it doesn't sound like everyone else's iPhone.

Customizing your iPhone can be fun but also useful too. Beyond changing colors or pictures, you can also customize your iPhone to rearrange app icons to make it easier to find the apps you use most often. More importantly, you might want to modify the privacy settings to protect the security of your personal data.

In this chapter, you'll learn different ways to customize your iPhone. Just remember that any time you change a setting, you can always change it back, so feel free to experiment and see how to make your iPhone uniquely your own.

In this chapter, we will go through the following topics:

- Getting an Apple ID
- Protecting your iPhone
- Making sure you don't lose your iPhone
- Changing the wallpaper
- Customizing sounds and haptics
- Blocking out disturbances
- Adjusting text size and screen brightness
- Customizing date/time formats
- Customizing the battery
- Defining an emergency SOS
- Protecting your privacy
- Defining notification settings
- Setting Wi-Fi, Bluetooth, and hotspots
- Updating an iPhone
- Using accessibility features

Since you'll likely want to download apps, listen to music, read e-books, or subscribe to news services, the first step when getting an iPhone is to set up an Apple ID.

Getting an Apple ID

To get the most out of your iPhone, you should create an Apple ID, which is an account that lets you access Apple's various services, such as the App Store, the iTunes Store, and iCloud. While it's possible to use an iPhone without an Apple ID, you will not be able to buy apps or subscribe to services such as Apple Music or Apple News without an Apple ID.

> **Important Note**
>
> If you already have an Apple ID, you do not need to create another Apple ID account.

Each user only needs one Apple ID. Since you cannot share Apple IDs, that means everyone in your family will need to create a separate Apple ID account. When you create an Apple ID, you'll need to define a unique password, along with several security questions that can help you access your Apple ID account in case you forget your password. To create an Apple ID, follow these steps:

1. Tap the **Settings** icon on the Home screen.
2. Tap the **Sign in to your iPhone** button at the top of the screen, as shown in *Figure 3.1*:

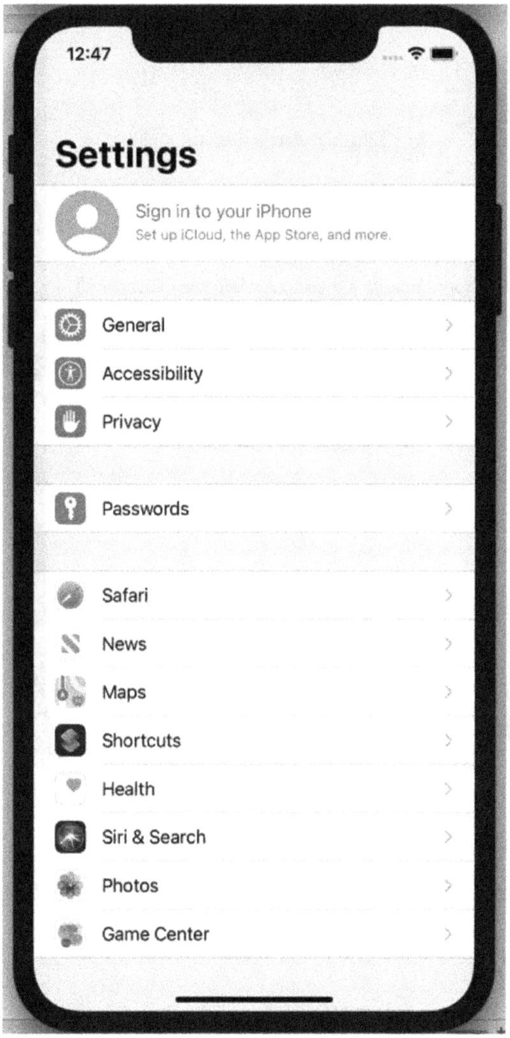

Figure 3.1 – Setting up an Apple ID

3. Tap the **Don't have an Apple ID or forgot it?** link, as shown in *Figure 3.2*:

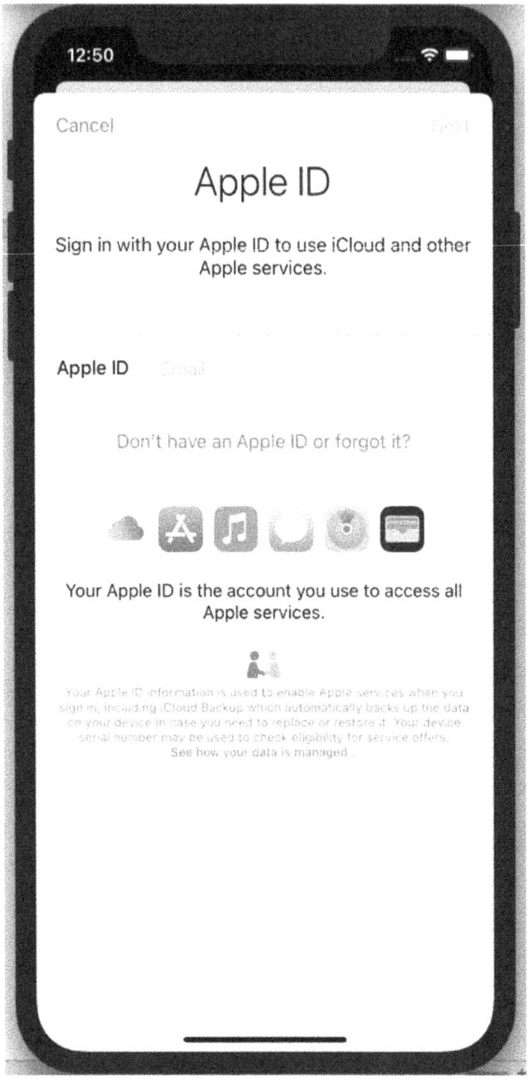

Figure 3.2 – Creating an Apple ID

A dialog pops up listing different options.

4. Tap the **Create Apple ID** link, as shown in *Figure 3.3*:

Figure 3.3 – The dialog for creating an Apple ID

5. Follow the steps to define an Apple ID (which is the email address you want to use), along with a password and credit card billing information. Although Apple stores your credit card information, you will not be charged for anything until you actually make purchases through a service such as the App Store.

Once you have set up an Apple ID, you'll now be able to make purchases through Apple's various services on your iPhone. To prevent unauthorized people from accessing your iPhone and making purchases on your stored credit card information, you should immediately take steps to protect your iPhone using a passcode and Touch ID or Face ID.

Protecting your iPhone

Since an iPhone can contain important information and private messages and photographs, you don't want anyone to use your iPhone without your permission. To block access to your iPhone, you need to set up one or more of the following:

- **Passcode**: Requires typing a six-digit number
- **Touch ID**: Requires your fingerprint
- **Face ID**: Requires recognizing your face

Remember, not all iPhone models offer all three forms of access control. Some iPhones only offer passcodes and Touch ID, while others may only offer passcodes and Face ID. Whatever iPhone model you might have, use two forms of access control, such as a passcode and Face ID. Since every iPhone offers passcodes, make sure you set a good passcode as soon as possible.

Using passcodes

A passcode represents the first line of defense restricting access to your iPhone. Until someone types in the correct six-digit code, your passcode will block access to your iPhone. Ideally, you want your passcode to be easy for you to remember but hard for someone else to guess.

Unfortunately, numbers that are easy for you to remember can also be easy for someone else to guess. That's why passcodes that contain nothing but the same number, such as 33333, might be easy to remember but are also easy for someone to guess.

Likewise, numbers that are hard for someone to guess can also be hard for you to remember. Ideally, choose a passcode that has some type of meaning to you that no one else will be able to guess or discover. For example, combining the year you were born with the month or day you were born is not a good idea because other people can easily discover those numbers by looking up your birthdate. Instead, choose numbers that other people cannot uncover, such as your first dog's birthdate (month and year) or some other number that has a unique meaning only to you.

For extra security, you may want to change your passcode periodically. By changing your passcode periodically, you can ensure that even if someone does discover your passcode, your new passcode will lock them out again.

To set up or change your passcode, follow these steps:

1. Tap the **Settings** app on the Home screen.
2. Tap **Face ID & Passcode** (for iPhones with Face ID) or **Touch ID & Passcode** (for iPhones with Touch ID). A screen appears, asking for your six-digit passcode (if you have already defined one).
3. Type in your six-digit passcode. A screen appears, as shown in *Figure 3.4*, with different options, as follows:

- **Turn Passcode Off**: This allows you to disable your passcode (not recommended).
- **Change Passcode**: This allows you to define a new six-digit passcode or a custom alphanumeric code.
- **ALLOW ACCESS WHEN LOCKED**: This allows you to turn on (or off) features that you may want to access without unlocking your iPhone, such as using Siri, viewing notifications, or replying to messages:

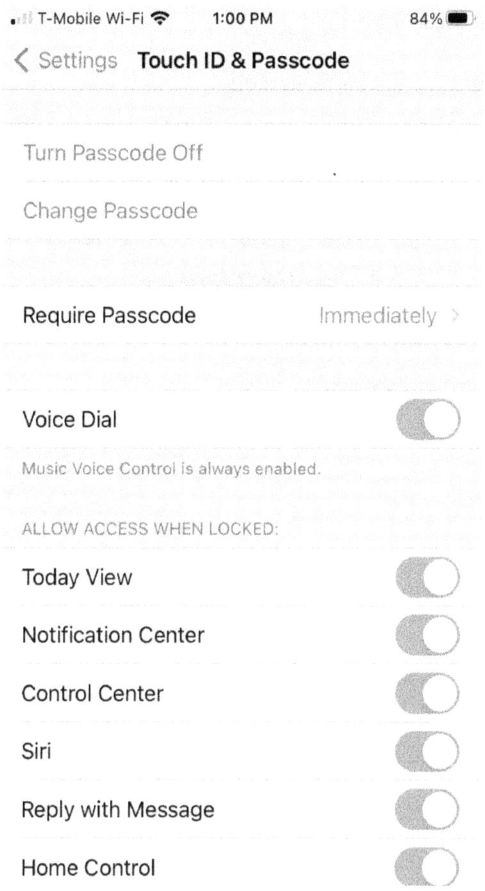

Figure 3.4 – Choosing passcode options

Remember, passcodes represent just the first line of protection. Once you've defined a passcode, make sure you also set up Touch ID or Face ID on your iPhone as well to provide additional security.

Using Touch ID

Touch ID lets you store up to five fingerprints, so you can store fingerprints from one or both hands. Many people use their thumb or index finger, but you can choose any combination of other fingers that you find most convenient to use.

The idea behind storing multiple fingerprints is to ensure that you will be able to access your iPhone with your fingerprint no matter which hand you may use or how you may be holding your iPhone.

To set up Touch ID, follow these steps:

1. Tap the **Settings** icon on the Home screen.
2. Tap **Touch ID & Passcode**. A screen appears asking for your six-digit passcode.
3. Type in your six-digit passcode. A new screen appears, as shown in *Figure 3.5*:

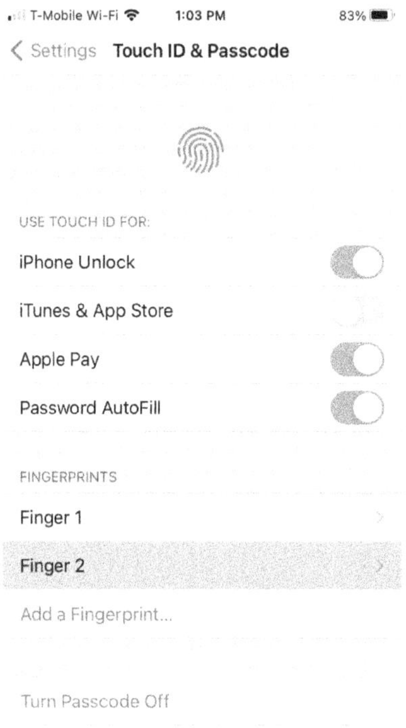

Figure 3.5 – Touch ID settings

4. Tap **Add a Fingerprint…** to recognize another fingerprint (you can swipe left on any fingerprint to either delete it or give it a more descriptive name than **Finger 1** and so on).

Each time you add a fingerprint, you'll need to roll your fingertip across the fingerprint sensor on the Home button until the iPhone recognizes the complete fingerprint. You may also want to define Touch ID to unlock your iPhone or use Apple Pay.

After you've captured your fingerprints in Touch ID, you'll be able to unlock your iPhone just by pressing a recognized fingertip on the Home button where the fingerprint sensor can recognize your fingerprint.

While Touch ID is popular on older iPhone models, Face ID has become the newer method for authorizing access.

Using Face ID

Face ID relies on the iPhone's camera to recognize your face, regardless of whether you wear glasses or contacts. The idea is to scan the front of your face from slightly different angles to capture a three-dimensional image. Then, any time you want to unlock your iPhone, you can just point your camera at your face.

To set up Face ID, follow these steps:

1. Tap the **Settings** icon on the Home screen.
2. Tap **Face ID & Passcode**. A screen appears asking for your six-digit passcode.
3. Type in your six-digit passcode. Another screen appears.
4. Tap **Set Up Face ID**. The screen shows a circle where you need to position your face inside.
5. Hold your iPhone an arm's length away in portrait mode (where the camera is oriented at the top of the iPhone).
6. Roll your head to one side then the other until the camera captures your face from all angles by highlighting the entire circle around your face, as shown in *Figure 3.6*:

Figure 3.6 – Training Face ID to recognize your face

7. Tap **Continue** and repeat the scan to ensure that Face ID can recognize your face, and then tap **Done**.

Once you've successfully captured your face in Face ID, you'll be able to unlock your iPhone by simply pointing your camera at your face. Make sure you hold the iPhone in portrait orientation with the camera at the top. An animated lock icon at the top of the screen will change from closed to open. When that happens, you can swipe up to access the Home screen of your iPhone.

Using passcodes, Touch ID, or Face ID can keep someone from accessing your iPhone without your permission, but you also need to know where your iPhone is so that you don't lose it.

Making sure you don't lose your iPhone

You can't use your iPhone if you can't find it. So, after securing your iPhone with passcodes, Touch ID, or Face ID, set up tracking so that you can find your iPhone in case you misplace it (or in case someone steals it).

The idea behind tracking a lost iPhone is that you can find it again. If for some reason you cannot retrieve your iPhone, then you can remotely wipe all the data so that a thief cannot access your personal data.

Tracking your iPhone requires using iCloud, which requires an Apple ID. Once you turn on tracking, you'll be able to track your iPhone using any device that can access iCloud, such as a computer or an iPad.

Setting up tracking

Since tracking requires an Apple ID, by default, tracking is turned off. To turn tracking on, follow these steps:

1. Tap the **Settings** icon on the Home screen.
2. Tap the Apple ID at the top of the screen that displays your name, as shown in *Figure 3.7*:

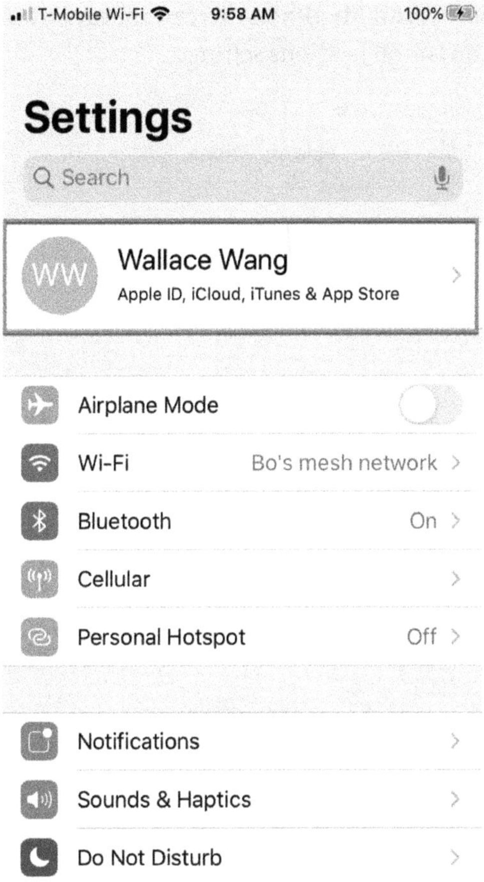

Figure 3.7 – The Apple ID button

3. Tap **Find My**. A **Find My** screen appears.

4. Tap **Find My iPhone**. A **Find My iPhone** screen appears, as shown in *Figure 3.8*, which lets you turn on (or off) various settings:

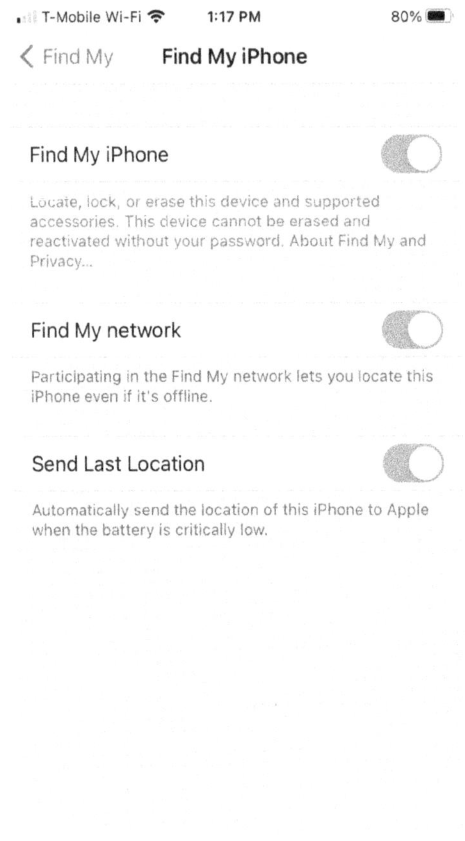

Figure 3.8 – The Find My iPhone screen

5. Turn on all the settings to track your iPhone. You will now be able to track your iPhone through iCloud using any computer's browser.

Locating a missing iPhone

After you've turned on iPhone tracking, you must set up an iCloud account by visiting `iCloud.com`. Once you've turned on iPhone tracking and set up an iCloud account, you'll be able to locate your iPhone through any browser by following these steps:

1. Visit `iCloud.com` using any browser and type in your email address and password.
2. Click the **Find iPhone** icon from the iCloud screen, as shown in *Figure 3.9*:

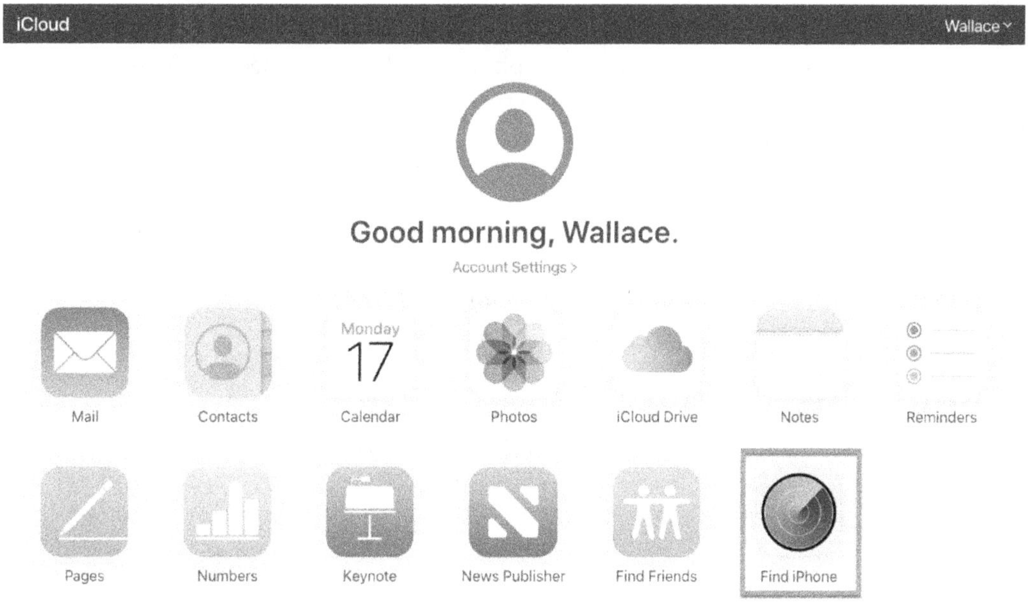

Figure 3.9 – Using Find My iPhone in iCloud

3. Type in your Apple ID password. iCloud displays a map showing the location of your iPhone.
4. Tap the circle that represents your iPhone's location. A menu appears, giving you the **Play Sound**, **Lost Mode**, and **Erase iPhone** options, as shown in *Figure 3.10*:

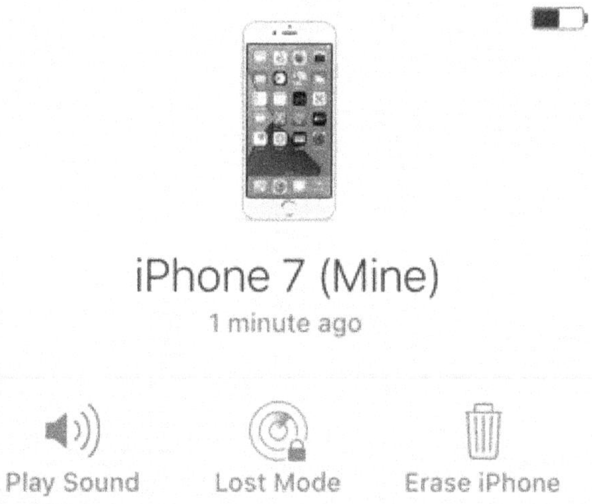

Figure 3.10 – Options for tracking an iPhone

Play Sound makes your iPhone play a noise so that you can find it in your home. **Lost Mode** lets you lock your iPhone and display a phone number for someone to contact you so that you can recover your lost iPhone. **Erase iPhone** lets you wipe everything important from your iPhone so that nobody can retrieve that data.

Once you've set up tracking to find a lost iPhone, and you have set up a passcode, Touch ID, or Face ID to block unauthorized access, it's time to start customizing your iPhone for fun. One way to personalize your iPhone is to change its wallpaper, which is the image that appears in the background whenever the Home screen appears.

Changing the wallpaper

Since you'll use the Home screen often, you might as well display an image that you like, such as an image that inspires you, or your favorite pet or person. Apple provides some wallpaper options, but you can always buy separate wallpaper images from other companies.

However, chances are good that you've taken pictures of something or someone you like, so you can use any image stored in the **Photos** library or any image you find on the internet.

To change your wallpaper, follow these steps:

1. Tap the **Settings** icon on the Home screen.
2. Tap **Wallpaper**. A **Wallpaper** screen appears.
3. Tap **Choose a New Wallpaper**. A new screen appears, listing the different wallpaper options you can choose from, such as choosing an image stored in your **Photos** library, as shown in *Figure 3.11*:

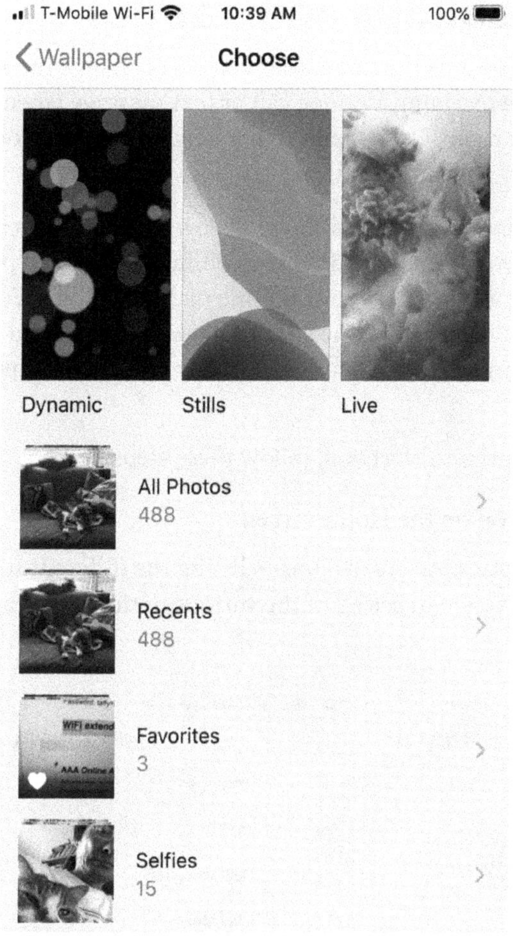

Figure 3.11 – Choosing a different image for the wallpaper

4. Tap an image you want to use. A preview of the image appears, letting you see how it looks on the iPhone screen. You may be able to move or zoom in on an image to change its appearance.
5. Tap **Cancel** or **Set**. If you choose **Set**, a dialog appears letting you define whether to use the image for the Home screen or Lock screen. The Lock screen appears when your iPhone is locked. The Home screen appears when your iPhone is unlocked. This lets you display two different images if you wish, such as a neutral image when your iPhone is locked and a more personal image when your iPhone is unlocked.

Changing the look of your iPhone's Home and Lock screens can make your iPhone unique, but you may want to also change the way your iPhone sounds every time you receive a message or phone call.

Customizing sounds and haptics

By default, every iPhone sounds the same, so if you don't change the sound settings, you may think your iPhone is receiving a phone call or text message when it's really someone else's iPhone in the same room. If you want to personalize the way your iPhone sounds, take some time to modify its sound settings.

In addition to changing the sound your iPhone makes when you receive a message, you can also define whether you want your iPhone to vibrate as a way to provide additional haptic feedback in case you can't hear your iPhone making a noise. For example, you can make it vibrate when you receive a phone call. That way, if you're in a noisy area and don't hear your iPhone ring, you'll still feel it vibrating to let you know you have an incoming call.

To define sounds and haptics to alert you, follow these steps:

1. Tap the **Settings** icon on the Home screen.
2. Tap **Sounds & Haptics**. A screen appears listing the different sound options. You may need to scroll down to see all of the various options you can select, as shown in *Figure 3.12*:

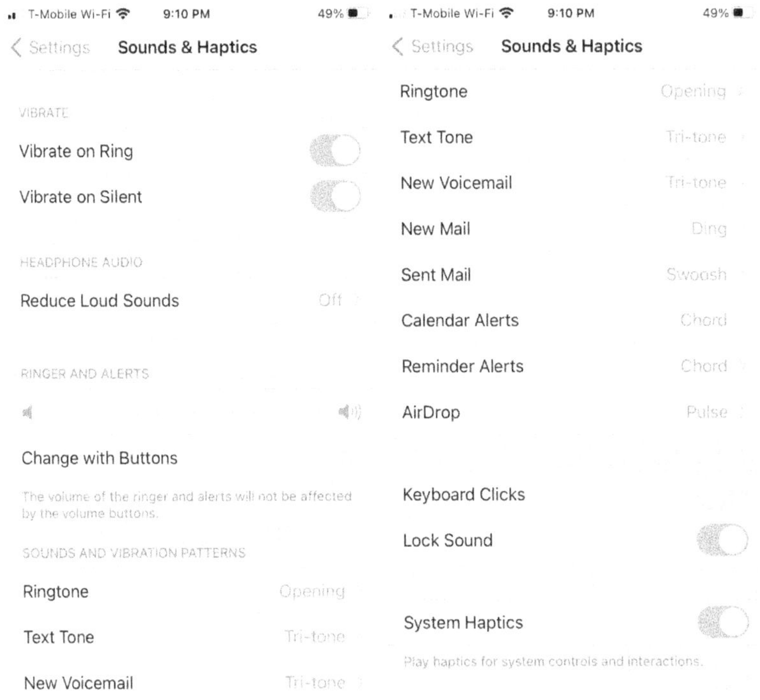

Figure 3.12 – The Sound & Haptics options

Before changing any of the sound and haptic options, determine where you use your iPhone most often. If you use your iPhone in crowded places often, such as in an office or school, you may want to choose softer sounds that won't annoy anyone nearby and rely on haptics to provide vibrations as feedback.

However, if you use your iPhone outdoors, you may want to choose more unique sounds, along with increasing the volume to make it easier to hear your iPhone. For additional feedback, turn **System Haptics** on so that even if you don't hear your iPhone, you can feel it vibrating to let you know when you've received a text message or phone call.

Everyone has different uses and needs for sound and haptics, so feel free to experiment to see what you like best. For example, you may want to change the **Keyboard Clicks** setting to give you audio feedback when you've tapped a key. If you find this clicking noise too annoying, you can always turn it off again.

Even if you prefer sounds, you may find them annoying when you want to work or concentrate. Rather than turn off all sound (and then turn it back on again later), you may want to temporarily disable sounds.

Blocking out disturbances

No matter how much you may love your iPhone and your friends, you may need to focus on a task and you don't want your iPhone to keep beeping or making noises while you're trying to get something done. One simple solution is to turn your iPhone off completely or leave it in another room so that you can't hear it.

Yet a simpler solution is to use the iPhone's **Do Not Disturb** features to temporarily quiet your iPhone. The iPhone gives you two options for blocking out disturbances through the **Do Not Disturb** feature:

- Manually turning **Do Not Disturb** on and off.
- Automatically turn **Do Not Disturb** on and off at a specific time every day.

Manually turning on the **Do Not Disturb** feature takes a conscious effort but can be handy when you temporarily need to block out potential disturbances. Automatically turning the **Do Not Disturb** feature on and off can be handy to encourage you to set aside a specific time when you won't be distracted by your iPhone.

To turn on the **Do Not Disturb** feature, follow these steps:

1. Tap the **Settings** icon on the Home screen.
2. Tap **Do Not Disturb**. A **Do Not Disturb** screen appears, as shown in *Figure 3.13*. You may need to scroll down to view all the options:

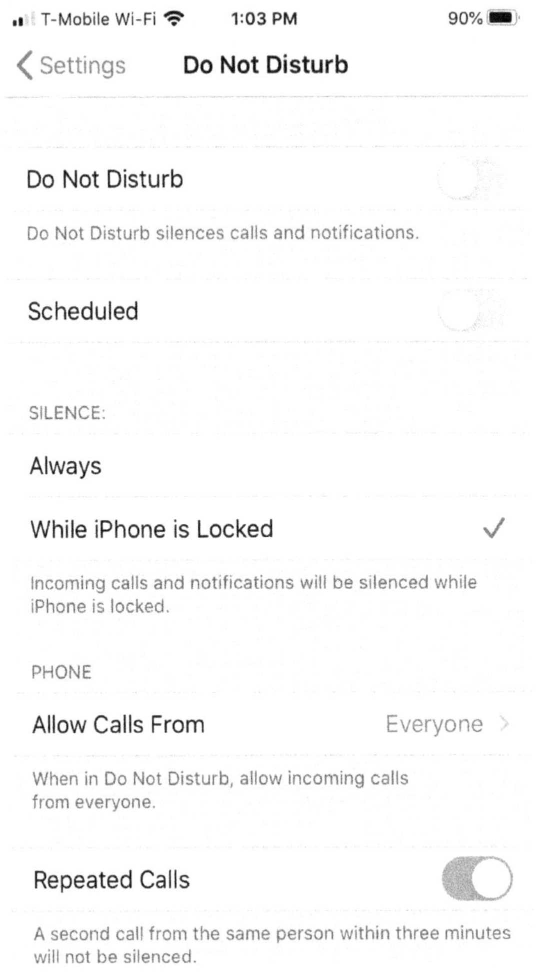

Figure 3.13 – The Do Not Disturb screen

3. Choose **Do Not Disturb** to silence your iPhone. If you choose this option, you'll need to select this option again to allow sounds on your iPhone again.
4. Choose **Scheduled** to define a starting and ending time to disable sounds. If you choose this option, your iPhone will automatically silence itself during the specified time you choose.
5. Choose **Always/While iPhone is Locked** to define whether you want your iPhone to be silent all the time or just when it's locked.
6. Choose **Allow Calls From** to define whether to receive calls from everyone, no one, or just people defined as your favorites or those stored in your **Contacts** app.
7. Choose **Repeated Calls** to allow repeated calls from the same person to get through.
8. Choose **Activate** to detect when you're driving. It lets your iPhone turn on **Do Not Disturb** when it detects you're driving, when it's connected to a car's Bluetooth, or manually.
9. Choose **Auto-Reply To** to send an automated reply to anyone who tries to contact you when you have **Do Not Disturb** turned on.

When you've defined the different audio settings just the way you like them, take a moment to customize the text and screen brightness as well.

Adjusting text size and screen brightness

Depending on your preference and eyesight, you may want to adjust the appearance of your iPhone's screen to modify the size of text and screen brightness. Changing the size of text can make text easier to read at the expense of showing less information, or showing more information at the expense of making text smaller and harder to read. By modifying text size, you can find the perfect balance for you.

You may also want to adjust the screen brightness to a comfortable level. A screen that's too dim or bright can be hard to read. In addition, a screen that's too bright uses up more power that can drain your iPhone's battery, so adjusting the screen brightness can be important for your eyes and your iPhone's battery life.

To adjust text size and screen brightness, follow these steps:

1. Tap the **Settings** icon on the Home screen.
2. Tap **Display & Brightness**. A **Display & Brightness** screen appears, as shown in *Figure 3.14*:

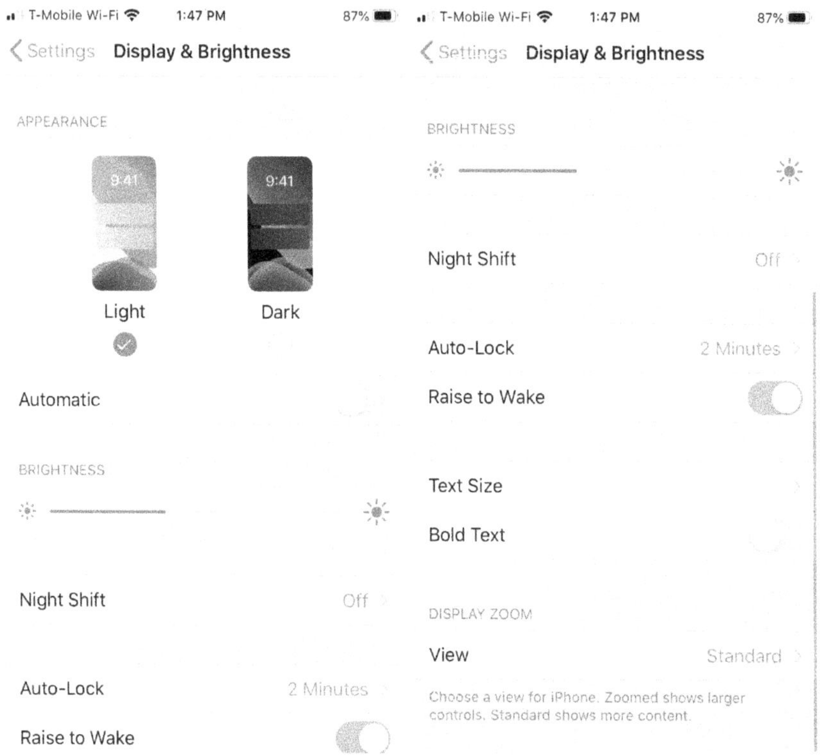

Figure 3.14 – The Display & Brightness screen for adjusting text size and screen brightness

3. Choose **Light/Dark** to select light or dark mode.
4. Choose **Automatic** to switch from light to dark mode based on sunset and sunrise or a scheduled time you define.
5. Choose **Brightness** to adjust a slider to increase or decrease the screen brightness.
6. Choose **Night Shift** to shift screen colors to adjust the closer it gets to the end of the day.
7. Choose **Auto-Lock** to define a time period to automatically lock your iPhone.
8. Choose **Raise to Wake** to turn the iPhone screen on when you raise it.
9. Choose **Text Size** to adjust the size of the text displayed on the screen.

10. Choose **Bold Text** to define the text as bold or not.
11. Choose **View** to set screen content larger or smaller.

Once you've gotten the text size and screen brightness the way you like, you may want to customize the way your iPhone displays information such as date and time.

Customizing date/time formats

Every region of the world displays times and dates differently. In America, dates are written in the month, day, year format—such as January 14, 2021—while in other parts of the world, dates may be written in the year, month, day format - such as 2021, January 14.

The same holds with time. Some people prefer a 24-hour time format, such as 13:25, while others prefer a 12-hour format, such as 1:25 P.M. However you prefer to see the date and time, you can change the format from the default setting.

To customize the format of date and time, follow these steps:

1. Tap the **Settings** icon on the Home screen.
2. Tap **General**.
3. Tap **Date & Time**. The **Date & Time** screen appears, as shown in *Figure 3.15*:

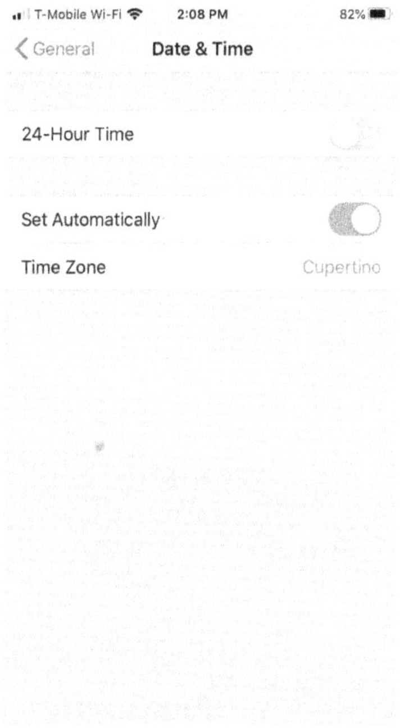

Figure 3.15 – The Date & Time screen for customizing times

4. Choose **24-Hour Time** to set or disable 24-hour time format, such as 14:31.
5. Choose **Set Automatically** to let your iPhone automatically set the time based on your current location.
6. Choose **Time Zone.** When **Set Automatically** is off, this option lets you define the current date and time, along with the time zone you want to use.
7. Tap the back button in the upper-left corner to return back to the **General** screen.
8. Tap **Language & Region**. The **Language & Region** screen appears for letting you choose your preferred languages, along with temperature units (**Celsius** or **Fahrenheit**) and a world region to define the format of times, dates, and currency, as shown in *Figure 3.16*:

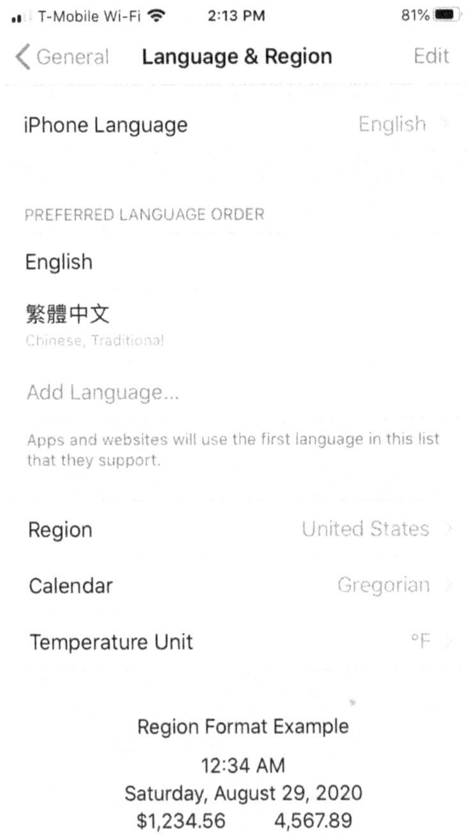

Figure 3.16 – Defining a language and region

9. Choose **Calendar** to define which calendar system to use: **Gregorian**, **Japanese**, or **Buddhist**.

In most cases, your iPhone will default to the most common settings used in your part of the world, but you always have the option of changing these settings if you wish. Regardless of where you live, one additional feature you should modify is how your iPhone uses its battery.

Customizing the battery

The iPhone's battery is designed to last for several years, but over time, it will wear out and hold less of a charge over time. Even if your battery is in optimum condition, it will lose its charge during the day as you use it, so you may want to take the time to optimize your battery and adjust your own behavior by seeing which apps you use that tend to consume the most power.

To see how to customize the battery on your iPhone, follow these steps:

1. Tap the **Settings** icon on the Home screen.
2. Tap **Battery**. The **Battery** screen appears, as shown in *Figure 3.17*. You may need to scroll down to see all the available options on the **Battery** screen:

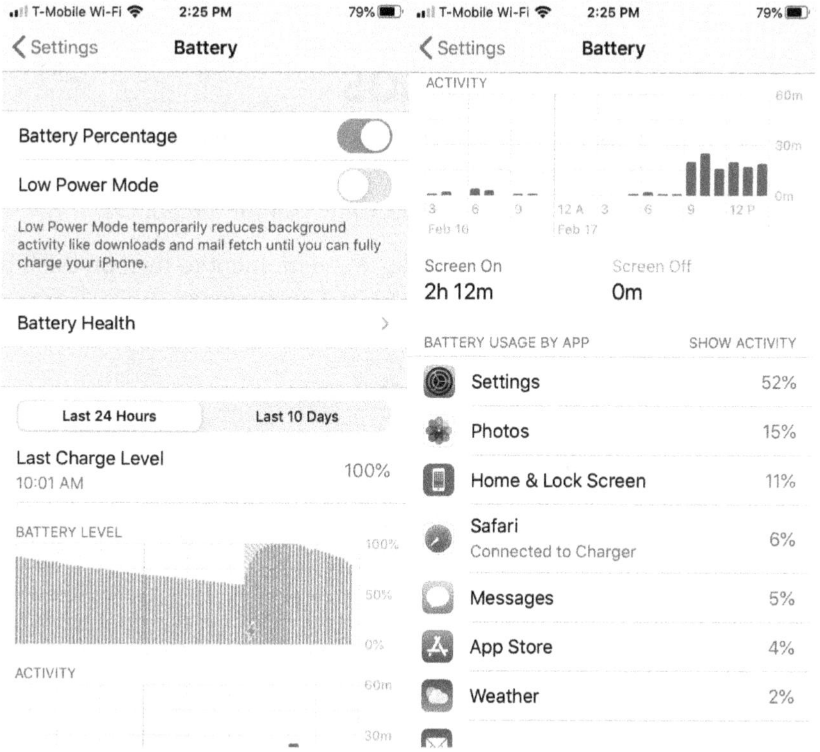

Figure 13.17 – Date pickers let you select different dates and times

3. Choose **Battery Percentage** to define whether to display the battery's remaining power as a percentage of its strength (such as 75%) or not.
4. Choose **Low Power Mode** to reduce background tasks to conserve battery life at the expense of slowing down tasks.
5. Choose **Battery Health** to view the strength of your battery and turn on optimized battery charging to reduce overcharging (and thus wearing out) your battery.

The bottom of the **Battery** screen lets you view your battery's charging levels over time, along with seeing which apps have been consuming the most power. By seeing which apps you use most often and that use the most power, you can adjust your usage to conserve power by using certain apps less often.

Expect over time that your iPhone's battery will hold less and less charge. This is common with all types of electronic devices, but by monitoring which apps use the most power, you can change how you use your iPhone to conserve battery power during ordinary use.

Battery life can be especially critical if you need to use your iPhone to call for help in an emergency. Since calling for help can take time, you might want to take a moment to set up emergency calls on your iPhone.

Defining an emergency SOS

Imagine the worse. What if you're in a car accident and are unable to use your hands to dial a phone number to call for help? Or what if you're in immediate danger from other people and don't have time to pull out your iPhone and call for the police?

The answer is simple. Before you get into trouble, take a moment to turn on the iPhone's **Emergency SOS** calling feature, which lets you contact emergency services by pressing the sleep/wake button five times to call for help.

To turn on this **Emergency SOS** feature, follow these steps:

1. Tap the **Settings** icon on the Home screen.
2. Tap **Emergency SOS**. The **Emergency SOS** screen appears, as shown in *Figure 3.18*:

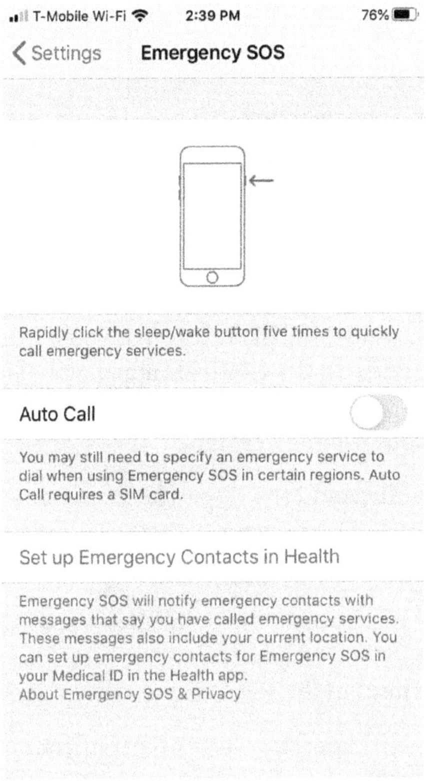

Figure 3.18 – Turning on the Emergency SOS calling feature

3. Tap **Auto-Call**. If **Auto-Call** is turned on, you'll also have the option of **Setting a Countdown Sound**, which will alert you when your iPhone is about to make an emergency call. This countdown sound can alert you in case you accidentally trigger the emergency calling feature so that you'll have time to turn it off if you don't need help.

> **Important Note**
>
> For the elderly or people experiencing illness or other ailments that could make calling for help through an iPhone difficult, consider pairing your iPhone with an Apple Watch. An iPhone can only call emergency services if you're carrying it with you when you need help. Since an Apple Watch is attached to your wrist, it's more likely to be available during an emergency if your iPhone is not within easy reach.

Turning **Emergency SOS** on can be critical, so it's generally a good idea to turn it on since you never know when you might need it.

One last feature you might want to customize is your privacy. Privacy extends beyond just keeping unauthorized people from accessing your iPhone, but also includes how other apps may access your personal data stored on your iPhone.

Protecting your privacy

The more you use your iPhone, the more likely it is that you'll store personal information, such as names and phone numbers in the **Contacts** app, personal and confidential messages in the **Messages** and Mail apps, or personal pictures in the **Photos** app that you may have captured through your iPhone's camera.

While using passcodes, Touch ID, and Face ID can keep unauthorized people from accessing this private data, none of these security measures can keep apps from accessing your private data.

For example, many apps may request permission to access your **Contacts** data to help you find contact information for your friends. Graphic-oriented apps may also request permission to access your pictures in the **Photos** app to use them.

If you're concerned that too many apps may have access to your private data, you can selectively block apps from specific data. That way, you can ensure that only the apps that are most important to you have access to your personal information.

To check and disable which apps are accessing data from your iPhone, follow these steps:

1. Tap the **Settings** icon on the Home screen.
2. Tap **Privacy**. The **Privacy** screen appears, listing all the apps and features available on your iPhone, such as **Calendars**, **Photos**, **Bluetooth**, **Microphone**, and **Health**, as shown in *Figure 3.19*

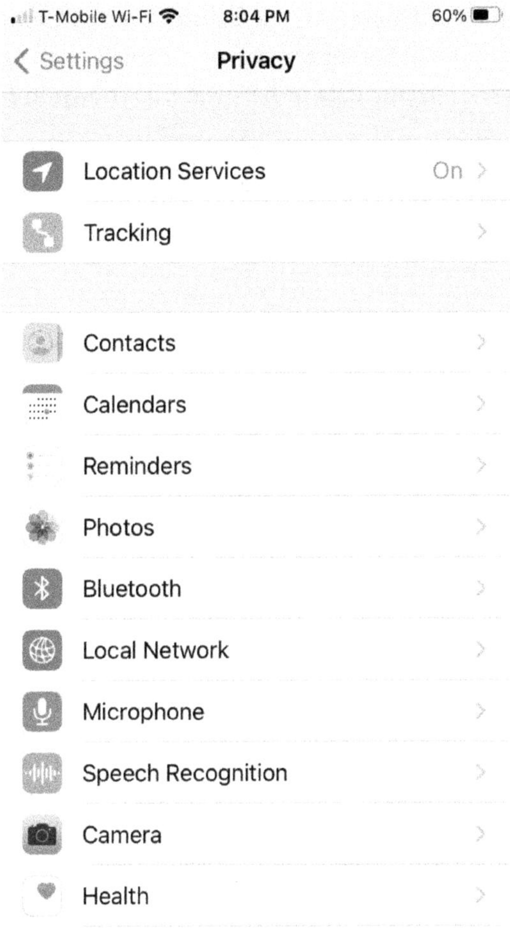

Figure 3.19 – Checking the privacy settings for different data and hardware

3. Tap an app name (such as **Contacts**) or a feature (such as **Camera** or **HomeKit**) that you want to examine. Another screen appears, listing all the apps that have requested access to the specific data or hardware, as shown in *Figure 3.20*:

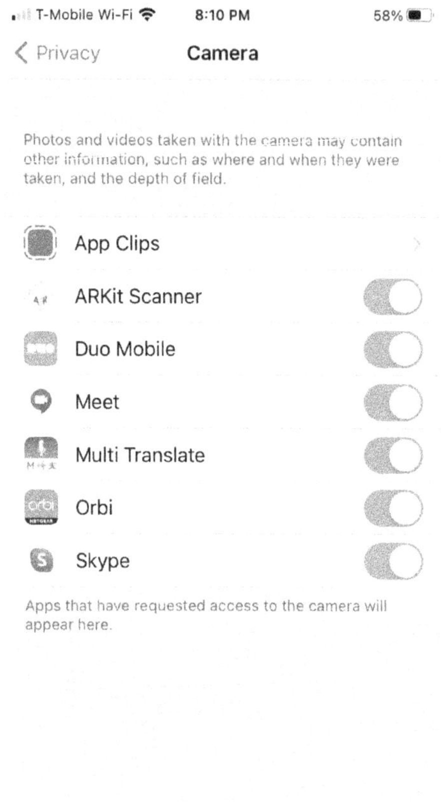

Figure 3.20 – A list of apps requesting access to data or hardware

4. Turn on/off any apps you do or do not want to access the selected data or service.

Often, when running a new app for the first time, it will ask for permission to access data or hardware, such as asking to use the camera. If you do not give an app permission, it likely won't work at all or will work but with limited capabilities. So, it's often easier to give an app permission right away.

However, you may want to periodically review which apps have permission to your data and services just to make sure you still want those apps to have access. While most apps won't maliciously steal your data, limiting access to your data and services can help you reduce the risk of losing important data, so review the privacy settings of different data and services to make sure you aren't giving too many apps access to your iPhone's data and services.

Besides checking your privacy settings periodically, you might also want to check your notification settings regularly as well. Notification settings let apps alert you when certain events occur. Since many apps want permission to notify you, you should define which apps are most important so that you aren't bombarded with notifications from apps that aren't that important to you.

Defining notification settings

Certain apps may need to notify you when certain events occur. For example, the Calendar app may notify you of an upcoming appointment and the Clock app may need to notify you when you've set an alarm.

Notifications allow apps to alert you when certain events occur, but you likely don't want every app to display notifications, or else they could prove annoying if notifications appear too often. You can set turning notifications on or off. If you turn notifications on, you can also define one or more of the following, as shown in *Figure 3.21*:

- **Alerts**: Pops a window in the middle of the screen to block everything until you dismiss the alert.
- **Banners**: Displays a skinny pane at the top of the screen that either appears temporarily or permanently until you tap to dismiss it.
- **Sounds**: Plays a distinctive noise when a notification appears.
- **Badges**: Displays a little red dot with a number (to define the number of alerts, such as the number of unread messages) in the upper-right corner of the app icon:

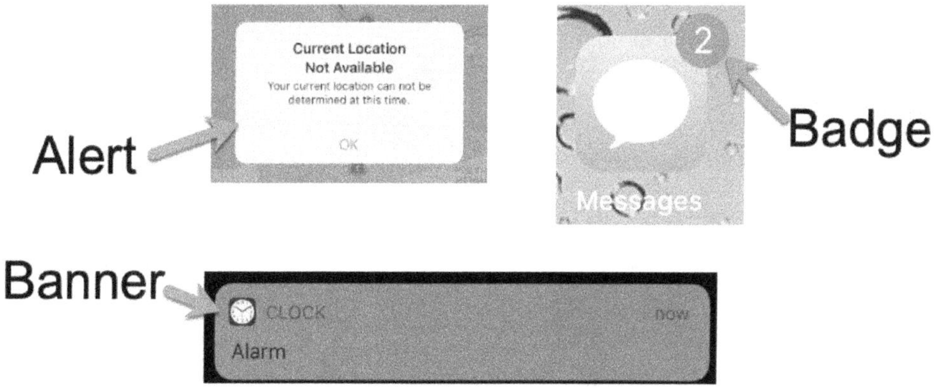

Figure 3.21 – Alerts, banners, and badges

To change the notification settings of different apps, follow these steps:

1. Tap the **Settings** icon on the Home screen.
2. Tap **Notifications**. A list of different app notification settings appears, as shown in *Figure 3.22*:

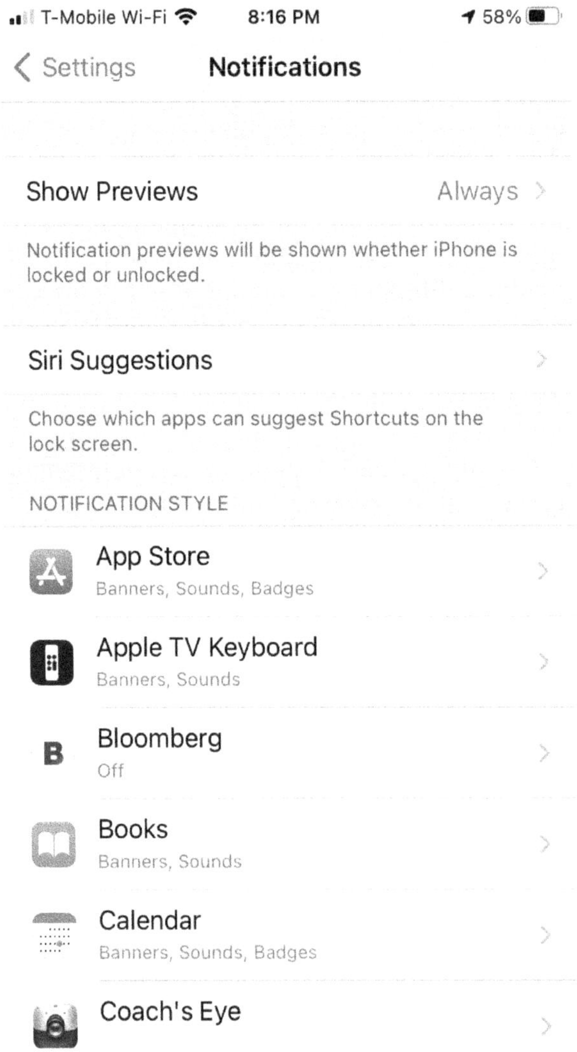

Figure 3.22 – Notification settings for different apps

3. Tap on an app (such as **Books** or **Calendar**) to modify its notification settings.
4. Tap the **Allow Notifications** switch to turn notifications on. As soon as notifications are turned on, a list of different events may appear, letting you specify a notification for each event, as shown in *Figure 3.23* (apps that do not allow notifications for multiple events will display a screen similar to *Figure 3.24* right away):

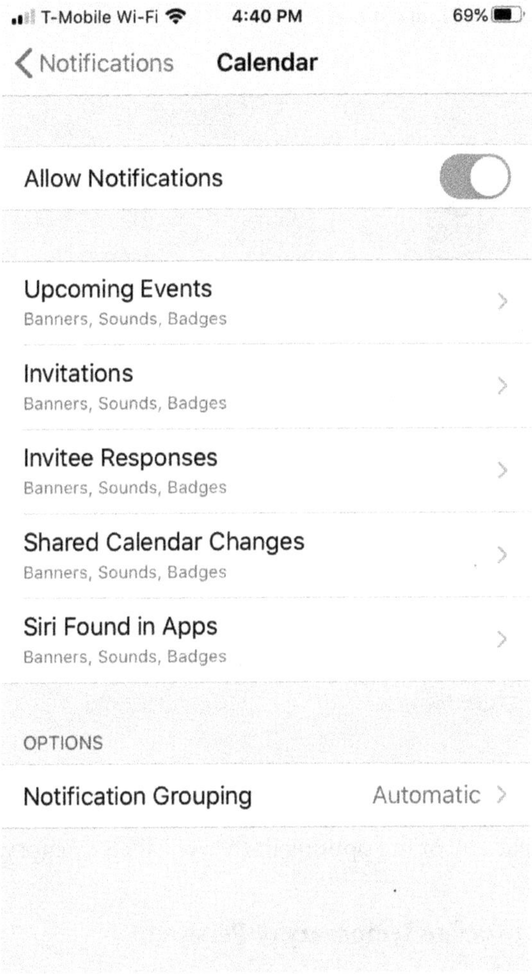

Figure 3.23 – Notification settings for different events

5. Tap an event to define its notifications. A list of options appears, as shown in *Figure 3.24*:

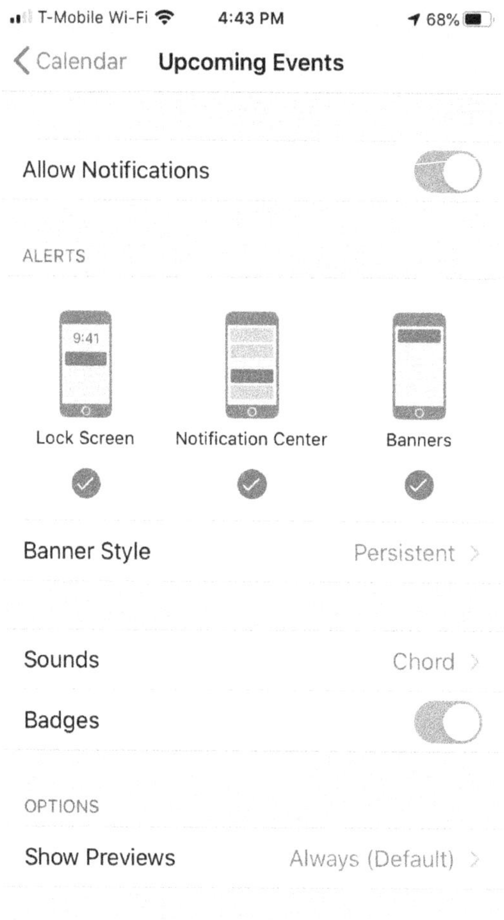

Figure 3.24 – Defining notifications for a specific event

6. Tap to select or clear any of the options in the **ALERTS** category, such as **Lock Screen** or **Banners**.
7. Tap **Banner Style** to define **Temporary** or **Persistent**.
8. Tap **Sounds** to choose a sound for the notification.
9. Tap the **Badges** switch to turn badges on or off.

By itself, an iPhone can connect to a cellular phone network so that you can access the internet. However, you may want to avoid relying on a cellular network in case you get charged for excess data usage or if a cellular network may be spotty or unreliable in a particular area. When you want to avoid a cellular network, you can often rely on Wi-Fi instead.

Setting Wi-Fi, Bluetooth, and hotspots

Wi-Fi lets you connect an iPhone to the internet without paying additional data usage charges through a cellular network. Bluetooth lets you connect an iPhone to accessories such as an external keyboard or speakers.

If a Wi-Fi hotspot does not exist but your iPhone can still connect to a cellular network, you can turn your iPhone into a Wi-Fi hotspot to let other devices (such as a laptop or tablet) connect to the internet through your iPhone.

By connecting to a Wi-Fi network or Bluetooth devices, or turning your iPhone into a Wi-Fi hotspot, you can make sure you always stay connected with your iPhone.

> **Important Note**
> When connecting your iPhone to a Wi-Fi network that you do not personally control, be extremely careful about sending sensitive data such as passwords, banking information, or credit card numbers. That's because it's possible for thieves to intercept data sent to a Wi-Fi router from your iPhone.

Connecting to a Wi-Fi network

In many places, connecting to a cellular network for an extended period of time costs extra. In that case, you may want to connect to a Wi-Fi network to avoid additional cellular network charges.

Even if you live in a place that provides unlimited data, you may still want to connect to a Wi-Fi network since Wi-Fi will often be faster than a cellular network for browsing the internet, sending emails, or even making phone calls.

To connect to a Wi-Fi network through your iPhone, follow these steps:

1. Tap the **Settings** icon on the Home screen.
2. Tap **Wi-Fi**. The **Wi-Fi** screen appears.

3. Tap the **Wi-Fi** switch to turn Wi-Fi on (or off). When the Wi-Fi switch is on, additional options appear, as shown in *Figure 3.25*:

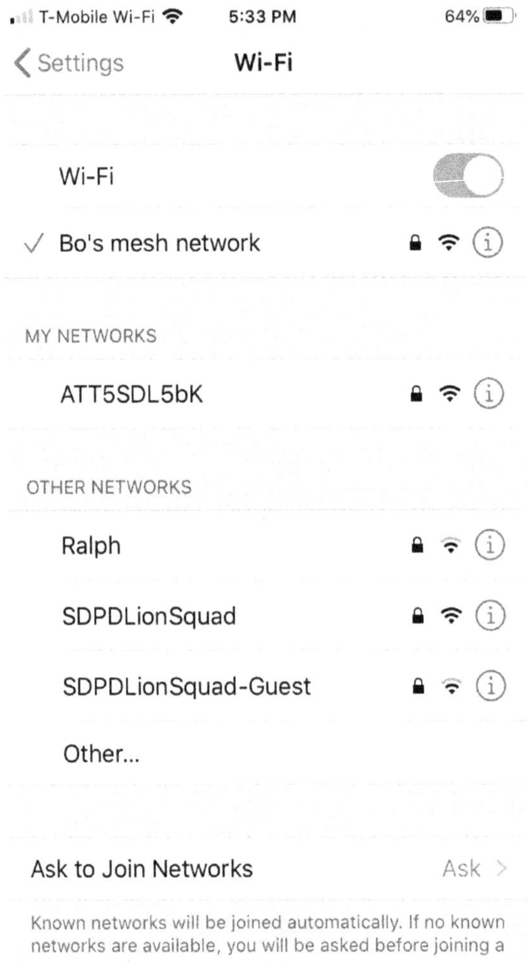

Figure 3.25 – The Wi-Fi screen for defining different connection settings

4. Tap on a Wi-Fi network that you want to join. Wi-Fi networks that require a password will display a lock icon, while those Wi-Fi networks that do not require a password will not display a lock icon. If you selected a locked Wi-Fi network, an **Enter Password** screen appears, as shown in *Figure 3.26*:

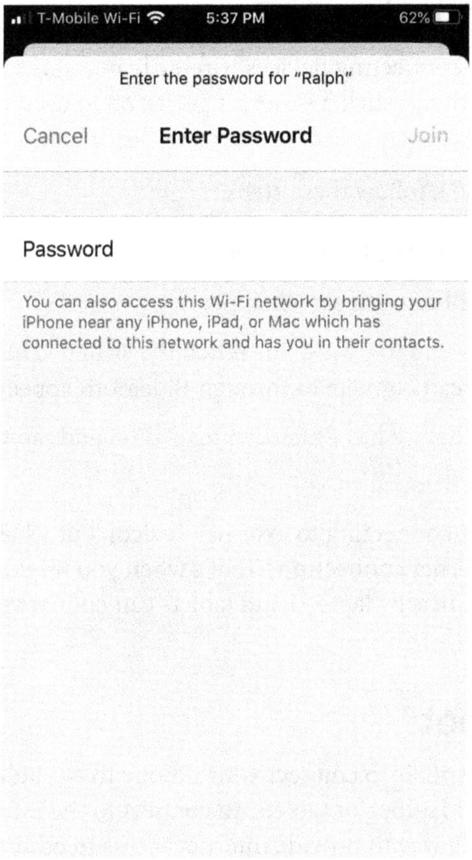

Figure 3.26 – The Enter Password screen for connecting to a locked Wi-Fi network

5. Tap on the **Password** text field and type the password to access the Wi-Fi network.
6. Tap **Join**. A checkmark appears to the left of a Wi-Fi network name to let you know which network your iPhone is currently connected to (you can only connect to one Wi-Fi network at a time).

Connecting to a Wi-Fi network lets you access the internet without relying on a cellular network that may be slower and that will charge you extra per minute. If you want to connect your iPhone to external devices, such as keyboards or speakers, you'll need to turn on Bluetooth as well.

Turning on Bluetooth

Bluetooth is a standard for connecting devices wirelessly in a short range (such as 1 meter or 3 feet). Because Bluetooth has such a short range, it's often used to connect external devices to an iPhone, such as a keyboard, speakers, or headphones.

To turn Bluetooth on (or off), follow these steps:

1. Tap the **Settings** icon on the Home screen.
2. Tap **Bluetooth**. The **Bluetooth** screen appears.
3. Tap the **Bluetooth** switch to turn it on. When the switch is turned on, a list of all the devices your iPhone can connect to through Bluetooth appears.
4. Make sure the other device has Bluetooth turned on and tap the device you want to connect to your iPhone.

Bluetooth can be handy for connecting to external devices, but what if you're stranded somewhere without an internet connection? That's when you might want to use your iPhone as a hotspot so that nearby laptops and tablets can connect to the nternet through your iPhone.

Creating a hotspot

The main purpose of a hotspot is to connect your iPhone to a cellular network and then allow other devices, such as laptops or tablets, to connect to the internet through your iPhone. This can be a handy way to provide internet access to others, but keep in mind that you may be charged extra for data usage and that the internet connection may not be fast. That means you probably don't want to use an iPhone as a hotspot for data-intensive activities, such as streaming movies or playing online video games.

To turn your iPhone into a hotspot, follow these steps:

1. Tap the **Settings** icon on the Home screen.
2. Tap **Personal Hotspot**. The **Personal Hotspot** screen appears.
3. Tap the **Allow Others to Join** switch to turn it on. When the switch is turned on, a list of instructions appears for connecting other devices to your iPhone, as shown in *Figure 3.27*:

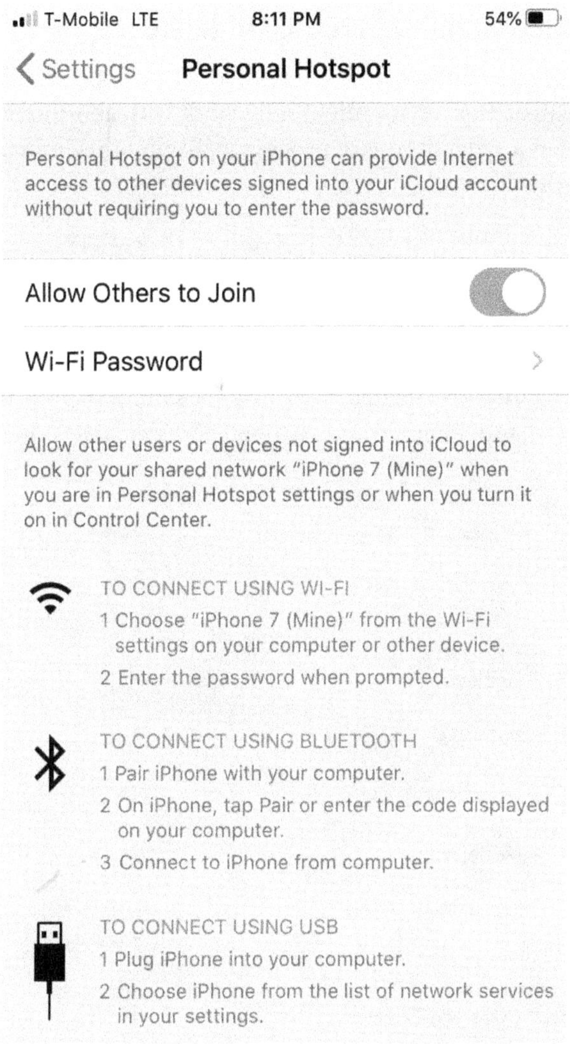

Figure 3.27 – The Personal Hotspot screen

4. Tap **Wi-Fi Password**. A Wi-Fi Password screen appears to let you define a password other people will need to type to connect to your iPhone.
5. Tap **Done**.

In most cases, you can use your iPhone with other devices without worrying about the technical details of your iPhone. However, in case you're curious or you need to know the specifics of your iPhone, you may need to know how to identify different parts of your iPhone, such as the version of iOS used or how much storage space you have left. To find out this information, you need to know how to look up your iPhone's technical details.

Finding information about your iPhone

In some cases, certain apps or hardware devices will only work on specific types of iPhones. For example, an app or device might only work with an iPhone running a certain version of iOS or that has a specific type of processor. To find this information, you can look up details about your iPhone.

To look up the technical features of your iPhone, follow these steps:

1. Tap the **Settings** icon on the Home screen.
2. Tap **General**.
3. Tap **About**. The **About** screen appears, listing the details of your iPhone, such as its software version, model name and number, and available storage space, as shown in *Figure 3.28*:

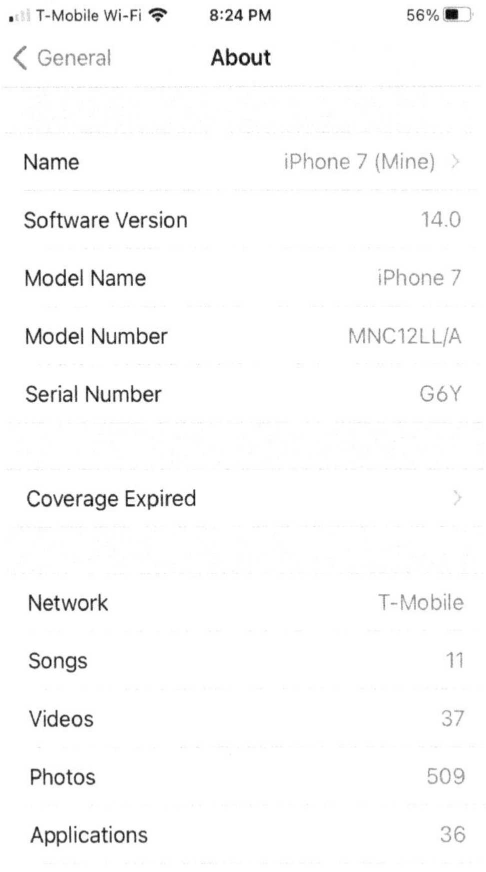

Figure 3.28 – The About screen for looking up information about an iPhone

Perhaps the most important information to check is whether you're running the latest version of iOS or not. The latest version of iOS often fixes bugs and increases security, so make sure you know how to update your iPhone's operating system.

Updating an iPhone

An iPhone is nothing more than a computer running an operating system. With the iPhone, the operating system is called iOS, which Apple updates annually with major changes and throughout the year with minor changes.

Generally, you want to keep your iPhone updated to the latest operating system version since that will offer the most features, along with fixing bugs from previous operating system versions. However, sometimes the latest software updates can prove buggy, which means if you install it on your iPhone, you could wreck its performance.

For that reason, you may want to turn off automatic updates. Automatic updates is designed to update your iPhone and keep it current without you having to consciously install the latest operating system yourself. However, you may want to wait before updating just in case people report troubles with the latest update.

To modify automatic updates, follow these steps:

1. Tap the **Settings** icon on the Home screen.
2. Tap **General**.
3. Tap **Software Update**.
4. Tap **Automatic Updates**. A switch appears so that you can turn automatic updates on or off.

Remember that the longer you keep your iPhone, the less likely it will be able to update to the latest version of iOS. Apple tends to support its products for around 5 years, so keeping your iPhone up to date ensures that it will be able to take advantage of the latest features of iOS. Even if your iPhone can no longer update to the latest version of iOS, it will still work just fine. As long as your iPhone continues doing what you need, that's all that matters anyway.

Using accessibility features

Some people have visual difficulties, while others have hearing or physical limitations. Fortunately, the iPhone comes with options to make all its features accessible for everyone just as long as you take a little time defining different accessibility features.

The iPhone divides accessibility features into the following categories: **Vision**, **Physical and Motor**, **Hearing**, and **General**. Although these accessibility features are designed for those who need them to be able to use the iPhone, anyone can use these accessibility features to make the iPhone easier to use.

To access the accessibility features, follow these steps:

1. Tap the **Settings** icon on the Home screen.
2. Tap **Accessibility**. The **Accessibility** screen appears, as shown in *Figure 3.29*:

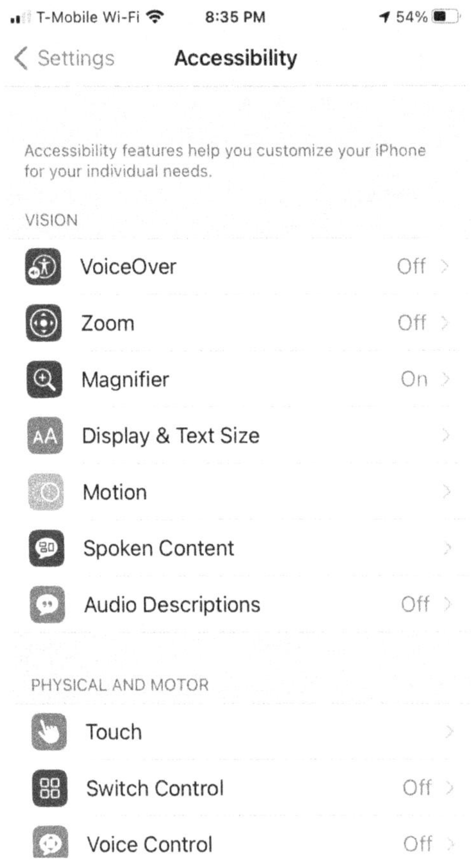

Figure 3.29 – The Accessibility screen

3. Tap an option you want to use, such as **Zoom** or **Touch**. Another screen appears, displaying various options you can define.

Everyone has different uses for the iPhone, so play around with the different accessibility features to see which ones might make your iPhone even easier to use.

Summary

The iPhone provides many different ways to customize its settings, but most settings fall into one of three categories. Fun and personal changes represent settings that have no effect on the performance of your iPhone, such as changing the wallpaper image.

Usability changes represent settings that can make your iPhone easier and more convenient to use, such as setting a **Do Not Disturb** schedule or increasing the text size to make text easier to read.

Potentially critical changes represent settings that could be important to your safety and the security of your data, such as setting up the **Emergency SOS** call feature or checking the privacy settings to make sure you aren't giving access to an app you no longer need.

Remember, you don't need to modify all the possible settings. The same procedure for turning on a particular setting can be used to turn off that same setting, so make sure you know the steps for turning a feature on or off just in case you need to reverse this setting later.

Once you've customized your iPhone's appearance and behavior, you may want to know how to use your iPhone to make phone calls, which is probably the main reason you bought an iPhone in the first place, and that's what the next chapter will cover.

4
Making Phone Calls

The iPhone is a combination of a music player, pocket computer, and mobile phone, but is sold as a phone, and so has the essential purpose of letting you make phone calls. While making and receiving calls sounds simple, there can be all kinds of variations involved in making and receiving calls.

For example, you might want to hold a conference call so you can chat with multiple people at the same time. Or, while on a call, you may get another call so you need to put one person on hold so you can answer the second call. You might also get calls from people you no longer want to hear from, so you block certain calls. Additionally, while on hold, you may be instructed to press a number to choose an option.

As you can see, just something as seemingly straightforward as making and receiving calls can range from simple to complicated, depending on what you want to do. In this chapter, you'll learn all the basics involved in making and receiving phone calls, along with additional features you may find useful as you talk on your iPhone.

The topics we will cover in the chapter are as follows:

- Making a call
- Receiving a call
- Taking multiple calls
- Blocking callers
- Blocking disturbances

Making a call

The most straightforward way of making a phone call is to dial a complete number. For example, many businesses advertise their phone number in public so people can call to get information or purchase a product or service.

Yet in most cases, few people memorize and type in anyone's complete phone number. Instead, it's far more common to store someone's phone number once and then simply tap that person's name to dial their phone number to reach them.

Another way to make a phone call is to view a phone number on a web page or in a text message. Then you can simply tap that phone number to call it without having to type in the number yourself. With so many different ways to make a phone call, you have lots of choice in how you make a phone call with your iPhone.

Typing a complete phone number

Oftentimes you'll need to call someone for the first time, but you don't need to store the phone number to call it again in the future. In this case, it's easier to type in that person's phone number once to make your call without storing that phone number for future use. To make a call by typing a complete phone number, follow these steps:

1. Tap the Phone icon on the Home screen, as shown in *Figure 4.1*:

Figure 4.1 – The Phone icon on the Home screen

2. Tap the **Keypad** button at the bottom of the screen, as shown in *Figure 4.2*. The keypad screen appears displaying a phone keypad:

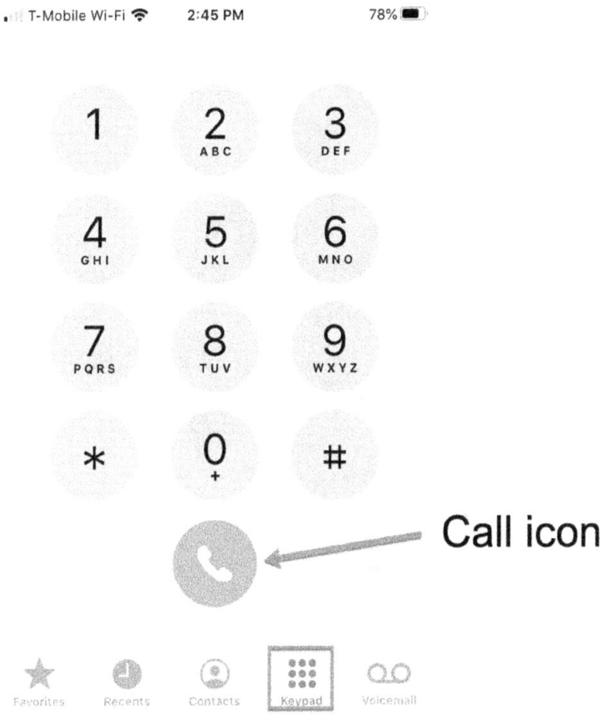

Figure 4.2 – The Keypad button

3. Tap the numbers of the telephone number you want to call (such as `1-800-555-1234`) and tap the green **Call icon** indicated in the preceding figure. After you press the green call icon, it will turn into a red hang-up icon that you can tap to end the call, as shown in *Figure 4.3*:

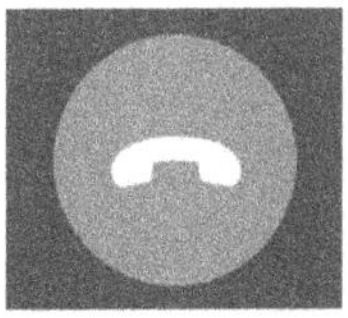

Figure 4.3 – The hang-up icon

The second way to end a phone call is to press the Sleep/Wake button on the side of the iPhone, as shown in *Figure 4.4*:

Figure 4.4 – The Sleep/Wake button

For phone numbers you may only need to call infrequently, typing in the entire phone number may be fine since you won't have to do it often. However, if that phone number already appears on the screen, there's no reason to type it in again.

Calling a phone number from the screen

Typing in a complete phone number can be tedious and error-prone because if you type the wrong number, you won't reach the person you expected. That's why it's more accurate to simply tap a phone number to let your iPhone dial that number for you automatically.

Some common places to find telephone numbers to tap and call are as follows:

- Websites
- Email messages
- Text messages
- Notes

To call a phone number displayed on the screen on a web page, message, note, or any other app, follow these steps:

1. Tap the number on the screen that you want to call. A menu of different options appears, as shown in *Figure 4.5*. The exact appearance will vary depending on whether you're tapping a phone number on a website or a phone number in a text message or note:

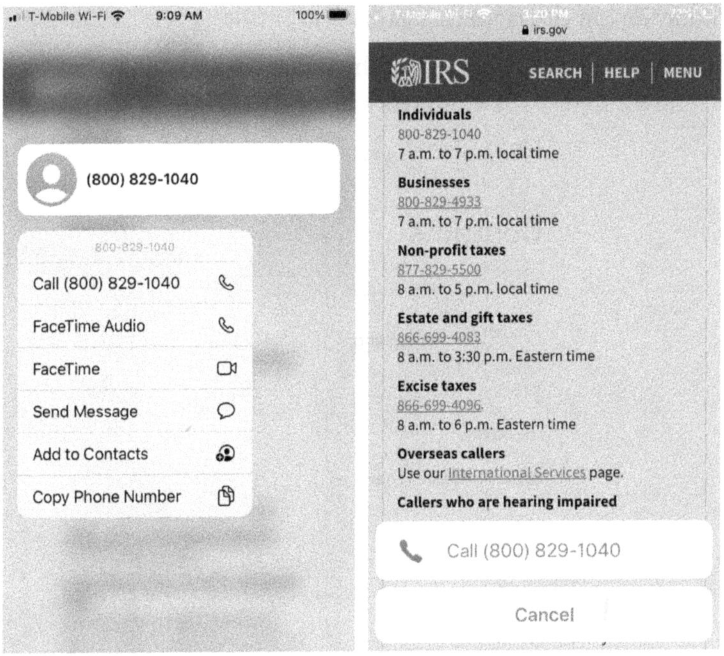

Figure 4.5 – The Call button appears after tapping a phone number displayed on the screen

2. Tap the **Call** button. If you tap the **Call** button, your iPhone dials the number for you. If you don't want to call, tap anywhere on the screen away from the menu to make it go away, or tap the **Cancel** button if one appears.

Calling numbers that appear on the screen can be convenient, but not every number you want to call will appear on the screen. To avoid memorizing and typing in multiple phone numbers, it's much easier to use the **Contacts** app to store phone numbers.

Storing and calling a number from the **Contacts** app

When you just need to call a number once, it's easier to type that number in. However, if you know you'll want to call someone again in the future, it's easier to store that number in the **Contacts** app. That way when you want to call that person again, you can just tap their phone number.

To store a phone number in the **Contacts** app, follow these steps:

1. Tap the Phone app on the Home screen.
2. Tap the **Contacts** icon at the bottom of the screen, as shown in *Figure 4.6*. A list of names currently stored in the **Contacts** app appears:

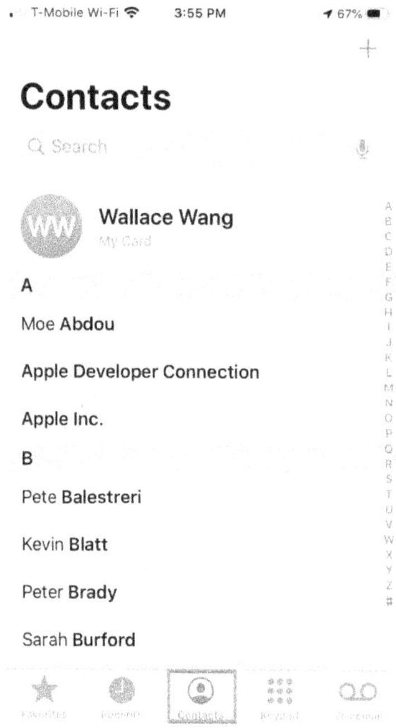

Figure 4.6 – The **Contacts** icon

3. Tap the + (add) icon in the upper-right corner to display a new contact screen.

4. Scroll down and tap the **+ add phone** button, as shown in *Figure 4.7*:

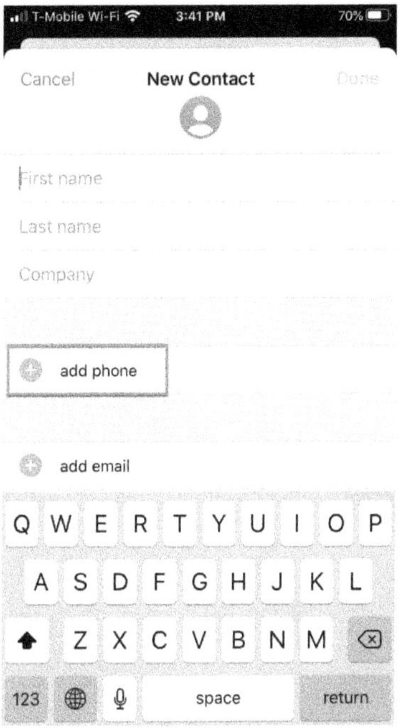

Figure 4.7 – The add phone button on the New Contact screen

5. Tap in that person's phone number and tap **Done** when you're finished adding in any other contact information, such as the person's name.

After you've stored a person's name and phone number in the **Contacts** app, you can call that person by simply tapping on that person's phone number. To call a number stored in the **Contacts** app, follow these steps:

1. Tap the **Contacts** icon on the Home screen.
2. Tap the name of the person you want to call.

3. Tap the phone number you want to call, as shown in *Figure 4.8*:

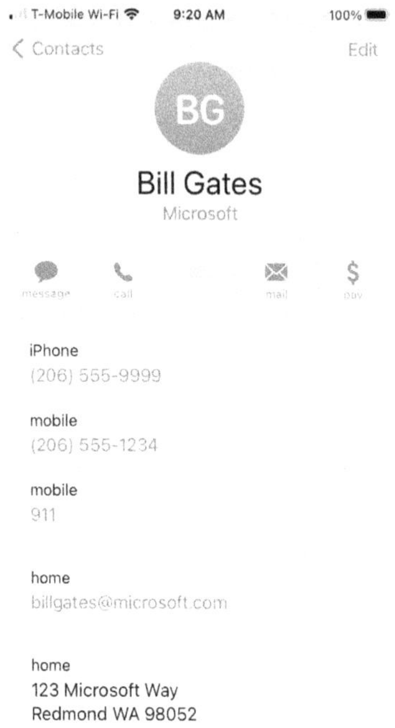

Figure 4.8 – Tap on a phone number to call

The **Contacts** app can be a handy way to store the phone numbers of friends, business associates, relatives, and anyone else important in your life. However, you'll likely store a large number of phone numbers in the **Contacts** app, but only call a handful of those numbers regularly. To make it faster to reach someone you call often, you can designate that person as a favorite person.

Calling a favorite person

Everyone has a small list of people they call most often, perhaps including a spouse, boyfriend/girlfriend, family members, and business associates. While you could constantly hunt for that person's phone number in the **Contacts** app, it's much faster to designate certain people as favorites.

Think of the favorites list as a subset of the names and phone numbers stored in the **Contacts** app. By creating a favorites list, you can quickly find the names and phone numbers of the people you care about the most. Even better, if someone has multiple phone numbers, your favorites list can store just the phone number that's most likely to reach that other person.

To create a favorites list, follow these steps:

1. Tap the Phone app on the Home screen.
2. Tap the **Favorites** icon at the bottom of the screen.
3. Tap the + icon in the upper-left corner of the screen. The **Contacts** app will list all names stored.
4. Tap a name that you want to identify as a favorite person. A dialog appears, listing **Message**, **Call**, or **Mail**, which lets you choose that person's contact information for text messaging, phone calls, or email, as shown in *Figure 4.9*:

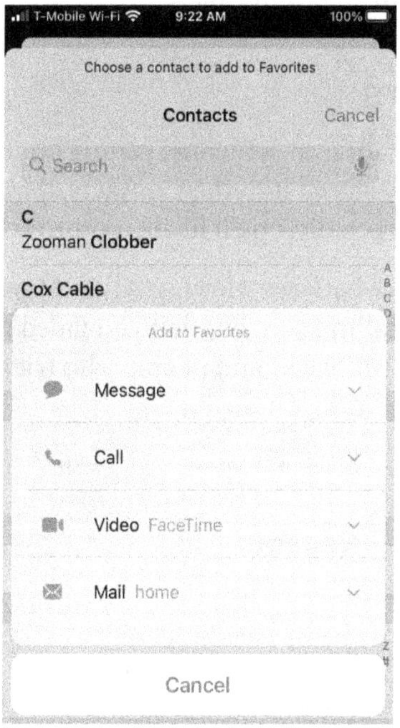

Figure 4.9 – Choosing which contact information to store in the favorites list

5. Tap **Call**. If the person you chose has multiple phone numbers, you'll be able to choose which number you want to store in your favorites list.
6. Tap a phone number.

Once you've stored one or more names and phone numbers in the **Favorites** list, you can make a call any time by viewing your **Favorites** list.

To make a call from the **Favorites** list, follow these steps:

1. Tap the Phone app on the Home screen.
2. Tap the **Favorites** icon at the bottom of the screen. A list of previously stored favorite names appears.
3. Tap on a name to call that person.

Adding names and phone numbers to your favorites list can help you find and call the people you talk to most often. However, sometimes you may not have stored someone's name and phone number in your favorites list. Fortunately, you can always call anyone back by simply looking up the list of recent callers.

Calling recent callers

Each time you call or receive a call from someone, your iPhone keeps track of that person's name (if you previously stored it in the **Contacts** app) or phone number. The idea is that if you spoke to someone recently, you'll likely want to talk to that person again.

The Phone app gives you a choice between viewing **All** or **Missed** calls. The **Missed** list only displays people who tried calling you, but that you failed to answer. The **All** list displays both people you called (in black) and people who tried calling you (in red), as shown in *Figure 4.10*:

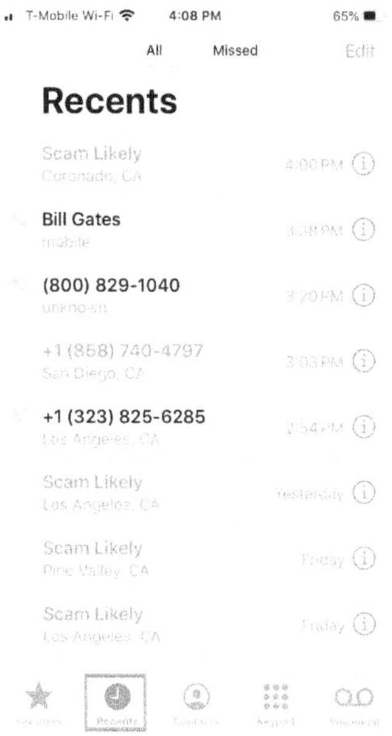

Figure 4.10 – The All list displays both people you called and those who called you

This list of recent calls can be particularly handy in case someone called you and you want to call them back but don't have their phone number saved on your iPhone.

To call a number stored in the **Recents** list, follow these steps:

1. Tap the Phone app on the Home screen.
2. Tap the **Recents** icon at the bottom of the screen.
3. Tap the **All** or **Missed** tab at the top of the screen.
4. Tap a name or phone number to call.

While you may call other people, others may call you. When someone calls, you'll have the option of answering that call or declining, so you need to understand your options for receiving a call.

Receiving a call

When you receive a phone call, your iPhone can play a sound (called a ringtone) and/or vibrate to provide you with additional haptic feedback in case you don't hear the ringtone. When you receive a call, your iPhone will display the calling phone number (or the name of the caller, if you previously stored that person's name and phone number in the **Contacts** app).

If your iPhone is currently locked, you'll see a screen asking you to swipe to answer the call, as shown in *Figure 4.11*:

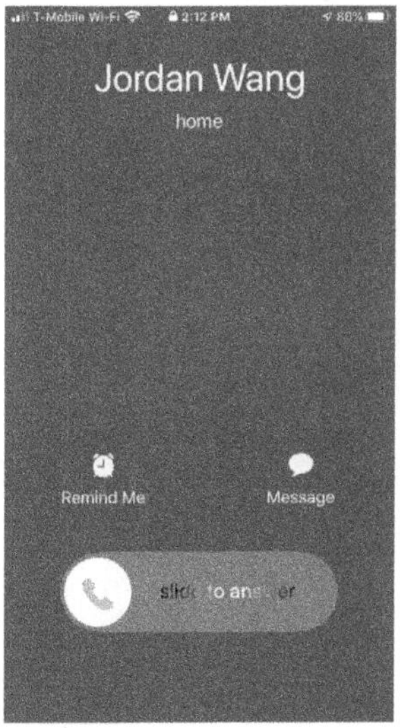

Figure 4.11 – Receiving a phone call on a locked iPhone

If your iPhone is unlocked and you receive a call, you'll see a slightly different screen that gives you the option of accepting or declining the call, as shown in *Figure 4.12*:

Figure 4.12 – Receiving a phone call on an unlocked iPhone

If you tap the banner shown in the preceding figure anywhere except either the red or green button, the banner expands to fill the entire screen, as shown in *Figure 4.13*:

Figure 4.13 – The expanded incoming call screen

To define whether an incoming phone call appears as a banner or fullscreen display, follow these steps:

1. Tap the **Settings** icon on the Home screen.
2. Tap **Phone**. The **Phone** screen appears.
3. Tap **Incoming Calls**. A screen appears, letting you choose between **Banner** and **Full Screen**.

When you receive a phone call, you have several options:

- Answer the call (slide to answer or tap the green **Accept** button).
- Decline the call (tap the red **Decline** button).
- Set a reminder to call back (tap the **Remind Me** icon).
- Send a pre-defined message to the caller (tap the **Message** icon).

Since you'll likely get calls from a variety of people, take some time now to define the ringtone and haptic feedback your iPhone will make each time you receive a call.

Defining a ringtone and haptic feedback

A ringtone plays a specific sound when you receive a call. Haptic feedback makes your iPhone vibrate to let you know someone's calling. Since you may not always want a ringtone to play when you receive a call (such as when you're in a movie theater), you can turn your iPhone's sound on or off by toggling the Ring/Silent switch that appears on the left side, as shown in *Figure 4.14*:

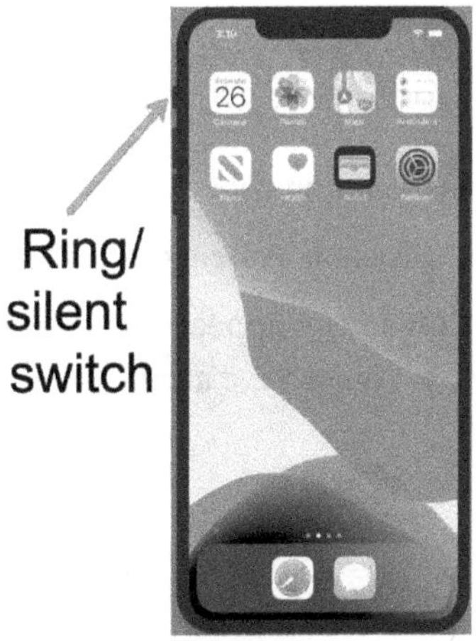

Figure 4.14 – The Ring/Silent switch on the iPhone

To set the ringtone and haptic feedback, follow the steps given below:

1. Tap the **Settings** icon on the Home screen.
2. Tap **Sounds & Haptics**. The **Sounds & Haptics** screen appears.
3. Tap **Ringtone**. A **Ringtone** screen appears, letting you choose between different ringtones or access the **Tone Store**, as shown in *Figure 4.15*:

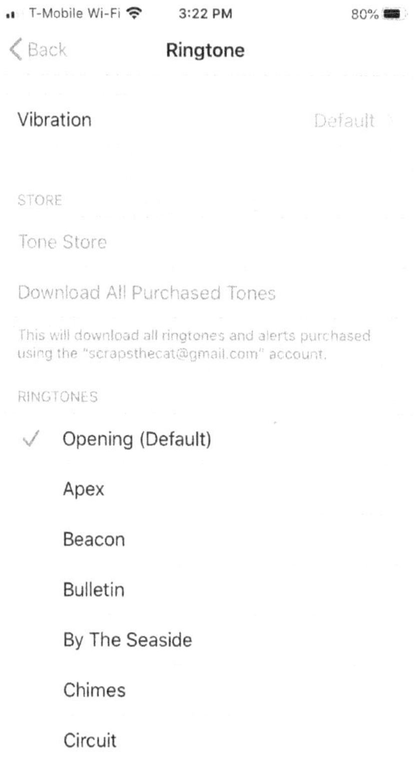

Figure 4.15 – Choosing a ringtone from the Ringtone screen

4. Tap a ringtone you want to use, such as **Beacon** or **Chimes**.
5. Tap **Vibration**. The **Vibration** screen appears, letting you choose from different haptic feedback options when you receive a call, as shown in *Figure 4.16*:

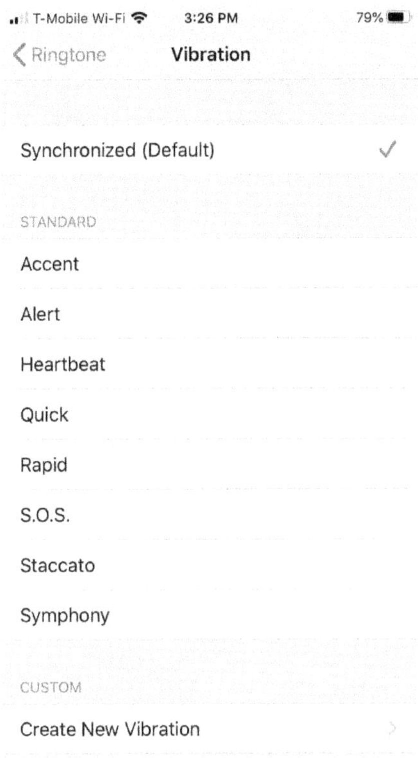

Figure 4.16 – Choosing a vibration pattern for haptic feedback when receiving a call

Once you've defined your chosen haptic feedback for when you receive a call, you might want to take time to specify whether you also want your iPhone to play a ringtone or stay silent. In addition, you can also adjust the volume of your ringtone to make it louder or softer.

To define whether to include haptic feedback with ringtones or when your iPhone is silent, follow these steps:

1. Tap the **Settings** icon on the Home screen.

2. Tap **Sounds & Haptics**. The **Sounds & Haptics** screen appears, letting you toggle the **Vibrate on Ring** and **Vibrate on Silent** switches, as shown in *Figure 4.17*:

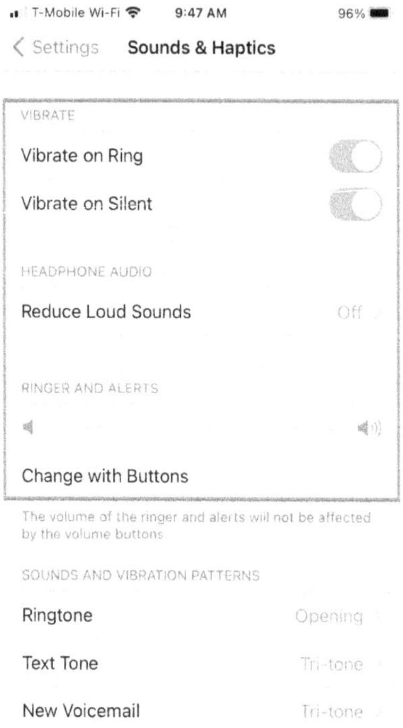

Figure 4.17 – Turning haptic feedback on or off for ringtones or silent mode

3. Tap the **Vibrate on Ring** and **Vibrate on Silent** switches to turn haptic feedback on or off.
4. Drag the volume slider to adjust the volume of your chosen ringtone.
5. Tap the **Change with Buttons** switch to allow you to adjust the volume of your ringtone using the volume buttons on the side of the iPhone. If this switch is off, the volume of your ringtone will be defined by the slider position in *step 4*.

Defining ringtones, volume, and haptic feedback is fine for notifying you of an incoming call. However, if you get an important call but can't answer it at the time, you have two choices:

- Create a reminder to yourself.
- Send a pre-defined message to the caller.

Creating a reminder for returning a call

When someone calls and you aren't able to answer the call right away, but don't want to forget about this call from someone important, set up a reminder. A reminder simply displays a note to yourself to return the call you missed.

There are two ways you can create a reminder. First, you can create a reminder that will pop up on your iPhone screen as soon as you leave your current location. Second, you can create a reminder that will pop up one hour later. In both cases, the reminders can help you return important calls.

To create a reminder when you are unable to answer a call, follow these steps:

1. Wait until you receive a call (see *Figures 4.11* and *4.13*).
2. Tap the **Remind Me** icon. A dialog appears giving you a choice to be reminded to call back when you leave your current location, or in one hour, as shown in *Figure 4.18*:

Figure 4.18 – Defining a reminder to return a call

3. Tap **When I leave** or **In 1 hour**. Both methods define a reminder that's stored in the **Reminders** app, as shown in *Figure 4.19*:

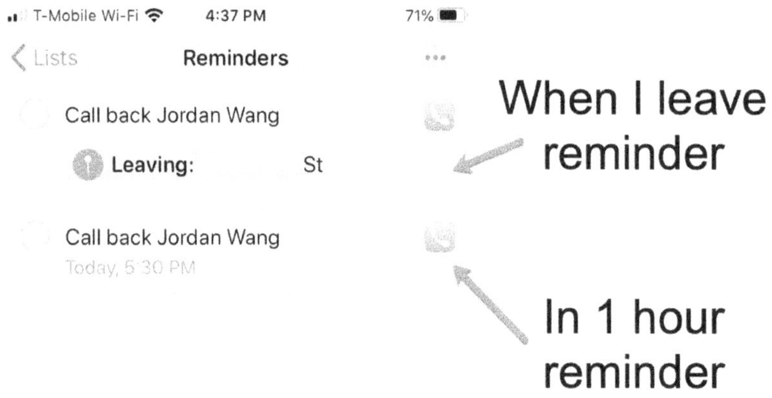

Figure 4.19 – Viewing callback reminders in the Reminders app

The moment you leave your current location or wait one hour, depending on your choice, a reminder will appear on your Home screen to call back the person who called you earlier. At this point, you can open the **Reminders** app and tap the green Phone icon to call that person back.

Reminders can be handy for dealing with calls right away. However, reminders don't let your caller know that you intend to call back. That's why you can prepare pre-defined messages that you can send back to someone right away to let your caller know you'll call back as soon as possible.

Creating messages for returning a call

When someone calls and you set up a reminder, your caller has no idea when or even if you will call back. To get around this problem, take some time to set up a pre-defined message. Now when someone important calls, you can send them this pre-defined message so they know you got their call but just weren't able to answer it at the moment, and that you'll get back to them.

The first step to sending a message to a caller is to create the message. Then you can choose which response you want to send.

To create a message to send to a caller, follow these steps:

1. Tap the **Settings** icon on the Home screen.
2. Tap **Phone**. The **Phone** screen appears, as shown in *Figure 4.20*:

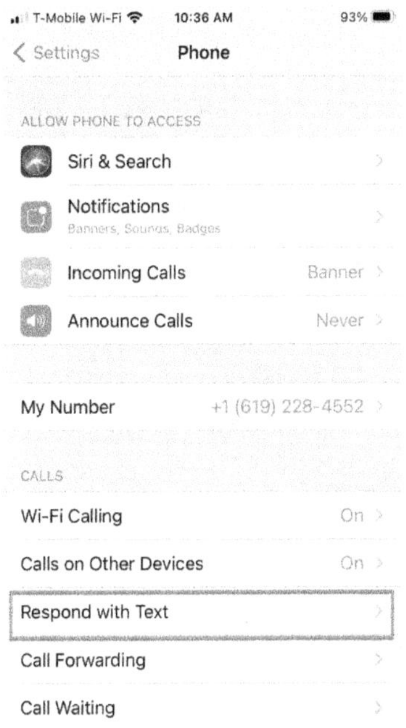

Figure 4.20 – The Respond with Text option on the Phone screen

3. Tap **Respond with Text**. A **Respond with Text** screen appears, listing several responses you can choose from as shown in *Figure 4.21*. You can either use the default responses or write your own:

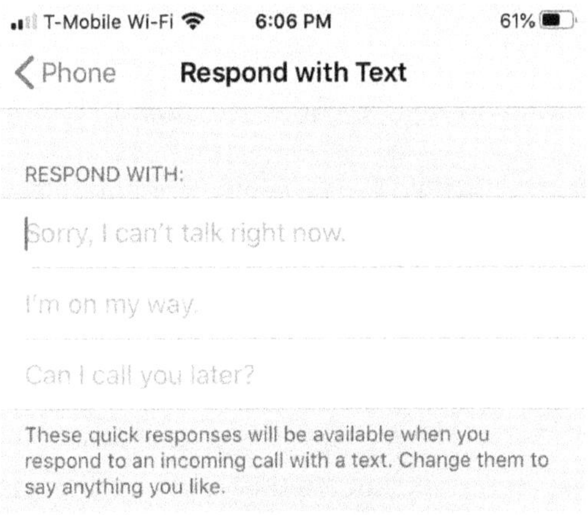

Figure 4.21 – Viewing and editing pre-defined responses

Whether you've defined your own messages or just want to use the default messages, you can set them to be sent to a caller to let them know you're not available now but will get back to them as soon as possible.

To send a message when receiving a call, follow these steps:

1. Wait until you receive a call (see *Figures 4.11* and *4.13*).
2. Tap the **Message** icon. A dialog appears, giving you a choice of which message to send, as shown in *Figure 4.22*:

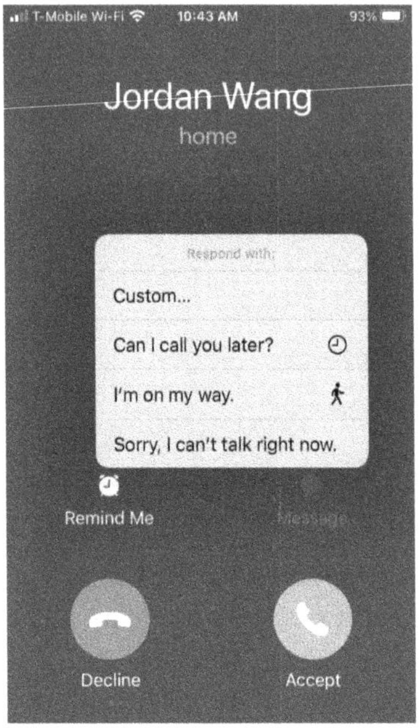

Figure 4.22 – Choosing the message to send to a caller

3. Tap the message you want to send or choose **Custom** to type a message to send.

By using reminders and messages, you can return important phone calls as soon as possible. In some cases, you may be talking to one person when another call comes in that you have to take at that moment. Rather than calling that person back, you might want to take that second call while still holding on to the first call.

Taking multiple calls

If you're talking to someone important and another crucial call comes in, you may want to keep both calls on the line. To do this, the iPhone gives you two options. First, you can put the first caller on hold temporarily while you talk to the second caller. When you're done with the second call, you can then return to the first caller.

Second, you can take both calls in a conference call. That way, multiple people can talk to each other at once.

Putting people on hold can be handy when you want to talk to one person at a time. Conference calls are useful when you want a group of people to talk to each other.

To create a conference call or put the current caller on hold so you can chat with a second person, follow these steps:

1. Call or accept a call from another person. When a second person calls while you're already connected to someone else, your iPhone gives you options to hold or end your current call, or switch to the second caller, as shown in *Figure 4.23*:

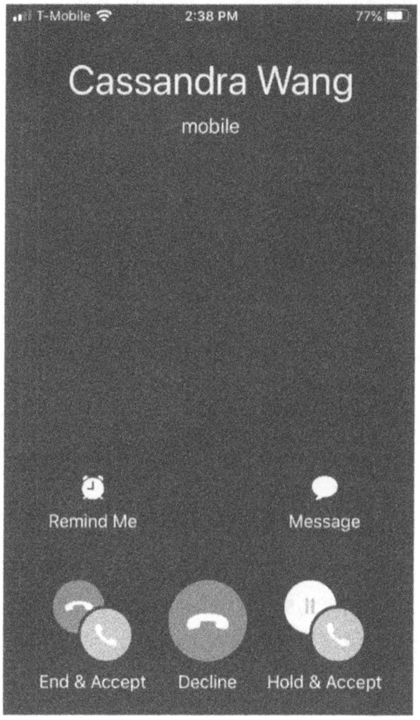

Figure 4.23 – Receiving a second call in the middle of another call

2. Tap **Hold & Accept**. This will let you put your current caller on hold while you speak to the second caller.

3. Tap **merge calls** to create a conference call (or tap **swap** to speak to the other person), as shown in *Figure 4.24*:

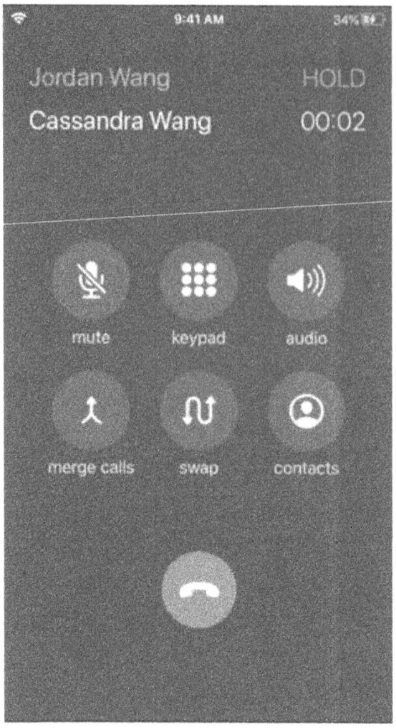

Figure 4.24 – Choosing to merge or swap callers

4. Tap the red hang-up button when you want to disconnect from the call.

In most cases, you'll be happy to receive phone calls on your iPhone. Unfortunately, many con artists, telemarketers, and just plain annoying people may try to call you. While you can ignore these calls, they might never stop calling periodically. When this happens, you might want to consider blocking these callers for good.

Blocking callers

Most likely you'll get phone calls from people you don't want to talk to, either because you no longer like them anymore or because they're unsolicited calls from people you don't know.

When you get a phone call, the caller's name appears on the screen if you've added that phone number and the caller's name in the **Contacts** app. If you have not added both the phone number and caller's name in the **Contacts** app, only the caller's phone number appears on the screen.

Once you receive a call from someone, you can block that phone number. To block a call, follow these steps:

1. Tap the Phone icon on the Home screen.
2. Tap the **Recents** icon at the bottom of the screen. A list of recent calls appears where an **i** is shown inside a circle icon to the right of each call, as shown in *Figure 4.25*:

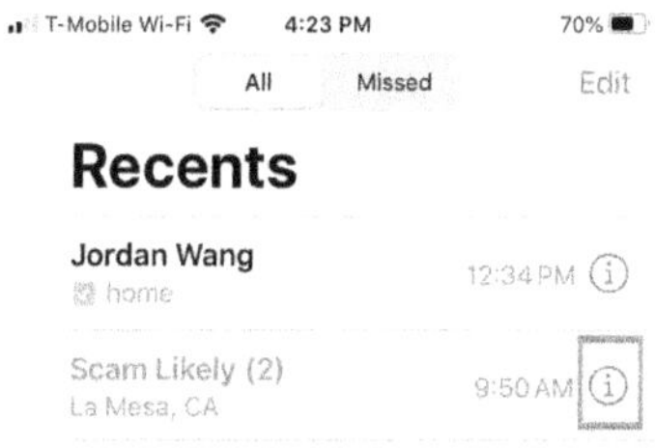

Figure 4.25 – The information icon appears next to each received call

3. Tap the **i**-inside-a-circle icon that appears to the right of the caller you want to block. A new screen appears listing details about the caller, such as their phone number and the time they called.
4. Scroll down this screen until you find the **Block this Caller** option near the bottom, as shown in *Figure 4.26*:

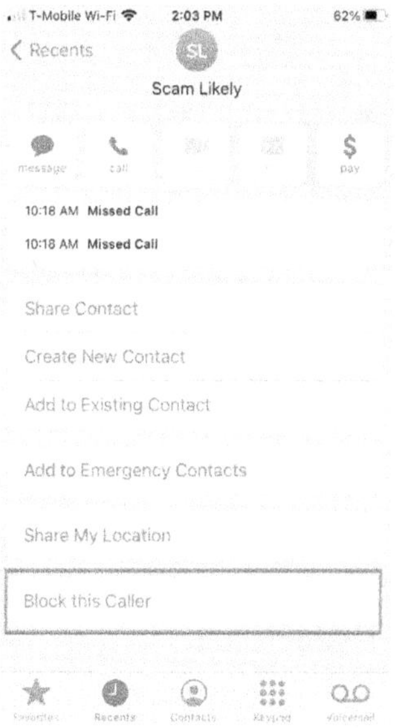

Figure 4.26 – The Block this Caller option

5. Tap **Block this Caller**.

Once you block a caller, that person can call you all they want and they'll never annoy you with their calls ringing or by appearing on your iPhone again. Feel free to block any callers you like, including people you no longer want to talk to, or complete strangers you never wanted to talk to in the first place.

Occasionally, you may need to stop blocking a particular phone number, such as one belonging to someone you're now willing to talk to again. To unblock a previously blocked phone number, follow these steps:

1. Tap the **Settings** icon on the Home screen.
2. Tap the **Phone** icon and scroll down to the bottom of the screen, as shown in *Figure 4.27*:

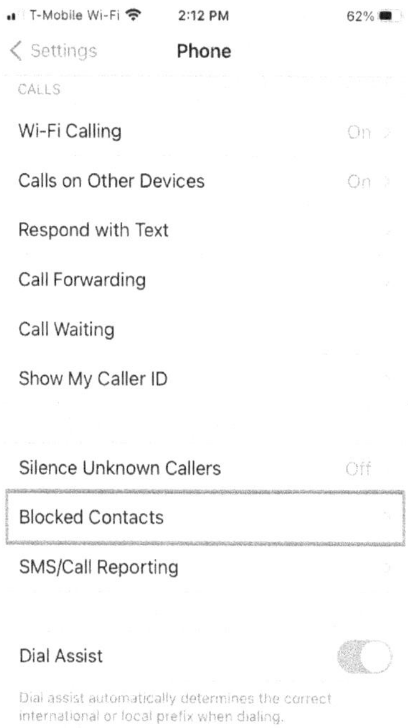

Figure 4.27 – The Blocked **Contacts** option on the Phone screen

3. Tap **Blocked Contacts**. A list of blocked phone numbers appears.
4. Tap on the phone number you want to unblock. A screen appears listing various options, including **Add to Existing Contact**.
5. Tap **Add to Existing Contact** to add the blocked phone number to your **Contacts** app.

After blocking callers, go through your list of blocked calls periodically to make sure you didn't accidentally block an unknown but valid caller. That way you can ensure that you only receive calls you want from people you already know.

Blocking disturbances

Sometimes you may want to set aside time for when you don't want your iPhone ringing or displaying alerts or notifications. When you want a little peace and quiet, you can turn on the **Do Not Disturb** feature. To turn this feature on, follow these steps:

1. Tap the **Settings** icon on the Home screen.
2. Tap the **Do Not Disturb** icon. The **Do Not Disturb** screen appears as shown in *Figure 4.28*:

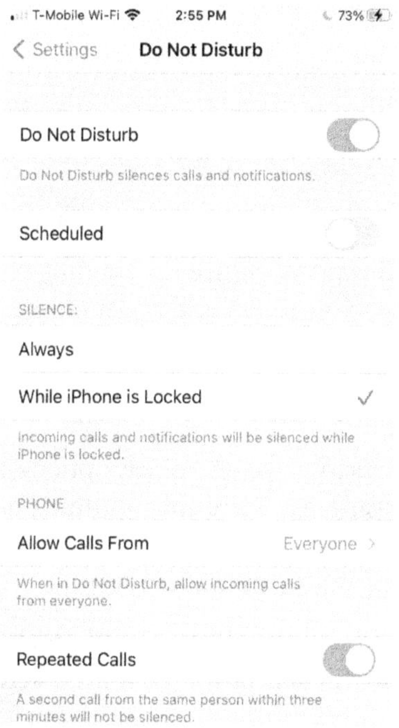

Figure 4.28 – The Do Not Disturb screen

3. Tap the **Do Not Disturb** switch to turn it on or off. When Do Not Disturb is on, a crescent moon icon appears in the upper-right corner of the screen.

Another way to toggle Do Not Disturb on or off is to open the Control Center (swipe up from the bottom on iPhones with a Home button, or swipe down from the upper right corner on iPhones without a Home button). Then tap the Do Not Disturb icon shown in *Figure 4.29*:

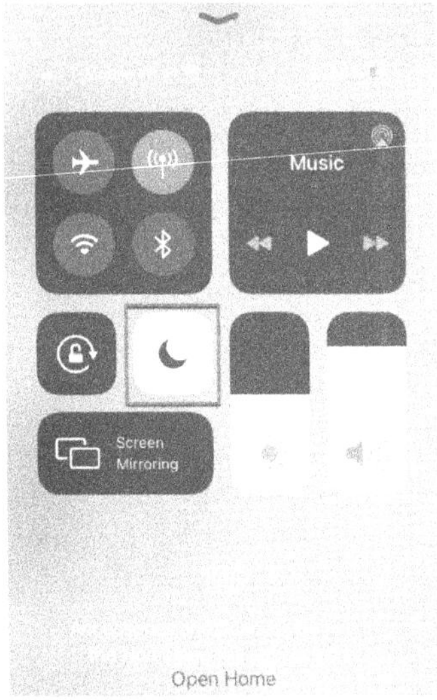

Figure 4.29 – The Do Not Disturb icon on the Control Center screen

Finally, if someone calls and you want to silence the ringing, press the Lock button. Remember, you can control when you accept and reject phone calls and notifications.

Summary

The main purpose of the iPhone is to make and receive phone calls. Making and receiving a phone call is fairly straightforward, but there are additional options you might want to use, such as creating a conference call, putting someone on hold, or using a keypad to choose different options while calling an automated service.

To help identify callers, it's best to store their names and phone numbers in the **Contacts** app. That way, the person's name will appear on the iPhone screen when they call, so you never have to guess.

Since you'll likely get unwanted calls, make sure you know how to block and unblock callers. You'll never be able to stop all unwanted calls, but by blocking certain phone numbers, you can make sure unwanted callers can't pester you anymore.

Making and receiving phone calls is a major use for your iPhone. However, there are other ways to communicate as well, such as text messaging, which many people use just as often as talking, so we will be covering this in the next chapter.

5
Sending Text Messages

Talking on the iPhone is just one of many ways you can communicate with others. Besides talking, another popular way to communicate is through text messages. Unlike phone calls, which require both parties to be free to chat at the same time, text messages allow you to carry on a conversation by typing in messages to each other and responding when it's convenient. Best of all, text messaging works for everyone who has a smartphone.

Text messaging was originally called **Short Message Service** (**SMS**) and was designed as a cheaper way to communicate. Sending audio over cellular networks required large amounts of data but sending text required far less data, making it faster and cheaper to use.

Text messaging has grown beyond alphanumeric characters to include pictures, audio, and video as well as emoji symbols, such as a smiling face. **Multimedia Messaging Service** (**MMS**) is an expanded version of text messaging that lets you share all types of data with others.

Whatever it's called, the basic idea is to send text, pictures, audio, or video to your friends without making an actual phone call. On the iPhone, you send and receive text messages through the **Messages** app.

In this chapter, you'll learn different ways to send and use text messages on an iPhone. Some of the topics covered include the following:

- Sending and receiving text messages
- Sending pictures
- Sending emojis and audio
- Sending video
- Sending animated drawings
- Sending money through Apple Pay

When you don't want to make a phone call, or if you live in an area that charges extra for cellular data, consider sending a text message as a cheap and fast way to communicate with others.

Understanding text messages

Text messages work by sending data to and from the phone number of a smartphone. That means you can't send or receive text messages to or from a landline telephone that requires a cable plugged into the wall.

> **Important Note**
>
> Do not send or read text messages while performing other actions such as driving or walking. Text messages can distract you from seeing obstacles and dangers around you, jeopardizing your own life as well as the lives of others. If you must send or read text messages, make sure you only do so from a safe location where you aren't driving or won't walk into obstacles such as walls or other people, and where you won't pose an obstacle to others.

You can freely send and receive text messages with any mobile phone that supports text messaging. However, when sending text messages to another iPhone via iMessage, messages will appear in a blue bubble. When sending text messages from any other mobile phone (such as an Android phone) or when using SMS from an iPhone, text messages will appear in a green bubble, as shown in *Figure 5.1*:

Figure 5.1 – Blue and green text message examples

One advantage of sending text messages to iPhone users is that you can verify when your message has been received by another iPhone. That way, you know for sure that your text message went through, which is impossible to verify when sending text messages using SMS.

Sending a text message

Text messages are sent to phone numbers, so it's usually best to store someone's name and phone number in the **Contacts** app. That way, you can send a message to an actual person's name.

If you do not want to store a name and phone number in the **Contacts** app, you can still send a text message by typing the person's phone number before sending the text message. This method is clumsy since it requires typing a complete phone number, but it can be handy if you don't want to store a person's name and phone number in the **Contacts** app for any reason.

To send a text message by typing in a mobile phone number, follow these steps:

1. Tap the **Messages** icon on the Home Screen. The **Messages** screen appears.

2. Tap the new message icon at the upper-right corner of the screen. A **New Message** screen appears, as shown in *Figure 5.2*:

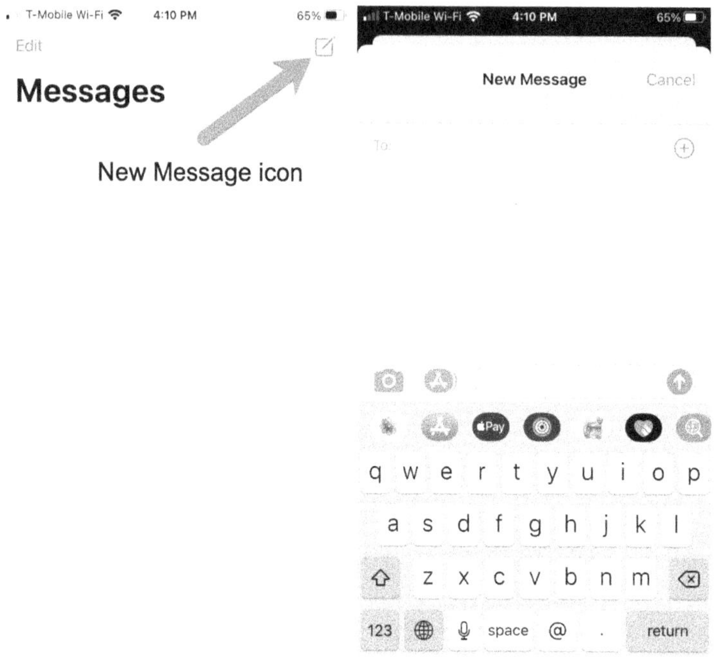

Figure 5.2 – The new message icon and the New Message screen

3. Tap in the **To:** text field and type a mobile phone number, including any area code or country code. Alternatively, tap the + sign inside the circle at the far right of the **To:** text field to display any names currently stored in the **Contacts** app. From this list, you can tap a person's name and mobile phone number to send a text message to.

4. Tap your text in the **Text Message** text field, and then tap the send icon at the far right when you're done, as shown in *Figure 5.3*:

Figure 5.3 – The Text Message text field and send icon

Most people just send plain text, but you can also send pictures as well. This lets you capture a picture using your iPhone's camera and send that image by text message.

Sending pictures as a text message

Once you've defined where to send your text message (by typing a specific mobile phone number or choosing a mobile phone number stored in your **Contacts** app), you can type text to send. Since a picture is worth a thousand words, you might want to send a picture as well.

This picture can be any picture stored in your iPhone's **Photos** app, or it can be any image you capture using the iPhone camera. To send a picture in a text message, follow these steps:

1. Open the **Messages** app and type in a mobile phone number or choose a mobile phone number from the **Contacts** app.
2. Tap the camera icon that appears to the left of the text message icon, as shown in *Figure 5.4*. Tapping the camera icon displays the Camera screen:

Figure 5.4 – The camera icon

3. Aim your iPhone's camera at an image and tap the white button at the bottom center of the screen. Alternatively, tap the **Photos** app icon at the upper-left corner of the screen, as shown in *Figure 5.5*, to open the **Photos** app so that you can select an image:

Figure 5.5 – The Camera screen

Whether you capture an image through the camera or choose an image stored in the **Photos** app, your chosen image appears in a text message bubble, as shown in *Figure 5.6*:

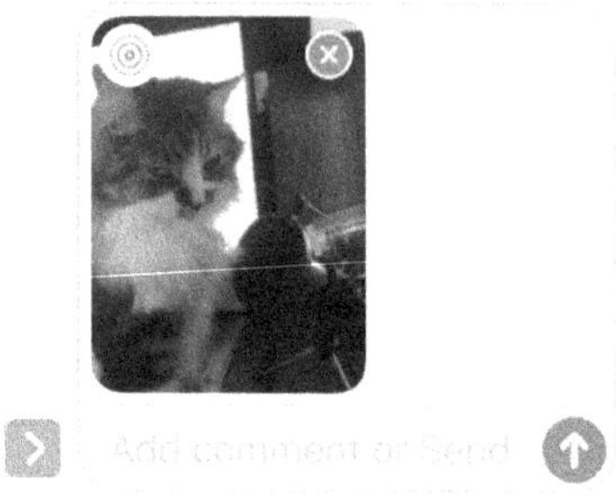

Figure 5.6 – An image selected to send as a text message

4. Tap in the text field and type a message to send with your picture (sending text with a picture is optional).
5. (Optional:) Tap the close icon (**x**) at the upper-right corner of your selected picture if you do not want to send the picture after all.
6. Tap the send icon at the far right of the text message field to send your chosen picture.

Sending pictures can be fun, but you might also want to send emojis as well to express your mood.

Sending emojis as a text message

Emojis represent silly and fun icons of different images, such as animals or smiley faces. Many people send emojis as pictorial comments or in addition to text to spice up a text message.

To send an emoji in a text message, follow these steps:

1. Open the **Messages** app and type in a mobile phone number or choose a mobile phone number from the **Contacts** app.
2. Tap in the **Text Message** text field so that the virtual keyboard appears.
3. Tap the globe icon at the bottom-left corner of the virtual keyboard, as shown in *Figure 5.7*:

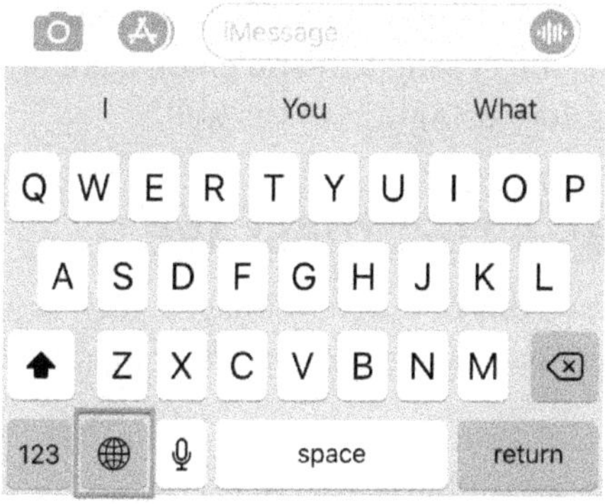

Figure 5.7 – The globe icon on the virtual keyboard displays different keyboard options

You may need to tap this globe icon multiple times to cycle through any other virtual keyboards that may appear. A list of emojis appears, as shown in *Figure 5.8*:

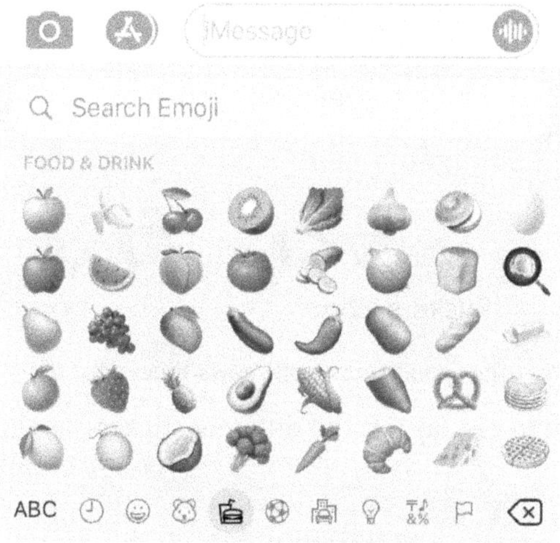

Figure 5.8 – The emoji keyboard

4. Tap an emoji category at the bottom of the screen to view a different set of emojis, such as smiley faces or sports images. You can also swipe left or right to view different emoji categories.
5. Tap on an emoji that you want to send. Your chosen emoji appears in the text bubble.
6. Tap in the text field and type a message to send with your emoji (sending text with an emoji is optional).
7. Tap the send icon at the far right of the text message field to send your chosen emoji.

Emojis represent different ways to express yourself in pictures instead of words. Some people just send emojis, while others send text and emojis. For another way to send pictures as text messages, consider using stickers as well.

Sending stickers as a text message

Stickers represent silly and fun icons of different images, such as animals or smiley faces. Many people also send stickers as pictorial comments or in addition to text to spice up a text message.

To send a sticker in a text message, follow these steps:

1. Open the **Messages** app and type in a mobile phone number, or choose a mobile phone number from the **Contacts** app.
2. Tap the applications icon to display a list of options, as shown in *Figure 5.9* (skip this step if the list of options is already visible):

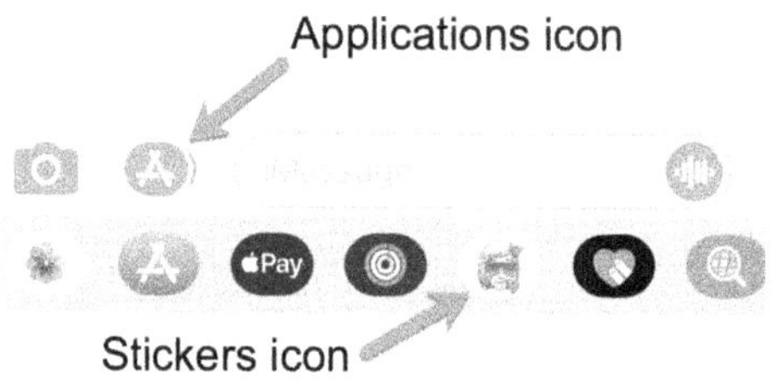

Figure 5.9 – The applications icon shows/hides a list of options

3. Tap the stickers icon to display a list of different stickers, as shown in *Figure 5.10*:

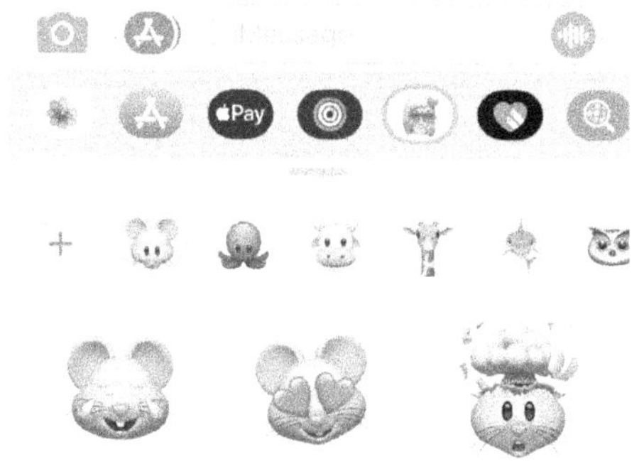

Figure 5.10 – The stickers icon displays different stickers to select

4. Tap on a sticker to send. Your selected sticker appears in a text bubble, as shown in *Figure 5.11*:

Figure 5.11 – Sending a sticker

5. Tap in the text field and type a message to send with your sticker (sending text with a sticker is optional).
6. (Optional:) Tap the close icon (**x**) at the upper-right corner of your selected sticker if you do not want to send the picture after all.
7. Tap the send icon at the far right of the text message field to send your chosen sticker.

Stickers are just another way to send cartoon images to others. While you can use the pre-designed stickers that Apple provides, you can also customize your own stickers. That way, you can make cartoon images of yourself or others.

Creating Memojis

Rather than sending pre-drawn stickers, take a moment to design your own stickers, called Memojis. Even if you aren't artistically inclined, you can simply choose different colors and options to create a Memoji that looks good, whether you have any drawing talent or not. In just a few minutes, you'll be surprised at how creative you can get making your own Memoji that either looks like you or looks like a cartoon version of another person.

To create a Memoji, follow these steps:

1. Open the **Messages** app and type in a mobile phone number, or choose a mobile phone number from the **Contacts** app.
2. Tap the applications icon to display a list of options (see *Figure 5.9*).
3. Tap the stickers icon to display a list of different stickers (see *Figure 5.10*).

4. Tap the + icon at the upper-left corner of the stickers screen. The Memoji creation screen appears, as shown in *Figure 5.12*:

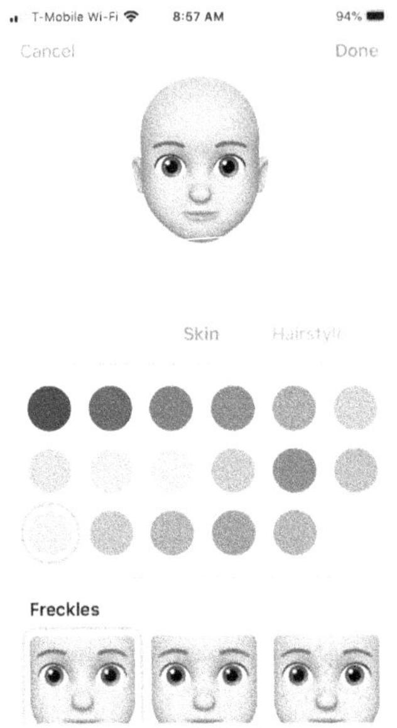

Figure 5.12 – Creating a custom Memoji

5. Tap a category, such as **Skin**, **Hairstyle**, **Brows**, **Eyes**, **Head**, **Nose**, **Mouth**, **Ears**, **Facial Hair**, **Eyewear**, and **Headwear**. Each category will display different options to select so that you can further customize your Memoji, as shown in *Figure 5.13*:

Figure 5.13 – Choosing different options for customizing a Memoji

6. Tap **Done** when you've finished creating your Memoji. After you've created at least one custom Memoji, you can select and view its variations any time you tap the stickers icon, as shown in *Figure 5.14*:

Figure 5.14 – Viewing variations of a custom Memoji

Once you've created one or more custom Memojis, you may later want to duplicate them, edit them, or delete them altogether. To duplicate, edit, or delete a Memoji, follow these steps:

1. Open the **Messages** app and type in a mobile phone number, or choose a mobile phone number from the **Contacts** app.
2. Tap the applications icon to display a list of options (see *Figure 5.9*).
3. Tap the stickers icon to display a list of different stickers (see *Figure 5.10*).
4. Tap the Memoji you want to edit. The three-dot icon inside a circle appears at the upper-left corner.

5. Tap this three-dot icon. A Memoji editing screen appears, as shown in *Figure 5.15*:

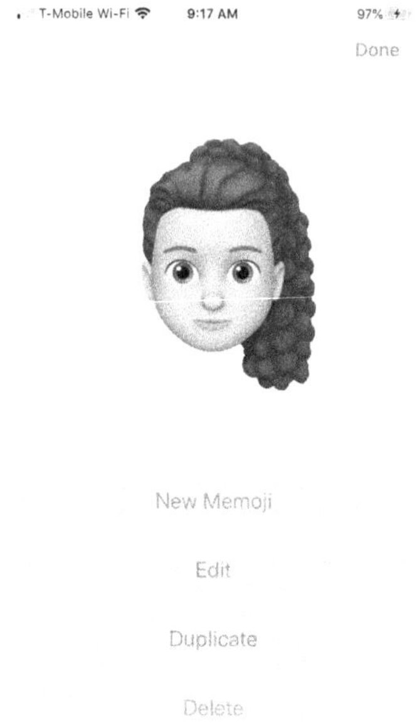

Figure 5.15 – The Memoji editing screen

6. Tap an option (**New Memoji**, **Edit**, **Duplicate**, or **Delete**).

Memojis are a unique way to send graphical images through a text message. For those who prefer exercising their artistic skills, you can also send drawings made with your fingertip.

Sending a Digital Touch drawing as a text message

Digital Touch is a way to draw simple pictures or letters with your fingertip. Then, you can send these simple finger drawings or writings as a text message.

As an option, you can also take a picture and add drawings to that picture. That way, you can highlight different parts of a picture, such as pointing out a problem or a specific item that you want someone to see.

To send a Digital Touch image in a text message, follow these steps:

1. Open the **Messages** app and type in a mobile phone number, or choose a mobile phone number from the **Contacts** app.
2. Tap the applications icon to display a list of options (see *Figure 5.9*).
3. Tap the Digital Touch icon to display a drawing area, as shown in *Figure 5.16*:

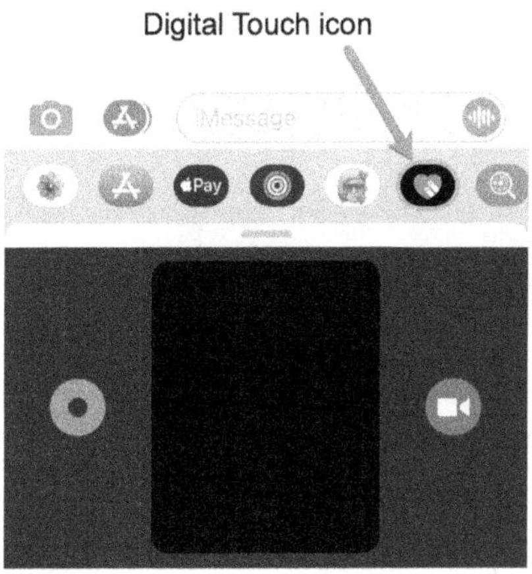

Figure 5.16 – The Digital Touch drawing area

4. Tap the color on the left side to display other colors. Then, tap the color you want to use. When you select a color, a camera icon appears on the right side of the drawing area.
5. Tap the camera icon that appears on the right side of the drawing area. A Digital Touch camera screen appears, letting you add drawings to an image that you can record, as shown in *Figure 5.17*:

Figure 5.17 – Adding Digital Touch drawings to a camera image

6. Tap a color and draw an image.
7. Tap the white button to capture a still image, or tap the red button to capture a video. A blue send icon appears at the bottom-right corner of the screen.
8. Tap the send icon.

Sending drawings that can include pictures can be fun, but another way to send a message is through audio.

Sending audio as a text message

Sometimes, typing a message can be troublesome or simply not possible due to physical limitations. For another way to communicate through text messaging, send audio clips. That way, you can speak your message and the other person can hear your message.

> **Note**
> Sending audio as a text message is only possible when texting another iPhone user. You cannot send audio to someone using a different smartphone, such as an Android device.

To send audio in a text message, follow these steps:

1. Open the **Messages** app and type in a mobile phone number, or choose a mobile phone number from the **Contacts** app. Make sure the person you're texting has an iPhone, which you can identify by seeing previous text messages appearing in blue text bubbles.
2. Tap the applications icon to display a list of options (see *Figure 5.9*).
3. Tap and hold the audio button that appears at the far right of the text message field, as shown in *Figure 5.18*:

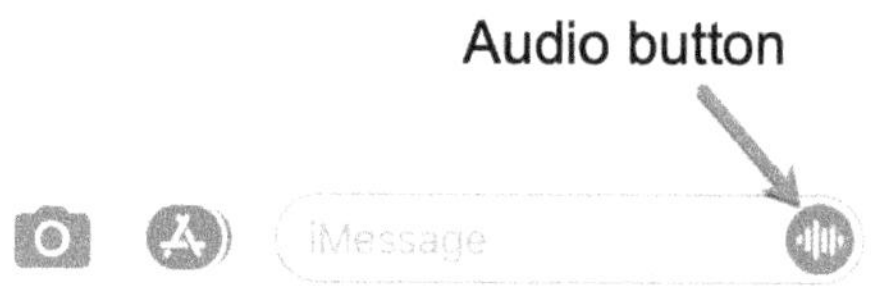

Figure 5.18 – The audio button

4. Speak your message while continuing to hold down the audio button. When you're done speaking, release the audio button. Your audio message appears, as shown in *Figure 5.19*:

Figure 5.19 – A recorded audio message ready to be sent

5. (Optional:) Tap the close button (**x**) to the left of the audio recording if you want to delete the audio recording without sending it.
6. Tap the send icon (an up arrow) to send your audio. Your audio appears, as shown in *Figure 5.20*:

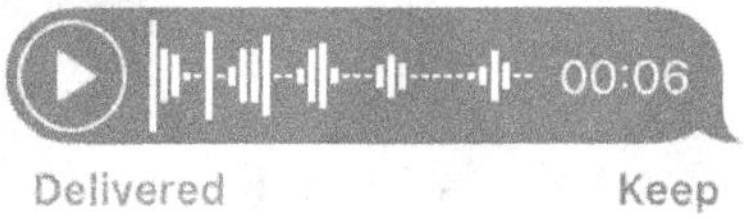

Figure 5.20 – A sent audio recording

7. Tap **Keep** if you want to save your audio recording. If you do not tap **Keep**, your audio recording will disappear after a few minutes.

Audio recordings make it easy to send messages without typing. For another way to send messages without typing, try sending animated activity images, which display simple animation, such as a rotating soccer ball or a waving flag. These animated images can spice up your text message and provide a fun addition to any text you might also want to type.

Sending animated fitness images as a text message

Animation can catch someone's eye much faster than a static image. If you want to add animated images to a text message, you can choose from the fitness category, which displays moving images.

To send an animated fitness image in a text message, follow these steps:

1. Open the **Messages** app and type in a mobile phone number, or choose a mobile phone number from the **Contacts** app.
2. Tap the applications icon to display a list of options (see *Figure 5.9*).

3. Tap the fitness icon to view a list of animated images, as shown in *Figure 5.21*:

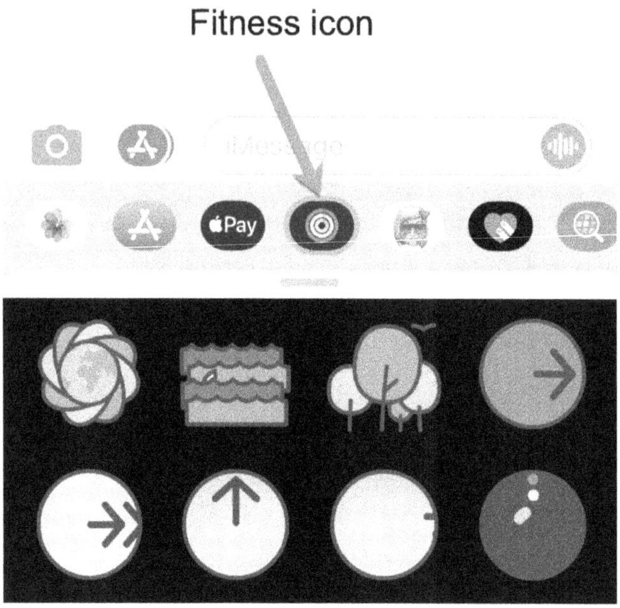

Figure 5.21 – The fitness animated images

4. Tap an animated image. Your chosen animated image appears in a text message bubble, as shown in *Figure 5.22*:

Figure 5.22 – Sending an animated image

5. (Optional:) Tap the close button (**x**) if you change your mind about sending the animated image.
6. (Optional:) Type some text to send along with your animated image.
7. Tap the send icon to send your animated image.

Let's take a look at another kind of animated image that we can send via text messages.

Sending animated images as a text message

Since a picture is worth a thousand words, you might want to send an animated image as a text message. Your iPhone comes with a collection of animated images, so you can select the one that best matches your mood. To send an animated image as a text message, follow these steps:

1. Open the **Messages** app and type in a mobile phone number, or choose a mobile phone number from the **Contacts** app.
2. Tap the applications icon to display a list of options (see *Figure 5.9*). You may need to swipe left or right to see all the available options.
3. Tap the images icon to view a list of animated images, as shown in *Figure 5.23*:

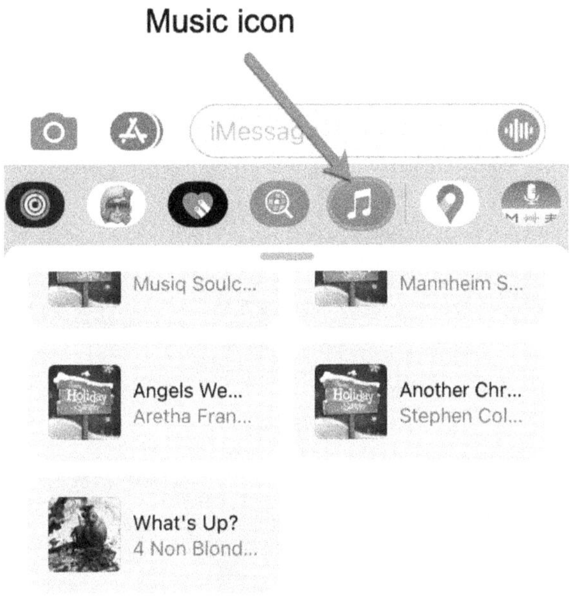

Figure 5.23 – Choosing an animated image

4. (Optional:) Tap the close button (**x**) if you change your mind about sending the animated image.
5. (Optional:) Type some text to send along with your animated image.
6. Tap the send icon to send your animated image.

Sending animated images can be a fun way to share your feelings and thoughts without typing. If you're listening to a particular song that reflects your mood, you can share your music taste with others as well without typing a thing.

Sending a song you're currently playing as a text message

Many people use their iPhones to play music that they can enjoy while moving around or sitting in place. As another fun way to share your feelings with others, you can let others know which songs you recently played without typing a single letter yourself.

To let others know your musical tastes in a text message, follow these steps:

1. Open the **Messages** app and type in a mobile phone number, or choose a mobile phone number from the **Contacts** app.
2. Tap the applications icon to display a list of options (see *Figure 5.9*). You may need to swipe left or right to see all the available options.
3. Tap the music icon to view a list of recently played songs, as shown in *Figure 5.24*:

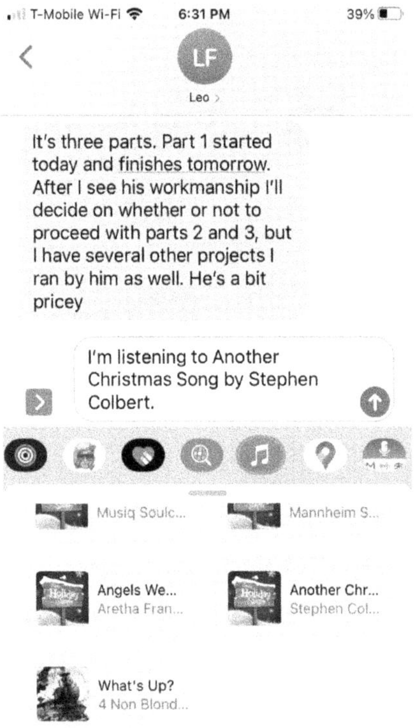

Figure 5.24 – Choosing from a list of recently played music

4. Tap a recently played song. Your iPhone automatically types text listing the song you chose, as shown in *Figure 5.25*:

Figure 5.25 – Text automatically created after choosing a recently played song

5. Tap the send icon to send your text message.

Sending your currently playing song can be fun, but sometimes you may want to send money as well, which you can do through Apple Pay (only available in certain regions of the world). By sending money through Apple Pay, you can easily transfer cash between iPhone users.

Sending money through a text message

These days, more people are relying on digital cash instead of carrying coins or paper bills, and for iPhone users, one of the most popular ways of carrying digital cash is through Apple Pay.

> **Note**
>
> Apple Pay is only available for iPhone or iPad users who have previously set up Apple Pay. That means you cannot send money through Apple Pay to Android devices or any non-iOS device. Both you and the recipient must also set up Apple Cash as well, which you can do when sending money through Apple Pay for the first time. Apple Cash will need to be linked to a debit card. Also, Apple Pay may not be available in all countries and regions

To send money through Apple Pay with a text message, follow these steps:

1. Open the **Messages** app and type in a mobile phone number, or choose a mobile phone number from the **Contacts** app. Make sure the person you're texting has an iPhone, which you can identify by seeing previous text messages appearing in blue text bubbles.

2. Tap the applications icon to display a list of options (see *Figure 5.9*).
3. Tap the Apple Pay icon. An Apple Pay screen appears, as shown in *Figure 5.26*:

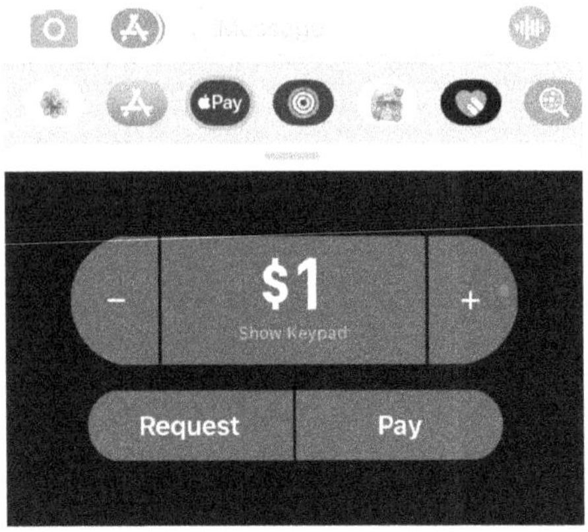

Figure 5.26 – Choosing an amount to send through Apple Pay

4. Tap the - or + keys to increment the amount you want to send.
5. (Optional:) Tap **Show Keypad** to display a numeric keypad so that you can type in the precise amount to send, as shown in *Figure 5.27*:

Figure 5.27 – Choosing an amount to send through Apple Pay with a numeric keypad

6. Tap **Pay**, and then tap the send icon.
7. Authorize the payment through Touch ID or Face ID.

Sending money through Apple Pay can be handy for sharing cash. However, sometimes you may just want to keep in touch with friends by sharing activities.

Sending text messages can be fun, but receiving them can be even better since it means other people want to communicate with you. It's time to learn how to read and respond to messages that you receive.

Receiving and responding to text messages

Each time you receive a text message, you'll see a notification number at the upper-right corner of the **Messages** icon on the Home Screen. This number displays the number of unread messages you've received, as shown in *Figure 5.28*:

Figure 5.28 – The **Messages** icon displaying notifications of new messages

If you're using your iPhone when you receive a message, you'll see a brief message at the top of the screen, as shown in *Figure 5.29*:

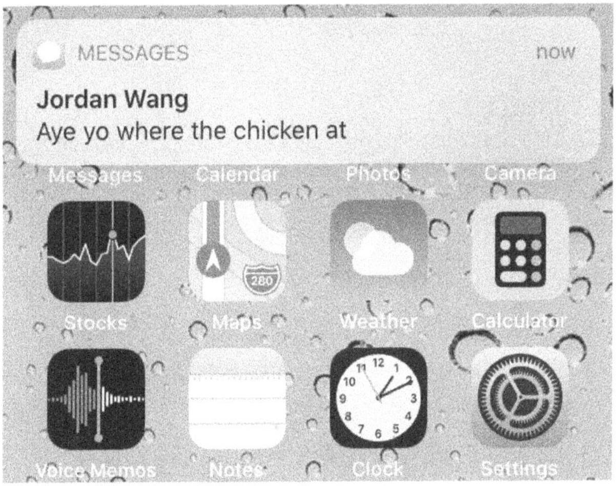

Figure 5.29 – Getting real-time notifications of an incoming message

The **Messages** app lists everyone who has contacted you in the past. If you have added their names and mobile phone numbers in the **Contacts** app, that person's name will appear. Otherwise, only that person's mobile phone number will appear.

When you receive a text message, you can read it by following these steps:

1. Tap the **Messages** app on the Home Screen. A blue dot appears to the left of any text message conversations containing unread messages, as shown in *Figure 5.30*:

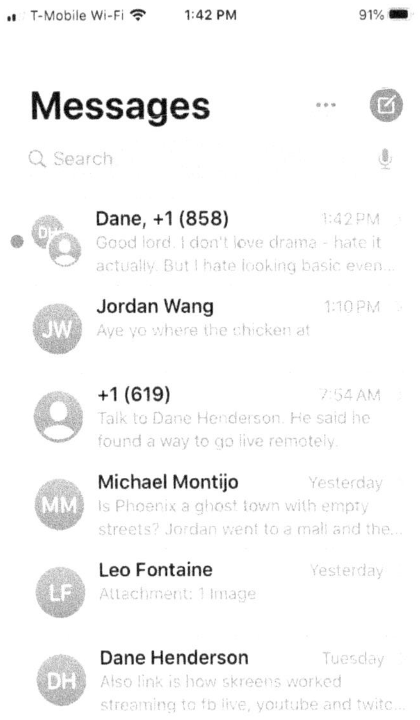

Figure 5.30 – Blue dots identify conversations containing unread messages

2. Tap a conversation that contains the messages you want to read. A list of past messages appears.
3. Scroll down to view the latest message you've received from someone.
4. Tap the **Text Message** text field, type in your text, and tap the send icon to send a response back to that person.

Responding to text messages with symbols

While text messages are meant to be short, even typing a few words can be troublesome. That's why the **Messages** app offers common symbols (such as a thumbs up or thumbs down) to let others know what you think without having to type a reply.

To respond to someone's message with a symbol, follow these steps:

1. Tap the **Messages** app on the Home Screen. A list of message conversations appears.
2. Tap on the conversation that contains a message you want to respond to.
3. Press and hold your fingertip over a message that you want to respond to. A list of symbols appears, as shown in *Figure 5.31*:

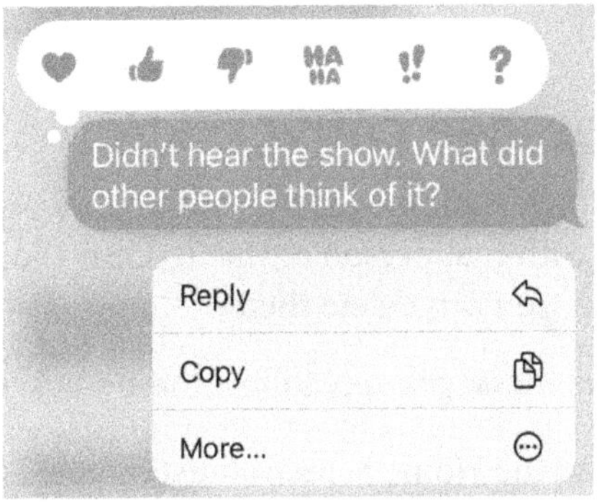

Figure 5.31 – Press and hold over a message to display symbols

4. Tap a symbol to send it in response to your chosen text message. (Note that in *Figure 5.31*, you also have the option of choosing **Copy** to copy an entire text message. That way, you can paste it anywhere you like, such as in the Notes app, a word processor, an email, or another text message.)

Hiding a text message conversation

If you belong to a particularly active conversation, you may receive messages constantly, which can be annoying if your iPhone constantly beeps or vibrates each time you get a new message. To mute any type of alerts when you receive a new message in a particular conversation, you can choose to hide alerts.

To hide alerts for a conversation in the **Messages** app, follow these steps:

1. Tap the **Messages** app on the Home Screen. A list of message conversations appears.
2. Swipe left on the conversation you want to modify. A blue hide alerts and a red delete button appear, as shown in *Figure 5.32*:

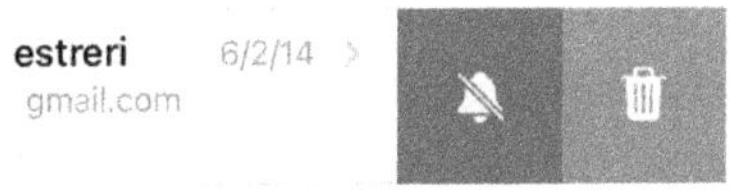

Figure 5.32 – Left swiping on a conversation displays a delete option

3. Tap hide alerts. From now on, you won't receive any alerts when a new message arrives in this conversation.

To turn alerts back on again, simply repeat the preceding steps, except instead of choosing hide alerts, you'll be able to choose a show alerts button.

If you no longer want to keep certain conversations because you don't need them or won't be communicating with that person again, you can choose to delete a conversation altogether.

Deleting a text message conversation

Sometimes, you may have a conversation with a friend or co-worker, but later you no longer need to communicate with that person again. To clear the number of conversations displayed in the **Messages** app, you can delete them.

To delete a conversation in the **Messages** app, follow these steps:

1. Tap the **Messages** app on the Home Screen. A list of message conversations appears.
2. Swipe left on the conversation you want to modify. A hide alerts and a delete button appear (see *Figure 5.32*). An action sheet appears at the bottom of the screen, as shown in *Figure 5.33*, asking you to verify that you want to delete the entire conversation and any messages stored inside:

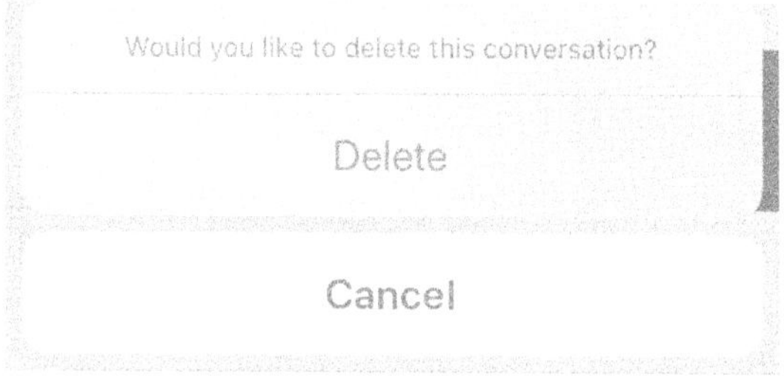

Figure 5.33 – An action sheet asking to verify deleting an entire **Messages** conversation

3. Tap **Delete**. The **Messages** app deletes your chosen conversation for good.

Go through your conversations periodically and delete the ones you no longer need. If you feel some messages might be important, simply copy and paste them to save them for future reference.

In general, delete any unnecessary conversations so that the **Messages** app will only contain conversations and messages that are actually important to you.

Summary

Text messaging is a common way to communicate quickly and easily with anyone with a mobile phone. While you can always share your thoughts and ideas as text, don't feel limited to just typing. Consider sending pictures, audio, or even digital cash through Apple Pay.

Text messaging is meant to help you stay in touch with important people or information, so consider hiding alerts if certain text messaging conversations alert you too often. Periodically, go through your text messaging conversations and delete the ones you no longer need so that you can focus attention on those conversations you currently want and need right now.

Text messaging can be a great way to communicate with others, but in the next chapter, you'll learn how to talk to Siri, Apple's voice assistant, who can answer questions and help you search the internet without you having to type anything at all.

6 Using Siri

Most people are familiar with using the touchscreen interface of the iPhone or a similar smartphone. While tapping, swiping, and pinching the screen can be powerful ways to control an iPhone, an even more revolutionary interface is to use your voice.

Siri represents the new user interface that relies solely on voice commands. By simply speaking to Siri, you can control many features of your iPhone, from making phone calls and scheduling events to searching the internet and changing settings. With Siri, you can control your iPhone with nothing more than your voice.

Just keep in mind that although Siri can understand and respond to a wide variety of voice commands, it's still not perfect. Sometimes when talking to Siri, you may need to rephrase your commands using different words or changing the order of your words.

The topics we will cover in the chapter are as follows:

- Setting up Siri
- Giving commands to Siri
- Asking Siri questions
- Dictating with Siri

Setting up Siri

You can start talking to Siri as soon as you get a new iPhone. However, you may want to take a moment to customize Siri's settings so that Siri behaves the way you want.

The first way to customize Siri is by defining how to start Siri in the first place. Three common ways to start Siri are the following:

- Press the Home button (for those iPhone models that have a physical Home button).
- Say "Hey Siri" out loud.
- Press the Side button (for newer iPhone models that do not have a Home button).

Another way to customize Siri is to define the voice and language. You can choose between a male or female voice with different types of accents, depending on your particular language. For example, English speakers can choose between several options, such as American, British, or Indian accents.

The language you choose will be whatever language you prefer speaking and hearing. Whatever language you choose, you'll likely have regional options as well. For example, French speakers can choose between France, Canada, or Belgium regions since each region tends to say words in a slightly different manner.

To customize Siri, follow these steps:

1. Tap the **Settings** icon on the Home Screen.
2. Tap **Siri & Search**. The **Siri & Search** screen appears, as shown in *Figure 6.1*:

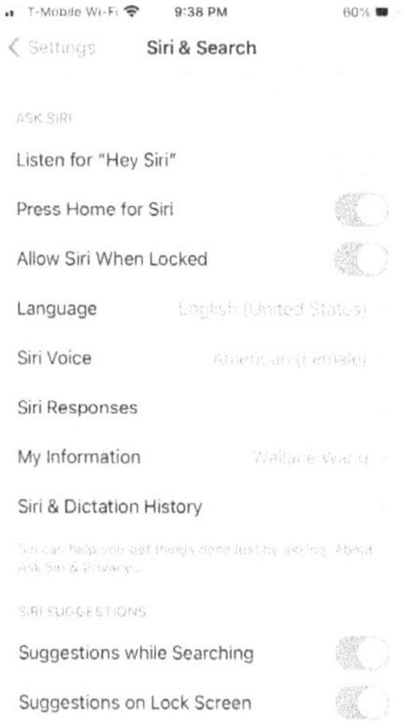

Figure 6.1 – The Siri & Search screen

3. Tap the **Listen for "Hey Siri"** switch to turn this option on or off.
4. Tap the **Press Side Button for Siri** or **Press Home for Siri** switch to turn this option on or off.
5. Tap the **Allow Siri When Locked** switch if you want to be able to talk to Siri even if your iPhone is locked (if you choose this option, you'll also need to type in your passcode to verify that you want this option on or off).
6. Tap **Language**. The **Language** screen appears, as shown in *Figure 6.2*:

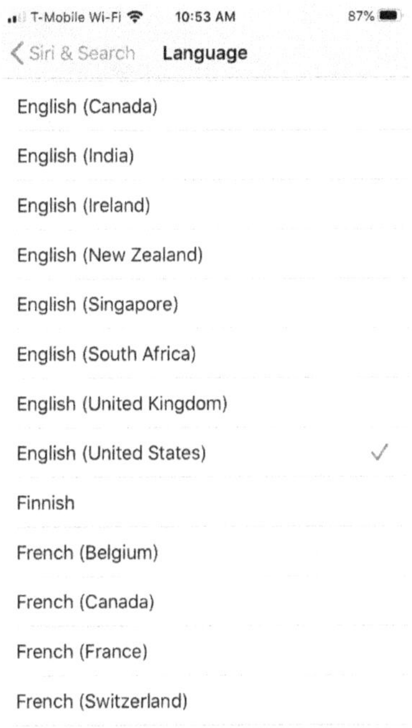

Figure 6.2 – The Language screen for selecting Siri's language

7. Tap the specific language you prefer, such as **English (India)** or **English (United Kingdom)**. Then, tap the **Siri & Search** button in the upper-left corner to return to the **Siri & Search** screen.

8. Tap **Siri Voice**. The **Siri Voice** screen appears, as shown in *Figure 6.3*:

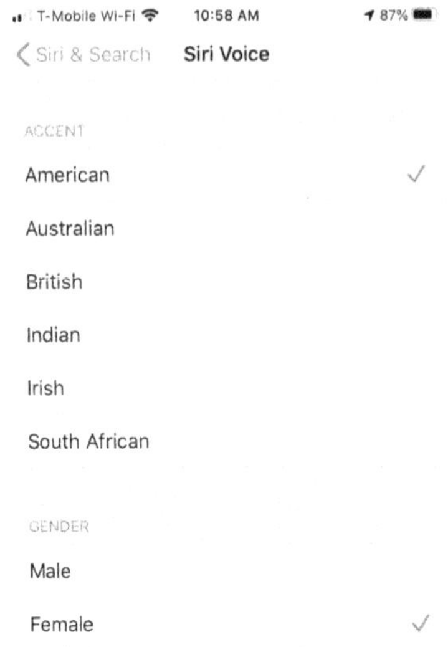

Figure 6.3 – The Siri Voice screen for choosing Siri's vocal personality

9. Tap an accent and gender (**Male** or **Female**). Then, tap the **Siri & Search** button in the upper-left corner to return to the **Siri & Search** screen if you want to make any additional changes to Siri.

Feel free to experiment with different Siri options until you find the ones you like best. For example, try using Siri with a male or female voice to see which one you like best. Even if you live in a particular area, try changing Siri to speak in an accent from another region. That might make Siri sound more pleasant to your ears.

Once you have Siri set up, you can always go back and change the options at any time. The first step is to try starting Siri in all the different ways you defined, such as pressing the Side button or Home button, or saying "Hey Siri."

Remember, Siri requires a connection to a cellular phone network or a Wi-Fi network. That's because Siri needs to send data back to Apple's servers to process requests and then send the answers back to your iPhone. If you do not have access to a cellular phone or Wi-Fi network, Siri may not work at all.

Asking Siri questions

One of the simplest ways to use Siri is to get information that you might ask a friend, such as finding the current weather forecast, getting the historical or geographical information about a place, or learning trivia about a popular movie.

Although Siri can understand spoken commands, it might not always give you the answer directly. Instead, Siri might just point you to a website where you might find the answer you're looking for. For example, ask Siri "How many books did Mark Twain write?" Then, Siri displays an answer on the screen with an option to tap on the Safari icon to view a web page containing the answer, as shown in *Figure 6.4*:

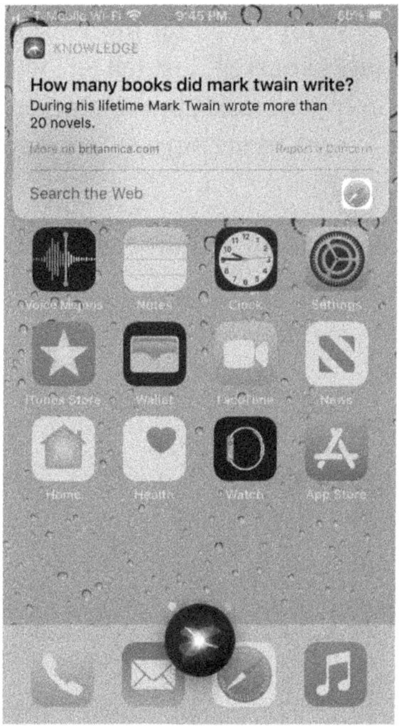

Figure 6.4 – Siri might display websites where you can find the answer

To ask Siri a question, follow these steps:

1. Start Siri the way you defined, such as pressing the Side or Home buttons, or saying "Hey Siri." The Siri icon appears at the bottom of the screen, as shown in *Figure 6.5*:

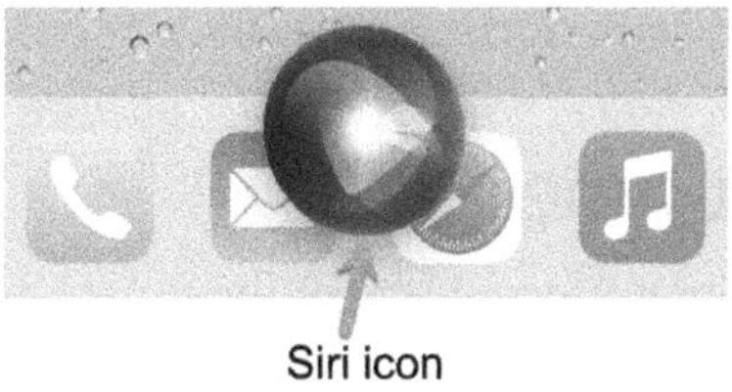

Figure 6.5 – The Siri screen waiting for you to speak

2. Ask a question. When you're finished asking your question, remain silent so that Siri will know that you are done. After a moment, Siri will respond with an answer.

Asking Siri questions can be fun, but you can also use Siri as an assistant to help you accomplish specific tasks.

Giving Siri commands

When you ask Siri a question, Siri may or may not know how to answer. Rather than asking questions covering a variety of topics, it's far more useful to use Siri to save time. Rather than performing specific tasks yourself, just tell Siri what to do. Not only is Siri far more accurate at performing common tasks, but relying on Siri can also save you the time of tapping through various screens to perform common tasks such as setting up appointments or alarms yourself.

Some of the different tasks Siri can perform include the following:

- Getting the current time
- Getting the current weather
- Translating words and phrases
- Setting, editing, and deleting an alarm
- Setting a timer
- Setting a reminder
- Setting an appointment
- Getting directions
- Sending and receiving text messages
- Making phone calls
- Opening an app
- Tracking flights above you

Let's look at how we can get Siri to perform these tasks.

Getting the current time

One of the simplest tasks Siri can perform is to get the time. You can just ask for the time, such as saying "Hey Siri, what time is it?" This will return the time in your current location.

Another option is to ask for the time in another city, just in case you want to know whether you can call someone in that city if they live in a different time zone. In that case, you might say, "Hey Siri, what time is it in Berlin?"

If you don't specify a location, Siri will assume that you want the time in your current location. So, if you want to know the time in another location, make sure you specify that location.

It's generally best to specify a particular city, rather than a country, since a country may be divided into separate time zones. By specifying a specific city, you can help Siri narrow down its answer to a specific time zone.

To ask for the current time, follow these steps:

1. Start Siri (by pressing the Side button or saying "Hey Siri").
2. Ask "What time is it"? or "What time is it in ______ (name a city)?" Siri responds with the time displayed, as shown in *Figure 6.6*. Notice that Siri also displays the number of hours the time in the other city might be ahead or behind your current time, such as +9 hours ahead:

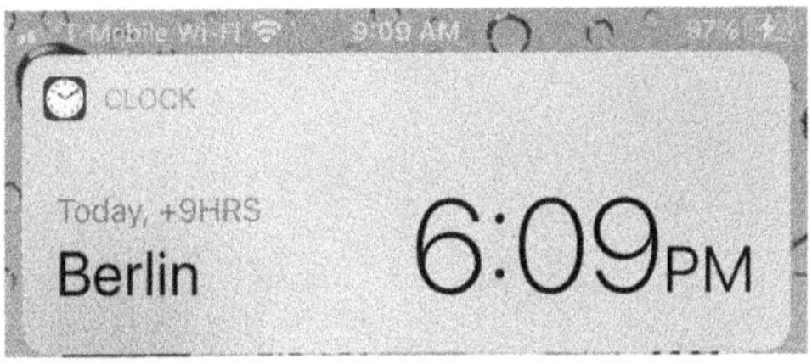

Figure 6.6 – Asking Siri for the time in another city

Knowing the time in your current location or another location can be handy, but you might also want to know the weather too, especially if you plan to travel to another city soon.

Getting the current weather

Knowing the time in another city can be handy if you want to call someone in that region and want to make sure they're awake. For travelers planning to visit another city, it can be handy to know the weather so that you can dress appropriately.

To ask about the weather, simply use a common weather-related term, such as "temperature," "hot," "cold," or "rain," or just say "weather."

Next, you can mention what day or time you want the weather information for, such as "today," "tomorrow," "next week," "morning," or "tonight."

If you don't specify a city, Siri will assume that you want the weather forecast for your current location. Otherwise, mention a specific city for that region's weather.

To get weather information, follow these steps:

1. Start Siri (by pressing the Side button or saying "Hey Siri").
2. Ask a question using a weather-related term (such as "How hot will it be"), a time (such as "tonight"), and a location (such as "in Tokyo"). Siri responds with the weather forecast, as shown in *Figure 6.7*:

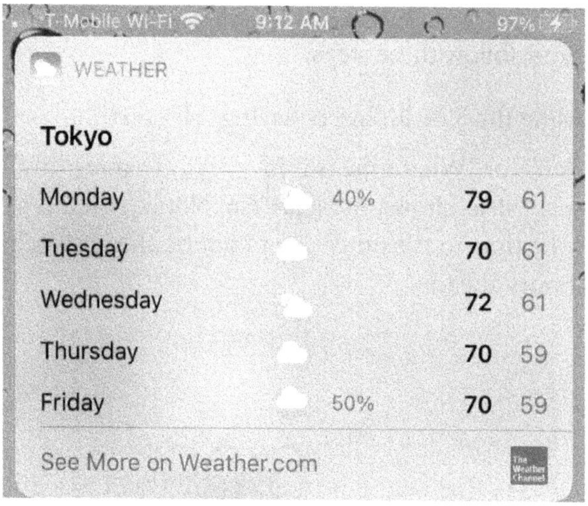

Figure 6.7 – Asking Siri for weather information

Knowing the weather in other parts of the world can be useful if you plan to travel there soon. If that region of the world speaks a different language, you might also want to know common words or phrases to say.

Translating words and phrases

Learning a foreign language can be difficult, so you might want to rely on Siri to help you learn certain words and phrases. By using your iPhone and Siri as a translator, you'll be able to communicate with people in other parts of the world enough to get the information you need without necessarily being fluent in another language.

Just ask Siri for the word or phrase you want to translate and the language you want, such as "Hey Siri, what's the French word for hotel?" or "How do you say taxi in Russian?"

When Siri responds, you'll see a written translation, along with hearing Siri pronounce the word or phrase correctly in the foreign language you chose.

To translate words or phrases into another language, follow these steps:

1. Start Siri (by pressing the Side button or saying "Hey Siri").
2. Ask a question and specify the word or phrase you want to translate and the language you want. Siri responds with the translation, as shown in *Figure 6.8*. You can tap the play button to hear Siri pronounce the word or phrase again:

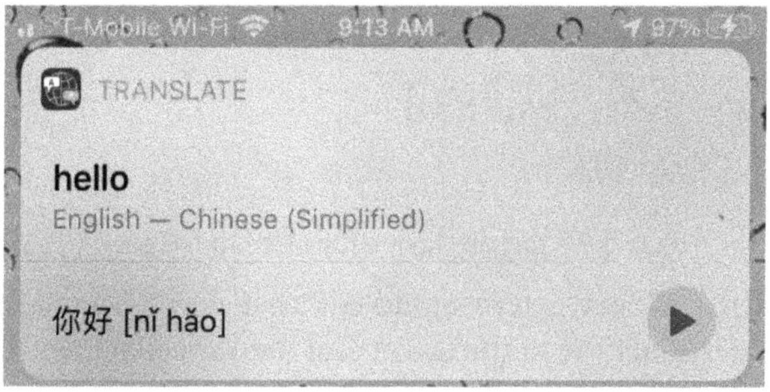

Figure 6.8 – Asking Siri to translate languages

No matter where you might be in the world, you'll likely need to keep track of time, such as knowing when to catch a plane or when to get to an appointment. To help you keep track of time, let Siri set alarms and timers for you.

Setting, editing, and deleting an alarm

Normally, you can set, edit, and delete alarms manually through the Clock app. However, doing any of these tasks takes several steps, so you might find that it's much easier to let Siri do the work for you.

An alarm can alert you when it gets to a specific time. If you need to get up early in the morning, you might set an alarm to wake you up at a specific time, such as 5 o'clock in the morning.

To set an alarm, specify a time for the alert and mention "alarm" or "wake me up." You can also specify a day or time, such as "Wake me up in an hour" or "Set an alarm at 8:00 AM every Saturday."

To set an alarm, follow these steps:

1. Start Siri (by pressing the Side button or saying "Hey Siri").
2. Mention "alarm" or "wake me up" followed by the time, such as 9:30 PM or 2 hours from now. Optionally, mention if you want it to occur on a specific day, such as "Monday." Siri displays the alarm so that you can verify that it's accurate, as shown in *Figure 6.9*:

Figure 6.9 – Siri displaying the alarm it has set

Once you've set an alarm, you may later want to edit that alarm. To modify an existing alarm, you need to tell Siri the time of the alarm and then specify a new time and/or day, such as "Change my 1:45 alarm to 2:15."

Rather than editing the time of an alarm, you can also turn off (or on) an alarm by saying "Turn on/off" followed by the time of your alarm, such as "2:00 PM alarm."

To edit an existing alarm, follow these steps:

1. Start Siri (by pressing the Side button or saying "Hey Siri").
2. State the alarm time you want to edit (such as "Change my 1:30 alarm") followed by the new time. Siri acknowledges your change verbally and shows the new alarm time.

Sometimes, you may create an alarm and later decide you don't need it anymore. One option is to turn off or disable the alarm. Another option is to delete the alarm altogether.

To delete or disable an alarm, follow these steps:

1. Start Siri (by pressing the Side button or saying "Hey Siri").
2. State the alarm time you want to edit (such as "my 1:30 alarm") preceded by "turn off," "disable," or "delete," which will be "turn off/disable/delete my 1:30 alarm." Siri acknowledges your change.

Alarms can be handy when you want to be alerted at a specific time, such as 1:30 PM. For another way to alert you when time passes, set a timer through Siri.

Setting a timer

While alarms are handy for alerting you when it gets to a specific time, you might also want to set a timer to let you know when a specific amount of time has passed, such as 5 or 10 minutes. By setting alarms and timers, you can make sure you never miss a meeting or overcook your food again.

To set a timer, say "Set a timer" or "Start a timer" followed by the amount of time you want, such as 10 minutes. Once a timer has started, you can also use Siri to pause, check, stop, or resume the timer by using phrases such as "Pause the timer" or "Resume the timer."

To set a timer, follow these steps:

1. Start Siri (by pressing the Side button or saying "Hey Siri").
2. State that you want to start or set a timer followed by the length of time, such as 20 minutes. Siri displays your timer information as it counts down, as shown in *Figure 6.10*:

Figure 6.10 – Setting a timer through Siri

You can use timers to measure a time period, such as the time to boil an egg or do an exercise workout. Similar to timers are reminders, which can be more useful when you want to be notified of an event further on in the future, such as a day, week, or month from now.

Setting a reminder

The moment you learn of an upcoming event, create a reminder. Reminders will pop up on your iPhone screen to notify you of a particular event, such as calling someone at a specific time. Reminders are similar to alarms, but alarms are linked to a specific time (such as 12:10 AM) while reminders can be linked to a date in the future, such as two days from now or next week.

To create a reminder with Siri, simply use the word "Remind" followed by the event and time, such as "next week," "on May 12," or "in 1 hour." Since your iPhone can track your location, you can also create a reminder to occur when you get to work or home.

To set a reminder, follow these steps:

1. Start Siri (by pressing the Side button or saying "Hey Siri").
2. State that you want to set a reminder by using the "Remind" word followed by an event and time, such as "tomorrow." Siri displays your reminder, as shown in *Figure 6.11*. Your reminder now appears in the Reminders app:

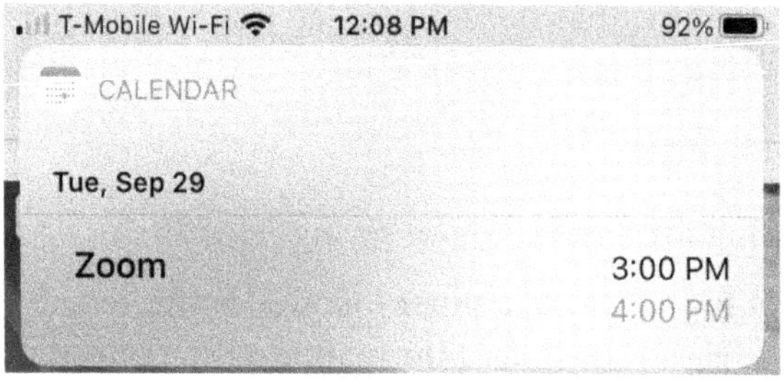

Figure 6.11 – Setting a reminder with Siri

Once you've set a reminder, you can delete it through Siri or manually by opening up the Reminders app.

To delete a reminder through Siri, follow these steps:

1. Start Siri (by pressing the Side button or saying "Hey Siri").
2. State the reminder you want to delete by stating a distinctive word used in the reminder followed by the "reminder" word. Siri displays the reminder it thinks you want to delete, as shown in *Figure 6.12*:

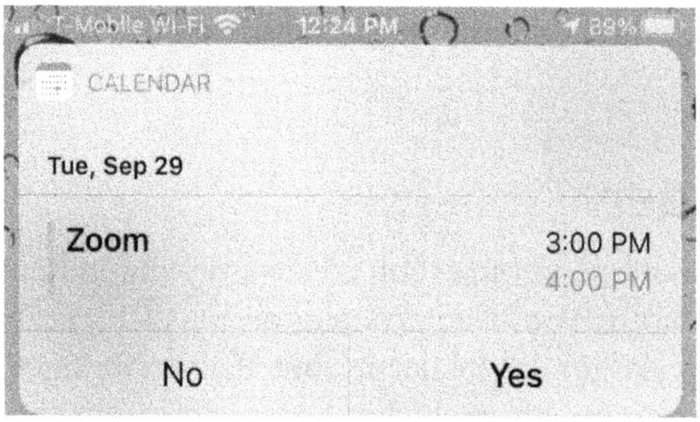

Figure 6.12 – Deleting a reminder

3. Tap **No** or **Yes**.

Reminders are one way to keep track of upcoming events, but another way is to store upcoming appointments in the Calendar app.

Setting an appointment

The Calendar app not only lets you see upcoming dates for the year, but it's also handy for storing future appointments on specific dates, such as doctor's appointments, business meetings, or important phone calls.

Rather than wasting time opening the Calendar app and checking your appointments for a particular day, it's much easier to let Siri remind you instead. Simply ask Siri "What's on my calendar?" or "What does my day look like?" and then choose a specific day, such as "today" or "May 13th."

To check your calendar, follow these steps:

1. Start Siri (by pressing the Side button or saying "Hey Siri").
2. Ask a question referencing "calendar" or "day" and a specific date. Siri displays a list of all appointments scheduled for that day, as shown in *Figure 6.13*:

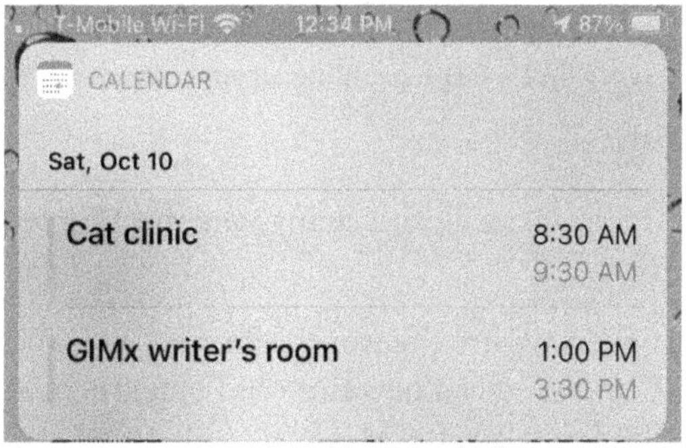

Figure 6.13 – Siri lists all appointments on a particular day

Seeing a list of scheduled appointments for a particular day can help you plan that day. However, you might also want to add, edit, or delete appointments as well. While you can do that manually through the Calendar app, you can also let Siri do it for you as well.

To schedule an appointment, say the words "appointment" or "meeting" to Siri, describe the meeting, such as "Meet with Dr. Gillian," and state a time and date, such as "August 8th at 10 AM."

To create an appointment for your calendar, follow these steps:

1. Start Siri (by pressing the Side button or saying "Hey Siri").
2. Make a statement using the words "meeting" or "schedule," describe the meeting, and give a specific date and time. Siri displays your meeting, as shown in *Figure 6.14*. If Siri needs more information, such as the time, date, or clarification on which person you want to meet (in case two people share similar names), an additional Siri screen will appear asking "What time is your appointment?" or something similar:

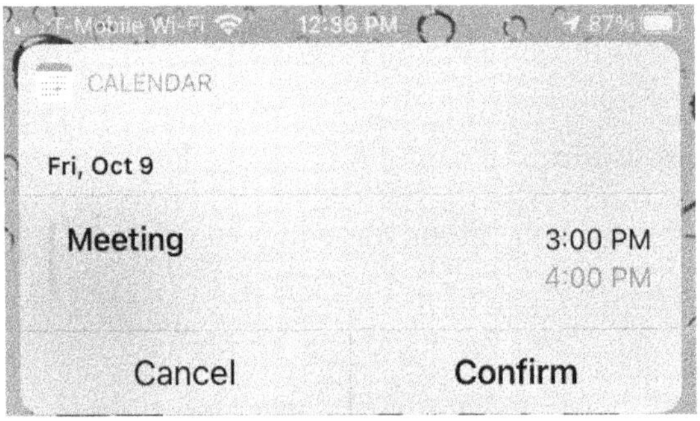

Figure 6.14 – Siri scheduling an appointment

3. Tap **Cancel** or **Confirm**.

Once you've set up a meeting, you can always change the meeting to another time or date, or you can delete it altogether.

To move or change an appointment, use the words "Change" or Move" followed by "meeting" or "appointment" and specify a new time and date, such as "Move my 9:00 PM meeting with John to next Friday at 10:30 AM."

If you want to edit an appointment without providing enough information, Siri will ask for clarification, such as when you want to reschedule the meeting.

To move or change an appointment, follow these steps:

1. Start Siri (by pressing the Side button or saying "Hey Siri").
2. Make a statement using the words "Change" or "Move" followed by identifying a "meeting" or "appointment." Then, give another time and date. If Siri needs more information, a message appears on the screen. When Siri has enough information to change an appointment, it displays the modified appointment, as shown in *Figure 6.15*:

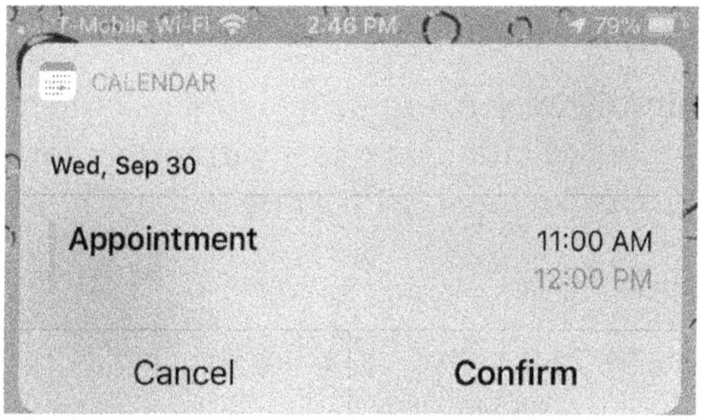

Figure 6.15 – Siri changing an appointment

3. Tap **Cancel** or **Confirm**.

While you may need to change appointments, you may also need to delete appointments altogether. To delete an appointment, use the words "Delete" or "Cancel" and specify the appointment you want to remove.

To remove an appointment, follow these steps:

1. Start Siri (by pressing the Side button or saying "Hey Siri").
2. Make a statement using the words "Cancel," "Remove," or "Delete" followed by identifying a "meeting" or "appointment" on a specific time and date. If Siri needs more information, a message appears on the screen. When Siri has enough information to change an appointment, it asks you to verify removing the appointment, as shown in *Figure 6.16*:

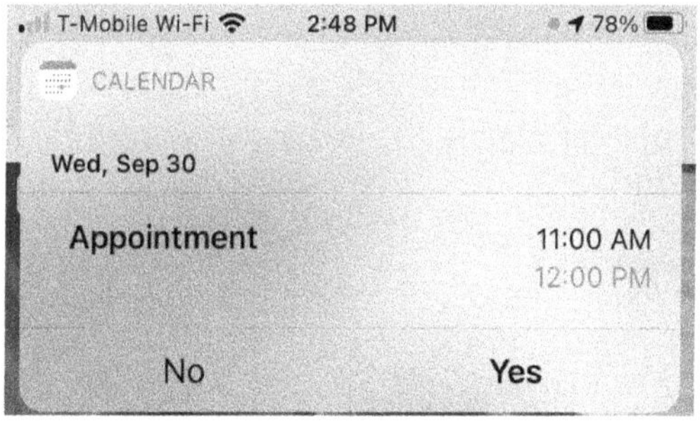

Figure 6.16 – Siri deleting an appointment

3. Tap **No** or **Yes**. If Siri misunderstood you, tap the **Tap to Edit** button and edit the text that Siri thinks you said. That way, you can fix any errors or confusion.

Appointments often take place in specific locations, so once you know what day and time you need to be somewhere, you might also need directions for how to get there.

Getting directions

To get directions, Siri has to know where you want to start and where you want to go. If you omit a starting location, Siri will assume your current location is your starting location. Once you identify a destination, Siri can display the Maps app with directions.

To get directions, follow these steps:

1. Start Siri (by pressing the Side button or saying "Hey Siri").
2. Ask a question using the words "directions" or "get" followed by a starting location and an ending destination. Siri will open the Maps app with directions, as shown in *Figure 6.17*. From this screen, you can choose driving, walking, transit, and cycling directions:

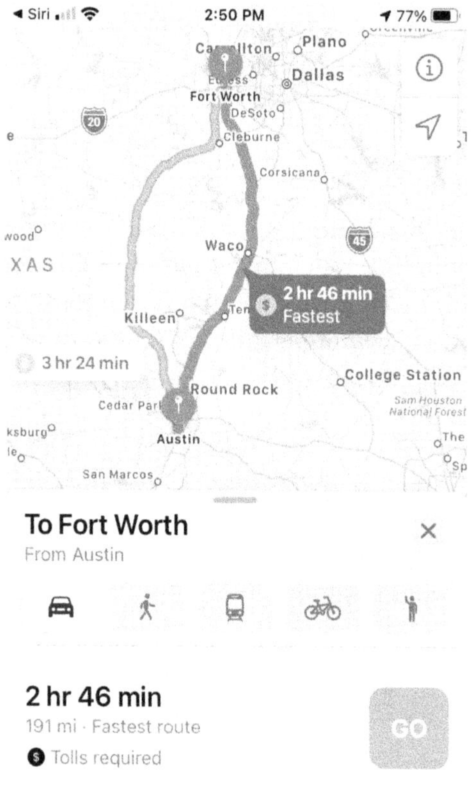

Figure 6.17 – Getting directions with Siri

Rather than get directions, you might be more interested in traffic around a certain area. By knowing whether traffic is light or heavy, you can choose the best route to your destination.

To get traffic information, follow these steps:

1. Start Siri (by pressing the Side button or saying "Hey Siri").
2. Ask a question using the words "traffic" followed by a location, such as "near me" or "in Chicago." Siri will open the Maps app and identify areas of heavy traffic.

Finding traffic jams or bottlenecks near you can be handy, but you can also use Siri to look for specific places nearby, such as finding a gas station or a Thai restaurant close by.

To find the location of a business or place, follow these steps:

1. Start Siri (by pressing the Side button or saying "Hey Siri").
2. Ask a question using the word "near" followed by the location or business you want, such as "What Brazilian restaurants are near me?" If you omit specifying a location, Siri will assume you want to use your current location. Siri displays a list of options, as shown in *Figure 6.18*:

Figure 6.18 – Finding locations nearby

When you're going to a specific location, you may want to meet others. You could call or text people, but it's often easier to let Siri help you so that you don't have to go through the steps manually, which can be especially useful if you're in cold weather and don't want to take your gloves off to tap your iPhone screen.

Sending and receiving text messages

Typing on the virtual keyboard of the iPhone can be clumsy for some people, especially if you want to text someone while wearing gloves in cold climates. That's when it's much easier to send a text message with Siri's help instead.

Siri can also be handy for reading text messages to you out loud. That way, you can reference a previous message before replying with your own. You can have Siri read the last text message you received (regardless of who sent it) or you can specify the last text message from a specific person.

To have Siri read text messages, follow these steps:

1. Start Siri (by pressing the Side button or saying "Hey Siri").
2. Give Siri a command using the words "read" and "text message." Optionally, describe the person whose text messages you want to read. That person's name and mobile phone number must be stored in the **Contacts** app. Siri reads the message and asks, "Would you like to reply?"
3. Say "Yes." Siri will ask, "What do you want to say?" and displays a text message bubble, as shown in *Figure 6.19*:

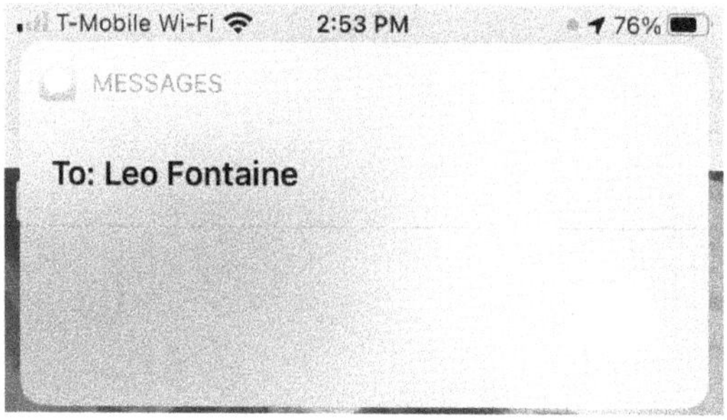

Figure 6.19 – Siri displaying a text message bubble for your reply

4. Dictate your reply. Siri displays your message along with the **Cancel** and **Send** buttons, as shown in *Figure 6.20*:

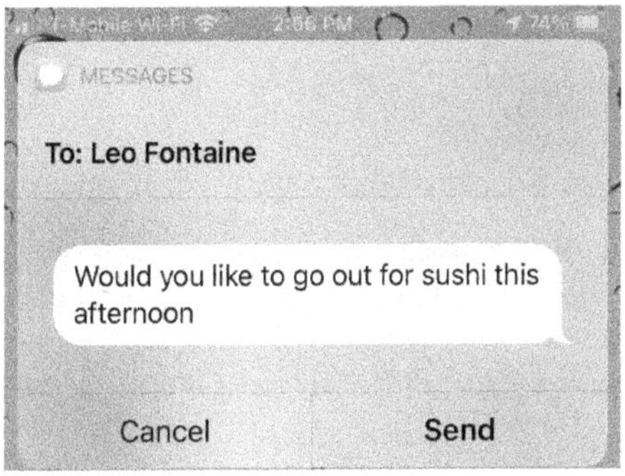

Figure 6.20 – Getting ready to send a text message

5. Tap the **Cancel** or **Send** button.

You might also want to send a text message to someone without reading any text messages. That's when you can simply state "Send text message" followed by a specific person or mobile phone number. Then, Siri will prompt you for a message to send.

To avoid this prompt, you can say "Send text" or "Send text message" followed by a specific person or mobile phone number, and the actual message, such as "Send text to Bob, What time can you be at my place?"

To send a text message, follow these steps:

1. Start Siri (by pressing the Side button or saying "Hey Siri").
2. Give Siri a command using the words "Send text" or "Send text message" followed by the person or mobile phone number. Optionally, include the message you want to send. If you do not include a message, Siri will prompt you to add a message.
3. Siri displays your text message along with a **Cancel** and **Send** button (see *Figure 6.20*).
4. Tap the **Cancel** or **Send** button.

Sending text messages through Siri can be handy, but sometimes you may want to talk to a person directly. That's when you can use Siri to help you make phone calls.

Making phone calls

To make a phone call with Siri, you must specify a mobile phone number to call or a person's name already stored in your **Contacts** app.

To make a call, follow these steps:

1. Start Siri (by pressing the Side button or saying "Hey Siri").
2. Give Siri a command using the word "Call" followed by the person or mobile phone number. Your iPhone starts dialing your chosen number.

Making a call with Siri simply opens the Phone app. Of course, you can use Siri to open any app on your iPhone.

Opening an app

You might have an app that you want to use, but it can be a nuisance to open the Home Screen and scroll through different icons to find the app you want to use. As a shortcut, just ask Siri to open a specific app for you by stating "Open" followed by the name of the app, such as "Calculator app."

To open an app, follow these steps:

1. Start Siri (by pressing the Side button or saying "Hey Siri").
2. Give Siri a command using the word "Open" followed by the app name, such as "Calculator app." Your chosen app appears on the screen.

One app that many people use frequently is the Music app so that they can play their favorite songs. While you can just ask Siri to open the Music app, you might want to specify a specific song as well.

To open the Music app and play a song stored in your music library, follow these steps:

1. Start Siri (by pressing the Side button or saying "Hey Siri").
2. Give Siri a command using the words "Play" and "song" followed by the name of the song you want to hear. Siri opens the Music app and starts playing your chosen song.

By using Siri to control the Music app, you won't have to search through your music library manually to find the song you want. While listening to music can be fun, you might also want to play with a neat Siri trick to check for commercial flights above your current location.

Tracking flights above you

At any given moment, there will be several commercial airplanes flying overhead. Just for fun, you can ask Siri about these flights and get a variety of information, such as the airline, flight number, altitude, and even the type of plane.

To find out what flights are above you, follow these steps:

1. Start Siri (by pressing the Side button or saying "Hey Siri").
2. Ask Siri "What flights are above me?" Siri displays the results, as shown in *Figure 6.21*:

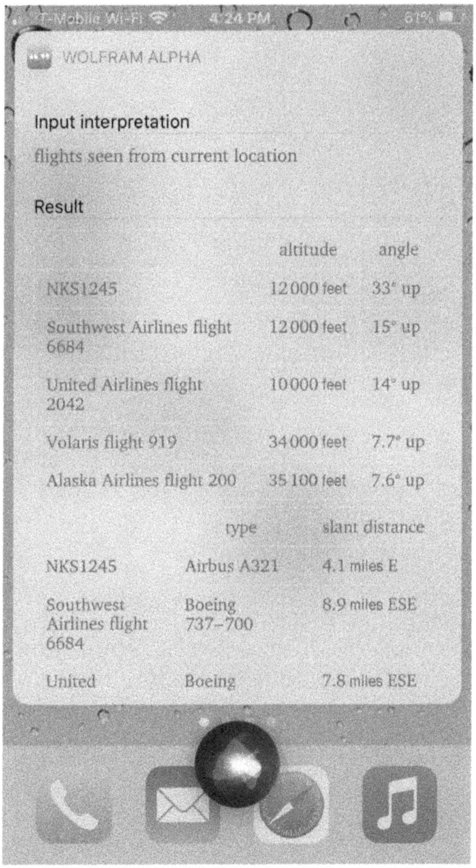

Figure 6.21 – Getting information about flights above your current location

Viewing flights above you can be interesting just to make you realize how many planes are flying over your current location at any time.

Summary

Think of having a courteous servant ready to obey your voice commands at all times, and that's what Siri can do for you and your iPhone. Not everyone may need Siri to play music, but chances are good that you use your iPhone for common tasks that can be made easier by relying on Siri.

Practice using different words and phrases to see which ones work most accurately with Siri. Depending on your pronunciation, some words and phrases may work better than others. Siri is handy when you can't use your hands to manually control your iPhone.

While Siri can control most features of your iPhone, the one feature that requires your complete attention is taking pictures through the iPhone's camera, which is the subject of the next chapter.

7

Taking and Sharing Pictures

You can't take a picture without a camera. That's why the best camera is one that you have with you, and for many people, that camera is in their iPhone. Over the years, the iPhone's camera has steadily improved, to the point where it's now equal or superior to many standalone cameras. Many professional photographers even rely solely on the iPhone's camera to capture both still and video images that are indistinguishable from still and video images captured by standalone cameras.

Of course, you don't have to know anything about photography to enjoy the iPhone's camera. All you need to know is how to take pictures, edit them later if you wish, save them, and share them with others. Taking pictures can be fun for anyone, so feel free to point your iPhone camera at any interesting image to capture your memories.

The topics we will cover in the chapter are as follows:

- Capturing still images and video
- Viewing and organizing pictures and videos
- Editing pictures and videos
- Sharing pictures and videos

Capturing still images

Despite its small size, the iPhone's camera can capture amazing pictures. To help you capture the best still images possible, the Camera app offers several options:

- **PHOTO**: Captures still images
- **SQUARE**: Captures still images in a square, which is the optimal photo size for many social media apps
- **PORTRAIT**: Captures a subject while blurring the background
- **PANO**: Captures panoramic still images

When capturing still images, you have several additional options, such as turning flash on (or off), using **HDR** (**High Dynamic Range**), turning Live **Photos** on (or off), setting a timer, or adjusting the color tone.

Flash is often used in poor lighting. If you turn flash on, you'll get to choose from three options:

- **Auto**: Auto means you let the iPhone decide whether to use flash or not.
- **On**: On means flash always occurs
- **Off**: Off means flash never occurs.

HDR is meant to capture differences between light and dark images. Without HDR, you can focus on a tree (slightly blurring everything else) or focus on the sky behind the tree (slightly blurring the tree). HDR captures all images equally well. Like the flash option, the HDR options are **Auto**, **On**, and **Off**.

Live **Photos** captures a 3-second moving image and audio, plus an additional 1.5 seconds after you capture the image. When viewing an image captured with Live Photos, you'll briefly see the images move.

Setting a timer lets you define a 3- or 10-second delay. This gives you time to set the camera and get into position before the camera actually captures an image.

Color tones lets you adjust the appearance of an image by making colors appear brighter or black and white. By choosing different color tones, you can improve an image or capture an artistic view of an image.

Capturing a photo or square image

The iPhone's camera makes it easy to simply point and shoot to capture any image. The **PHOTO** option is the most common setting for capturing still images, but the **SQUARE** option can be handy for capturing images in a size best suited for social media apps.

To capture a still image with the **PHOTO** or **SQUARE** settings, follow these steps:

1. Tap the **Camera** app on the Home Screen. The Camera screen appears.
2. Swipe left or right on the settings options to choose **PHOTO** or **SQUARE** so that it appears directly over the white button and appears highlighted in yellow, as shown in *Figure 7.1*:

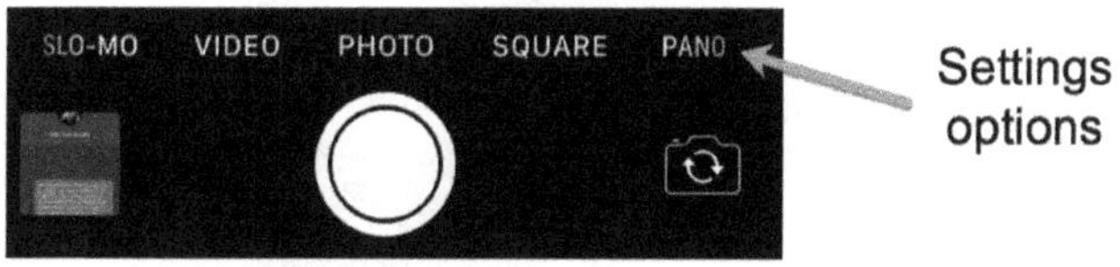

Figure 7.1 – The Camera app's settings options

3. (Optional) tap the camera icon with two circular arrows in the bottom-right corner of the screen to toggle between the front and back camera.
4. (Optional) tap the flash icon in the upper-left corner of the screen, as shown in *Figure 7.2*, and choose **Auto**, **On**, or **Off**:

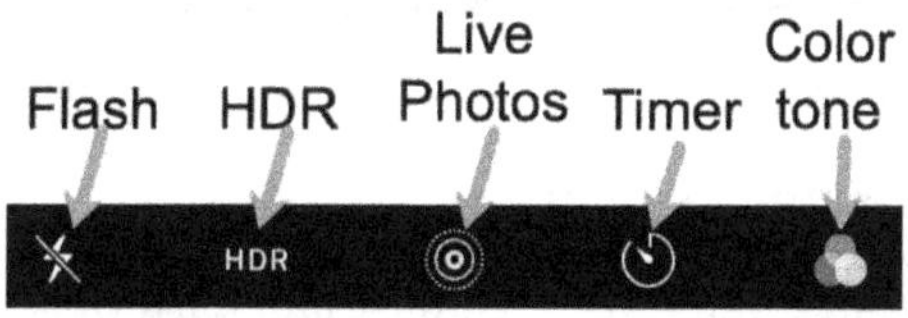

Figure 7.2 – The options at the top of the screen

5. (Optional) tap the **HDR** icon at the top of the screen (see *Figure 7.2*) and choose **Auto**, **On**, or **Off**.
6. (Optional) tap the Live **Photos** icon at the top of the screen (see *Figure 7.2*) to toggle Live **Photos** on or off.
7. (Optional) tap the timer icon at the top of the screen (see *Figure 7.2*) and choose **Off**, **3s**, or **10s**.

8. (Optional) tap the color tone icon at the top of the screen (see *Figure 7.2*) and scroll left and right through the list of color options near the bottom of the screen, such as **VIVID WARM** or **DRAMATIC COOL**, as shown in *Figure 7.3*:

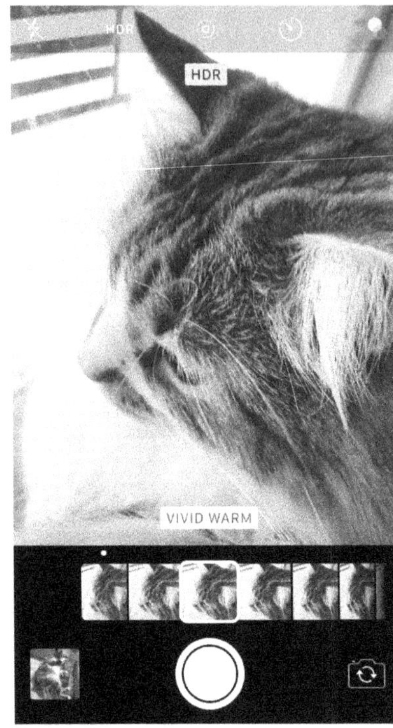

Figure 7.3 – Choosing different color tones for a still image

9. Tap the white shutter button to capture your image.

Still images are useful for almost any type of subject you wish to capture, from landscapes and people to objects and animals. However, if you want to capture a person, you might want to use a special setting called **PORTRAIT**.

Capturing a portrait image

Portrait mode is best when you want to focus on a person and blur any background images around that person. When capturing a still image in portrait mode, you can choose between several light settings:

- **NATURAL LIGHT**: Keeps the person's face in focus and blurs the background
- **STUDIO LIGHT**: Lights up a person's face and blurs the background

- **CONTOUR LIGHT**: Casts shadows on a person's face to provide greater contrast
- **STAGE LIGHT**: Blacks out the background so that only the person's face is seen
- **STAGE LIGHT MONO**: Just like **Stage Light** except displays everything in black and white.
- **HIGH-KEY MONO**: Just like **Stage Light Mono** but displays a white background

To capture a still image with the **PORTRAIT** setting, follow these steps:

1. Tap the **Camera** app on the Home Screen. The Camera screen appears.
2. Swipe left or right on the settings options to choose **PORTRAIT** so that it appears directly over the white button and appears highlighted in yellow (see *Figure 7.1*). Frame your subject within the white corner borders, as shown in *Figure 7.4*:

Figure 7.4 – PORTRAIT displays four white corners to frame your subject

3. (Optional) tap a lighting option, such as **NATURAL LIGHT** or **CONTOUR LIGHT**, as shown in *Figure 7.5*:

Figure 7.5 – Choosing a lighting option

4. Tap the white button.

Portrait mode is optimized just for capturing images of people. If you want to capture landscapes, then you might prefer the panoramic setting.

Capturing a panoramic image

The **PANO** option to capture panoramic views can be useful for capturing an image wider than the iPhone's camera can normally capture. By moving your iPhone from left to right, you can capture a wide image, such as the Grand Canyon.

To capture a panoramic view, follow these steps:

1. Tap the **Camera** app on the Home Screen. The Camera screen appears.
2. Choose **PANO** in the settings options (see *Figure 7.1*). A white arrow appears next to a yellow horizontal line, as shown in *Figure 7.6*:

Figure 7.6 – Starting to capture a panoramic view

3. Aim the iPhone camera to the left of the panoramic view you want to capture and then tap the white button to start capturing a panoramic view.
4. Slowly move the iPhone to the right, keeping the white arrow as level as possible along the yellow horizontal line, as shown in *Figure 7.7*:

Figure 7.7 – Capturing a panoramic view

5. Tap the white stop button when you're done capturing the panoramic view.

While you can use the iPhone cameras to capture any image you can point at, what if you want to show someone a picture of your current screen? Since the iPhone's camera can't point at the screen, you'll need to know how to capture screenshots.

Capturing screenshots

Screenshots let you capture images that appear on your screen. If you find an interesting website or a unique app, you might want to capture an image to share with others.

To capture a screenshot, follow these steps:

1. Display something on your iPhone screen that you want to capture, such as a game or a web page.
2. For iPhone models without a Home button, press the Side button and volume up button at the same time, as shown in *Figure 7.8* (for iPhone models with a Home button, press the Home button and the Side button at the same time):

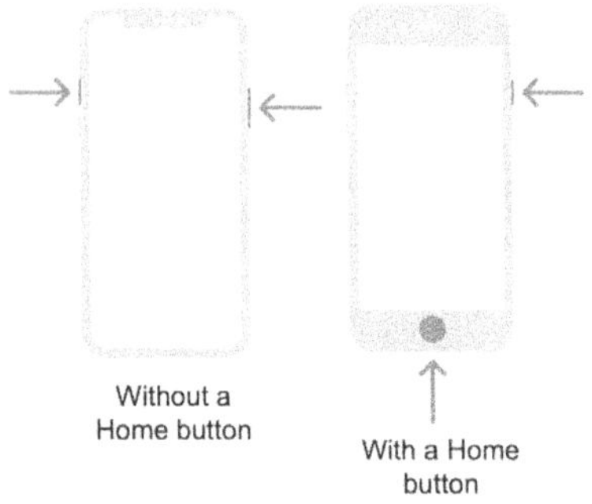

Figure 7.8 – Capturing a screenshot with different iPhone models

Capturing still images can be fun, but sometimes, you may wish to record video images instead. Fortunately, the iPhone camera can double as both a still image camera and a video camera.

Recording video

Besides capturing still images, the iPhone camera can also record video. Instead of carrying around a camera and a camcorder, the iPhone gives you both in one camera.

Some of the different ways you can capture video include the following:

- **Video**
- **Time lapse**
- **Slow motion**

Recording ordinary video

The **VIDEO** option lets you capture events as they happen without any added modification. By shooting video instead of still images, you can not only capture motion but also ensure that you capture that perfect shot.

To record video, follow these steps:

1. Tap the **Camera** app on the Home Screen. The Camera screen appears.
2. Choose **VIDEO** in the settings options. The record button appears as a red circle, replacing the white shutter button, as shown in *Figure 7.9*:

Figure 7.9 – A red record button lets you know that you're recording video

3. (Optional) tap the camera icon with the two circular arrows in the bottom-right corner of the screen to toggle between the front and back camera.
4. Tap the red recording button to start recording video. The bottom of the Camera app screen now displays a white button and a red square button, as shown in *Figure 7.10*. The white button lets you capture still images, while the red square button represents the stop recording button:

Figure 7.10 – The white and red buttons

5. (Optional) tap the white button to capture a still image.
6. Tap the red square stop button to stop recording video.

Recording ordinary video is fine for most occasions, but you might also want to record a time-lapse video, which can be handy for creating interesting visual effects.

Recording time-lapse video

If you've ever seen videos of LEGO pieces moving around, or inanimate objects such as pencils, coffee mugs, or toy cars appearing to move on their own, it was likely captured using time-lapse photography.

Time-lapse photography works by capturing images periodically. This gives you time to move inanimate objects around or just capture ordinary images, which creates an unusual video effect like old-fashioned video cameras that couldn't capture motion smoothly.

To record a time-lapse video, follow these steps:

1. Tap the **Camera** app on the Home Screen. The Camera screen appears.
2. Choose **TIME-LAPSE** in the settings options. The record button appears as a red circle with tick marks surrounding it, as shown in *Figure 7.11*:

Figure 7.11 – Capturing time-lapse video

3. Tap the red record button to start recording a time-lapse video. The white tick marks around the record button start filling the outer edges to let you know when the camera will capture another image, as shown in *Figure 7.12*:

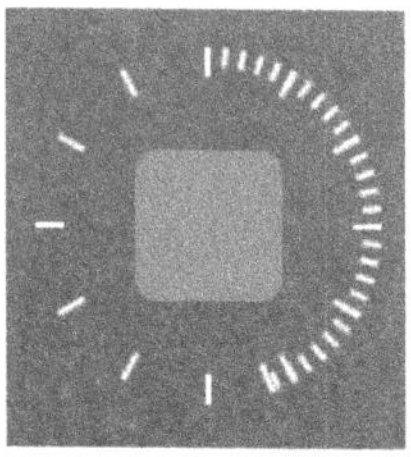

Figure 7.12 – Displaying the time until the camera captures another image

4. Tap the red square to stop recording the time-lapse video.

Time-lapse video may be good at creating interesting visual effects, but if you're capturing fast motion, you may want to capture it in slow motion instead. That way, you'll be able to study the motion in more detail.

Recording slow motion video

If you've ever watched a sporting event, the broadcasters often replay particularly interesting scenes in slow motion. That way, you can clearly see the details that were easily missed in the speed and short time frame of the activity.

So, if you want to capture fast-moving action, or just want to experiment with an interesting visual effect, the iPhone can also capture slow motion video.

To record slow motion video, follow these steps:

1. Tap the **Camera** app on the Home Screen. The Camera screen appears.
2. Choose **SLO-MO** in the settings options. The record button appears as a red circle with tick marks surrounding it, as shown in *Figure 7.13*:

Figure 7.13 – Recording slow motion video

3. Tap the red button again to stop recording the slow motion video.

Each time you capture either still images or videos, your iPhone stores those images in the **Photos** app. That's where you can search, sort, edit, and delete any pictures or videos.

Using the Photos app

The **Photos** app stores all captured still images and videos. Within the **Photos** app, you can view, edit, and send images and videos. By keeping all your pictures and videos in one place, the **Photos** app ensures you never lose track of any important pictures or videos.

The **Photos** app hold all your still images and videos, whether you have one image or a thousand. To help you find a particular image or video, you can organize items into several categories:

- **Library**
- **For You**
- **Albums**

The **Library** category contains all images and videos, organized in chronological order. By scrolling up and down, you can view past and current images and videos, as shown in *Figure 7.14*:

Figure 7.14 – The Library category displays images in rows and columns

When browsing through your images and videos, you can identify videos because they display their time length in the bottom-right corner, such as **7:29** or **1:36**, as shown in *Figure 7.15*:

Figure 7.15 – Identifying a video by its time length display

The **For You** category automatically organizes related image and videos based on time, location, or subject. That way, you can find related images that form a memory of an occasion or subject, as shown in *Figure 7.16*:

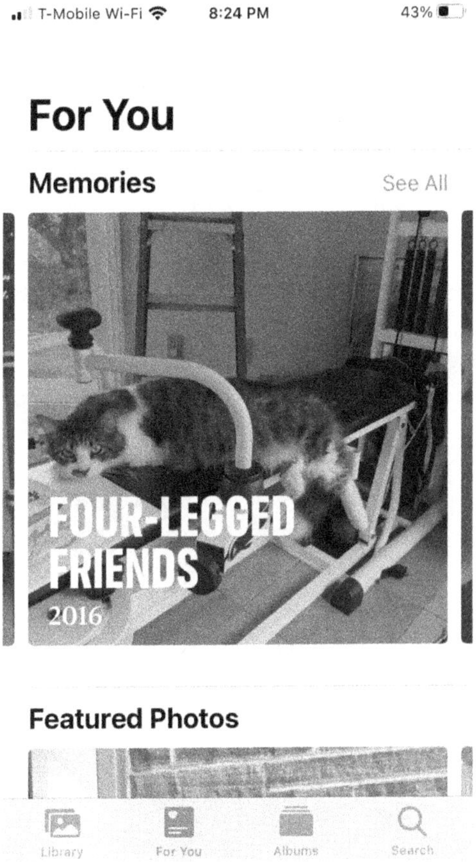

Figure 7.16 – The For You category automatically groups related items

The **Albums** category lets you manually choose which images and videos to group together. This lets you create albums that reflect certain moods or that contain items from different time periods or locations.

Viewing images and videos in the photos category

Viewing images and videos in the photos category lets you see everything saved on your iPhone. This ensures that you won't miss an item but can also be troublesome if you store hundreds or thousands of images.

When viewing images and videos in the photos category, you can increase or decrease the size of each item so that it appears smaller or larger. That way, you'll be able to see more items or focus on the details of fewer items.

To view items in the photos category, follow these steps:

1. Tap the **Photos** app on the Home Screen. The **Photos** screen appears.
2. Tap **Library** on the tab bar at the bottom of the screen.
3. Tap **All Photos** at the bottom of the screen. Your images and videos appear as thumbnail tiles on the screen (see *Figure 7.14*).
4. Tap the **...** icon in the upper-right corner of the screen. This will display a menu, so you can choose **Zoom In** or **Zoom Out** to increase or decrease the magnification of the list of stored images, as shown in *Figure 7.17*:

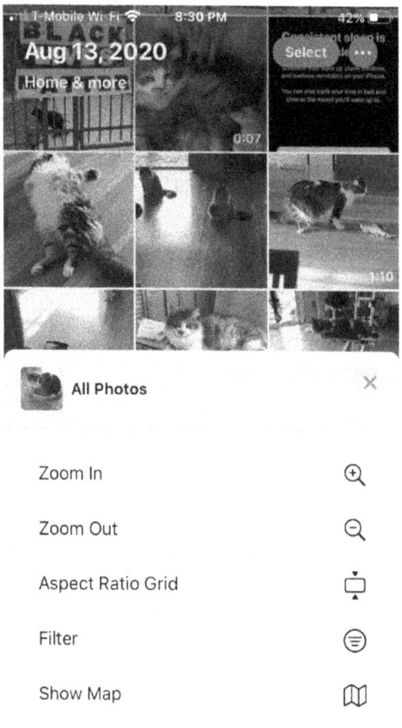

Figure 7.17 – Zooming in or out lets you view more or fewer stored images

5. Tap **Years**, **Months**, or **Days** at the bottom of the screen. This groups your images by year, month, or day, as shown in *Figure 7.18* (**All Photos** lets you view all images and videos stored in the **Photos** app):

Figure 7.18 – Grouping images by time

6. Tap the image you want to view.

Selecting an image to view through the **Library** category can be cumbersome if you have a large number of images. For a potentially faster method, consider browsing the **For You** category.

Viewing images and videos in the For You category

The **For You** category automatically groups related images and videos together, which makes it easier to look for similar images.

To view images in the **For You** category, follow these steps:

1. Tap the **Photos** app on the Home Screen. The **Photos** screen appears.
2. Tap **For You** on the tab bar at the bottom of the screen. Categories of your images appear (see *Figure 7.16*).
3. Scroll through your images and tap the one you want to view.

One unique feature of the **For You** category is that it lets you create slideshows, complete with music, so you can enjoy your images and share them with others.

To view a **For You** slideshow, follow these steps:

1. Tap the **Photos** app on the Home Screen. The **Photos** screen appears.
2. Tap **For You** on the tab bar at the bottom of the screen. Categories of your images appear, as shown in *Figure 7.19*:

Figure 7.19 – Viewing categories of images in the For You option

3. Tap on a category to display a play button at the bottom-right corner of a **For You** category. Then, tap the play button to watch a slideshow presentation, complete with music.
4. Tap a different type of music to play, such as **GENTLE** or **CHILL**, as shown in *Figure 7.20*:

Figure 7.20 – Modifying a For You slideshow

5. Tap **SHORT** or **MEDIUM** to choose a different length for your slideshow.
6. Tap the play/pause button to play or pause your slideshow.

Creating albums to organize images and videos

The **Photos** app can automatically organize images and videos by time, location, or subject. However, you may want to organize images and videos into your own groups, called albums.

Just as you can put different pictures in physical album binders, so can you put different pictures in virtual albums in the **Photos** app. Unlike the physical world, where you can only put a picture in one album, the **Photos** app lets you store the same picture in as many different albums as you wish.

The **Albums** category automatically sorts images and video into albums such as **Videos**, **Selfies**, **Live Photos**, or **Panoramas**, as shown in *Figure 7.21*:

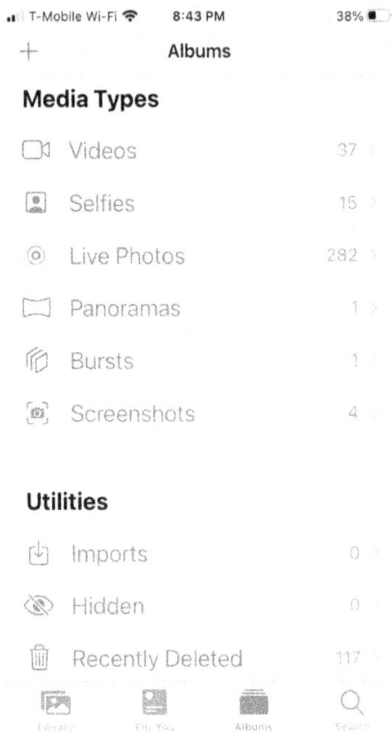

Figure 7.21 – Default albums in the **Photos** app

To browse an existing album, follow these steps:

1. Tap the **Photos** app on the Home Screen. The **Photos** screen appears.
2. Tap **Albums** on the tab bar at the bottom of the screen. A list of all available albums appears, such as **My Albums** and **People & Places**. You may need to scroll down to see all your albums.
3. Tap an album name. The album displays all the stored images and videos in rows and columns.
4. Tap on the image you want to view.

While the default albums available might be handy for organizing your images and videos, you might want to organize images yourself. In that case, you can create an album and choose which images to store.

When creating an album, you can create an ordinary album or a shared album. A shared album lets others view and edit the album by storing images in iCloud, while an ordinary album is stored on your iPhone.

> **Note**
> To create a shared album, you'll need to make sure you turn on iCloud by going to **Settings** | **[your name]** | **iCloud** | **Photos**, then turning on **Shared Albums**.

To create an album and fill it with images and videos, follow these steps:

1. Tap the **Photos** app on the Home Screen. The **Photos** screen appears.
2. Tap **Albums** on the tab bar at the bottom of the screen.
3. Tap the + icon in the upper-left corner of the screen. A list of options appears at the bottom of the screen, as shown in *Figure 7.22*:

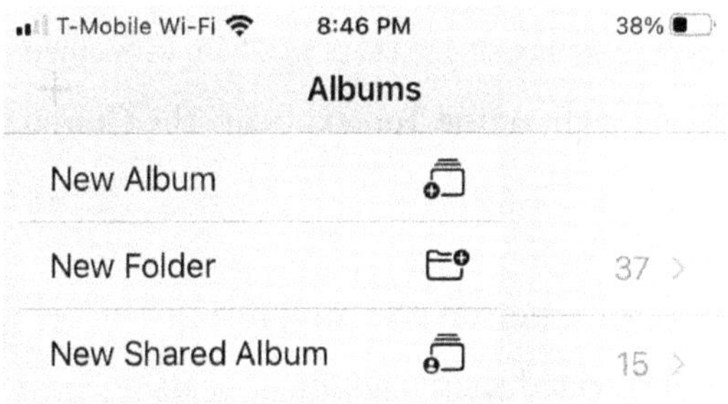

Figure 7.22 – Choosing to create an album or shared album

4. Tap **New Album** or **New Shared Album**. A dialog appears, asking you to choose a name for your album.
5. Type a descriptive name for your album.

If you chose **New Album** in *Step 4*, follow these steps:

1. After typing a descriptive name for your album, tap **Save**. The **All Photos** category appears, showing every image and video stored on your iPhone.
2. Tap on each image and video you want to add to the album.
3. Tap **Done**. All your chosen images and videos now appear in your album.

If you chose **New Shared Album** in *Step 4*, follow these steps:

1. After typing a descriptive name for your album, tap **Next**. An iCloud dialog appears, letting you choose people to share the album with, as shown in *Figure 7.23*:

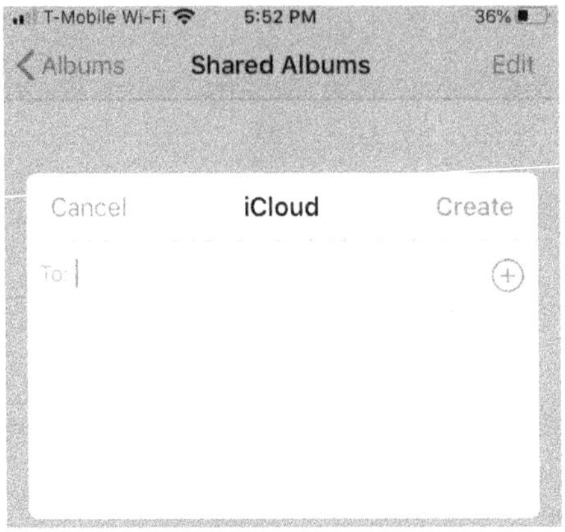

Figure 7.23 – Choosing to share an album with others

2. Tap the + icon on the far right of the **To:** text field. The **Contacts** app displays a list of your stored names.
3. Tap on a name.
4. Repeat *Steps 2* and *3* for each person you want to add.
5. Tap **Create**. Your newly created shared album appears.
6. Tap the shared album. A + icon appears inside a box, as shown in *Figure 7.24*:

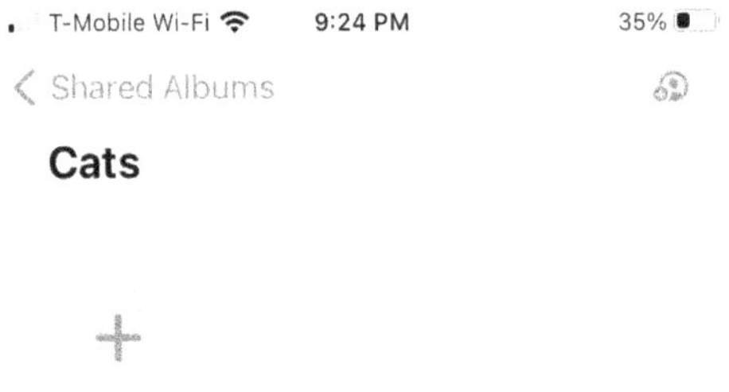

Figure 7.24 – Adding images and videos to a shared album

7. Tap the + icon inside the box. An **All Photos** screen appears, letting you tap the images and videos to add in the shared album.
8. Tap **Done** when you're finished selecting images and videos.

Once you've created an album, you can/may want to delete that album later. Deleting an album does not delete any images or videos stored in that album.

To delete an album, follow these steps:

1. Tap the **Photos** app on the Home Screen. The **Photos** screen appears.
2. Tap **Albums** on the tab bar at the bottom of the screen.
3. Scroll to the **My Albums** or **Shared Albums** categories.
4. Tap **See All** in the upper-right corner. All your albums appear in rows and columns.
5. Tap **Edit** in the upper right-hand corner. A red – sign icon appears in the upper-left corner of the album, as shown in *Figure 7.25*:

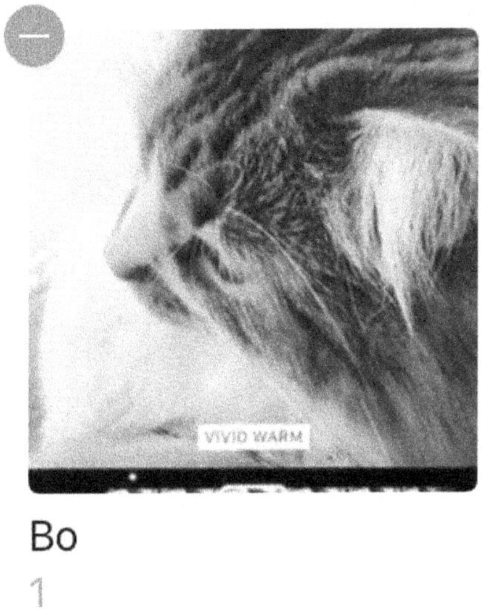

Figure 7.25 – The red – icon lets you delete an album

6. Tap this red – icon. A list of options appears at the bottom of the screen, letting you choose **Delete Album** or **Cancel**.
7. Tap **Delete Album** (or **Cancel**).
8. Tap **Done**.

Albums can be a handy way to organize your pictures and videos. Each time you capture a picture, it might be perfect, or it might be almost perfect. For those almost-perfect pictures, consider modifying them to make them exactly how you want.

Editing images and videos

Many people happily use the **Photos** app simply to view their pictures. However, you might want to modify any pictures you capture, either to improve them or to get creative and silly with them. To edit images and videos, the first step is to select the image or video you want to modify.

If you want to modify images or videos, you can choose from one of the following categories of editing tools:

- **Live Photos** (still images only): Lets you choose which frame within a live photo to use
- **Video** (video only): Lets you adjust the starting and ending point of a video
- **Adjust**: Lets you modify brightness, exposure, contrast, and other features
- **Filters**: Lets you choose different ways to alter the overall appearance of an image or video
- **Reset**: Lets you rotate, crop, and adjust the position of an image or video

Editing Live Photos

Live **Photos** capture a 1.5-second recording before and after you take a picture. That way, you get a brief amount of movement and sound. Not only do Live **Photos** move when you first look at them, but they also give you the option of selecting which frame within a Live Photo might look best.

For example, suppose you took a picture of a little kid. However, just as you captured the picture, the kid shut their eyes. With Live Photo editing, you could view the 1.5-second images before and after the picture to see whether you actually caught a picture with the kid's eyes open. Then, you could select that frame to use instead.

To edit a Live Photo, follow these steps:

1. Select the Live Photo you want to edit. You can identify Live **Photos** because they display **LIVE** at the upper-left corner, as shown in *Figure 7.26*:

Figure 7.26 – Identifying a Live Photo

2. Swipe up on the Live Photo. A list of visual effects appears, as shown in *Figure 7.27*:

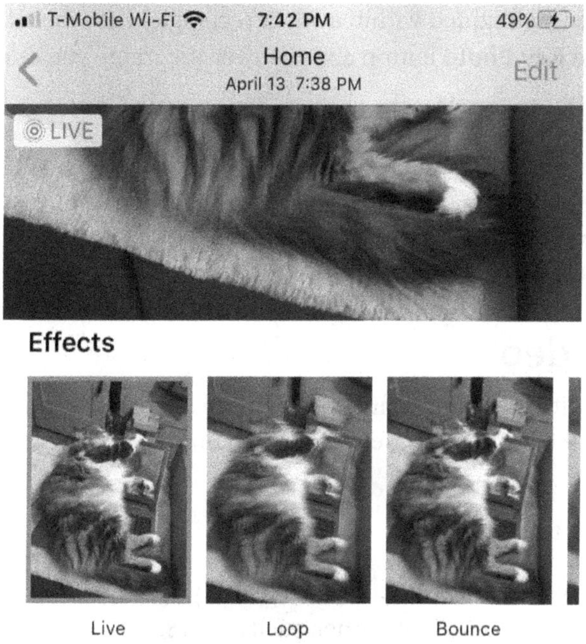

Figure 7.27 – Choosing a visual effect for a Live Photo

3. Tap on a visual effect you want to use, such as **Loop** or **Bounce**.
4. Tap **Edit** in the upper-right corner of the screen. A list of different editing icons appears at the bottom of the screen, as shown in *Figure 7.28*:

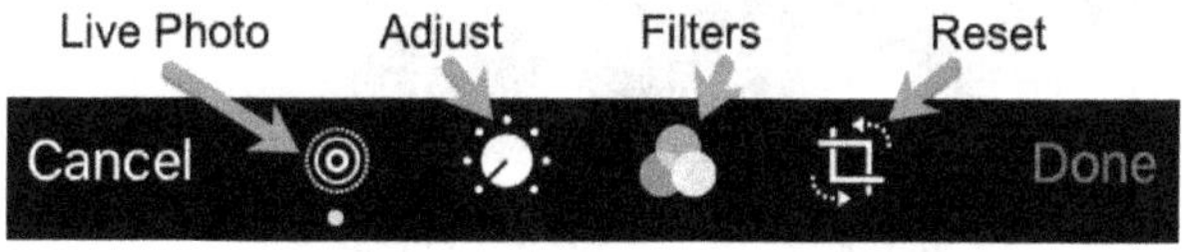

Figure 7.28 – The list of editing icons

5. Tap the **Live Photo** icon. Multiple frames of your Live Photo appear, as shown in *Figure 7.29*:

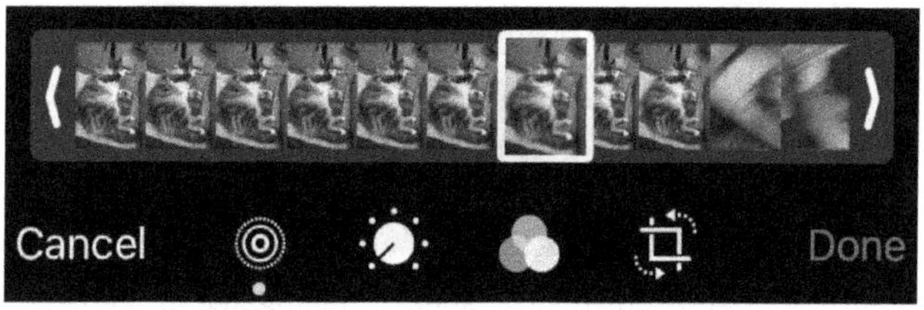

Figure 7.29 – Viewing multiple frames of a Live Photo

6. Select the frame (highlighted within a white rectangle) that you want to use for your picture. A **Make Key Photo** button appears over the frame you selected.
7. Tap **Make Key Photo** to select the chosen frame, or tap **Cancel**.

By default, your iPhone will capture Live Photos, but you can always turn this feature on and off at any time. In most cases, you want to capture Live **Photos** because it gives you the option later of selecting a better image. For another way to capture the best possible image, consider capturing video instead.

Trimming a video

The simplest way to edit video is to define the beginning and end to make the video shorter. By trimming the beginning or end, you can eliminate extra scenes that you don't need.

To trim a video, follow these steps:

1. Select the video you want to edit. You can identify videos because they display their time length in the bottom-right corner, such as **4:18**.
2. Tap **Edit** in the upper-right corner of the screen. The individual frames of the video appear underneath the video, with a white curved line representing the beginning and end of the video, as shown in *Figure 7.30*:

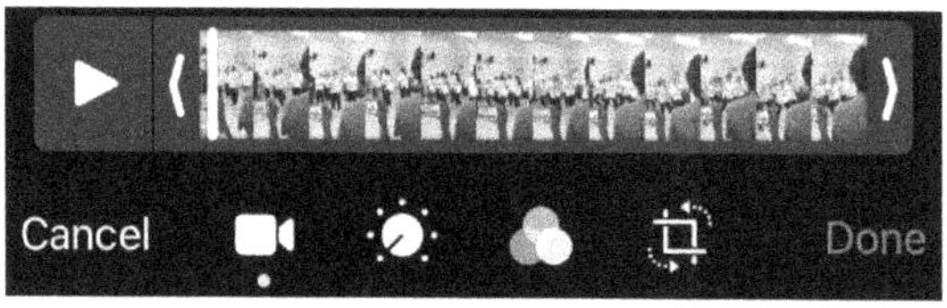

Figure 7.30 – Trimming a video

3. Drag the beginning and/or end of the video to define a new start and end time, as shown in *Figure 7.31*:

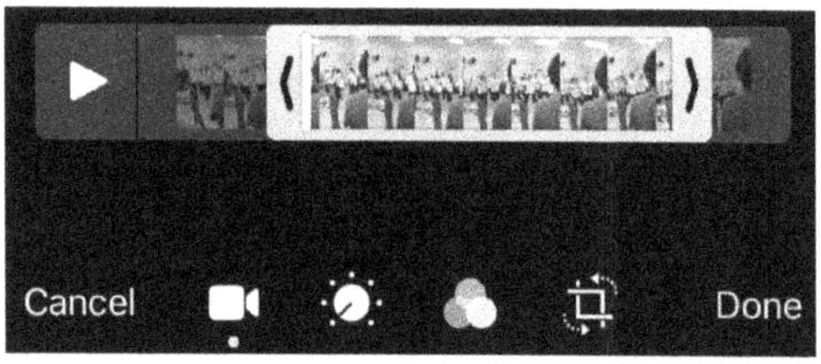

Figure 7.31 – A trimmed video appears highlighted in yellow

4. Tap **Done**.

Many times, you might capture an image or video that looks almost perfect, but not quite. That's why you might want to spend a little time modifying the appearance of an image or video, such as changing the contrast, brightness, or saturation.

Adjusting the appearance of an image or video

Sometimes, you may capture an image or video that's too bright or too dark, but might otherwise be perfect. Rather than trying to capture that same image again (which might be impossible), you can try adjusting the image or video's appearance by lightening or darkening the image or video.

To lighten or darken an image or video, follow these steps:

1. Select the image or video you want to edit.
2. Tap **Edit** in the upper-right corner of the screen.
3. Tap the adjust icon at the bottom of the screen. Icons appear for adjusting the lightness or darkness of the image.
4. Tap an icon such as **EXPOSURE** or **BRILLIANCE**. A horizontal scale appears, as shown in *Figure 7.32*:

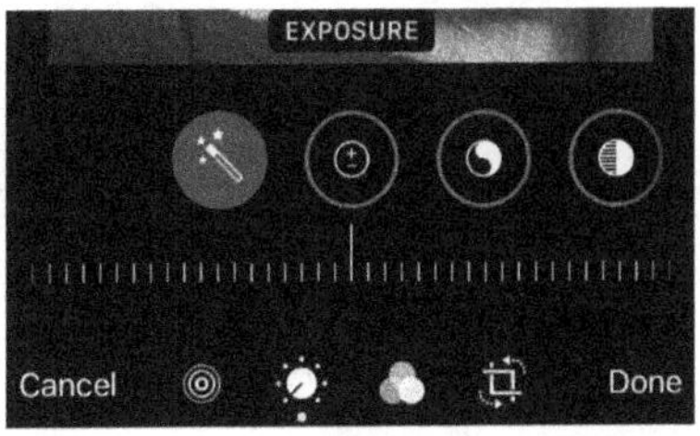

Figure 7.32 – Different options for adjusting lightness and darkness

5. Swipe left or right on this horizontal scale to adjust your chosen options by a positive or negative numerical value, as shown in *Figure 7.33*:

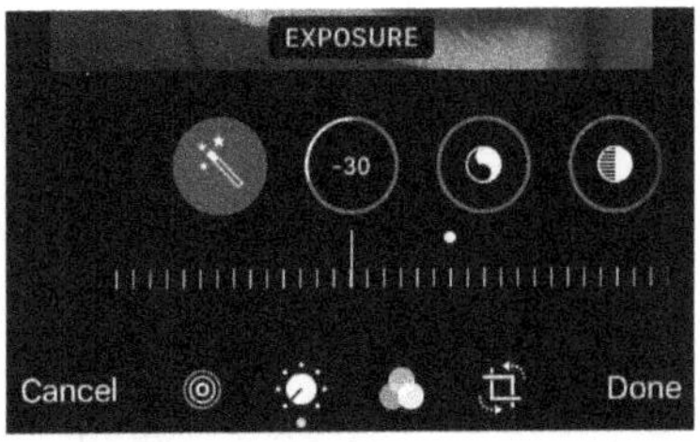

Figure 7.33 – Different options for adjusting lightness and darkness

6. Tap **Done** when you're happy with the appearance (or tap **Cancel**).

Lightening or darkening an image or video is one way to correct an image, but for a more artistic option, you can apply filters over an image or video. Filters simply modify an image in a uniform manner, such as making it appear black and white or brighter.

Applying filters to an image or video

Filters offer a quick way to modify an image or video by applying a uniform change, such as muting or sharpening the appearance of colors. By experimenting with different filters, you can either correct an image or video, or create a unique visual effect.

To apply a filter to an image or video, follow these steps:

1. Select the image or video you want to edit.
2. Tap **Edit** in the upper-right corner of the screen.
3. Tap the filters icon at the bottom of the screen. Frames appear, showing how the image or video will look under each filter, as shown in *Figure 7.34*:

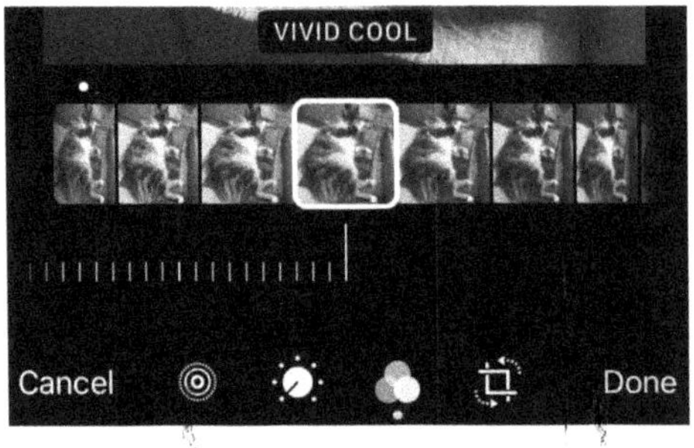

Figure 7.34 – Choosing a filter

4. Tap a filter, and then tap **Done** (or **Cancel**).

Filters can alter the overall appearance of an image or video, but what if you captured the perfect shot but it's slightly crooked? That's when you may need to choose a reset option to flip, rotate, or change the physical orientation of an image or video.

Resetting the orientation of an image or video

Resetting an image or video lets you adjust its physical orientation in the following ways:

- **Flip**: Displays the mirror image of an image or video
- **Rotate**: Rotates an image or video 90 degrees to the right
- **Resize**: Changes the shape of an image, such as making it square or wider
- **Straighten**: Rotates an image or video around the *x*, *y*, and *z* axes

To straighten the orientation of an image or video, follow these steps:

1. Select the image or video you want to edit.
2. Tap **Edit** in the upper-right corner of the screen.
3. Tap the reset icon at the bottom of the screen, as shown in *Figure 7.35*:

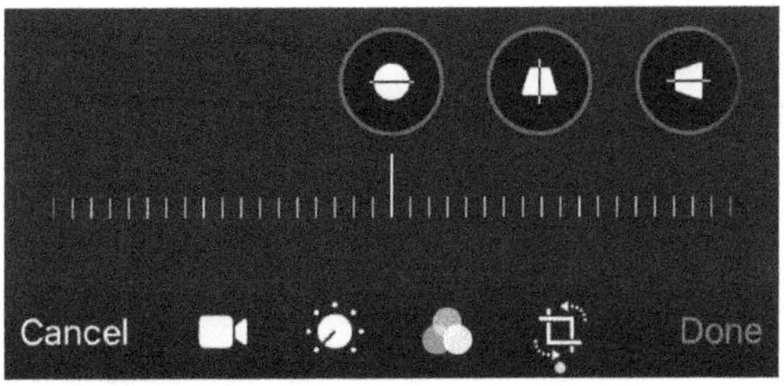

Figure 7.35 – The reset options

4. Tap one of the straighten icons that appear underneath the image or video. A grid appears over the image or video.
5. Swipe left or right on the horizontal row of white vertical lines to adjust how much to modify the image or video, as shown in *Figure 7.36*:

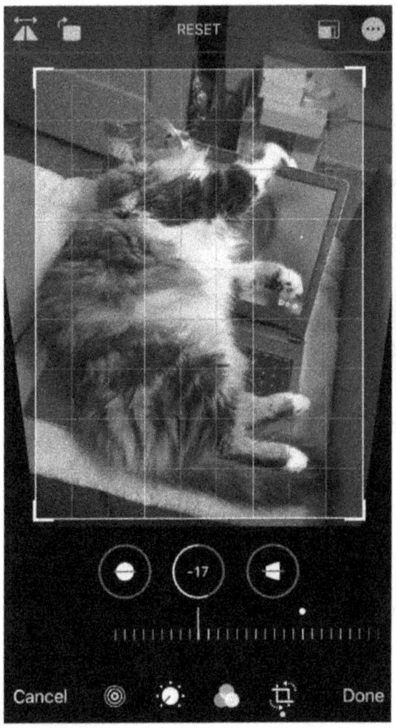

Figure 7.36 – A grid appears to help you modify an image or video

6. Tap **Done** (or **Cancel**).

Manually adjusting an image gives you complete control over its appearance. However, this can be time-consuming, so you might want a faster solution to flip, rotate, or resize an image or video.

To flip, rotate, or resize an image or video, follow these steps:

1. Select the image or video you want to edit.
2. Tap **Edit** in the upper-right corner of the screen.
3. Tap the reset icon at the bottom of the screen (see *Figure 7.35*).
4. (Optional) tap the flip icon in the upper-left corner of the screen, as shown in *Figure 7.37*:

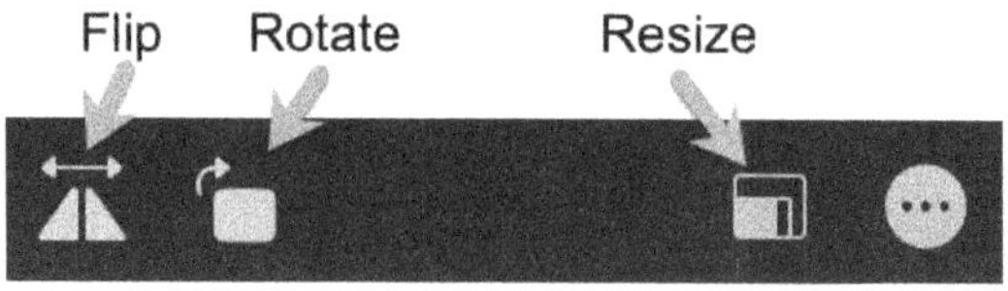

Figure 7.37 – The flip, rotate, and resize icons

5. (Optional) tap the rotate icon in the upper-left corner of the screen (see *Figure 7.37*). Each time you tap the rotate icon, the image or video rotates 90 degrees to the right.
6. (Optional) tap the resize icon. A list of resizing options appears near the bottom of the screen, such as **FREEFORM**, **SQUARE**, and **9:16**, as shown in *Figure 7.38*:

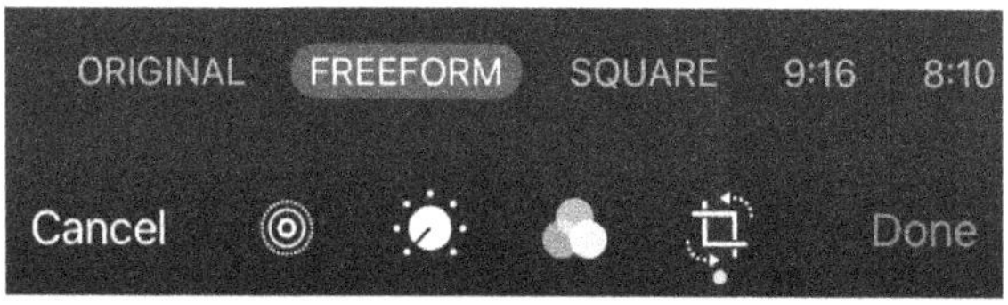

Figure 7.38 – Resizing options

7. Tap a resize option, such as **SQUARE** or **8:10**.
8. Tap **Done** (or **Cancel**).

One final way you might want to modify an image or video is by cropping, which essentially lets you shrink the area you want to keep. Cropping can be handy to cut off the tops or edges of an image or video to delete the parts of an image or video that aren't necessary.

Cropping an image or video

Cropping lets you use virtual scissors to cut the edges from an image or video. Cropping always removes parts from an image or video, so you can eliminate the edges that you don't need to keep.

To crop an image or video, follow these steps:

1. Select the image or video you want to edit.
2. Tap **Edit** in the upper-right corner of the screen.
3. Tap the reset icon at the bottom of the screen (see *Figure 7.35*). Four thick white crop marks appear around the four corners of the image.
4. Move the crop marks to define the part of the picture you want to keep. Any area outside of the crop marks will appear dimmed to show what will be cut out, as shown in *Figure 7.39*:

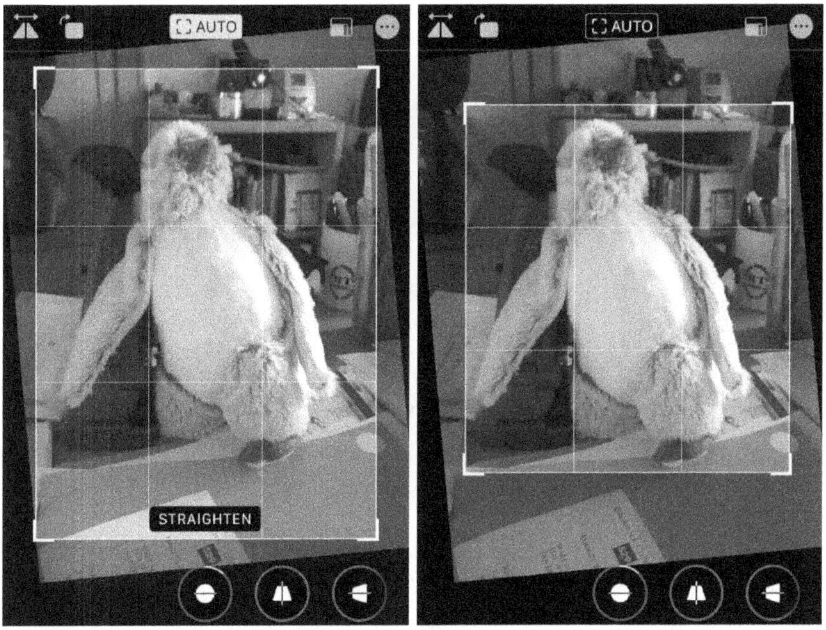

Figure 7.39 – Cropping an image

5. Tap **Done**.

After you are done fixing or modifying an image or video, you might want to share the image or tag it as a favorite. Sharing lets others see your pictures, while tagging an image or video as a favorite automatically makes that item appear in the **Favorites** album.

Tagging and sharing images and videos

Not every picture or video you capture will be great, but for those that you like the best, you can tag them as a favorite. That way, they'll automatically show up in your **Favorites** album.

Whether you like a picture or not, you might want to share it with others. Sharing lets you send images or videos by email, text messaging, or through AirDrop, where you can send items to another Apple device, such as a Macintosh, iPad, or iPhone.

Tagging an image or video

Tagging an image or video as a favorite helps you find your best pictures quickly and easily.

To tag an image or video, follow these steps:

1. Select the image or video you want to tag.
2. Tap the favorites icon (the heart) at the bottom of the screen, as shown in *Figure 7.40*:

Figure 7.40 – Using the favorites tag

Sharing an image or video

Half the fun of taking pictures is sharing them with others, whether privately through email or publicly through a social media app. Some of the different ways to share an image or video include the following:

- **AirDrop**: Send an item to another Apple device, such as a Macintosh, iPhone, or iPad.
- **Messages**: Send an item by text message.
- **Mail**: Send an item as a file attachment by email.

Depending on the apps installed on your iPhone, you may also have the option of sharing an item directly to a social media app such as Twitter or Facebook.

To share an image or video, follow these steps:

1. Select the image or video you want to share.
2. Tap the share icon (see *Figure 7.40*). Your chosen picture appears as a thumbnail along with a blue checkmark in the bottom-right corner.
3. (Optional) tap any other pictures or videos you want to send as well if you want to share more than one item. A horizontal row of circular icons appears underneath your thumbnail image, listing any nearby AirDrop devices, along with the names of people you've sent a text message to recently. Another horizontal row lists different sharing options, such as **AirDrop**, **Messages**, and **Mail**, as shown in *Figure 7.41*:

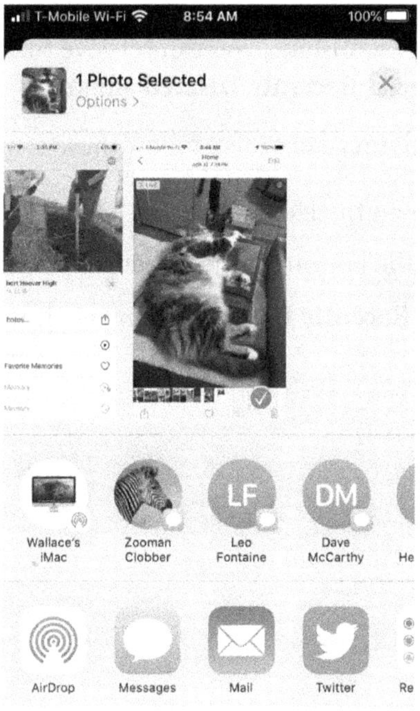

Figure 7.41 – Choosing how to share an item

4. Tap either a destination (nearby Macintosh computers or people you've previously texted) or a sharing option (**AirDrop**, **Messages**, **Mail**, or so on). If you've chosen a sharing option such as **Mail** or **Messages**, you'll need to type in additional information, such as an email address or mobile phone number to send your selected item to.

You can share items to as many people as you wish, as often as you like. After you share certain pictures or videos, you may not want to keep them, so you need to learn how to delete items as well.

Deleting images and videos

When you no longer want to keep an item, delete it. If you change your mind, you can even recover a deleted item right away. By deleting images and videos, you can make sure your iPhone never runs out of storage.

To delete an image or video, follow these steps:

1. Select the image or video you want to delete.
2. Tap the delete icon (see *Figure 7.40*). A **Delete** and **Cancel** button appear at the bottom of the screen.
3. Tap **Delete** (or **Cancel**).

If you delete an image or video by mistake, you can retrieve that item because the iPhone stores all deleted items in a special **Recently Deleted** album.

To retrieve a previously deleted image or video, follow these steps:

1. Tap the **Photos** app icon on the Home Screen.
2. Tap the **Albums** icon at the bottom of the screen.
3. Scroll down and tap the **Recently Deleted** album, as shown in *Figure 7.42*:

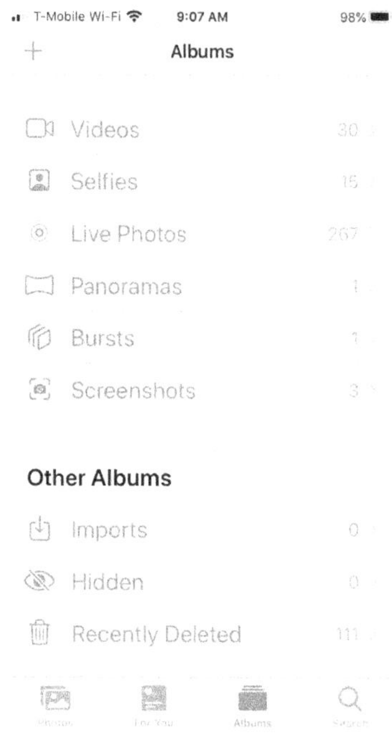

Figure 7.42 – The Recently Deleted album

4. Tap on the image or video you want to retrieve. A **Delete** and **Recover** button appear at the bottom of the screen.
5. Tap **Retrieve** to retrieve the deleted item (or tap **Delete** to permanently delete the item from the **Recently Deleted** album).

It's a good idea to review the **Recently Deleted** album periodically to permanently delete any images or videos you know you'll never want to keep again. That way, you can save storage space on your iPhone for important items, such as apps or new images and videos.

Summary

Taking pictures and videos can be a fun way to capture moments in your life and share them with others. Even if you're not a professional photographer, you can still enjoy capturing images and modifying them slightly to correct flaws, or apply unique visual effects for fun.

While the camera is one of the iPhone's most entertaining features, you might also want to turn your iPhone into a portable music player so that you can listen to music, radio stations, and podcasts wherever you go, which is the subject of the next chapter.

8
Listening to Music

In the old days, you could only listen to music outside if you carried a portable radio with you. Sony's introduction of the Walkman started a music revolution because you could now play cassette tapes wherever you went. Then, Apple changed the music world forever with their combination of iTunes and the iPod, one of the most popular portable music players ever.

Instead of carrying bulky tape cassettes or audio CDs, the iPod lets you store digital copies of your favorite songs. With an iPod, you can carry thousands of your favorite songs with you wherever you go.

When Apple introduced the iPhone, they combined the features of a mobile phone with the music-playing capabilities of an iPod. As long as you have your iPhone, you essentially get an iPod for free.

The topics we will cover in the chapter are the following:

- Listening to the radio
- Listening to podcasts
- Transferring music to an iPhone
- Storing and organizing audio files on an iPhone
- Playing an audio file
- Deleting audio files

Listening to the radio

While the iPhone can play music, it cannot tune into AM/FM radio broadcasts that an ordinary radio can play. Instead of receiving AM/FM broadcasts, your iPhone can simply access the radio through the internet (either through Wi-Fi or a cellular phone network). This allows you to access internet radio.

Apple offers Music 1, a 24-hour live radio station broadcast by Apple's DJs in Los Angeles, New York, and London. Best of all, Music 1 is free, so you can enjoy live shows, exclusive interviews, and new music from around the world.

The Music app on the iPhone can also access internet radio stations from around the world. Now you can tune into your favorite radio stations in another country or language, so you can choose between talk shows, different types of music, or sports broadcasts from anywhere on the planet.

> **Note:**
> Access to Music 1 and other radio shows may be limited depending on the area of the world you're in.

Listening to Music 1

The main goal of Music 1 is to help listeners discover new music based on lists curated by prominent DJs. To tune into Music 1, follow these steps:

1. Tap the **Music** app on the Home Screen. The Music app screen appears.
2. Tap the **Radio** icon at the bottom of the screen, as shown in *Figure 8.1*:

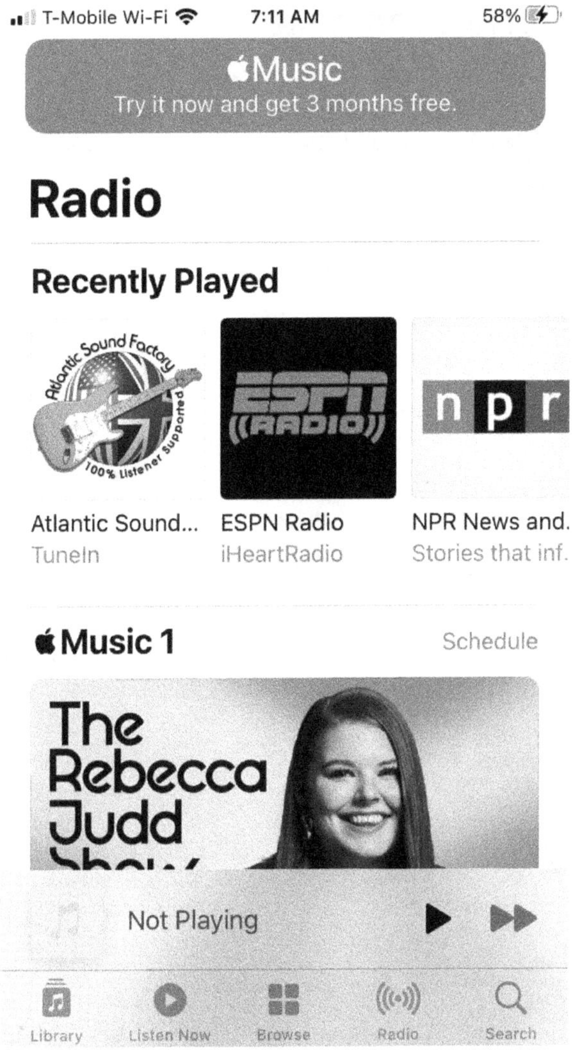

Figure 8.1 – The Radio icon to access Music 1

3. Scroll left and right under the **Radio** category until you find the Music 1 image.
4. Tap the Music 1 image to start playing the Music 1 station.

While Music 1 tries to play a variety of different types of music, you might want to pay for an Apple Music membership (`www.apple.com/apple-music/`), which gives you access to over 70 million songs of all genres that you can play whenever you want. You may also want to listen to a radio station that focuses on a certain market, such as country music, talk radio, or classic rock. In that case, you can listen to any radio station across the world that streams its content over the internet.

Listening to internet radio stations

Many people listen to local radio stations in their car or through a radio at home. Fortunately, most radio stations now also stream their broadcasts over the internet. That means as long as your iPhone has internet access, it can receive and play any broadcast stream from any radio station around the world.

If you have a favorite radio station from home (either in another city or another country), you can tune into that station through the Music app. To listen to any internet radio station, follow these steps:

1. Tap the **Music** app on the Home Screen. The Music app screen appears.
2. Tap the **Search** icon at the bottom of the screen, as shown in *Figure 8.2*:

Figure 8.2 – The Search icon

3. Tap in the search text field at the top of the screen and tap the **Apple Music** tab, as shown in *Figure 8.3*:

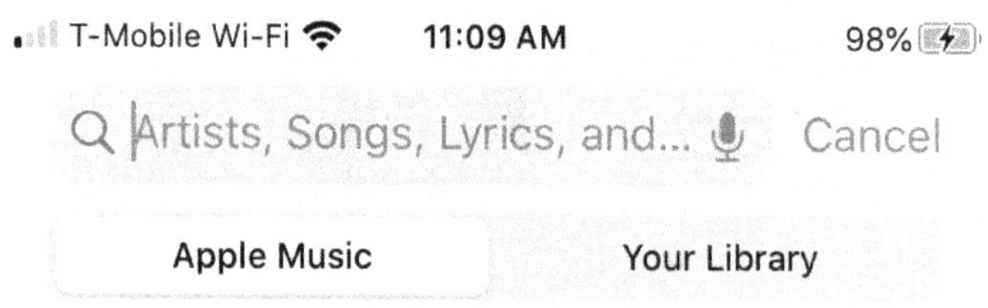

Figure 8.3 – The search text field

4. Type a radio station's name, call sign, frequency, nickname, or the type of station you want to find, such as `news station`. The Music app displays a radio station category with different stations that match your search criteria, as shown in *Figure 8.4*:

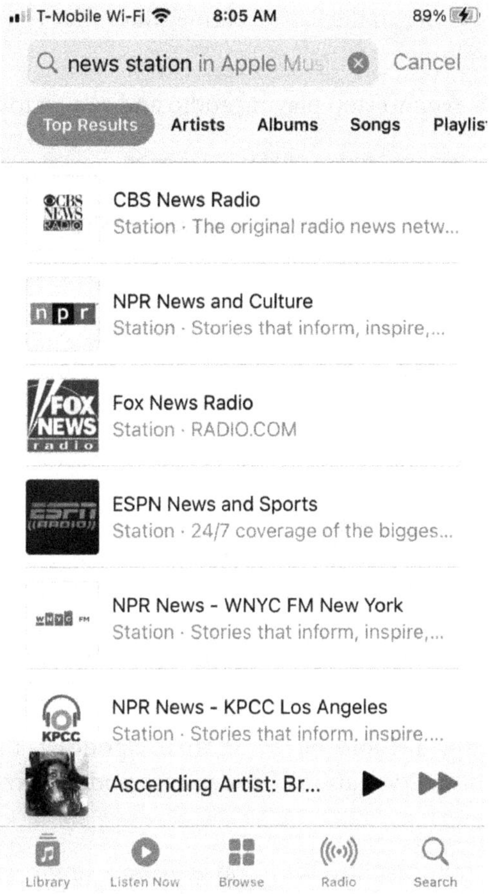

Figure 8.4 – The radio station category lists stations matching your criteria

5. Tap on a radio station. Your chosen radio station logo appears as a banner at the bottom of the screen and starts playing its streaming audio, as shown in *Figure 8.5*:

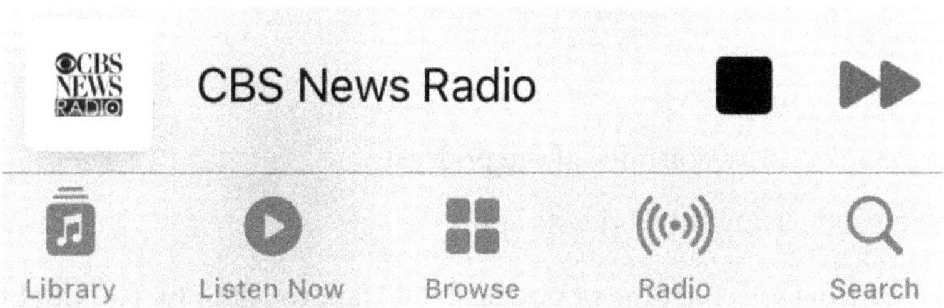

Figure 8.5 – Listening to a radio station

6. (Optional:) Tap the play/pause button (to toggle between playing and pausing the audio).

7. (Optional:) Tap the banner to display a volume slider that you can drag left or right to adjust the audio volume.
8. Swipe down on the screen to stop playing audio and return to the Music app.

> **Note:**
> You can also start Siri and say something such as, "Hey Siri, play ESPN radio" or any other radio station you want to hear.

Radio stations tend to focus on certain markets, but they may offer multiple shows that you may not like. Instead of listening to a particular radio station, you might prefer listening to a particular show. One way that many people promote themselves and provide useful information is through podcasts.

Listening to podcasts

Podcasts are informative and entertaining shows that focus on a specific topic, such as business marketing. Each episode typically involves one or more hosts talking for a fixed amount of time. Listeners can download one or more episodes of a podcast and listen to them at their convenience.

Most podcasts are recorded in a studio, but some are live podcasts that are recorded in front of a live audience. Another variation of podcasts is podcast novels, which are similar to audiobooks.

The main difference is that podcast novels can range from a single narrator reading a book to a group of voice actors combining sound effects to create an audio performance. Podcast novels are often a way for novelists to distribute their work, even if their novel hasn't been printed by a publisher.

No matter what type of podcast you want to hear, the basic steps to playing podcasts are as follows:

- Find a podcast to listen to.
- Download one or more episodes of the podcast.
- Play each episode using the Podcasts app.

If you have no idea what specific type of podcast you want to listen to, you might want to browse through lists of popular podcasts and see which one catches your attention.

To browse through podcasts, follow these steps:

1. Tap the **Podcasts** app on the Home Screen. The Podcasts screen appears.
2. Tap the **Browse** icon at the bottom of the screen. Different new and popular podcasts appear, as shown in *Figure 8.6*:

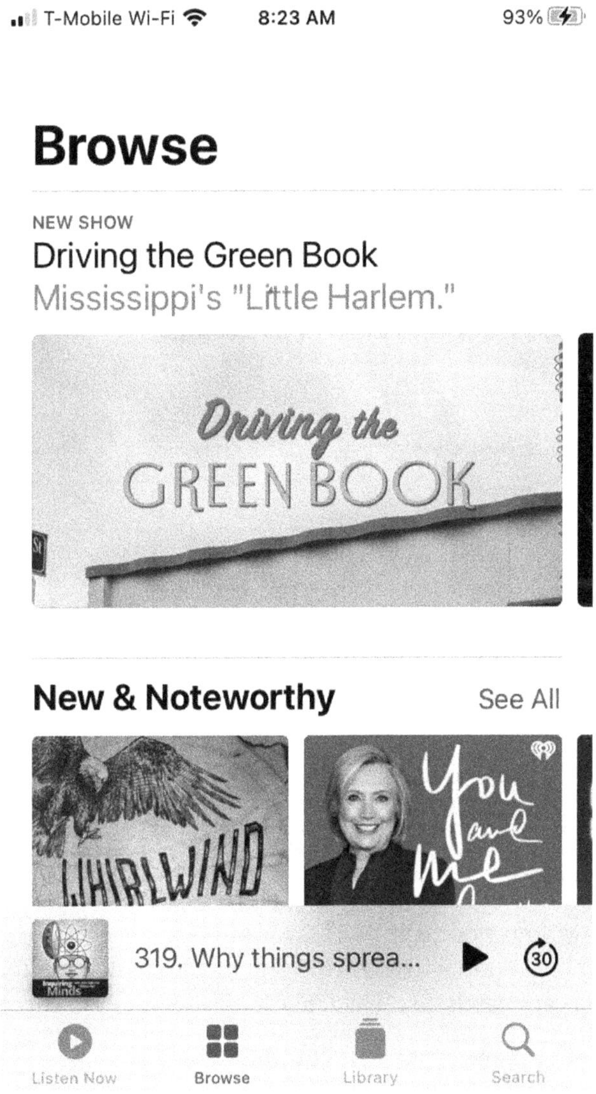

Figure 8.6 – Browsing through lists of popular podcasts

3. Tap a podcast that you want to hear. A brief description of that podcast appears, along with a list of episodes, as shown in *Figure 8.7*:

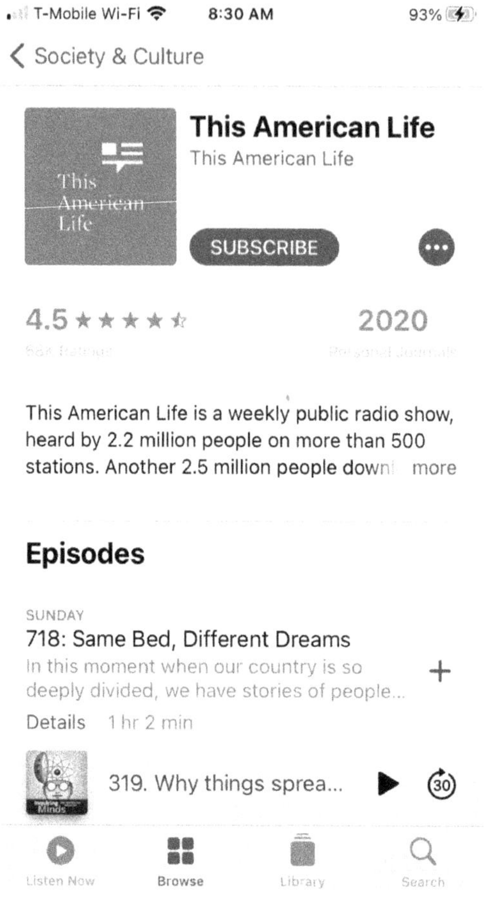

Figure 8.7 – Details about a podcast

4. Tap on an episode to listen to it.

By browsing through various podcasts, you may stumble across an interesting podcast that you may never have thought about before. However, if you know what topic you want to know more about, you can search for a particular type of podcast that meets your needs.

To search for a podcast by name or topic, follow these steps:

1. Tap the **Podcasts** app on the Home Screen. The Podcasts screen appears.
2. Tap the **Search** icon at the bottom of the screen. A search text field appears at the top of the screen.

3. Type a podcast name or topic you want to find and tap the **Search** key on the virtual keyboard. A list of podcasts matching your search criteria appears, as shown in *Figure 8.8*:

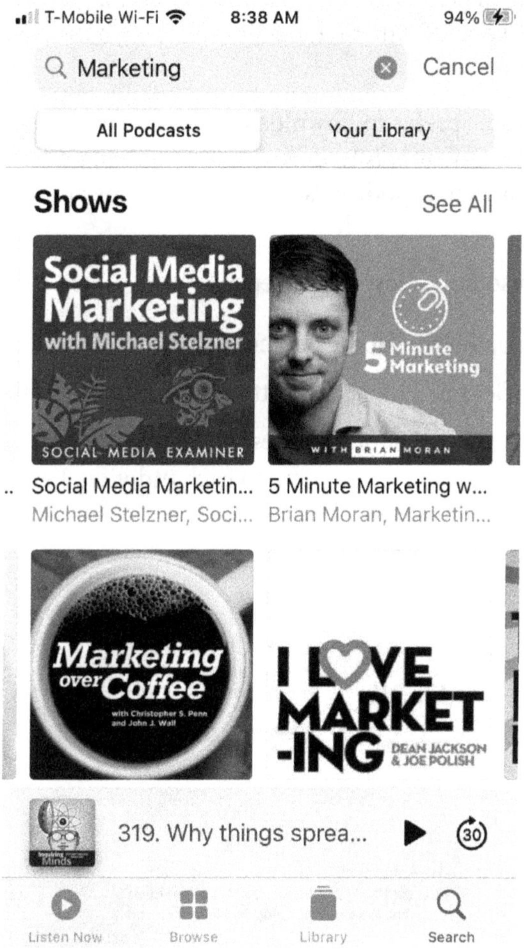

Figure 8.8 – Searching for a podcast

4. Tap a podcast that you want to hear. A brief description of that podcast appears, along with a list of episodes (see *Figure 8.7*).
5. Tap on an episode to hear it.

Listening to podcasts is fine, as long as you have an internet connection. However, for those times when you might want to listen to a podcast but won't have an internet connection (such as in an airplane or while bicycling on the road), you can still listen to your favorite podcasts by downloading them to your iPhone first.

Downloading podcast episodes

The two ways to listen to a podcast is as streaming audio and as a digital audio file. When you listen to a podcast as streaming audio, you need an internet connection, but it won't take up any storage. When you listen to a podcast as a digital audio file, you must download and store it on your iPhone first, but you can play it even without internet access.

For that reason, many people prefer to download podcast episodes so that they can play them at their convenience. One way is to download individual podcast episodes. A second way is to subscribe to a particular podcast so that your iPhone automatically downloads each episode.

To download podcast episodes, follow these steps:

1. Tap the **Podcasts** app on the Home Screen. The Podcasts screen appears.
2. Tap the **Browse** or **Search** icon at the bottom of the screen to find a podcast.
3. Tap on a podcast to view a list of episodes. The description of the podcast shows a **SUBSCRIBE** button and a + icon next to each individual episode, as shown in *Figure 8.9*:

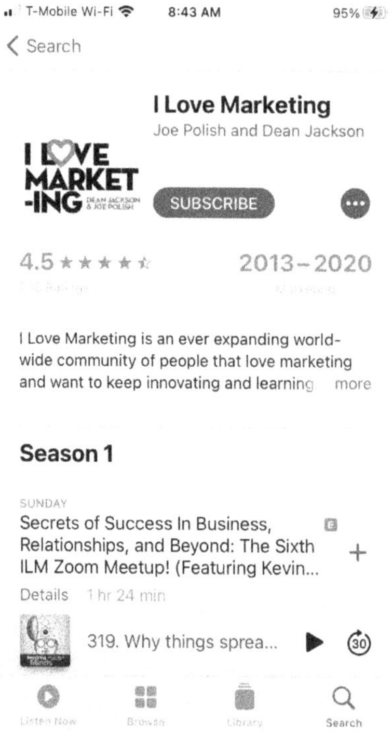

Figure 8.9 – Downloading a podcast episode

4. Tap the **SUBSCRIBE** button if you want to automatically download each new episode, or tap the + icon that appears to the right of an individual episode. Then, tap the cloud icon with a down arrow in it to download just that one episode.

Once you start downloading podcast episodes, you can listen to them over and over again. Fortunately, you can always free up space by deleting individual podcast episodes or stop a podcast subscription altogether.

Deleting downloaded podcast episodes

After 24 hours, your iPhone will delete a podcast episode after you listen to it, but you can also delete it manually.

To delete a podcast episode that you have previously downloaded, follow these steps:

1. Tap the **Podcasts** app on the Home Screen. The Podcasts screen appears.
2. Tap the podcast show that contains the episode you want to delete.
3. Tap on an episode you have downloaded (it will lack a + icon in the right margin). Your chosen podcast episode appears. Near the volume slider, you'll see a **...** icon, as shown in *Figure 8.10*:

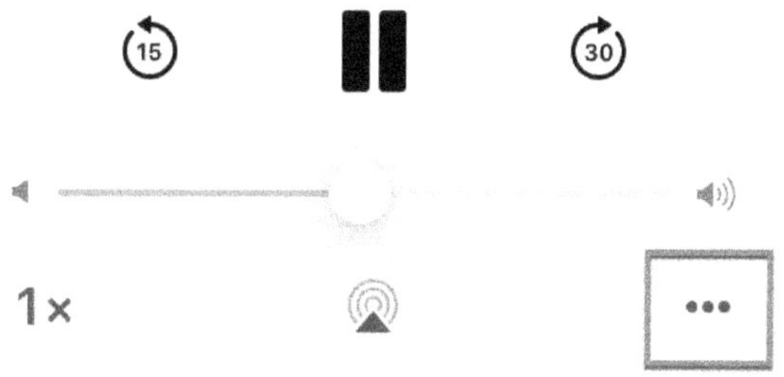

Figure 8.10 – The ... icon displayed by a podcast episode

4. Tap the **...** icon on the episode you want to delete. A list of options appears at the bottom of the screen, as shown in *Figure 8.11*:

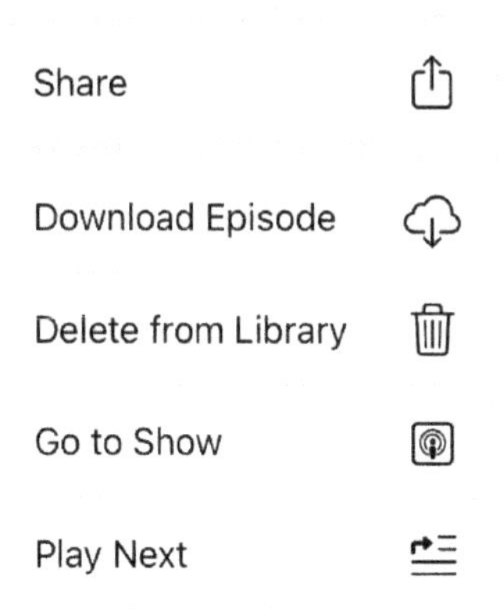

Figure 8.11 – Options appear for your chosen podcast episode

5. Tap **Delete from Library**. A list of options appears, as shown in *Figure 8.12*. You'll have the choice of **Cancel** or **Delete from Library**:

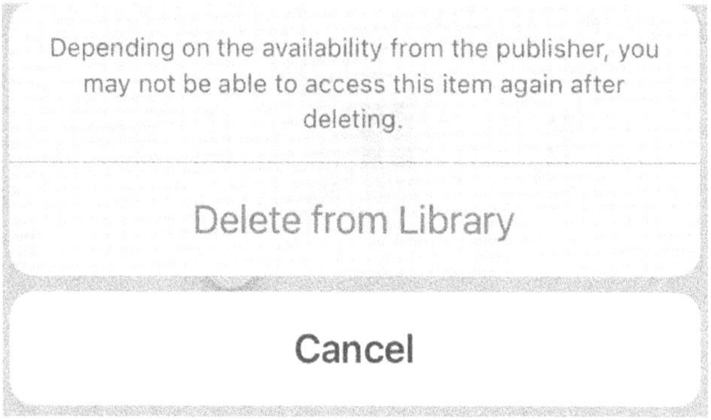

Figure 8.12 – Options appear for your chosen podcast episode

6. Tap **Cancel** or **Delete from Library**.

Rather than deleting individual podcast episodes, you might want to unsubscribe from a podcast altogether. That way, you won't keep getting podcast episodes that you'll need to delete anyway.

Unsubscribing from a podcast

Subscribing to a podcast ensures that you'll download each new episode as it arrives. However, you may eventually want to stop receiving podcast episodes automatically. In that case, you may want to unsubscribe from a podcast.

To unsubscribe from a podcast, follow these steps:

1. Tap the **Settings** app on the Home Screen. The **Settings** screen appears.
2. Tap **Podcasts** and scroll down.
3. Tap **Download Episodes**. A list of choices appears, as shown in *Figure 8.13*:

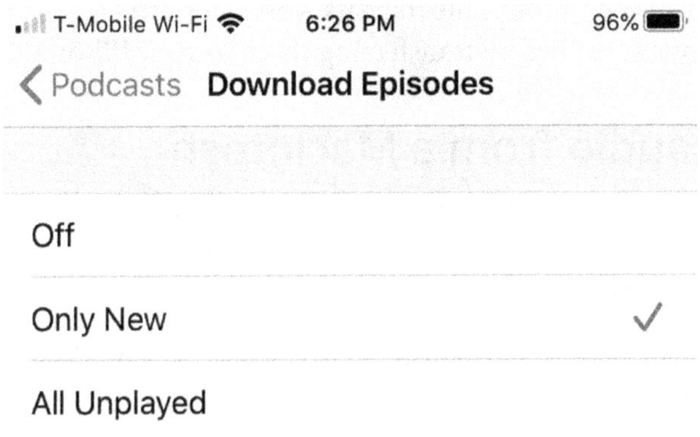

Figure 8.13 – Options appear for your chosen podcast episode

4. Tap **Off**.

Podcasts are often spoken audio that is mostly educational and informative while also being entertaining. Although almost anyone can find a podcast that might interest them, not everyone likes the idea of listening to podcasts. However, almost everyone enjoys listening to music of some kind. As a result, you'll find that playing music can be one of the most common functions you might use an iPhone for.

Transferring music to an iPhone

If you have audio files stored on a computer, you can transfer them to your iPhone using either a USB cable or Wi-Fi.

Before transferring any audio files to your iPhone, first make sure that the audio file is stored in a format that the iPhone can use. Some of the more common audio file formats that the iPhone supports are the following:

- **AAC** (**Advanced Audio Coding**)
- **M4A** (**MPEG-4 Audio**)
- **FLAC** (**Free Lossless Audio Codec**)
- **WAV** (**Waveform Audio**)
- **MP3** (**MPEG-2 Audio Layer III**)

If you have audio files stored in other file formats, you'll need to convert them to one of the preceding file formats first before transferring them to your iPhone.

Transferring audio from a Macintosh

The Music app, which comes with the latest version of macOS Catalina (or higher), replaces the old iTunes program. You can transfer any audio files stored in the Music app on your Macintosh onto your iPhone.

On a Macintosh, you can import audio files into the Music app by choosing **File** | **Import**. Once you've added audio files to the Music app on a Macintosh, you can transfer that audio file to the Music app on your iPhone.

To transfer audio files from a Macintosh to an iPhone, follow these steps:

1. Connect your iPhone to your Macintosh using a USB cable.
2. Click the **Finder** icon on the dock to open the Finder window.
3. Click on the name of your iPhone under the **Locations** category in the left sidebar, as shown in *Figure 8.14*:

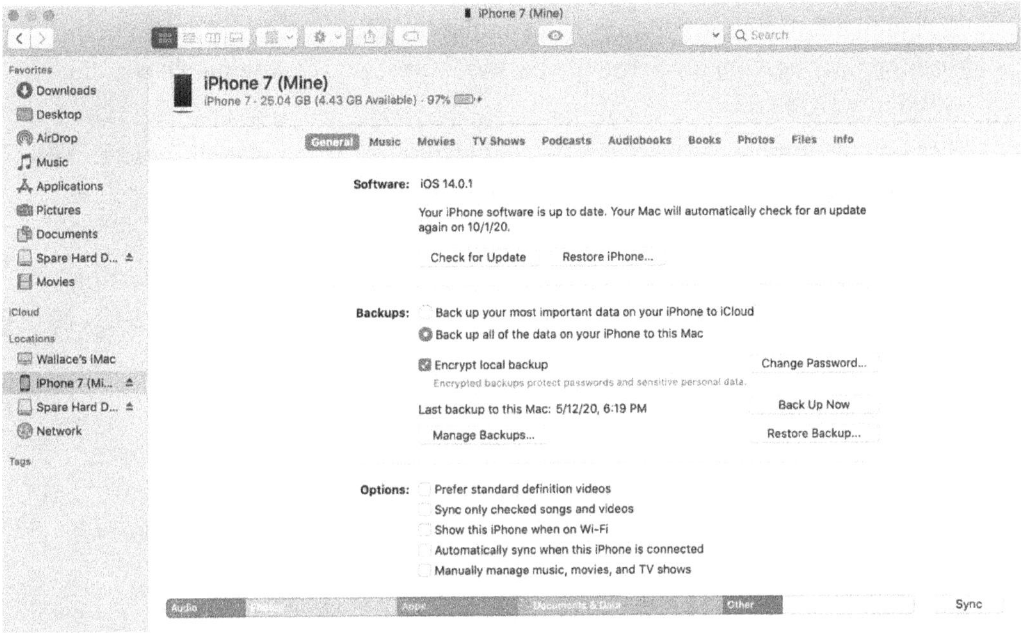

Figure 8.14 – Selecting an iPhone in the Finder window

4. Click the **Music** tab in the button bar. A list of options appears, as shown in *Figure 8.15*:

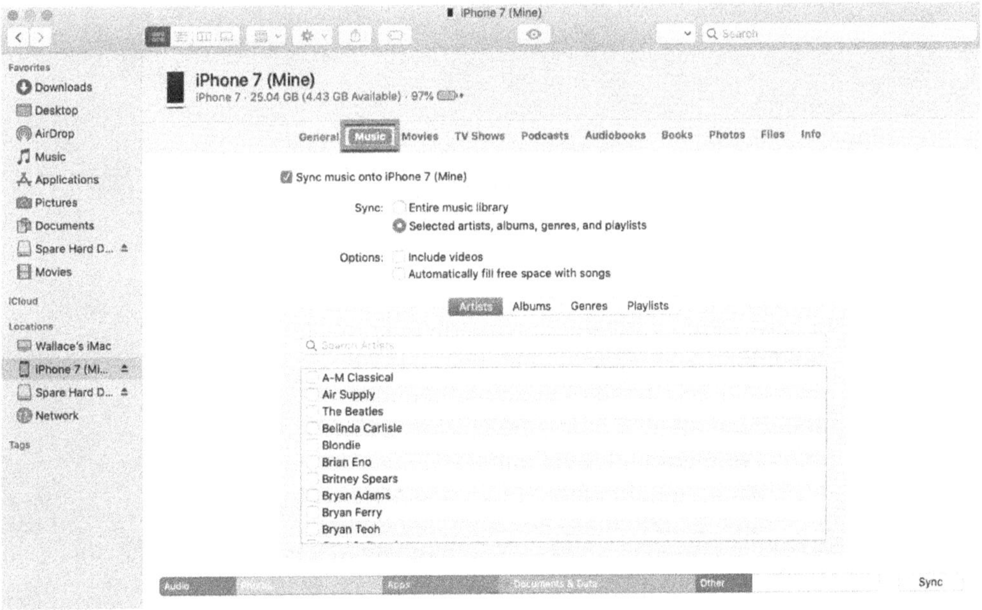

Figure 8.15 – Viewing a list of music options in the Finder window

5. Click on the **Entire music library** radio button (to select everything stored in the Music app), or click on the **Selected artists, albums, genres, and playlists** radio button (see *Figure 8.15*).
6. Click on one or more checkboxes to select the different artists of each audio file you want to transfer to your iPhone (skip this step if you chose to transfer the entire music library in *Step 5*).
7. Click the **Apply** button. Depending on how many audio files you're transferring, this process may take some time.
8. Click the eject icon in the Finder window next to your iPhone, as shown in *Figure 8.16*:

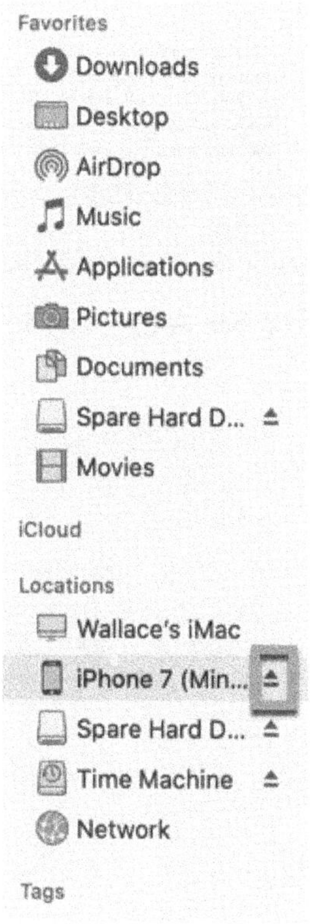

Figure 8.16 – The eject icon lets you safely disconnect your iPhone from a Macintosh

The preceding steps work with the newer Macintosh models. However, if you want to transfer audio files from an older Macintosh or a Windows PC, you'll need to use the iTunes program.

Transferring audio files with iTunes

Until the Music app arrived with macOS Catalina (and higher), older Macintosh computers and Windows PCs stored and organized audio files using the iTunes program.

To transfer audio files from iTunes (on either an older Macintosh or a Windows PC), follow these steps:

1. Start iTunes.
2. Connect your iPhone to the computer using a USB cable.
3. Click on the device icon in the upper-left corner of the iTunes window, as shown in *Figure 8.17*:

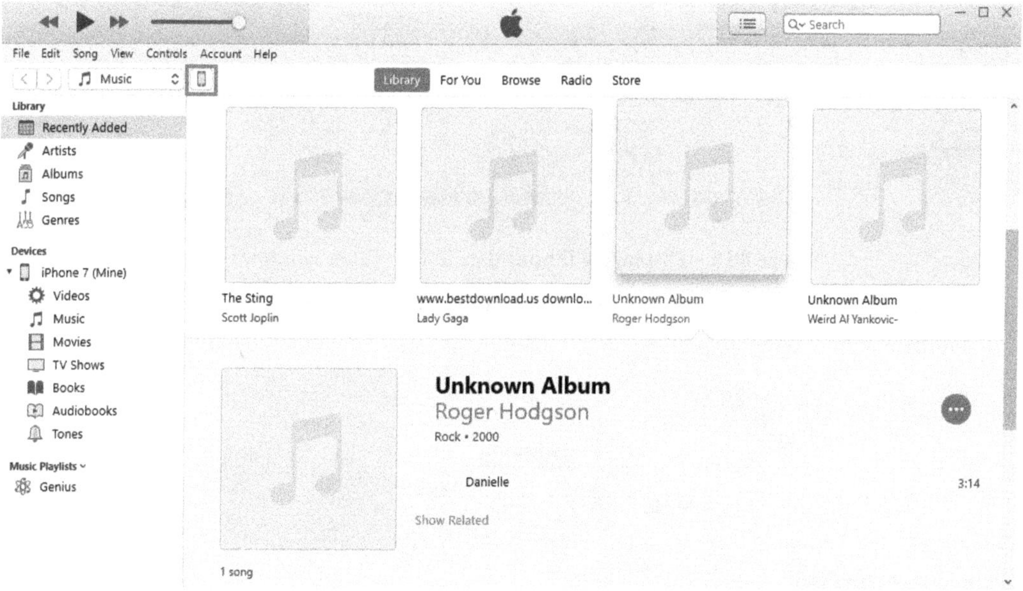

Figure 8.17 – Using iTunes to connect to an iPhone

The **Settings** pane appears on the left side of the iTunes window, as shown in *Figure 8.18*:

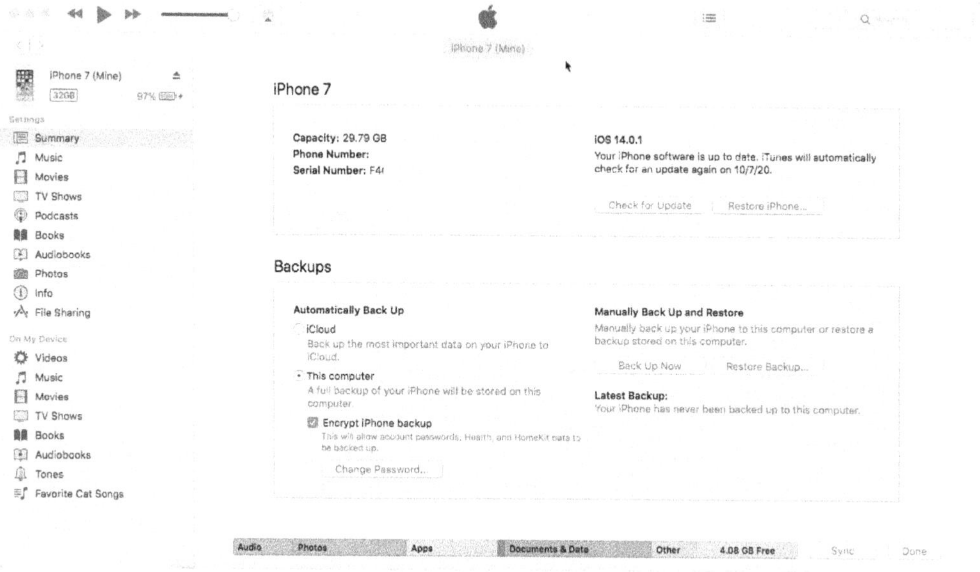

Figure 8.18 – Displaying iPhone data in the iTunes window

4. Click on **Music** in the left pane and click the **Sync Music** checkbox, as shown in *Figure 8.19*:

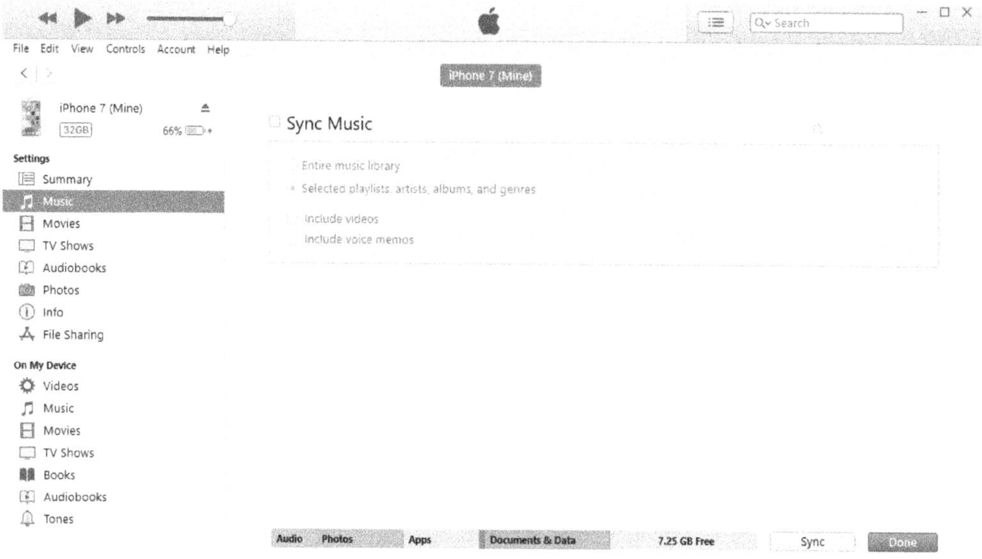

Figure 8.19 – Defining which audio files to transfer from iTunes to your iPhone

5. Click on the **Entire music library** radio button (to select everything stored in the Music app), or click on the **Selected artists, albums, genres, and playlists** radio button (see *Figure 8.19*).
6. Click on one or more checkboxes to select the different artists of each audio file you want to transfer to your iPhone (skip this step if you chose to transfer the entire music library in *Step 5*).
7. Click the **Apply** button. Depending on how many audio files you're transferring, this process may take time.
8. Click the eject icon in the upper-left corner of the iTunes window next to your iPhone, as shown in *Figure 8.20*:

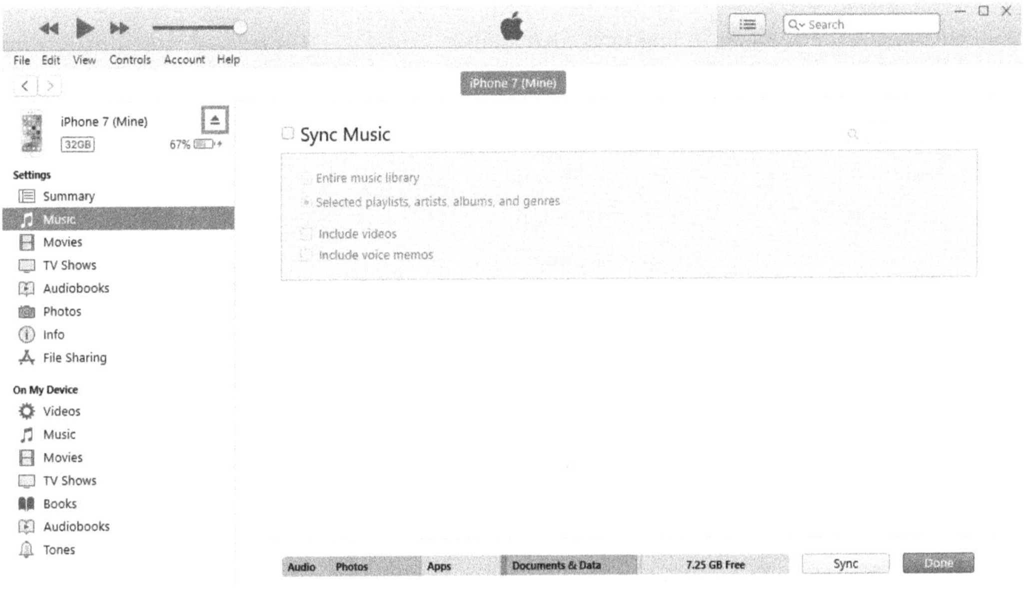

Figure 8.20 – Ejecting your iPhone from iTunes

Once you've transferred audio files from your computer to your iPhone, you'll likely want to play one or more audio files later. To do that, you need to understand the different ways your iPhone organizes audio files.

Storing and organizing audio files on an iPhone

The Music app on your iPhone automatically stores and organizes audio files in an audio library that's divided into several categories, as shown in *Figure 8.21*:

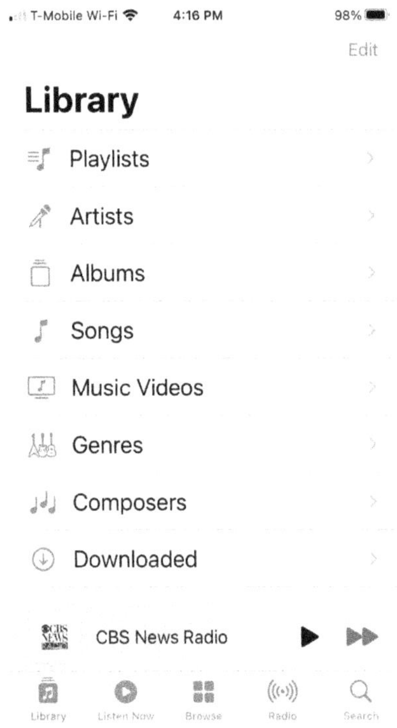

Figure 8.21 – The Music app organizes audio files into categories

Let's see how each of these categories organizes our music:

- **Playlists**: Playlists organize audio files into favorites, such as music from the 90s, love songs, classical music, or any arbitrary grouping you want to make.
- **Artists**: This organizes audio files alphabetically by recording artist, such as the band or individual artist.
- **Albums**: Albums organize audio files by album name, so you can find all audio files that come from the same album.
- **Songs**: This organizes audio files alphabetically by song title.
- **Music Videos**: Videos that contain songs from a recording artist.
- **Genres**: Songs defined by musical genre, such as blues, rock, or pop.

- **Composers**: Songs written by specific people.
- **Downloaded**: This displays only those audio files physically stored on your iPhone. In comparison, the other categories can list audio files that you may have selected within the Music app or iTunes program, but haven't physically transferred to your iPhone yet.

Creating playlists

A playlist contains audio files grouped according to different categories. You could create a playlist of love songs, another playlist of songs from the 90s, and still another playlist of songs that use the bagpipes. Playlists can group audio files of any type you wish.

The Music app creates some playlists automatically, such as the **Top 25 Most Played** or **Recently Played** audio files. If you want to create your own playlist, follow these steps:

1. Open the Music app and tap the **Library** icon at the bottom of the screen.
2. Tap **Playlists** to display the **Playlists** screen, as shown in *Figure 8.22*:

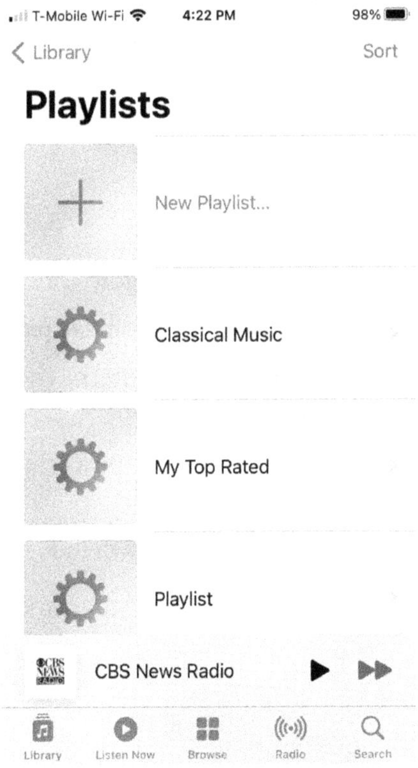

Figure 8.22 – The Playlists screen

3. Tap **New Playlist**. A **New Playlist** screen appears, as shown in *Figure 8.23*:

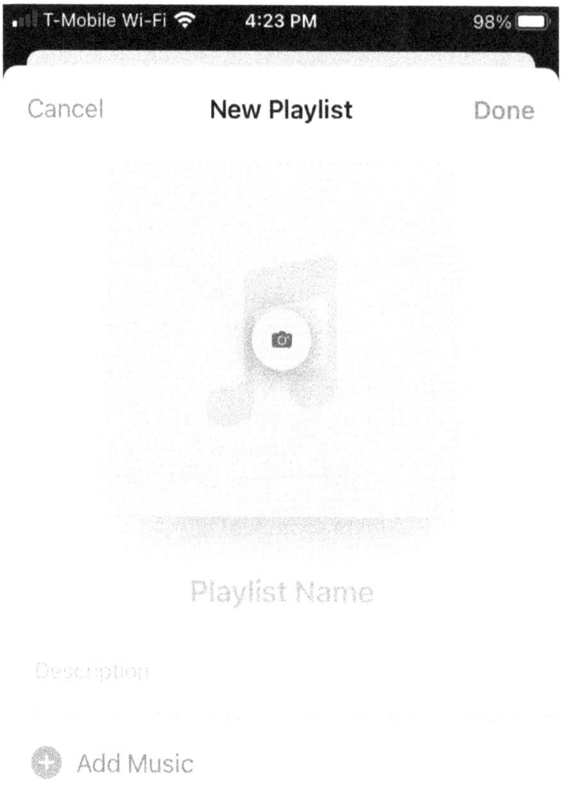

Figure 8.23 – The New Playlist screen

4. Tap the **Playlist Name** text field and type a descriptive name for your playlist.
5. (Optional:) Tap the camera icon and take a picture, or choose a photo stored in the **Photos** app to represent your playlist.
6. (Optional:) Tap the **Description** text field and type a brief description of your playlist.
7. Tap **Add Music**. A **Music** screen appears, as shown in *Figure 8.24*:

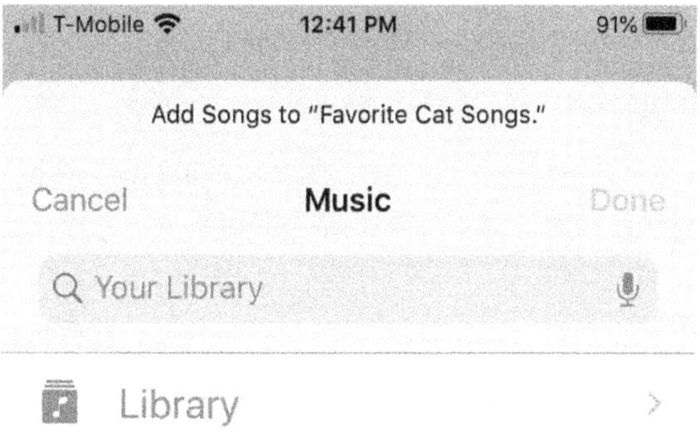

Figure 8.24 – The Music screen

8. Tap **Library**. A **Library** screen appears, listing all your audio file categories, such as **Artists**, **Albums**, **Songs**, or **Genres**.
9. Tap on a category, such as **Music Videos** or **Composers**, and tap any additional categories until you see a list of audio files.
10. Tap the + icon that appears to the right of each audio file you want to add to a playlist, as shown in *Figure 8.25*:

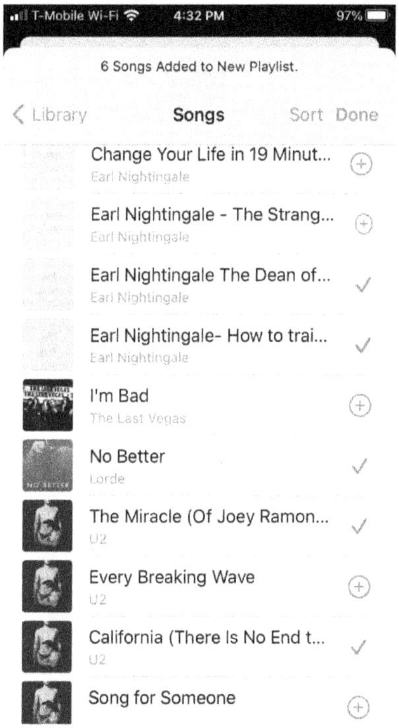

Figure 8.25 – The + icon lets you choose which audio files to add to a playlist

11. Repeat *Steps 9* and *10* as often as necessary.
12. Tap **Done** twice to finish creating your playlist.

After you finish creating a playlist, you can listen to that playlist at any time. Of course, you may want to add or remove audio files from a playlist, which you can do at any time.

Editing a playlist

Once you create a playlist, you can always add or remove audio files from that playlist at any time.

To edit a playlist, follow these steps:

1. Open the **Music** app, tap the **Library** icon at the bottom of the screen, and then tap **Playlists**.
2. Tap on the playlist you want to modify. Your chosen playlist appears.
3. Tap **Done** in the upper-right corner of the screen. A green + icon and a red – icon appears, as shown in *Figure 8.26*:

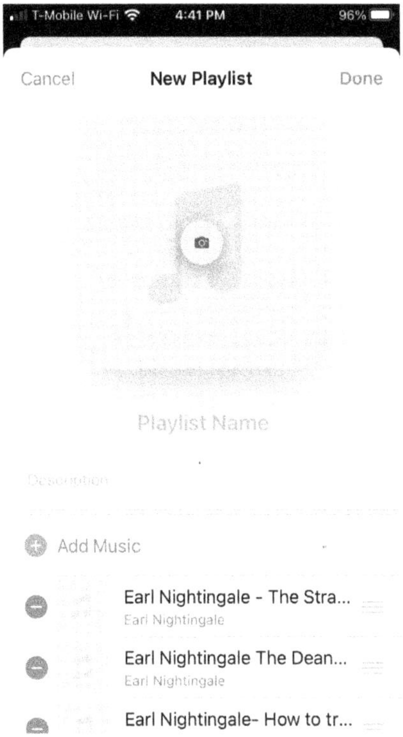

Figure 8.26 – The add and remove icons

4. (Optional:) Tap the green + icon to add a new audio file to the playlist. Then, tap **Library** and choose a category and audio file to add.
5. (Optional:) Tap the red – icon to remove an audio file from the playlist (note: removing an audio file from a playlist does not delete the audio file from your iPhone).
6. (Optional:) Drag the three horizontal lines icon that appears to the right of an audio file up or down to rearrange its order in the playlist.
7. Tap **Done**.

Playlists let you add, remove, and rearrange audio files, but whether you use a playlist or not, you'll eventually want to know how to listen to your audio files.

Playing an audio file

Once you store multiple audio files on your iPhone, you can listen to those audio files at any time. Audio files are often songs, but can also be motivational talks, speeches, nature sounds, or anything you want to hear on a regular basis.

One way to play an audio file is to play just a single audio file. This can be handy if you just want to listen to a single song or motivational speech.

A second way to play an audio file is within a collection of related files, such as all audio files in a single album. With a collection of related files, you can play them in order or use the shuffle command to let your iPhone play audio files in random order.

To play a single audio file, follow these steps:

1. Open the Music app and tap the **Library** icon at the bottom of the screen.
2. Tap a category, such as **Playlists**, **Artists**, or **Songs**, to view a list of audio files.
3. Tap on the audio file you want to play. A thumbnail of your currently playing audio file appears at the bottom of the screen, displaying a pause button, as shown in *Figure 8.27*:

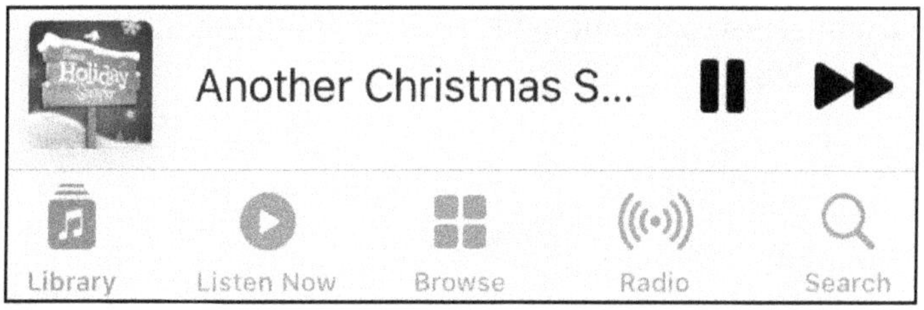

Figure 8.27 – The currently playing audio file appears at the bottom of the screen

In many cases, you may not want to listen to a single audio file but a group of audio files, such as songs stored in a playlist or music off the same album. When you want to play multiple audio files, you can choose to play them in order or have the **Music** app shuffle audio files in a random order.

To play groups of audio files in order or in a random order, follow these steps:

1. Open the Music app and tap the **Library** icon at the bottom of the screen.
2. Tap a category, such as **Playlists**, **Artists**, or **Songs**, to view a list of audio files.
3. Tap either **Play** or **Shuffle**, as shown in *Figure 8.28*:

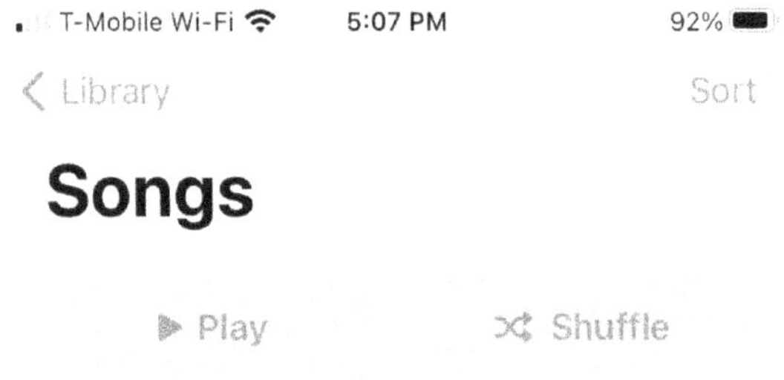

Figure 8.28 – The Play and Shuffle buttons

Playing audio files in random order can be like listening to your favorite radio station that plays the songs you like best. You know you'll like the next song, but you have no idea what that next song might be.

Deleting audio files

When you no longer want to keep an audio file, delete it. That way, you can keep your audio file lists uncluttered, keeping only the files you want to hear again and again.

To delete an audio file, follow these steps:

1. Open the Music app and tap the **Library** icon at the bottom of the screen.
2. Tap a category, such as **Playlists**, **Artists**, or **Songs**, to view a list of audio files.
3. Tap and hold a finger over the audio file you want to delete. A menu appears, as shown in *Figure 8.29*:

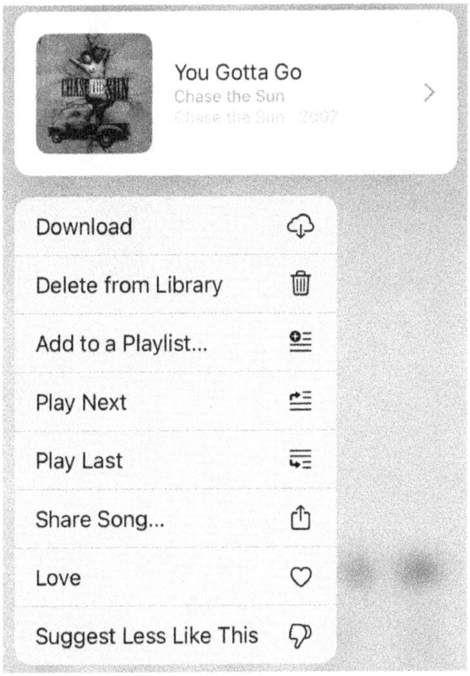

Figure 8.29 – Deleting an audio file from the Music app

4. Tap **Delete from Library**. **Delete Song** and **Cancel** buttons appear at the bottom of the screen.
5. Tap **Delete Song**.

Deleting audio files can be handy when you no longer need them and want to free up storage space on your iPhone. If you have the audio file saved on your computer, you can always copy it back onto your iPhone at a later date.

Summary

Listening to audio files, such as music, is an activity that people all over the world enjoy. Although everyone has different musical tastes, everyone will likely want to keep audio files on their iPhone to listen to whether they're at work, waiting, or driving a car.

Take the time to put all your favorite audio files onto your iPhone so that you can listen to them wherever you go. With the right audio files, you can turn your iPhone into a portable music player or educational tool to help you learn just by listening.

While listening to music is an activity everyone enjoys, surfing the internet to read the latest news is another common activity that all kinds of people enjoy, and that's the topic of the next chapter.

9
Browsing the Internet with Safari

One appeal of the iPhone is that it puts a computer in your pocket. When the internet first arose for public use, people relied on personal computers to browse websites. However, the iPhone made web browsing possible on a mobile device.

Now, if you want to find information on the internet, you don't have to wait until you get home to use a bulky computer. Instead, you can visit websites on your iPhone and do everything from online shopping and watching videos to reading news and responding to blog posts.

Although web browsing on the iPhone is different because of the smaller iPhone screen compared to the larger screen of desktop or laptop computers, the principles remain the same: load a browser and visit a website. The difference is just learning how to type and view websites on the smaller screen and virtual keyboard of the iPhone.

The topics that this chapter covers are as follows:

- Browsing websites
- Navigating between web pages
- Opening and switching between multiple web pages
- Private browsing

- Bookmarking websites
- Viewing browsing history
- Using reading lists
- Sharing websites
- Searching with Safari

Browsing websites

Every iPhone comes with the Safari browser, which is similar to the Safari browser found on every Macintosh (you can always download and install other browsers on your iPhone, but this chapter focuses exclusively on using Safari).

To browse any website, you just need to know the website address, such as `www.yahoo.com` or just `apple.com`. Once you know which website to visit, you need to type that information into Safari.

> **Note**
>
> You do not need to type in the complete website address, such as `https://www.yahoo.com`. It's often simpler and faster to type only the website name (such as `yahoo`) and its domain (such as `.com`), rather than typing in `https://` or www.

Typing a website address

The first time you start Safari, you must type a website address to visit anything on the internet. From that point on, Safari keeps track of the websites you've visited, so you won't have to type the complete website address again to visit that site.

To type a website address into Safari, follow these steps:

1. Tap the **Safari** app on the Home Screen. The Safari app screen appears.
2. Tap the text field at the top of the screen, as shown in *Figure 9.1*. This text field lets you type a website address or a search query. As soon as you tap inside the text field, a keyboard appears at the bottom of the screen:

Figure 9.1 – The text field at the top of the screen in Safari

3. Type a website address, such as `microsoft.com` or `nasa.gov`, and tap the **go** button that appears highlighted in blue in the bottom-right corner of the virtual keyboard, as shown in *Figure 9.2*. If you typed a valid website address, the website appears on the screen:

Figure 9.2 – The go button on the virtual keyboard

4. Tilt your iPhone in portrait or landscape orientation to view any website in different ways, as shown in *Figure 9.3*. Most (but not all) websites will adjust their content based on the orientation of the iPhone:

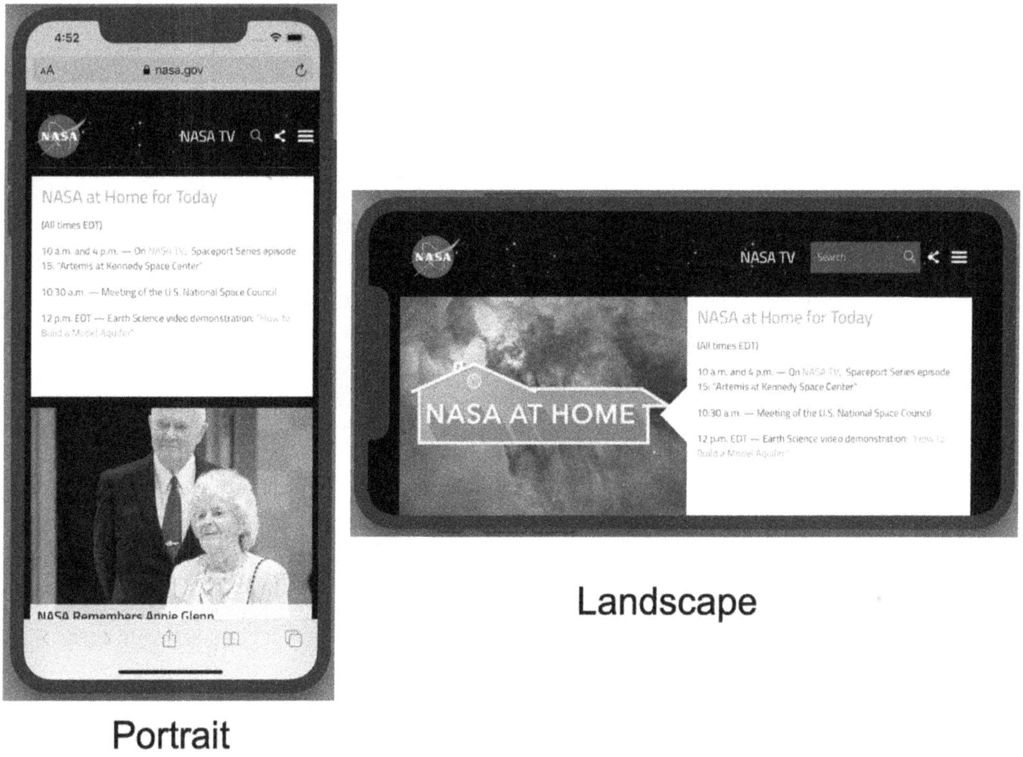

Figure 9.3 – You can view any website in portrait or landscape orientation

Once you visit a website, you can slide your finger up/down to scroll through all the available content. Since the iPhone screen is much smaller than a traditional computer monitor, you might want to shrink or enlarge the text or reload a website to make sure you're viewing the latest content.

Changing text size

For some people, Safari displays text too small, which makes it hard to read. For others, Safari displays text too large, which makes it hard to see all the content on a web page.

To help you adjust the size of text displayed on a website, Safari lets you shrink or enlarge text. To shrink or enlarge text, follow these steps:

1. Tap the **Safari** app on the Home Screen. The Safari app screen appears.
2. Tap the text field at the top of the screen (see *Figure 9.1*) and type a website address, such as `yahoo.com`. A font size and reload icon appear, as shown in *Figure 9.4*:

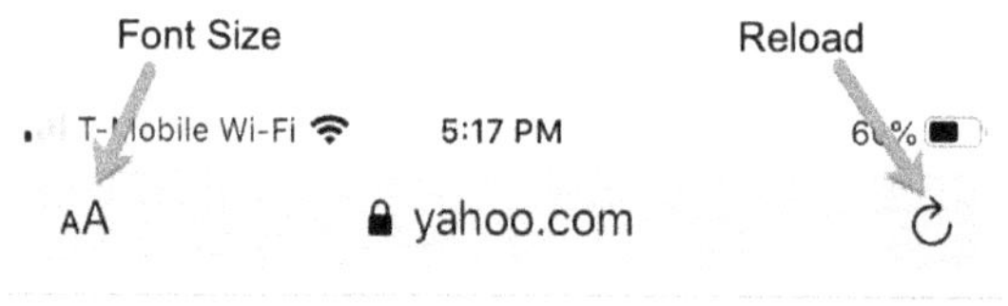

Figure 9.4 – The font size and reload icons

3. Tap the font size icon. A menu appears, showing the font size percentage, such as **100%**. A small **A** icon appears to the left, which shrinks the font size, while a larger **A** icon appears to the right, which increases the font size, as shown in *Figure 9.5*:

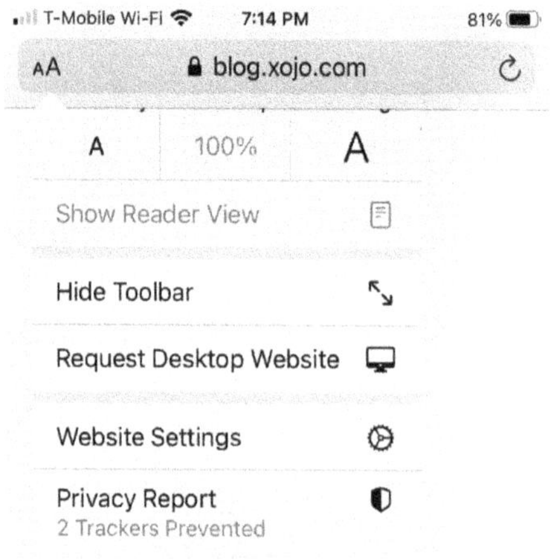

Figure 9.5 – Changing the font size of text on a website

4. Tap the small **A** or large **A** icon to adjust the font size.

The font size icon lets you adjust the text size on each website you visit. If you prefer a specific font size for all websites, you can define a font size other than **100%**, which is the default setting.

To define a font size magnification for all websites, follow these steps:

1. Tap the **Settings** app on the Home Screen. The **Settings** app screen appears.
2. Tap **Safari**. A list of Safari settings appears. Scroll down until you see **Page Zoom**.
3. Tap **Page Zoom**. The **Page Zoom** screen appears, as shown in *Figure 9.6*. The current website loaded in Safari appears at the top, such as **yahoo.com**:

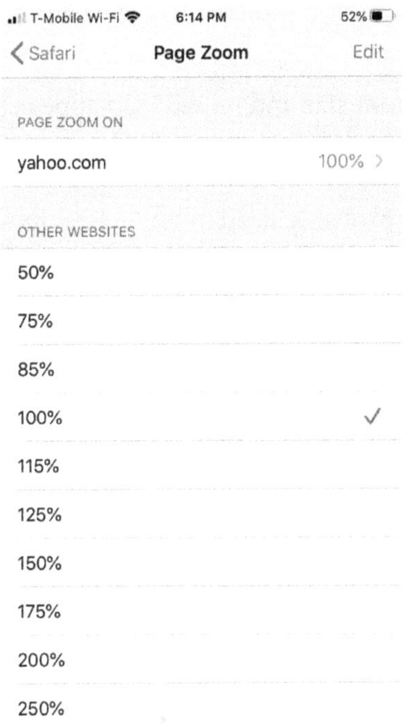

Figure 9.6 – The Page Zoom screen lets you define a font size magnification for all websites

4. Tap on the name of the currently loaded website, such as **yahoo.com**, to adjust its font size, and then tap a magnification option, such as **75%** or **125%**.
5. Tap the **Page Zoom** back button in the upper-left corner of the screen to return to the **Page Zoom** screen.
6. Tap a magnification option under the **Other Websites** category to define a magnification for all other websites.

By changing the font size magnification for a single website or all websites, you can make browsing the internet comfortable for your eyes.

In some cases, the font size magnification is fine, but the website content itself may be old. To make sure you have the latest content, you may want to reload a web page.

Reloading web pages

If you visit a website, you'll usually get the latest content. However, if that content changes, Safari may not always display any changed content. To make sure you're viewing the latest content displayed on a website, you may need to periodically reload the web page.

To reload a web page, follow these steps:

1. Tap the **Safari** app on the Home Screen. The Safari app screen appears.
2. Tap the text field at the top of the screen (see *Figure 9.1*) and type a website address, such as `yahoo.com`. A font size and reload icon appear (see *Figure 9.4*).
3. Tap the reload icon.

Once you visit a website, you'll probably need to know how to tap on links, as well as go back and forth between previous web pages. Fortunately, browsing the internet on an iPhone works identically to browsing the internet on a computer, except you need to use touch gestures and look for icons at the top and bottom of the screen.

Navigating between web pages

Most websites consist of multiple web pages, and its common to jump from one website to another. The three main ways to navigate from one web page to another are as follows:

- Tap on a hyperlink.
- Tap the back icon.
- Tap the forward icon.

Hyperlinks appear as blue text that will jump to another web page on either the same website or an entirely different website. *Figure 9.7* shows what a typical hyperlink looks like:

Figure 9.7 – A hyperlink displayed on a web page

The back and forward icons appear at the bottom of the screen, as shown in *Figure 9.8*, any time you tap in the text field at the top of the screen:

Figure 9.8 – The back and forward icons

> **Note**
> The forward icon will appear dimmed until you tap the back icon at least once.

To see how to use hyperlinks and the back/forward icons, follow these steps:

1. Tap the **Safari** app on the Home Screen. The Safari screen appears.
2. Tap in the text field at the top of the screen and type a website address, such as `apple.com`.

3. Tap on any blue hyperlink to visit another web page.
4. Tap the text field at the top of the screen to make the back and forward icons appear at the bottom of the screen.
5. Tap the back icon. Notice that the previous web page appears.
6. Tap the forward icon. Notice that the web page you viewed before tapping the back icon appears.

Hyperlinks can take you to new web pages, while the back icon lets you return to previously viewed web pages. Once you tap the back icon at least once, you'll be able to tap the forward icon. The back and forward icons let you go back and forth between two or more previously viewed web pages.

However, you may want to keep two or more web pages open and switch between them, which you can do in Safari on an iPhone as well.

Opening and switching between multiple web pages

If you're familiar with using a browser on a desktop or laptop computer, you probably know about tabs. Tabs let you keep multiple web pages open and switch between them whenever you want.

Opening additional web pages

To open additional web pages, follow these steps:

1. Tap the **Safari** app on the Home Screen. The Safari screen appears.
2. Tap in the text field at the top of the screen and type a website address, such as `apple.com`. A tab bar appears at the bottom of the screen, as shown in *Figure 9.9*:

Figure 9.9 – The show all tabs icon

3. Tap the show all tabs icon in the bottom-right corner of the screen. All open web pages appear and a + icon appears at the bottom of the screen, as shown in *Figure 9.10*:

Figure 9.10 – The + icon lets you open a new web page

4. Tap the + icon. A text field appears at the top of the screen, along with a list of favorite and frequently visited websites, as shown in *Figure 9.11*:

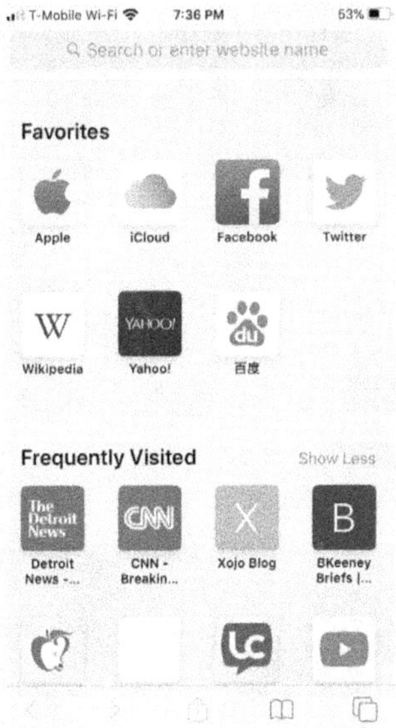

Figure 9.11 – Choosing a new web page to open

5. Type a website address, or tap on an icon that displays a previously visited website. Safari opens your chosen website.

Once you've opened two or more websites, you need to know how to switch quickly between one and the other.

Switching between open web pages

The advantage of opening multiple web pages is that you can jump from one web page to another. For example, you might display a weather forecast, a sports score, and a news site on separate web pages so that you can view the information you want without the hassle of typing in a website address and waiting for a web page to load.

To switch between web pages, follow these steps:

1. Make sure you have opened two or more web pages by following the instructions in the *Opening additional web pages* section.
2. Tap in the text field at the top of the screen. The show all tabs icon appears at the bottom of the screen (see *Figure 9.9*).
3. Tap the show all tabs icon. All open web pages appear like stacked cards, as shown in *Figure 9.12*:

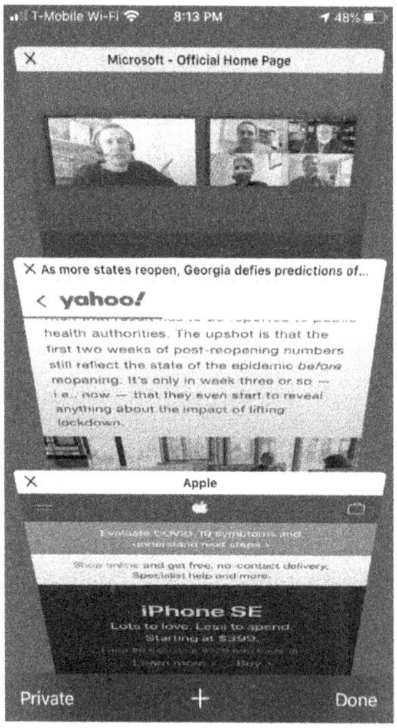

Figure 9.12 – Viewing multiple open web pages

4. Tap on the web page you want to view. Your chosen web page appears in Safari.

Having multiple web pages open can be convenient since you don't have to close one web page and wait to load another one. However, you'll likely want to close one or more open web pages eventually when you no longer need them anymore.

Closing web pages

The more web pages you open, the harder it can be to see them all. That's why you'll probably want to keep the number of open web pages to a reasonable amount and close any web pages you no longer want.

To close a web page, follow these steps:

1. Make sure you have opened two or more web pages by following the instructions in the *Opening additional web pages* section.
2. Tap in the text field at the top of the screen. The show all tabs icon appears at the bottom of the screen (see *Figure 9.9*).
3. Tap the show all tabs icon. All open web pages appear like stacked cards (see *Figure 9.12*).
4. Tap the close icon (the **X** icon) in the upper-left corner of the web page that you want to close, as shown in *Figure 9.13*:

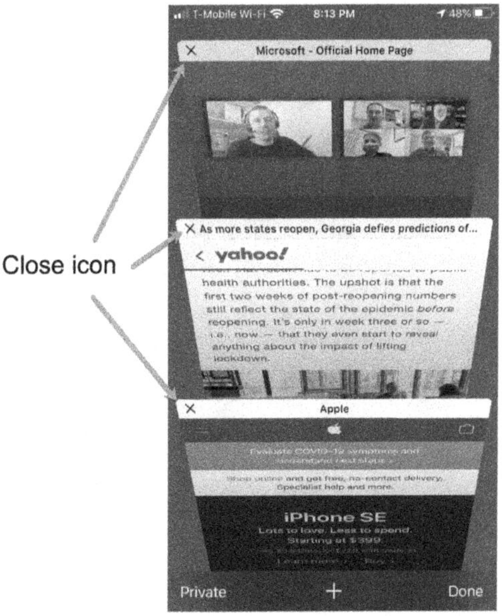

Figure 9.13 – The close icon on web pages

5. Tap **Done**.

Each time you browse a website, you risk giving away information such as your current location or what type of information you've been searching for. If you want to protect your privacy, you should use Safari's private browsing options.

Private browsing

Private browsing lets you visit websites without tracking the history of the pages you visit, blocks **AutoFill** to prevent remembering passwords typed in a web page, and deletes any cookies when you close the web page that sent the browser a cookie.

To use private browsing, follow these steps:

1. Tap the **Safari** app on the Home Screen. The Safari screen appears.
2. Tap the show all tabs icon.
3. Tap **Private**. Safari displays a **Private Browsing Mode** message and highlights **Private** in the bottom-left corner, as shown in *Figure 9.14*:

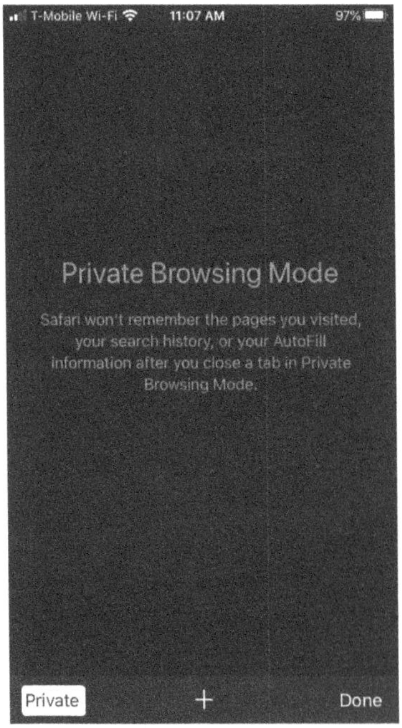

Figure 9.14 – Private Browsing Mode

4. Tap the + icon to open a website in private browsing mode.
5. Tap in the text field at the top of the screen and type a website address, such as `apple.com`.

Once you start browsing in private mode, you may want to turn private browsing mode off eventually. To turn off private browsing mode, follow these steps:

1. Tap the show all tabs icon.
2. Tap **Private**.

Toggling in and out of private browsing mode can be handy, but you may want to define specific privacy settings within Safari as well.

Defining privacy settings in Safari

Privacy settings let you define how much (or how little) information Safari gives out to websites; the following are some of the settings available:

- **Prevent Cross-Site Tracking**: Blocks websites from tracking the websites you visit
- **Block All Cookies**: Blocks websites from storing data about your activities in a file referred to as a cookie
- **Fraudulent Website Warning**: Displays a warning if Safari detects a suspected phishing website, which is a site that mimics a known site for the purpose of stealing passwords and other important information
- **Check for Apple Pay**: Checks whether you can pay for products on websites through Apple Pay
- **Clear History and Website Data**: Removes your browsing history and data stored from visiting websites

To define one or more privacy settings for Safari, follow these steps:

1. Tap the **Settings** app on the Home Screen. The **Settings** screen appears.
2. Tap **Safari**. The **Safari** settings screen appears.

3. Scroll down to the **PRIVACY & SECURITY** category, as shown in *Figure 9.15*:

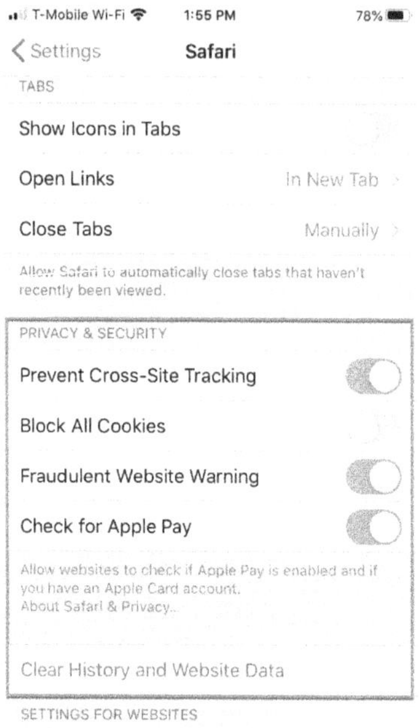

Figure 9.15 – Safari's privacy and security settings

4. (Optional) tap the green switch to turn on or off **Prevent Cross-Site Tracking**.
5. (Optional) tap the green switch to turn on or off **Block All Cookies**.
6. (Optional) tap the green switch to turn on or off **Fraudulent Website Warning**.
7. (Optional) tap the green switch to turn on or off **Check for Apple Pay**.
8. (Optional) tap **Clear History and Website Data** to erase your browsing history.

Whether you browse with or without privacy settings, you'll likely visit some websites more than others. Rather than constantly typing in the domain names of your favorite websites, it's much easier to bookmark favorite websites so that you can visit them with the tap of a finger.

Bookmarking websites

Bookmarks let you save your favorite website addresses so that you don't have to type them in again when you want to visit them. Safari lets you organize bookmarks in folders, so that way, you might create a folder of just news websites, a second folder of entertainment websites, and a third folder of work-related websites. Folders simply help you keep your bookmarks organized.

Creating a bookmark

To bookmark a favorite website, follow these steps:

1. Tap the **Safari** app on the Home Screen. The Safari screen appears.
2. Tap in the text field at the top of the screen and type a website address, such as `aljazeera.com`. A tab bar appears at the bottom of the screen and displays the share icon, as shown in *Figure 9.16*:

Figure 9.16 – The share icon

3. Tap the share icon at the bottom of the screen. A sheet appears from the bottom of the screen.
4. Scroll down this sheet until you see a list of options, as shown in *Figure 9.17*:

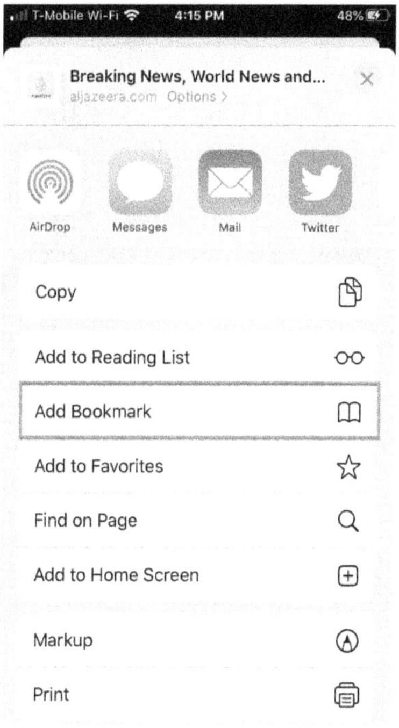

Figure 9.17 – The Add Bookmark command

5. Tap **Add Bookmark**. (If you tap **Add to Favorites**, you can add a bookmark to the **Favorites** folder. If you tap **Add to Home Screen**, you can add a bookmark that will appear on the Home Screen.) An **Add Bookmark** screen appears, which lets you edit a descriptive name of the bookmark, the website address, and a location to save the bookmark, as shown in *Figure 9.18*:

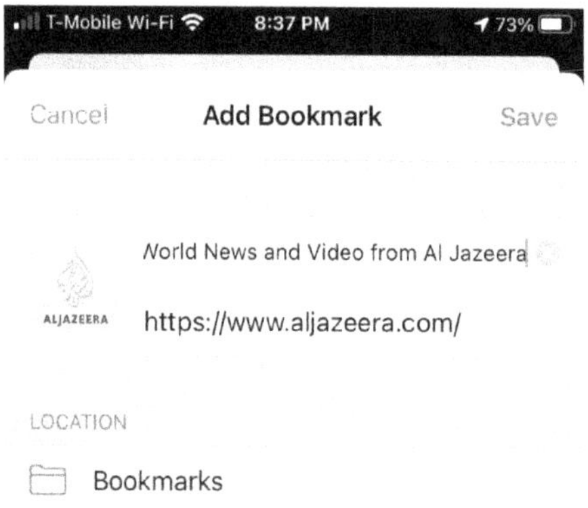

Figure 9.18 – The Add Bookmark screen

6. (Optional) Edit the name of the bookmark (tap the **X** icon on the far right of the bookmark name text field to clear all text).
7. Tap **Bookmarks** under the **LOCATION** category. The **LOCATION** category displays a **Favorites** folder, a **Bookmarks** folder, and a **New Folder** option, as shown in *Figure 9.19*:

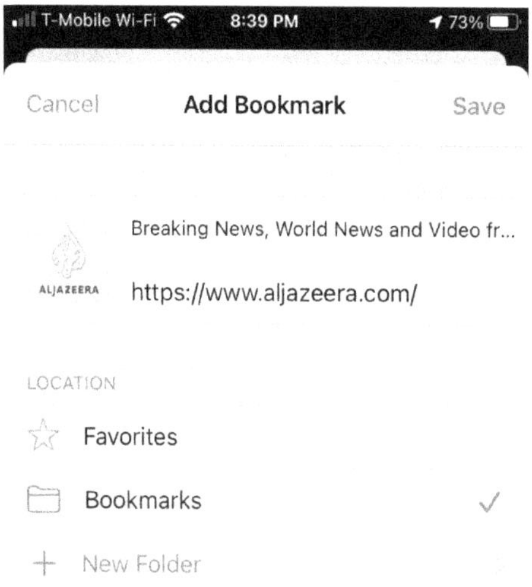

Figure 9.19 – Defining a location to store a bookmark

8. Tap a location to store your bookmark, such as **Favorites** or **Bookmarks**. If you tap **New Folder**, a **New Folder** screen appears, letting you type a descriptive folder name, as shown in *Figure 9.20*:

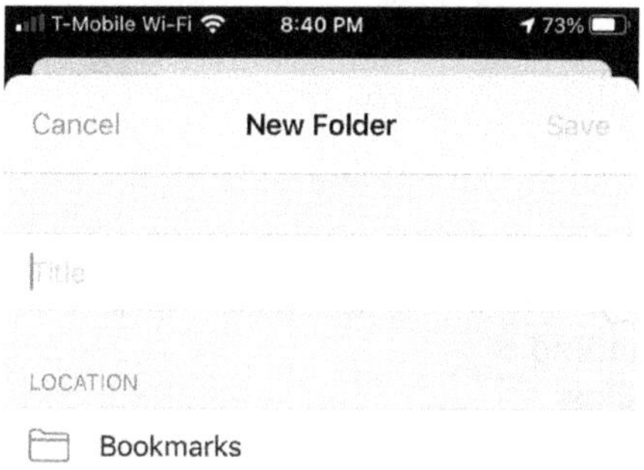

Figure 9.20 – The New Folder screen

9. Tap **Save**.

Once you bookmark one or more websites, you can open those websites quickly without typing in a website address.

Using a bookmark

Bookmarks let you jump to a favorite website with one tap. To visit a bookmarked website, follow these steps:

1. Tap the **Safari** app on the Home Screen. The Safari screen appears and displays the bookmarks icon at the bottom of the screen, as shown in *Figure 9.21*:

Figure 9.21 – The bookmarks icon

2. Tap the bookmarks icon. The **Bookmarks** screen appears, listing all previously saved bookmarked websites, as shown in *Figure 9.22*:

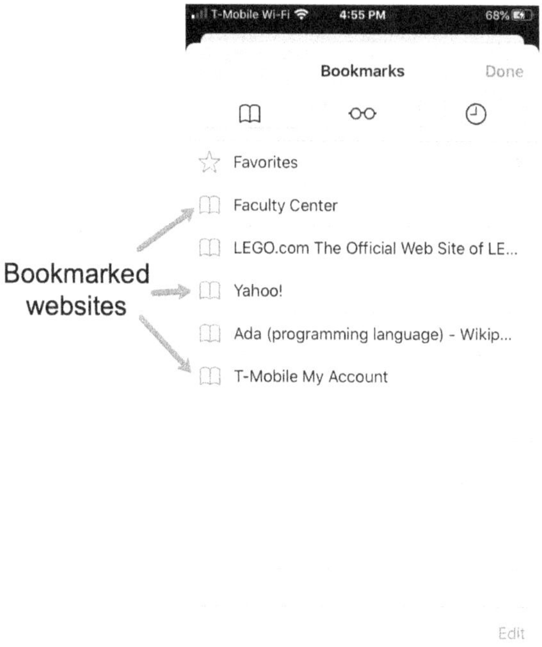

Figure 9.22 – The Bookmarks screen

3. Tap a bookmark to load that website.

Bookmarks can be handy for loading your favorite websites quickly. However, the longer your list of bookmarks is, the harder it can be to find a particular website. That's why you need to know how to delete bookmarks as well.

Deleting and moving a bookmark

When Safari adds a bookmark, the list of bookmarks may not be in the order you like. Fortunately, you can rearrange or even delete bookmarks to make your bookmark list more manageable.

To rearrange bookmarks, follow these steps:

1. Tap the **Safari** app on the Home Screen. The Safari screen appears and displays the bookmarks icon at the bottom of the screen (see *Figure 9.21*).
2. Tap the bookmarks icon. The **Bookmarks** screen appears, listing all previously saved bookmarked websites (see *Figure 9.22*).

3. Tap **Edit** in the bottom-right corner of the screen. Delete icons appear to the left of each bookmark and move icons appear to the right, as shown in *Figure 9.23*:

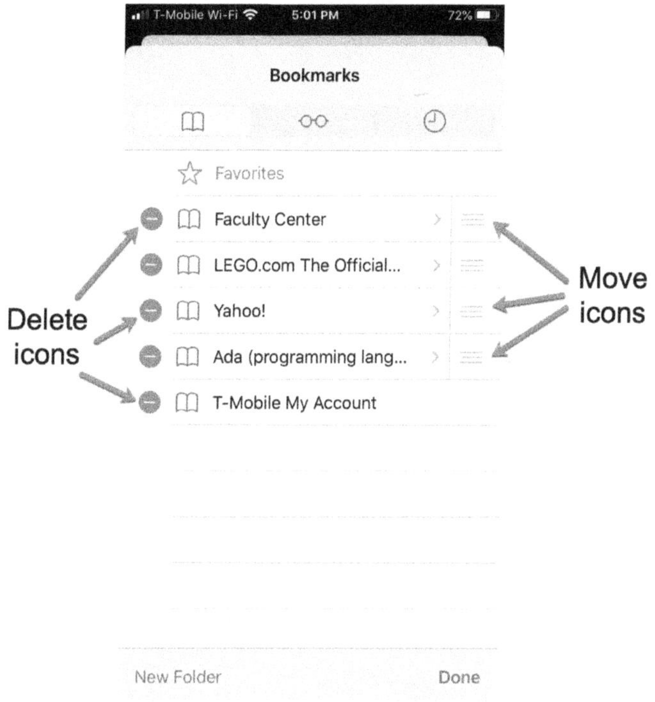

Figure 9.23 – Editing a bookmark list

4. Place your fingertip over the move icon of the bookmark you want to move and slide your finger up or down.
5. Tap **Done**.

Rearranging the order of bookmarks can help you organize your bookmarks, but sometimes you may want to delete a bookmark altogether. To delete a bookmark, follow these steps:

1. Tap the **Safari** app on the Home Screen. The Safari screen appears and displays the bookmarks icon at the bottom of the screen (see *Figure 9.21*).
2. Tap the bookmarks icon. The **Bookmarks** screen appears, listing all previously saved bookmarked websites (see *Figure 9.22*).
3. Tap **Edit** in the bottom-right corner of the screen. Delete icons appear to the left of each bookmark and move icons appear to the right (see *Figure 9.23*).

4. Tap the delete icon to the left of the bookmark you want to remove. A red **Delete** button appears to the right of the bookmark, as shown in *Figure 9.24*:

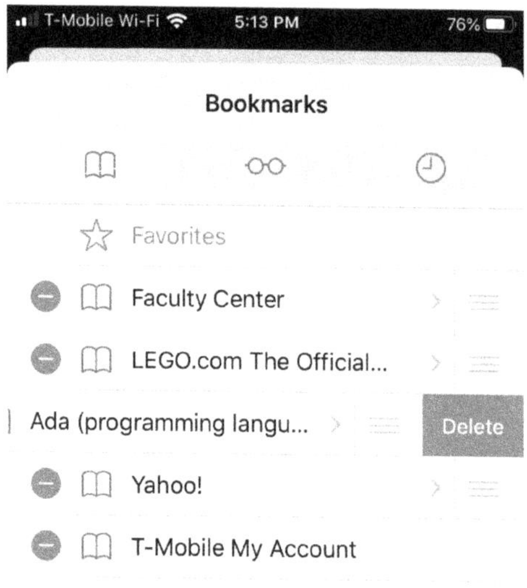

Figure 9.24 – Deleting a bookmark

5. Tap the **Delete** button.
6. Tap **Done**.

Bookmarks are handy for saving your favorite websites, but bookmarks are only useful if you remember to bookmark a specific website. For another way to visit a previously visited website, consider using your browsing history instead.

Viewing browsing history

As you visit various websites, Safari keeps track of all the website addresses (unless you use **Private Browsing Mode**). By reviewing your browsing history, you can return to any previously viewed website.

To reopen a website that you visited previously, follow these steps:

1. Tap the **Safari** app on the Home Screen. The Safari screen appears and displays the bookmarks icon at the bottom of the screen (see *Figure 9.21*).
2. Tap the bookmarks icon. The **Bookmarks** screen appears, listing all previously saved bookmarked websites (see *Figure 9.22*).
3. Tap the history icon. A list of previously viewed website addresses appears, as shown in *Figure 9.25*:

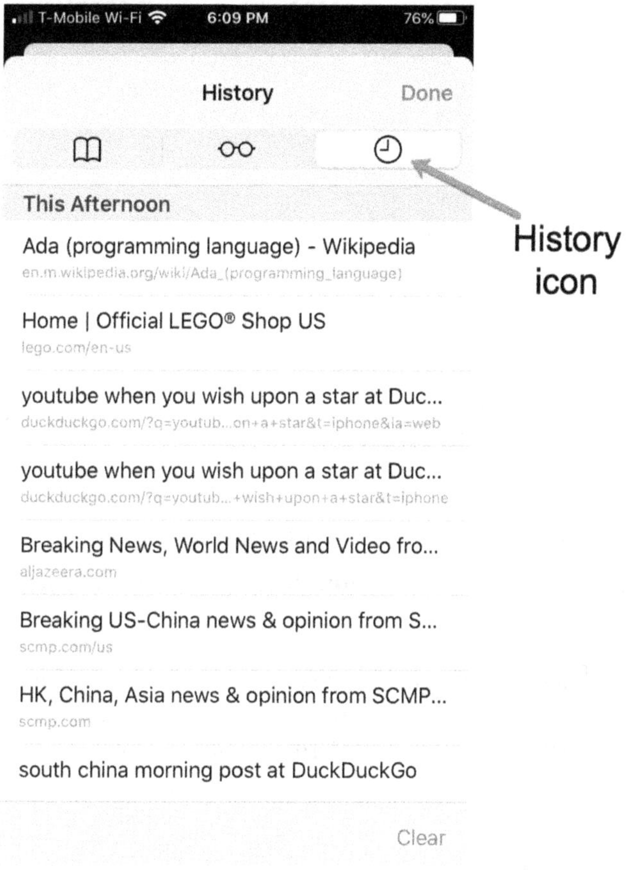

Figure 9.25 – Previously viewed website list

4. Tap on a previously viewed website to see it again.

Keeping track of your browsing history can be handy if you remember visiting a website but can't remember its address. However, you may eventually want to clear your browsing history to protect your privacy.

To clear your browsing history, follow these steps:

1. Tap the **Safari** app on the Home Screen. The Safari screen appears and displays the bookmarks icon at the bottom of the screen (see *Figure 9.21*).
2. Tap the bookmarks icon. The **Bookmarks** screen appears, listing all previously saved bookmarked websites (see *Figure 9.22*).
3. Tap the history icon. A list of previously viewed website addresses appears (see *Figure 9.25*).

4. Tap **Clear** in the bottom-right corner of the screen. A list of options appears, as shown in *Figure 9.26*:

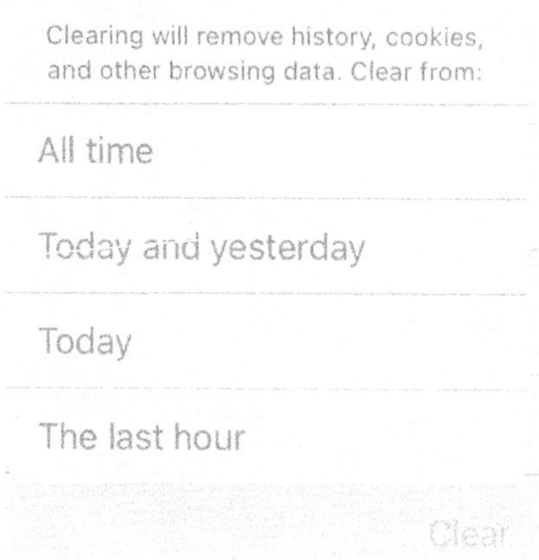

Figure 9.26 – Choosing how to clear the browsing history

5. Tap an option, such as **Today** or **All time**. Safari deletes your browsing history based on the time span you choose.

Using bookmarks or browsing through your history can be handy to view a previously opened website, but what happens if you're in an area where you lack internet or cellular phone network access, such as in an airplane? Then, you can rely on something called a reading list.

Using reading lists

Normally, if you lack access to the internet or a cellular phone network, you cannot read web pages. However, if you download and save web pages in a reading list, you can later read saved web pages anywhere you go, even if you lack access to the internet or cellular phone network.

Storing web pages in a reading list

Before you can read anything, you need to store items in a reading list. To store a web page in a reading list, follow these steps:

1. Tap the **Safari** app on the Home Screen. The Safari screen appears.
2. Tap the text field at the top of the screen and type a website address, and then navigate to a web page that you want to save.

3. Tap the share icon. A sheet of icons appears at the bottom of the screen.
4. Slide down the sheet of icons until you see a list of commands, as shown in *Figure 9.27*:

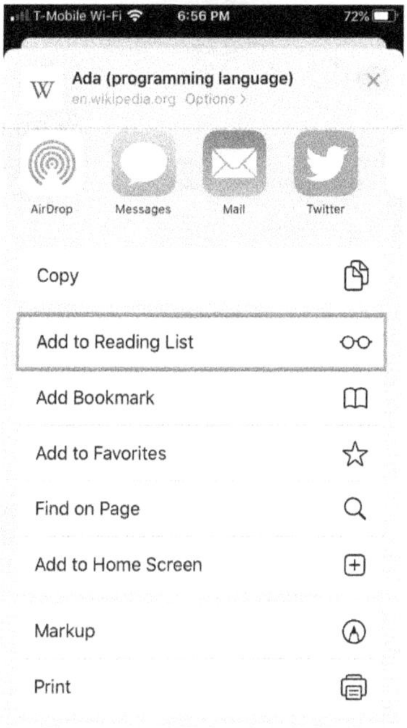

Figure 9.27 – The Add to Reading List command

5. Tap **Add to Reading List**.

Once you save one or more web pages to your reading list, you will be able to read them any time in the future.

Viewing web pages in a reading list

A reading list lets you keep a list of web pages to read. Just remember that if the contents of that web page changes in the future, you can only read the content you saved at the time you added it to the reading list.

To read a web page saved in a reading list, follow these steps:

1. Tap the **Safari** app on the Home Screen. The Safari screen appears.
2. Tap the bookmarks icon at the bottom of the screen.

3. Tap the reading list icon. A list of saved web pages appears, as shown in *Figure 9.28*:

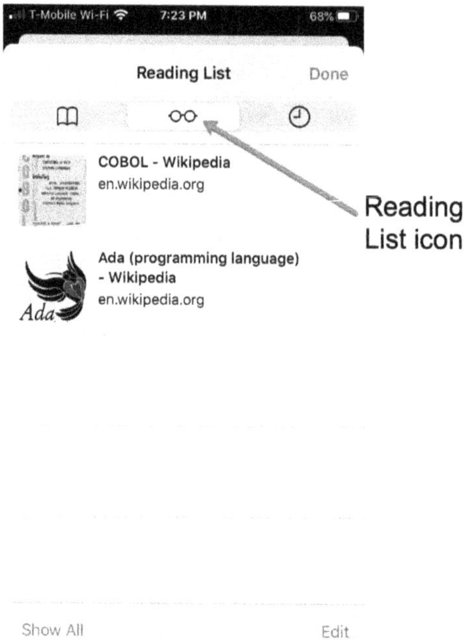

Figure 9.28 – The reading list

4. Tap on a web page to read.

When you choose a saved web page to read, Safari automatically removes that web page from the reading list.

Deleting web pages in a reading list

Sometimes, you may save a web page in your reading list but later decide you want to remove it without reading it. To delete a web page from the reading list, follow these steps:

1. Tap the **Safari** app on the Home Screen. The Safari screen appears.
2. Tap the bookmarks icon at the bottom of the screen.
3. Tap the reading list icon. A list of saved web pages appears (see *Figure 9.28*).
4. Tap **Edit** in the bottom-right corner of the screen. Empty circles appear to the left of each saved web page.
5. Tap in the circle to the left of one or more web pages you want to delete, as shown in *Figure 9.29*:

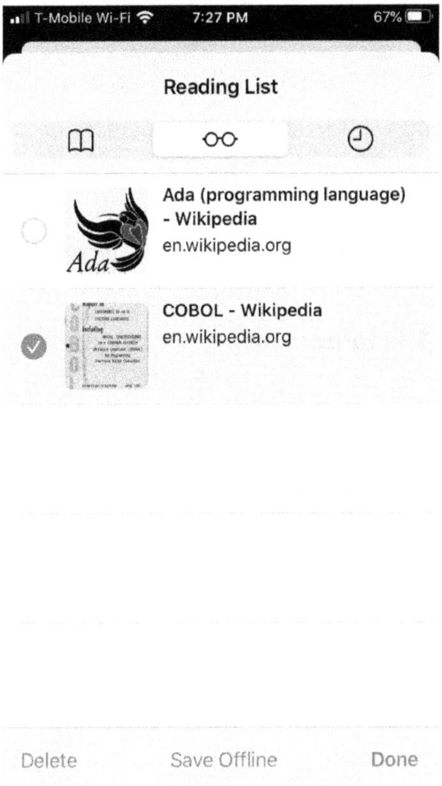

Figure 9.29 – Selecting web pages to delete in a reading list

6. Tap **Delete** in the bottom-left corner of the screen.
7. Tap **Done** in the upper-right corner of the screen.

Saving web pages in a reading list can give you something to read in the future, but if you want to share interesting web pages with others, you need to know how to share websites easily.

Sharing websites

Chances are good that you'll run across a web page with interesting, funny, or useful information that you may want to share with friends, relatives, or co-workers. Three common ways to share websites are the following:

- Through email
- Through text message
- Through AirDrop

To share a website, follow these steps:

1. Tap the **Safari** app on the Home Screen. The Safari screen appears.
2. Visit a web page that you want to share with others.
3. Tap the share icon at the bottom of the screen. A sheet appears at the bottom of the screen, showing icons that represent people you recently contacted, along with the **AirDrop**, **Messages**, and **Mail** icons, as shown in *Figure 9.30*:

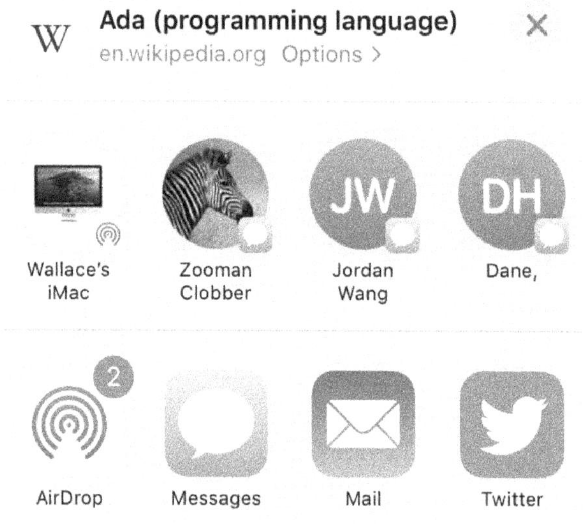

Figure 9.30 – Sharing web pages

4. Tap on an icon that represents a recent contact, or tap the **AirDrop**, **Messages**, or **Mail** icon. Then, specify the person you want to send your chosen website to.

By sharing websites with others, you can pass along information that others might never find on their own. When people receive your website link, they can just tap or click on it to visit that website without typing any long website address.

Searching with Safari

When you know a specific website you want to visit, you can type in that website address. However, many times, you may know what information you want to find but you don't know a specific website to visit.

That's when you need to search for the information you want. To search in Safari, follow these steps:

1. Tap the **Safari** app on the Home Screen. The Safari screen appears.
2. Tap in the text field at the top of the screen and type a word or phrase that defines what you want to find, such as `cat breeds` or `fish recipes`.
3. Tap the blue **go** button in the bottom-right corner of the virtual keyboard. Safari displays a list of websites that match your search criteria.

When Safari searches the internet, it relies on a search engine such as Google. If you aren't happy with the results you get when searching for information, try changing the search engine Safari uses.

To define the search engine for Safari, follow these steps:

1. Tap the **Settings** app on the Home Screen. The **Settings** screen appears.
2. Tap **Safari**. The **Safari** settings screen appears.
3. Tap **Search Engine**. A list of search engines appears, as shown in *Figure 9.31*:

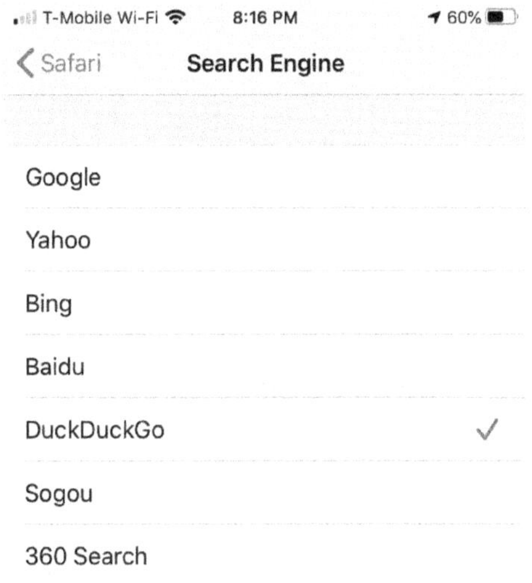

Figure 9.31 – Choosing a search engine for Safari

4. Tap on a search engine to use, such as **Yahoo** or **Baidu**.

Search engines all have their strengths and weaknesses, so experiment with different search engines until you find the one that consistently gives you the best results every time you search with Safari.

Summary

Part of the iPhone's usefulness isn't just in making and sending phone calls or text messages, but also in putting a computer in your pocket so that you can access the internet. Through Safari, you can browse any websites on the internet.

Almost everyone needs to search the internet at one time or another, so make sure you know how to search and switch search engines if necessary. If you find a particularly useful or interesting website, share it with your friends or bookmark it so that you can find it later.

You can also share websites by email, so read the next chapter, which focuses on all the different ways to read, write, and sort through email messages.

10
Sending and Receiving Email

The three most popular ways to communicate through an iPhone is by phone calls, text messaging, and email. Since people cannot always take a phone call and text messages are often brief, email can be a great way to communicate large amounts of information that others can review at their leisure.

With email, you can send text and file attachments such as pictures or video. By sending and receiving email on your iPhone, you can choose which method of communicating is best for your needs.

The topics covered in this chapter are as follows:

- Setting up an email account
- Sending email
- Reading messages
- Creating a VIP list
- Filtering email
- Flagging messages
- Dealing with junk email

Setting up an email account

Before you can send and receive email messages, you need an email account such as a free one through Gmail or Yahoo, or one provided through your work. When adding a popular and common email account, such as Gmail, your iPhone can set up the email account with little more than your email address and password. When adding a work or unusual email account, you may need to manually enter technical details, such as POP or IMAP server names.

Setting up a common email account

Your iPhone can automatically recognize and set up the following types of email accounts:

- iCloud
- Microsoft Exchange
- Google (Gmail)
- Yahoo
- AOL
- Outlook

To set up an email account through one of these email providers, follow these steps:

1. Tap the **Settings** app on the Home Screen. The **Settings** screen appears.
2. Tap **Mail**. A **Mail** screen appears.
3. Tap **Accounts**. An **Account** screen appears.
4. Tap **Add Account**. An **Add Account** screen appears, as shown in *Figure 10.1*:

5. cTap the name of your email provider (such as **AOL** or **Yahoo**) and follow the instructions to type in your email address and password.

Most people use one of the previously mentioned popular email providers, such as iCloud or Yahoo. However, in some cases, you may need to enter email account information manually.

Manually setting up an email account

If your email account is not one of the more popular ones, such as a work or school email account, you may need to manually enter your email account information. That means you'll need to get information beforehand, such as host names and other technical information that you may need to obtain from an IT administrator.

To manually set up an email account, follow these steps:

1. Tap the **Settings** app on the Home Screen. The **Settings** screen appears.
2. Tap **Mail**. A **Mail** screen appears.
3. Tap **Accounts**. An **Account** screen appears.
4. Tap **Add Account**. An **Add Account** screen appears (see *Figure 10.1*).
5. Tap **Other**. An **Add Account** screen appears, as shown in *Figure 10.2*:

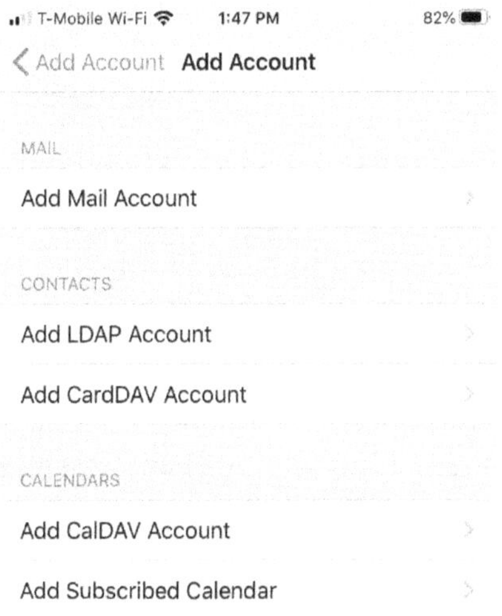

Figure 10.2 – The Add Account screen

6. Tap **Add Mail Account**. A **New Account** screen appears, as shown in *Figure 10.3*:

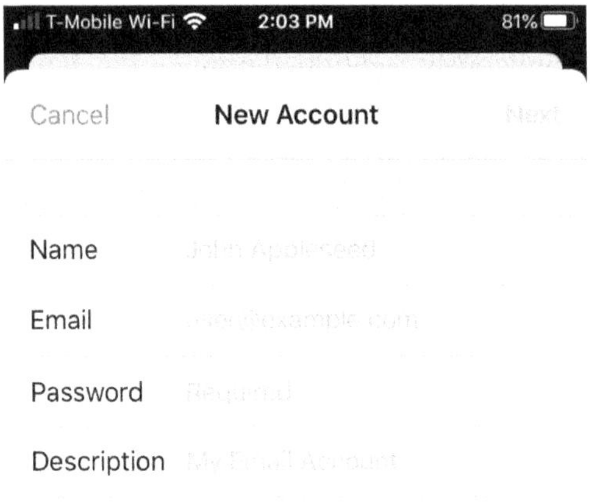

Figure 10.3 – The New Account screen

7. Type in your name, email address, password, and a description of your email account, and then tap **Next**.
8. If your iPhone can successfully connect to your email account, you can tap **Done**. Otherwise, you will need to tap **Next** and enter additional information, such as mail server names and whether your email account is IMAP or POP.

To make sure you successfully connected to your email account, you may want to get a friend to send an email message to make sure you can receive it. Once you know you've successfully connected an email account, you can start sending and receiving email.

Sending email

Sending email involves defining an email address, subject line, and text that makes up the bulk of your message. You can type an email address, but it's far easier to select an email address that you previously stored in the **Contacts** app.

When you send email, you need to specify at least one email address. You can also specify additional email addresses in the **Cc:** (carbon copy) or **Bcc:** (blind copy) text fields.

Carbon copy means everyone who receives the message can also see all the additional email addresses that received the same message.

Blind copy means no one can see any of the additional email addresses who may have received the same message.

Writing and sending email

To create an email to send, you need to specify a recipient's email address, a subject line, and the actual message itself.

To send email, follow these steps:

1. Tap the **Mail** app on the Home Screen. The **Mail** app screen appears and displays the New Message icon at the bottom-right corner of the screen, as shown in *Figure 10.4*:

Figure 10.4 – The New Message icon

2. Tap the New Message icon. A **New Message** screen appears, as shown in *Figure 10.5*:

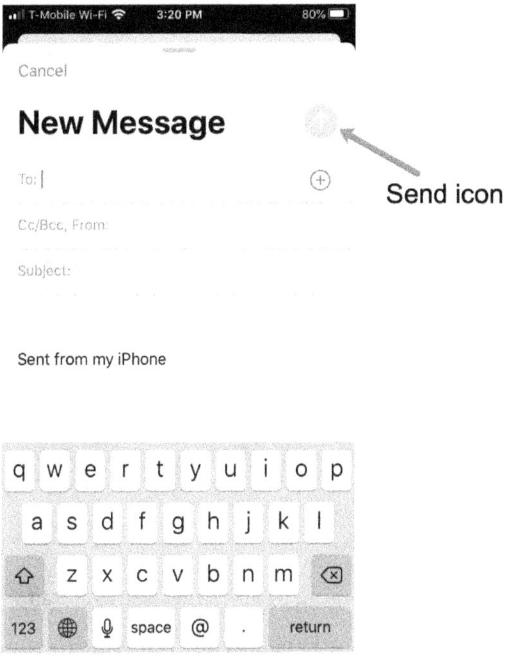

Figure 10.5 – The New Message screen

3. Type an email address in the **To:** text field, or tap the + icon on the far right to open the **Contacts** app and then tap a name.
4. (Optional) Tap in the **Cc/Bcc, From:** text field and type any additional email addresses that you want to receive your message as well.

5. Type a description of your message in the **Subject:** text field.
6. Type your message in the message text field that appears above the **Sent from my iPhone** text.
7. Tap the Send icon (it looks like an up arrow inside a circle) in the upper-right corner of the screen.

The preceding steps assume you want to write and send an email message right away. However, sometimes you may want to start writing a message and save it as a draft so that you can go back to it later.

Saving email as a draft

Sometimes you may want to write part of a message and then come back later to edit the text before sending it out. So, instead of writing and sending a message, you write a message and then save it in a special Drafts folder. Then you can go back and edit that message when you're ready to send it.

To save a message as a draft, follow these steps:

1. Tap the **Mail** app on the Home Screen and then tap the New Message icon at the bottom-right corner of the screen (see *Figure 10.4*).
2. Type text in the blank email message.
3. Tap **Cancel** in the upper-left corner of the screen. A list of options appears at the bottom of the screen, as shown in *Figure 10.6*:

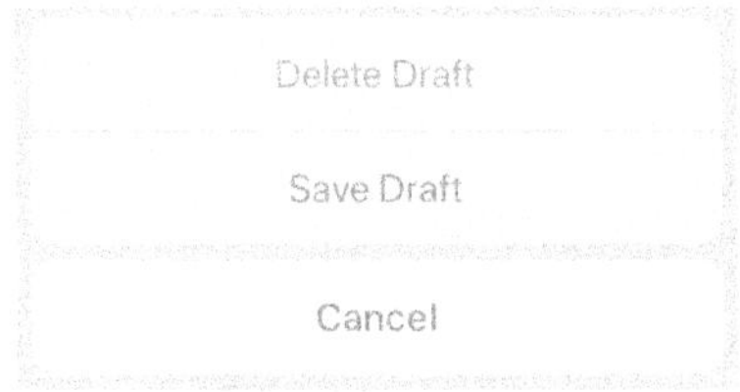

Figure 10.6 – Choosing to save a message as a draft

4. Tap **Save Draft**. (**Cancel** lets you go back to editing your message, while **Delete Draft** deletes your entire message without sending it.)

Once you've saved a message as a draft, you can return to that message at any time to edit it and eventually send it off. To edit a message stored in the **Drafts** folder, follow these steps:

1. Tap the **Mail** app on the Home Screen. The **Mail** screen appears.
2. Tap the Back arrow in the upper-left corner until the **Mailboxes** screen appears, which displays a number showing how many messages are stored in the **Drafts** folder, as shown in *Figure 10.7*:

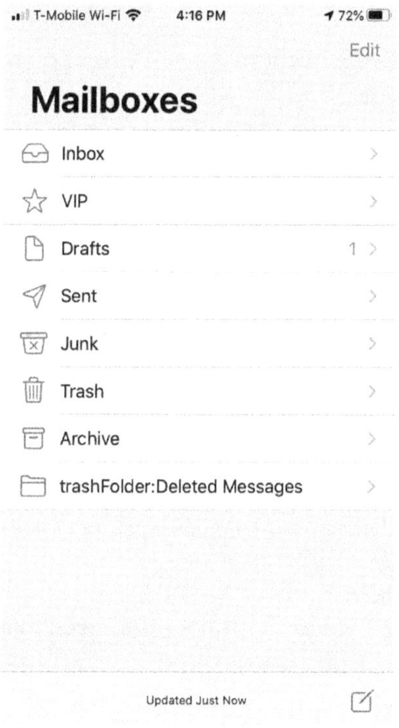

Figure 10.7 – The Mailboxes screen showing the Drafts folder

3. Tap **Drafts**. The **Drafts** screen appears, listing all the messages that you haven't sent out yet.
4. Tap on the message you want to edit. Your chosen message appears, letting you type or edit the email address, subject line, and text.
5. Edit your message.
6. Tap the **Send** icon to send your message or tap **Cancel** and then tap **Save Draft** to save the message back in the **Drafts** folder.

Eventually you'll either want to send a message or delete it. To delete a message from the **Drafts** folder, follow these steps:

1. Tap the **Mail** app on the Home Screen. The **Mail** screen appears.
2. Tap the Back arrow in the upper-left corner until the **Mailboxes** screen appears, which displays a number showing how many messages are stored in the **Drafts** folder (see *Figure 10.7*).
3. Tap **Drafts**. The **Drafts** screen appears, listing all the messages that you haven't sent out yet.
4. Swipe left on the message you want to delete. A red **Trash** icon appears on the far right, as shown in *Figure 10.8*:

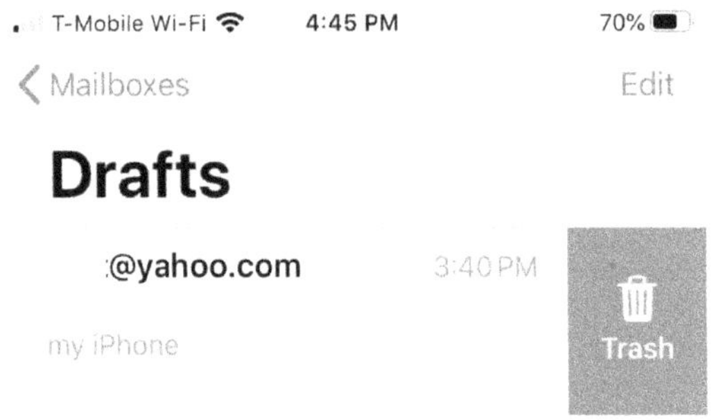

Figure 10.8 – The Trash icon lets you delete a message

5. Tap the Trash icon to delete the message from the **Drafts** folder.

Email can be handy for sending text, but occasionally you may want to send a file such as a word processor document or a video. To do this, you need to attach a file to a message.

Attaching files to an email message

Oftentimes, you need to share a word processor, spreadsheet, or presentation file, or a video file. To share any type of file, you need to attach that file to your email. Then you can send text along with the file or just the file itself.

To attach a file to an email message, follow these steps:

1. Tap the **Mail** app on the Home Screen. The **Mail** screen appears.
2. Tap the New Message icon. A **New Message** screen appears (see *Figure 10.5*).

3. Press and hold a fingertip in the message text field (above the **Sent from my iPhone** text) until a menu appears, as shown in *Figure 10.9*:

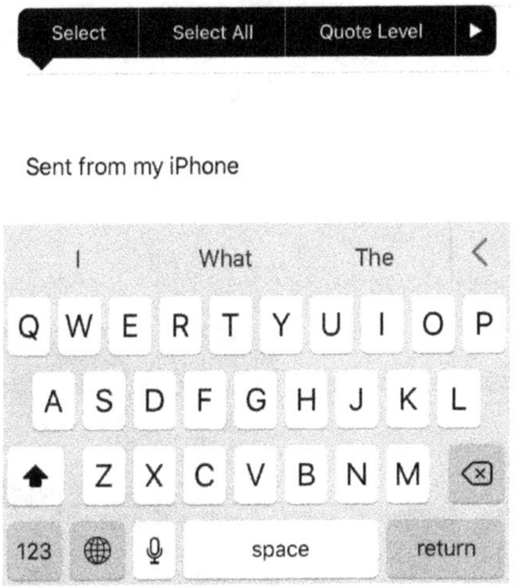

Figure 10.9 – A pop-up menu appears when you press and hold in a message text field

4. Tap the right arrow on the far right of the pop-up menu to see more options, as shown in *Figure 10.10*:

Figure 10.10 – Adding a picture or document to an email message

5. Tap on the type of file you want to attach, such as **Insert Photo or Video** or **Add Document**. Your chosen types of files appear, as shown in *Figure 10.11*:

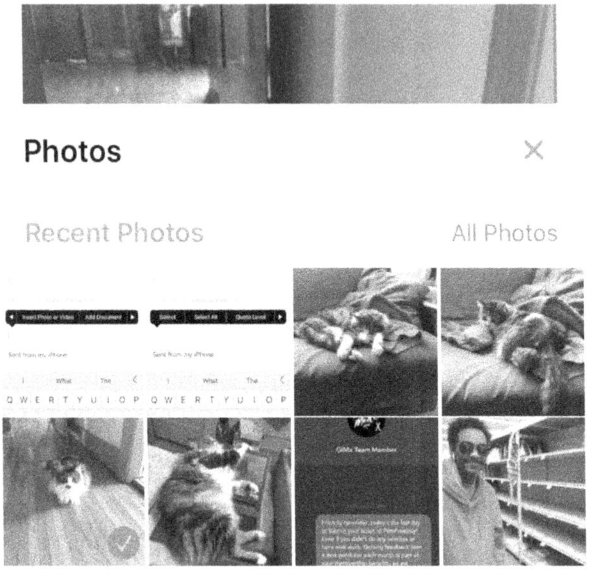

Figure 10.11 – Choosing a file to attach to an email message

6. Tap on the file you want to attach to an email message. If you want to add a picture or video, you can tap on multiple files and then tap the close icon (**X**) when you're done. You can repeat the preceding steps to add multiple files to a single email message. Just make sure your email account will allow you to send large amounts of data.

> **Note**
> Most email providers set a maximum file size limit that you can send in a single email message, such as 10 MB or 25 MB. Check with your email provider so you'll know the largest file you can send.

Sending messages is only half the use of email. The other half involves receiving and reading messages that other people send to you.

Reading messages

Once you give out your email address to others, they'll likely send you messages. When you receive a message, you'll have the option of reading it, replying to it, forwarding it to others, storing it in a folder for future reference, or deleting it altogether.

Choosing a message to read

Before you can read a message, you need to select the message you want to read. To read a message, follow these steps:

1. Tap the **Mail** app on the Home Screen. The **Mail** screen appears.
2. Tap the Back arrow in the upper-left corner until the **Mailboxes** screen appears.
3. Tap **Inbox**. A list of messages appears.
4. Tap on a message you want to read. Your chosen message appears.
5. Tap the Previous or Next icons in the upper-right corner of the screen to read the previous or next message, as shown in *Figure 10.12*:

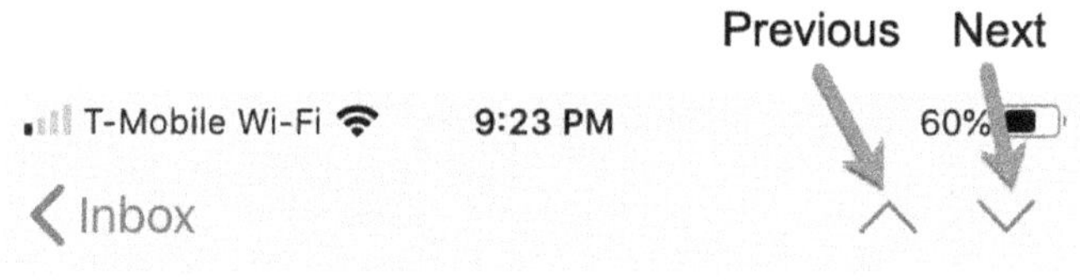

Figure 10.12 – The Inbox, Previous, and Next icons

6. Tap the **Inbox** button in the upper-left corner of the screen to go back to seeing a list of messages in the **Inbox** folder.

You may just want to read a message and keep it, but it's likely you'll want to reply to that message.

Responding to a message

When you reply to an existing message, your reply contains any new text you type, along with the entire contents of the previous message. This lets the recipient understand the context of your new message based on the text that you're responding to.

There are three options for responding to a message:

- **Reply**: Sends a message only to the person who sent you the message
- **Reply All**: Sends a message to everyone who received the same message through **Cc:** (carbon copy) or **Bcc:** (blind copy)
- **Forward**: Sends a message to someone whose email address wasn't originally on the message

To reply to a message, follow these steps:

1. Tap the **Mail** app on the Home Screen. The **Mail** screen appears.
2. Tap the Back arrow in the upper-left corner until the **Mailboxes** screen appears.
3. Tap **Inbox**. A list of messages appears.
4. Tap on a message you want to read. Your chosen message appears and displays a Reply icon at the bottom of the screen, as shown in *Figure 10.13*:

Figure 10.13 – The Reply icon

5. Tap the Reply icon. A sheet of options appears at the bottom of the screen, as shown in *Figure 10.14*:

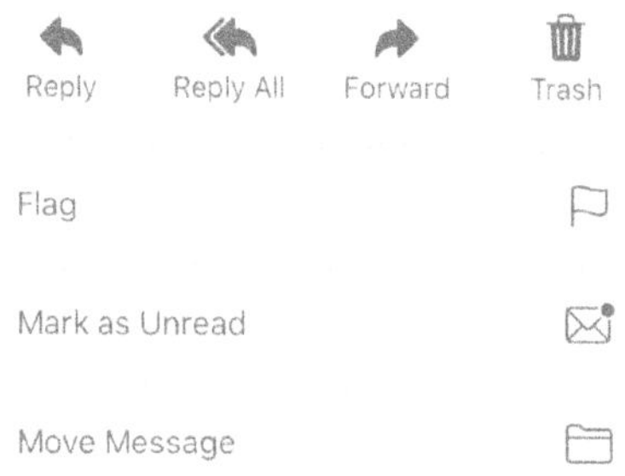

Figure 10.14 – Options appear at the bottom of the screen

6. Tap **Reply** (to send a message to the person who sent you the message), **Reply All** (to send a message to everyone who received the message), or **Forward** (to send a message to a completely new email address). A new message screen appears that contains all the text of the previously viewed message.
7. (Optional) If you chose **Forward** in *Step 6*, type an email address that you want to receive your forwarded message.
8. Type any additional text you wish above the **Sent from my iPhone** text.
9. Tap the Send icon in the upper-right corner of the screen to send your message.

Replying to a message can be a fast way to send a message to the person who sent a message to you. Once you read or reply to a message, you might want to move a message to another folder to keep your **Inbox** folder uncluttered.

Moving a message to the Archive folder

Every time you receive a message, it automatically goes to your **Inbox** folder. Since this can clutter up your **Inbox** folder, you may want to move messages to the **Archive** folder. That way, you can keep a message and keep the **Inbox** folder uncluttered.

To move a message to the **Archive** folder, follow these steps:

1. Tap the **Mail** app on the Home Screen. The **Mail** screen appears.
2. Tap the Back arrow in the upper-left corner until the **Mailboxes** screen appears.
3. Tap **Inbox**. A list of messages appears.
4. Tap on a message you want to move to the **Archive** folder. The Folder icon appears at the bottom of the screen, as shown in *Figure 10.15*:

Figure 10.15 – The Folder icon

5. Tap the Folder icon. A list of folders appears, as shown in *Figure 10.16*:

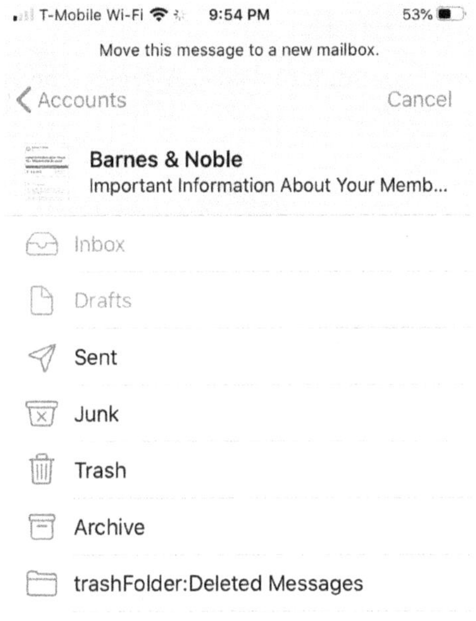

Figure 10.16 – A list of available folders

6. Tap the **Archive** folder. Your selected message moves to the **Archive** folder.

Once you've moved a message to the **Archive** folder, you'll probably want to view it later. To view any messages in the **Archive** folder, follow these steps:

1. Tap the **Mail** app on the Home Screen. The **Mail** screen appears.
2. Tap the Back arrow in the upper-left corner until the **Mailboxes** screen appears.
3. Tap **Archive**. A list of messages in the **Archive** folder appears.

Whether you move a message to the **Archive** folder or keep it in the **Inbox** folder, you may eventually want to delete a message when you no longer need it.

Deleting a message

Every time you receive a message, it automatically goes to your **Inbox** folder. Since this can clutter up your **Inbox** folder, you may want to move messages to the **Archive** folder. That way, you can keep a message and keep the **Inbox** folder uncluttered.

To delete a single message, follow these steps:

1. Tap the **Mail** app on the Home Screen. The **Mail** screen appears.
2. Tap the Back arrow in the upper-left corner until the **Mailboxes** screen appears.
3. Tap the folder that contains the message you want to delete, such as **Inbox** or **Archive**. A list of messages appears.
4. Swipe left on the message you want to delete. A **Trash** icon appears on the right, as shown in *Figure 10.17*:

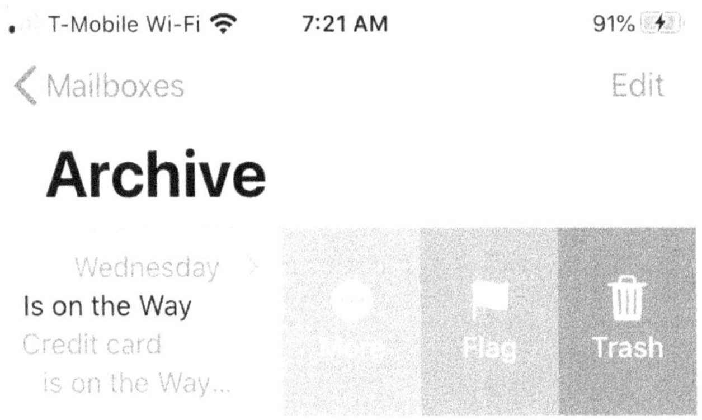

Figure 10.17 – The Trash icon appears when you swipe left

5. Tap the **Trash** icon.

Before deleting a message, you might want to review it first. To delete a message after reading it, follow these steps:

1. Tap the **Mail** app on the Home Screen. The **Mail** screen appears.
2. Tap the Back arrow in the upper-left corner until the **Mailboxes** screen appears.
3. Tap the folder that contains the message you want to delete, such as **Inbox** or **Archive**. A list of messages appears.
4. Tap on the message you want to read before deleting it.
5. Tap the trash icon in the bottom-left corner of the screen, as shown in *Figure 10.18*:

Figure 10.18 – The trash icon appears in the bottom-left corner

If you want to delete multiple messages, you could swipe left on each message or open them up individually and tap the trash icon, but that would be tedious, and there is a faster way.

To delete multiple messages, follow these steps:

1. Tap the **Mail** app on the Home Screen. The **Mail** screen appears.
2. Tap the Back arrow in the upper-left corner until the **Mailboxes** screen appears.
3. Tap the folder that contains the messages you want to delete, such as **Inbox** or **Archive**. A list of messages appears.
4. Tap **Edit** in the upper-right corner of the screen. Radio buttons (empty circles) appear to the left of each message.

5. Tap in the radio button of each message you want to delete, as shown in *Figure 10.19*:

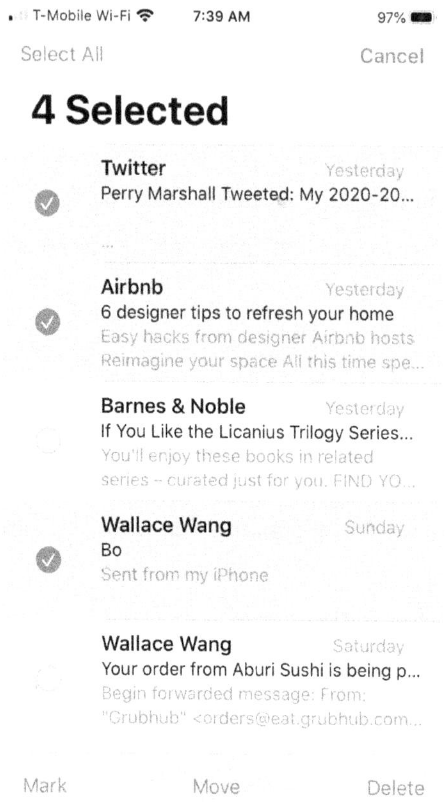

Figure 10.19 – Selecting multiple messages to delete

6. Tap **Delete** in the bottom-right corner of the screen.

If you delete a message by mistake and later want to retrieve it, you can find it in the **Trash** folder. To retrieve messages from the **Trash** folder, follow these steps:

1. Tap the **Mail** app on the Home Screen. The **Mail** screen appears.
2. Tap the Back arrow in the upper-left corner until the **Mailboxes** screen appears.
3. Tap the **Trash** folder. A list of messages appears.
4. Tap the message you want to retrieve.
5. Tap the Folder icon at the bottom of the screen (see *Figure 10.15*). A list of folders appears.
6. Tap the **Inbox** folder.

Getting email can be fun, but over time you may wind up with a flood of email from important people to useless messages. How can you sort through the clutter? By creating a special VIP list.

Creating a VIP list

The main idea behind a VIP list is to automatically route email from certain people into a special VIP folder. Now you can first check your VIP folder for important messages and then later check your regular **Inbox** folder for messages from everyone else.

> **Note**
>
> To create a VIP list, you must first store a name and email address in the **Contacts** app.

To create a VIP list, follow these steps:

1. Tap the **Mail** app on the Home Screen. The **Mail** screen appears.
2. Tap the Back arrow in the upper-left corner until the **Mailboxes** screen appears.
3. Tap the **VIP** folder. The **VIP List** screen appears and displays an **Add VIP** button.
4. Tap the **Add VIP** button. The **Contacts** screen appears, listing all the names stored in the **Contacts** app. If a name appears dimmed, it's because you have not stored an email address for that name.
5. Tap a name to store in your VIP list.

Once you store a name in your VIP list, you'll receive a notification any time you receive an email in your VIP folder. **Messages** from a VIP appear in both your **Inbox** and **VIP** folders.

A gold star to the left of a message identifies messages from people on your VIP list, as shown in *Figure 10.20*:

Figure 10.20 – Identifying messages also stored in the VIP list

Eventually, you may want to remove people from your VIP list. To remove someone from your VIP list, follow these steps:

1. Tap the **Mail** app on the Home Screen. The **Mail** screen appears.
2. Tap the Back arrow in the upper-left corner until the **Mailboxes** screen appears. An Info icon appears to the right of the VIP folder, as shown in *Figure 10.21*. This Info icon appears as long as you have identified at least one person from your **Contacts** app as a VIP:

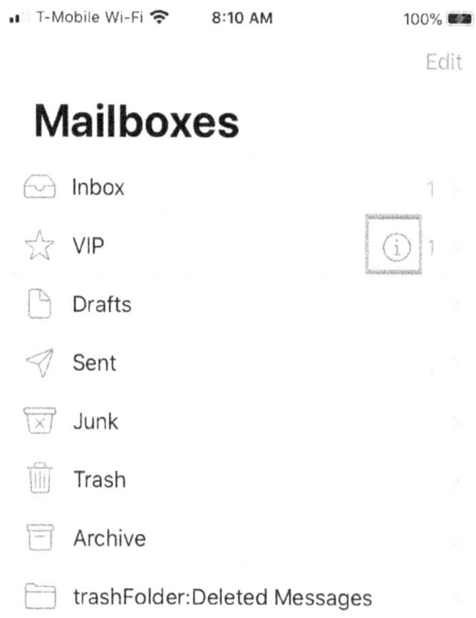

Figure 10.21 – The Info icon near the VIP folder

3. Tap the Info icon that appears to the right of the VIP folder. The **VIP List** screen appears, listing all the names currently stored in your VIP List.
4. Swipe left on the name you want to remove from your VIP list. A **Delete** icon appear to the right of that name, as shown in *Figure 10.22*:

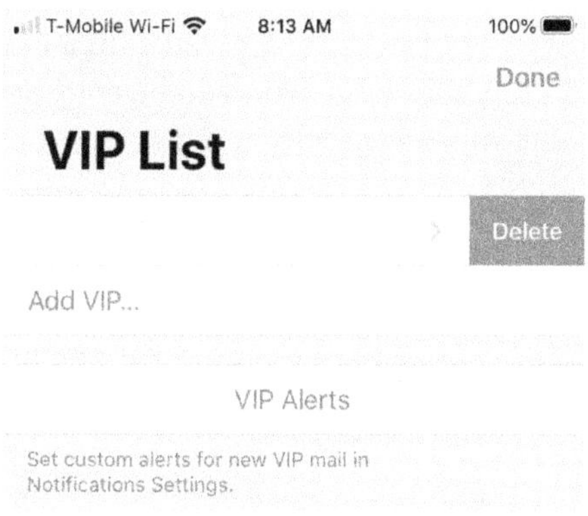

Figure 10.22 – Removing a name from the VIP list

5. Tap **Delete**.

The VIP list can be one way to make it easier to find important messages. Another way is to toggle between displaying all messages and displaying only new messages.

Filtering email

Normally, the **Inbox** folder lists all messages, both those you have read and those you have not read. To make it easier to find and read all unread messages, you can filter your folder to show only unread messages. Then you can turn off the filter to display all messages (read and unread) again.

To filter a folder, follow these steps:

1. Tap the **Mail** app on the Home Screen. The **Mail** screen appears.
2. Tap the Back arrow in the upper-left corner until the **Mailboxes** screen appears.
3. Tap the folder you want to filter, such as the **Inbox** folder. The list of messages in that folder appears.
4. Tap the Filter icon in the bottom-left corner of the screen, as shown in *Figure 10.23*. When the Filter icon is highlighted, the screen only shows unread messages:

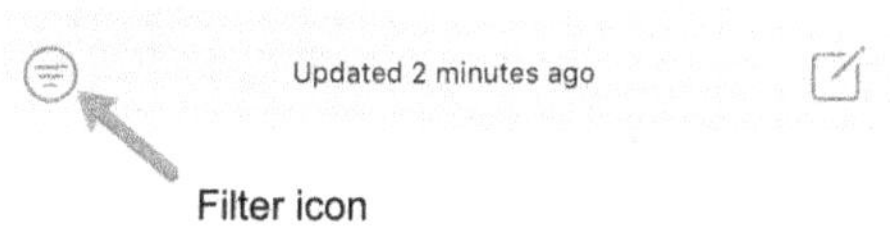

Figure 10.23 – The Filter icon

5. Tap the Filter icon again. When the Filter icon is no longer highlighted, the screen will show both read and unread messages.

When you first receive a message, it's marked as unread with a blue dot to the left of that message. As soon as you read it, that message will then be considered read. However, you can mark a message as unread to make it easy to find it again when you use the Filter icon.

To mark a message as unread (even if you have already read it), follow these steps:

1. Tap the **Mail** app on the Home Screen. The **Mail** screen appears.
2. Tap the Back arrow in the upper-left corner until the **Mailboxes** screen appears.
3. Tap a folder that contains the message you want to mark as unread.
4. Swipe left on the message you want to mark as unread. **More**, **Flag**, and **Trash** icons appear on the right.
5. Tap **More**. A list of options appears at the bottom of the screen, as shown in *Figure 10.24*:

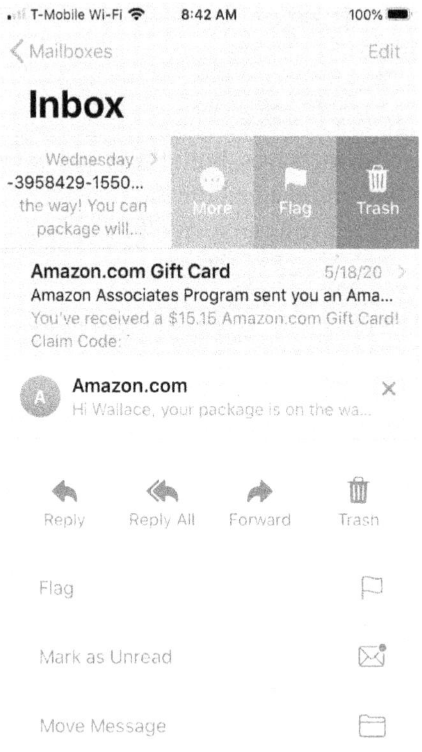

Figure 10.24 – Options for marking a message

6. Tap **Mark as Unread**. A blue dot now appears to the left of that message until you open and read that message again.

When you mark a message unread, you can easily find it using the Filter icon. However, each time you open that message again, that message is no longer considered unread. For another way to identify certain messages, consider flagging them instead.

Flagging messages

Not all messages you receive may be equally important. To make it easy to find the important messages, you can flag them. That way, you can visually spot all the important messages and skip over the less important ones.

To flag a message, follow these steps:

1. Tap the **Mail** app on the Home Screen. The **Mail** screen appears.
2. Tap the Back arrow in the upper-left corner until the **Mailboxes** screen appears.
3. Tap a folder that contains the message you want to flag.
4. Swipe left on the message you want to flag. **More**, **Flag**, and **Trash** icons appear on the right (see *Figure 10.24*).
5. Tap the **Flag** icon. A tiny colored flag appears in the right margin, as shown in *Figure 10.25*:

Figure 10.25 – A flagged message displays a flag icon in the right-hand margin

To remove a flag from a message, just repeat the preceding steps.

Dealing with junk email

Junk email typically involves scams, unwanted sales messages, and fake warnings. The **Mail** app on your iPhone does not sort junk messages from legitimate ones, but relies on your email provider to identify possible junk messages.

Any time your email provider isn't sure whether a message is junk, it will send it to your **Junk** folder. That means you should periodically check for missing messages that have been sent to the **Junk** folder by mistake.

Despite the efforts of your email provider, junk messages will still slip through, so you need to know how to deal with junk when you receive it.

To send a message to the **Junk** folder, follow these steps:

1. Tap the **Mail** app on the Home Screen. The **Mail** screen appears.
2. Tap the Back arrow in the upper-left corner until the **Mailboxes** screen appears.
3. Tap a folder.
4. Swipe left on the message that you want to mark as junk. **More**, **Flag**, and **Trash** icons appear on the right.
5. Tap **More**. A list of options appears at the bottom of the screen.
6. Scroll up to view all the options, as shown in *Figure 10.26*:

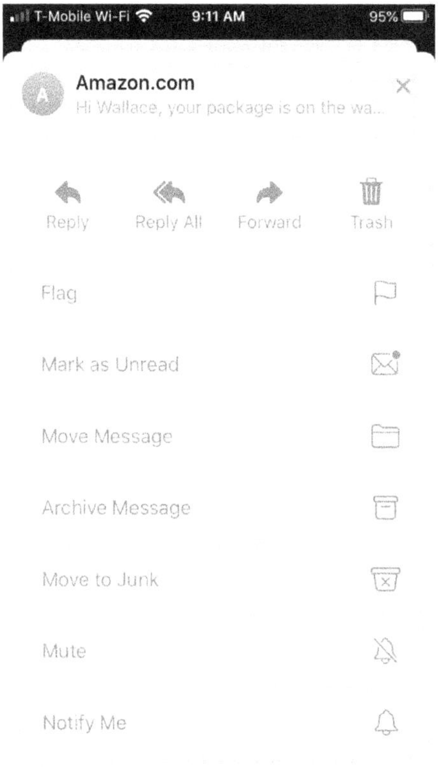

Figure 10.26 – The complete list of options displayed by tapping the More icon

7. Tap **Move to Junk**.

Once you've moved messages to the **Junk** folder or just want to check whether your email provider has sent any messages to the **Junk** folder for you to review, you'll need to browse inside the **Junk** folder.

To browse through your **Junk** folder, follow these steps:

1. Tap the **Mail** app on the Home Screen. The **Mail** screen appears.
2. Tap the Back arrow in the upper-left corner until the **Mailboxes** screen appears.
3. Tap the **Junk** folder. A list of zero or more messages inside the **Junk** folder appears.
4. Tap a message to read it, or swipe left and tap **Delete** to remove it.

To avoid flooding your **Junk** folder with obvious junk messages, your email provider may simply store all blatant junk messages on their own server. This means that if you want to check whether any important messages have been flagged as junk by mistake, you'll need to first check the **Junk** folder on your iPhone and then check the **Spam** folder of your email provider. To do this, you'll need to contact your email provider for details on how to examine the **Spam** folder of your email account.

Summary

Sending and receiving email can help you stay in touch with important people and their messages wherever you go with your iPhone. At a basic level, make sure you know how to read and write messages.

For greater convenience, learn how to reply to and forward messages. Replying to a message lets you include the text of a previous message and show your response. You can reply to the person sending that message or to everyone who received that same message.

Forwarding lets you pass a message along to someone else. That way, you can share messages with your friends and co-workers so that they don't miss out on something important.

On a more advanced level, use folders, filters, VIP lists, and flags to make it easier to find messages. The more messages you receive, the more you'll want to use these methods to help you find the messages that are most important to you.

While email can be convenient, you might want to talk to someone right away. Instead of making a phone call, consider making a video call instead using FaceTime, which is the topic of the next chapter.

11
Using FaceTime

Making a phone call can put you in touch with your friends and loved ones, but sometimes hearing their voice isn't enough. That's when you might want to use FaceTime, so that way people can hear your voice and see you at the same time.

FaceTime lets you talk and see up to 32 people at once, although it's far more likely you'll just talk to one person at a time or a handful of people at once.

> **Important note**
>
> FaceTime calls only work if everyone uses an iPhone, iPad, or Macintosh. You cannot use FaceTime with someone using a Windows PC, Linux, or an Android smartphone or tablet. Also, FaceTime may not be available in all countries and regions.

The topics covered in this chapter are as follows:

- Setting up FaceTime
- Making a FaceTime call
- Talking in a FaceTime call

Setting up FaceTime

Before you can use FaceTime, you must define a phone number, Apple ID, or email address that people can use to call you through FaceTime. Two FaceTime options you may want to modify are **Speaking** and **FaceTime Live Photos**.

Speaking enlarges the title of the person speaking in a Group FaceTime chat so it's easier to see who's talking at any given time. If the **Speaking** option is turned off, the person's name will not appear enlarged.

FaceTime Live Photos lets you capture live photos during a FaceTime call.

To set up FaceTime, follow these steps:

1. Tap the **Settings** app on the Home Screen. The **Settings** screen will appear.
2. Scroll down and tap on **FaceTime**. A **FaceTime** screen will appear.
3. Enter your phone number, email address, and Apple ID.
4. (Optional) Tap the **Speaking** switch to turn it off or on.
5. (Optional) Tap the **FaceTime Live Photos** switch to turn it off or on, as shown in *Figure 11.1*:

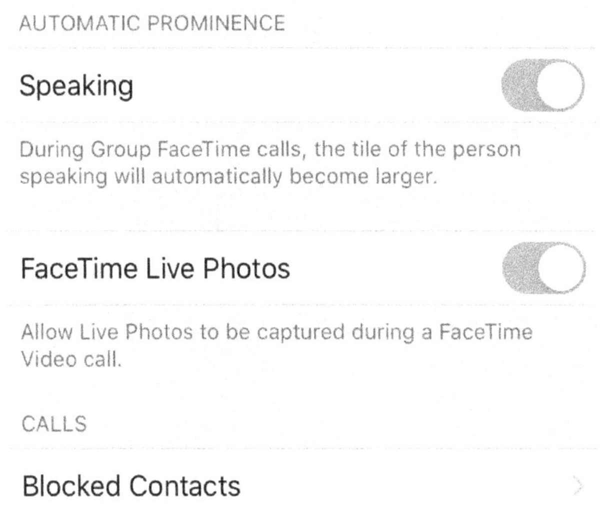

Figure 11.1 – Choosing the Speaking and FaceTime Live **Photos** switches

You can repeat the preceding steps in case you want to modify your FaceTime settings at any time. Once you've set up FaceTime on your iPhone, you can make and receive FaceTime calls.

Using Wi-Fi for a FaceTime call

In many parts of the world, users only get a monthly data allotment. The moment they exceed this monthly data allotment, the cellular phone company charges extra. If you do not have an unlimited data plan, you may want to take some precautions first before using FaceTime.

When you make a Facetime call, FaceTime first searches for a Wi-Fi network to connect to. Thus, FaceTime can be a handy way to make audio or video phone calls without using any cellular data whatsoever.

If FaceTime cannot connect to a Wi-Fi network, then it will rely on a cellular data network. For those who must pay extra for data, a FaceTime video call will use up far more data than an ordinary phone call.

So, if you want to make phone calls without paying for cellular data, make sure your iPhone is connected to a Wi-Fi network. You can check for a Wi-Fi connection by looking for the Wi-Fi icon in the upper-left corner of the iPhone screen, as shown in *Figure 11.2*:

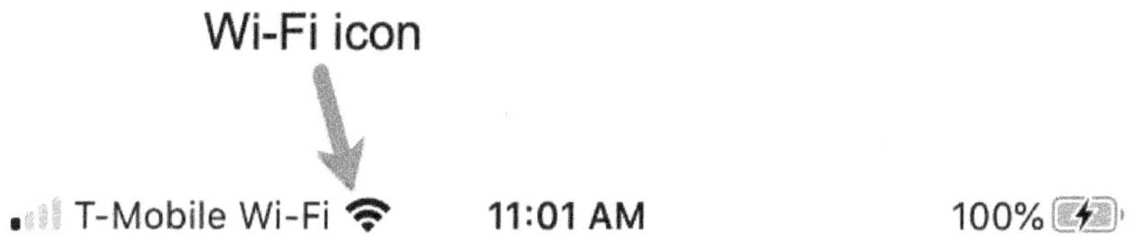

Figure 11.2 – Checking for a Wi-Fi connection

To ensure that FaceTime won't use cellular data, you might want to temporarily turn off your iPhone's use of cellular data when you're making a FaceTime call. Then you can turn cellular data back on again afterward.

To turn cellular data off (or on again), follow these steps:

1. Tap the **Settings** app on the Home Screen. The **Settings** screen appears.
2. Tap **Cellular**. The **Cellular** screen appears, as shown in *Figure 11.3*. Depending on the region, you'll either see Cellular or Mobile Data:

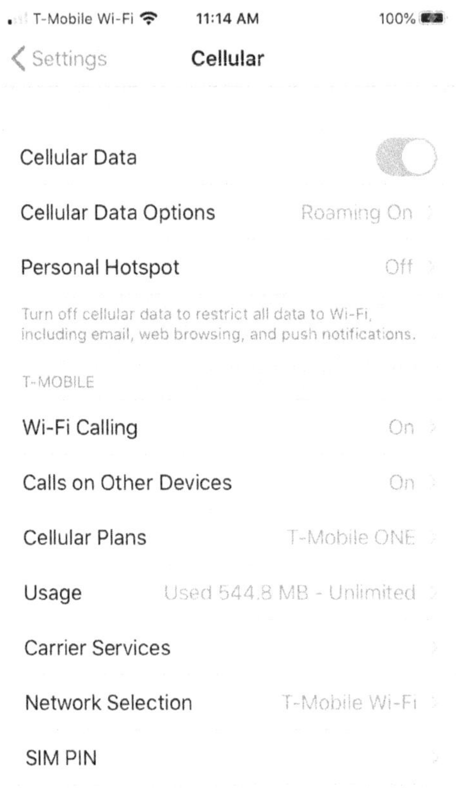

Figure 11.3 – The Cellular screen

3. Tap the **Cellular Data** switch to turn it off (or on). When cellular data is off, your iPhone won't use any cellular data and will rely solely on a Wi-Fi network connection if one exists.

FaceTime, through a Wi-Fi network, lets you make free phone calls without affecting your cellular data usage. If you have to watch your cellular data usage every month, consider using FaceTime to make free audio and/or video calls to everyone who owns an Apple product such as an iPhone, iPad, or Macintosh.

Making a FaceTime call

Once you have set up FaceTime, you can make calls to anyone you know who also has an iPhone, an iPad, or a Macintosh. (If someone uses an Android smartphone or tablet, or a computer that runs Windows, Linux, or Chrome OS, you will not be able to contact them using FaceTime.)

Since FaceTime calls use the camera, make sure you're in an area where your camera won't accidentally capture images that you'd rather not broadcast to others. For example, it's easy to talk on a regular phone call while going to the restroom, but you probably wouldn't want to do that with a FaceTime call since someone could see exactly where you are and what you might be doing.

To make a FaceTime call, follow these steps:

1. Tap the **FaceTime** app on the Home Screen. The **FaceTime** screen will appear. If you have made or received FaceTime calls in the past, a list of all your previous calls appears, as shown in *Figure 11.4*:

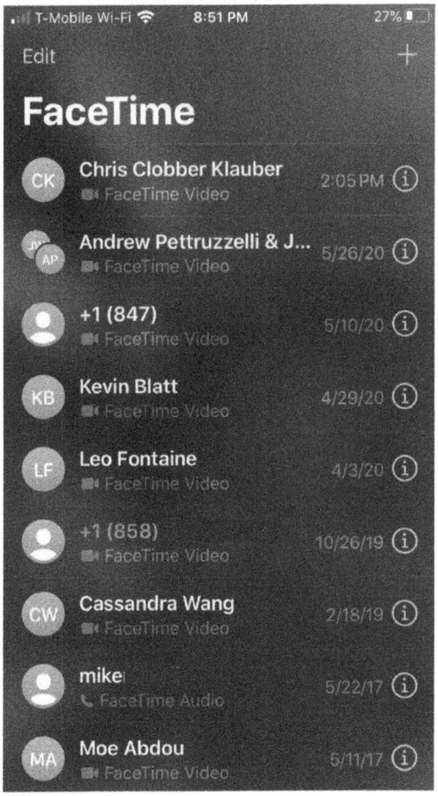

Figure 11.4 – The FaceTime screen

2. Tap a name, email address, or phone number that you want to call. If you want to call someone who's name, email address, or phone number does not appear on the FaceTime list of previous calls, tap the + button in the upper-right corner to display a **New FaceTime** screen, as shown in *Figure 11.5*:

Figure 11.5 – The New FaceTime screen

3. Tap on the **To**: text field and type an email address or phone number that you want to call. If you tap the + icon inside the circle, the **Contacts** app opens, allowing you to choose a name stored in the **Contacts** app.
4. Tap the FaceTime icon displayed under the name of the person you want to call. **Audio** and **Video** buttons appear, as shown in *Figure 11.6*:

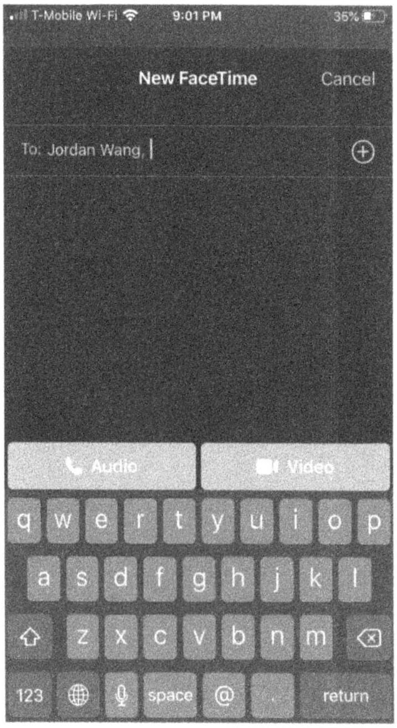

Figure 11.6 – Choosing to make an audio or video call

5. (Optional) Repeat *Step 3* for each additional person you want to join the FaceTime call.
6. Tap the **Audio** or **Video** button.

When you call using FaceTime, each person will see a banner at the top of the screen that they can tap to display an incoming FaceTime screen, as shown in *Figure 11.7*:

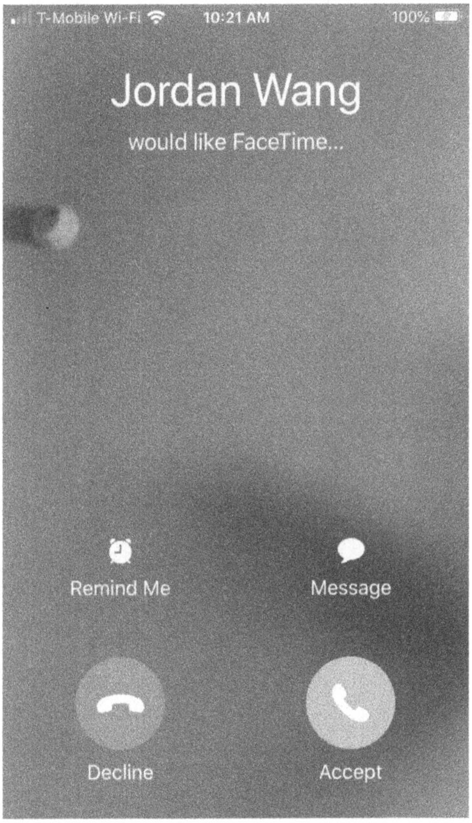

Figure 11.7 – Receiving a FaceTime call request

At this point, each person can tap **Decline** or **Accept**. If someone tries to FaceTime you but you fail to answer because you're busy or just didn't have your iPhone with you at the time the FaceTime call request arrived, a notification appears in the upper-right corner of the FaceTime app on the Home Screen, as shown in *Figure 11.8*:

Figure 11.8 – FaceTime notifications

This notification lets you know not only that someone tried to FaceTime you, but also how many FaceTime requests you may have missed.

Talking in a FaceTime call

Once you connect through FaceTime as a video call, you'll see your own video image, along with video images of all the other callers, as shown in *Figure 11.9*:

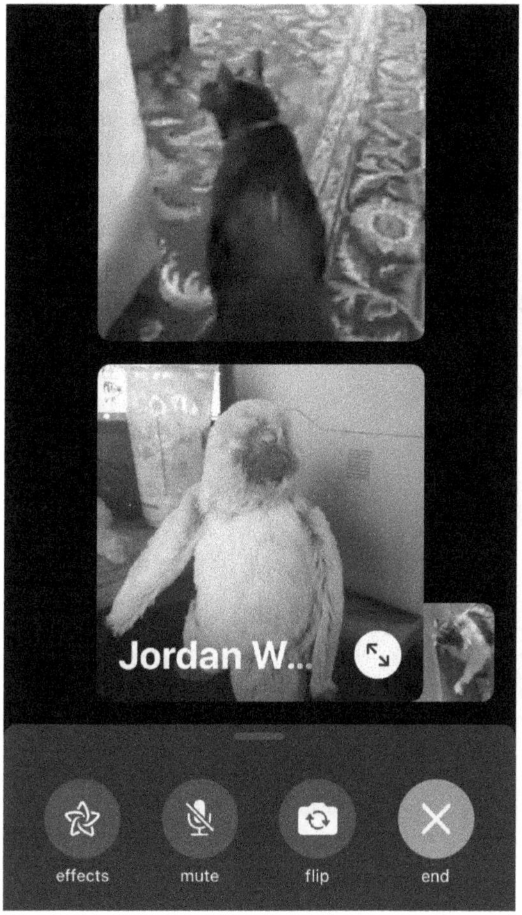

Figure 11.9 – Viewing different callers in FaceTime

Now, let's look at the different options we can use once we are on the call.

Adding multiple people to a FaceTime call

In many cases, FaceTime calls occur between two people. However, you can have up to 32 people involved in a FaceTime call. When you create a FaceTime call, you can simply add as many people as you wish by tapping the + icon when you initiate a FaceTime call (see *Figure 11.6*).

While you're in the middle of a FaceTime call, you can always include more people as well. To add more people during a FaceTime call, follow these steps:

1. Swipe up from the horizontal handle above the **mute** and **flip** icons (see *Figure 11.9*). The entire screen displays FaceTime options, as shown in *Figure 11.10*:

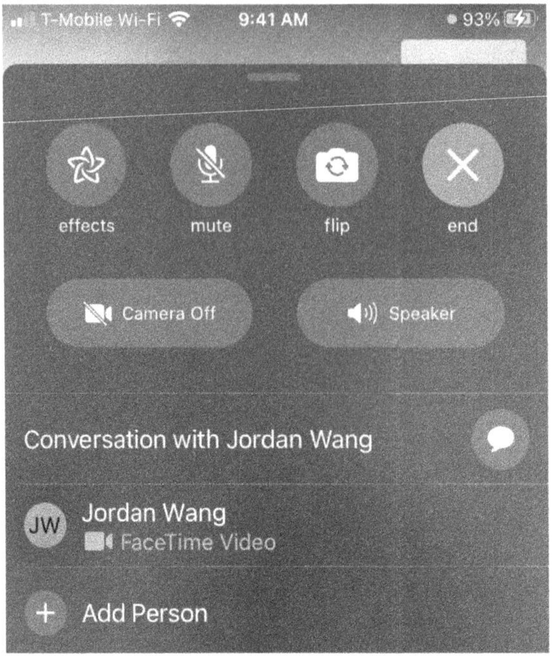

Figure 11.10 – Viewing different callers in FaceTime

2. Tap the + **Add Person** button. An **Add Person** screen appears (see *Figure 11.5*).
3. Repeat *Step 2* for each additional person you want to add to the FaceTime call, up to a maximum of 32 people.

Having multiple people on a FaceTime call can be fun to share ideas, but remember that everyone needs a fast cellular or Wi-Fi connection to make the FaceTime call work. Once you start talking to one or more people, you might want to add different effects to your image for fun.

Using visual effect filters in FaceTime

Visual effect filters let you alter the picture of the person you're talking to through FaceTime. That way, you can alter their video image to make it easier to see them or just to get creative and make them look odd or funny.

You can modify your own image in different ways by tapping any of the following buttons at the bottom of a FaceTime screen:

- **Effects**: Offers different visual effects for your own video image
- **Mute**: Toggles between turning your microphone on or off
- **Flip**: Toggles between the front-facing or back-facing camera
- **End**: Ends a FaceTime call

When you modify your own image, other people on the FaceTime call will see your changes as well. This lets you create humorous effects or allows you to highlight something important to others.

To apply a visual effect filter during a FaceTime call, follow these steps:

1. Tap the **effects** button on the FaceTime screen. Buttons representing different types of effects appear as the **effects** button appears highlighted, as shown in *Figure 11.11*:

Figure 11.11 – Various effects options

2. Tap the **Filter button** on the far left to see a list of different filters you can apply to the currently displayed image. Then, scroll left or right until you find a filter you like, as shown in *Figure 11.12*:

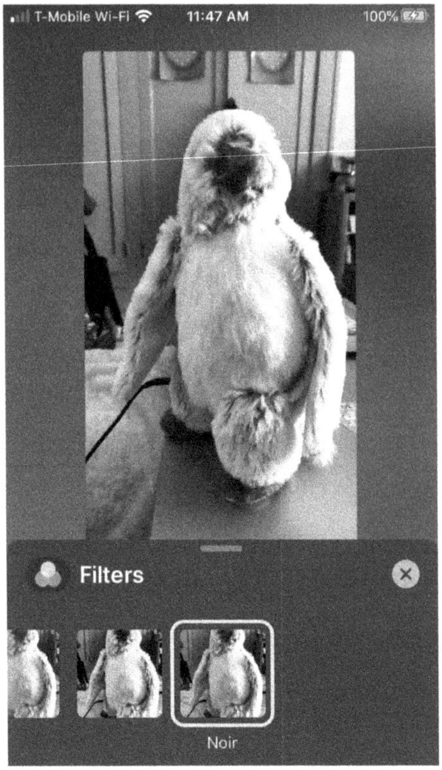

Figure 11.12 – Choosing a filter

3. Tap the close (**X**) icon in the upper-right corner of the **Filters** area to exit out of the filters options and the list of visual effect option buttons appears again (see *Figure 11.11*).

Filters can alter the visual appearance of images, but you may want to add text to an image so you can identify items for other people to see.

Adding text to a FaceTime image

Text can appear on your image, which can be handy if you point your camera at something and type text to identify it, such as while showing others how to repair an appliance. Then, text can identify the name of the parts others are seeing.

To add text to your image during a FaceTime call, follow these steps:

1. Tap the **effects** button on the FaceTime screen. Buttons representing different types of effects appear as the **effects** button appears highlighted (see *Figure 11.11*).
2. Tap the **Text** button (which appears as the second button from the left). A list of different text styles appears at the bottom of the screen, as shown in *Figure 11.13*:

Figure 11.13 – Choosing a variety of text styles

3. Tap a text style. The word **Text** appears on the image and a virtual keyboard appears at the bottom of the screen, as shown in *Figure 11.14*:

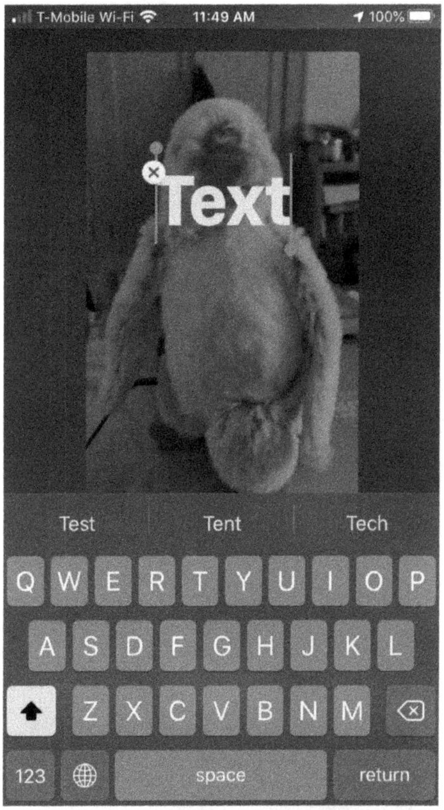

Figure 11.14 – Creating text on an image

4. Type any text you wish. If you want to delete text, tap the close (**x**) icon that appears in the upper-left corner of the text.
5. Tap the close (**x**) icon in the upper-right corner of the Text area to exit out of the text options. The list of visual effect option buttons appears again (see *Figure 11.11*).

Text can help describe items in an image, but sometimes you may just want to add silly pictures to an image for fun.

Adding shapes to a FaceTime image

FaceTime provides a collection of silly images and shapes you can put on an image. These provide simple animation that can highlight certain parts of an image for others to see.

To add a shape to a FaceTime image, follow these steps:

1. Tap the **effects** button on the FaceTime screen. Buttons representing different types of effects appear as the **effects** button appears highlighted (see *Figure 11.11*).
2. Tap the **Shapes** button (which appears as the third button from the left). A list of different shapes appears at the bottom of the screen.
3. Double-tap on a shape to place it on the image, as shown in *Figure 11.15*. If you want to delete a shape, tap the close (**x**) icon that appears in the upper-left corner of the shape:

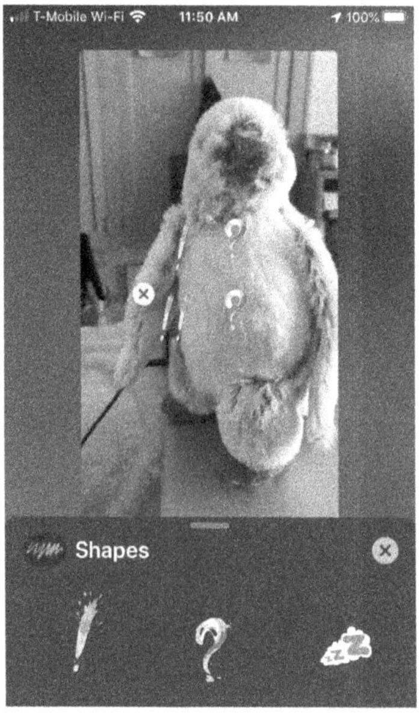

Figure 11.15 – Adding a shape to an image

4. Tap the close (**x**) icon in the upper-right corner of the **Shapes** area to exit out of the shapes options. The list of visual effect option buttons appears again (see *Figure 11.11*).

Similar to shapes are activities, which provide animated images such as miniature cartoons.

Adding activities to a FaceTime image

Activities give you yet another way to spice up images with tiny cartoons. To add an activity to a FaceTime image, follow these steps:

1. Tap the **effects** button on the FaceTime screen. Buttons representing different types of effects appear as the **effects** button appears highlighted (see *Figure 11.11*).
2. Tap the **Fitness** button (which appears as the fourth button from the left). A list of different activities will appear at the bottom of the screen.
3. Double-tap on an activity to place it on the image, as shown in *Figure 11.16*. If you want to delete an activity, tap the close (**x**) icon that appears in the upper-left corner:

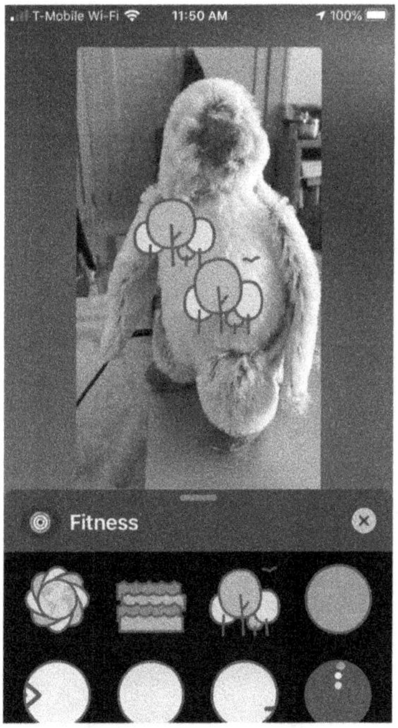

Figure 11.16 – Adding an activity to a FaceTime image

4. Tap the close (**x**) icon in the upper-right corner of the activities area to exit out of the activity options. The list of visual effect option buttons appears again (see *Figure 11.11*).

Yet another way to create interesting visual effects is to add memojis, which are little cartoon faces.

Adding memojis to a FaceTime image

Memojis represent silly cartoon faces of animals such as a cow, mouse, or shark. Adding memojis are mostly for humorous and entertainment purposes.

To add a memoji to a FaceTime image, follow these steps:

1. Tap the **effects** button on the FaceTime screen. Buttons representing different types of effects appear as the **effects** button appears highlighted (see *Figure 11.11*).
2. Tap the **Memoji** button (which appears as the fifth button from the left). A list of different memojis appears at the bottom of the screen.
3. Double-tap on a memoji to place it on the image, as shown in *Figure 11.17*. If you want to delete a memoji, tap the close (**x**) icon that appears in the upper-left corner:

Figure 11.17 – Adding a memoji to a FaceTime image

4. Tap the close (**x**) icon in the upper-right corner of the memoji area to exit out of the memoji options. The list of visual effect option buttons appears again (see *Figure 11.11*).

A final way to spice up a FaceTime image is to add emojis, which are animated images of common objects, such as stars, hearts, or light bulbs.

Adding emojis to a FaceTime image

An emoji represents a simple, animated image that you can place in a FaceTime image for humorous or decorative purposes, or to express emotions in a visual manner.

To add an emoji to a FaceTime image, follow these steps:

1. Tap the **effects** button on the FaceTime screen. Buttons representing different types of effects appear as the **effects** button appears highlighted (see *Figure 11.11*).
2. Tap the **Emoji** button (which appears as the sixth button from the left). A list of different emojis appears at the bottom of the screen.
3. Double-tap on an emoji to place it on the image, as shown in *Figure 11.18*. If you want to delete an emoji, tap the close (**x**) icon that appears in the upper-left corner:

Figure 11.18 – Adding an emoji to a FaceTime image

4. Tap the close (**x**) icon in the upper-right corner of the Emoji area to exit out of the emoji options. The list of visual effect option buttons appears again (see *Figure 11.11*).

Emojis, like all visual effects, give you different ways to express yourself while chatting through FaceTime. You can use all, some, or none of these options. For example, you might not want to use any visual effects when chatting in relation to a business call, but you may want to get creative when chatting with a loved one or close friend.

Summary

FaceTime gives you a chance to make visual phone calls, which can be handy for talking and seeing a loved one or helping you show someone an item or scene around you. By connecting to a Wi-Fi network, you can make free phone calls without affecting any monthly data allotment that might restrict how many phone calls you can make.

For entertainment, consider using FaceTime's various visual effects, such as displaying text or animated cartoon images. Such visual effects can make a video call through FaceTime even more entertaining and enjoyable.

FaceTime gives you yet another way to communicate with others with your iPhone, just as long as you only want to talk to people who also have an iPhone, iPad, or Macintosh.

While FaceTime can be a way to entertain yourself with others, you can also turn your iPhone into an ebook reader so that you can entertain yourself wherever you take your iPhone.

12
Reading eBooks

If you've ever traveled by plane or train, you've probably taken a book with you. The problem with printed books is that they're bulky, which means you can only take a handful at the most before they become unwieldy. Even worse, it's far too easy to forget or misplace a book – and then be stuck without it.

Fortunately, you can turn your iPhone into an eBook reader. Not only can you carry hundreds or even thousands of books to read wherever you take your iPhone, but you can read any time you get a chance, such as waiting in line or traveling on a plane or train.

With eBooks, you literally have access to any book in the world that you can read at your convenience from your iPhone. If you prefer to read without looking at text, you can also buy and listen to audiobooks as well.

The topics covered in this chapter are as follows:

- Getting eBooks from Apple's bookstore
- Adding eBooks to the Books app
- Opening an eBook
- Reading an eBook

Getting eBooks from Apple's bookstore

There are two ways to put eBooks on your iPhone. First, you can buy them from Apple's bookstore. When you get eBooks from Apple, those eBooks can be free or cost money.

A second option is to get eBooks from another source and then copy those files into the Books app so you can read them on your iPhone. Two popular types of eBook file formats are **PDF** (**Portable Digital Format**) and **EPUB** (**Electronic Publication**) files that you can either buy or get for free from various third parties on the internet.

Generally speaking, you will need to pay for eBooks such as the latest bestsellers from your favorite authors. However, you can find many free eBooks containing classics such as writings by Mark Twain, Jane Austen, or Charles Dickens. You may also find free eBooks containing useful information that individuals or corporations provide to market their services or products.

First, let's take a look at how to buy eBooks through Apple's bookstore. To access Apple's bookstore, follow these steps:

1. Tap the **Books** app on the Home Screen.
2. Tap the **Book Store** icon at the bottom of the screen. The **Book Store** screen appears, as shown in *Figure 12.1*. (If you want an audio book, tap the **Audiobooks** icon at the bottom of the screen instead.):

Figure 12.1 – The Book Store screen

3. Tap on **Browse Sections**. A list of options will appear, as shown in *Figure 12.2*:

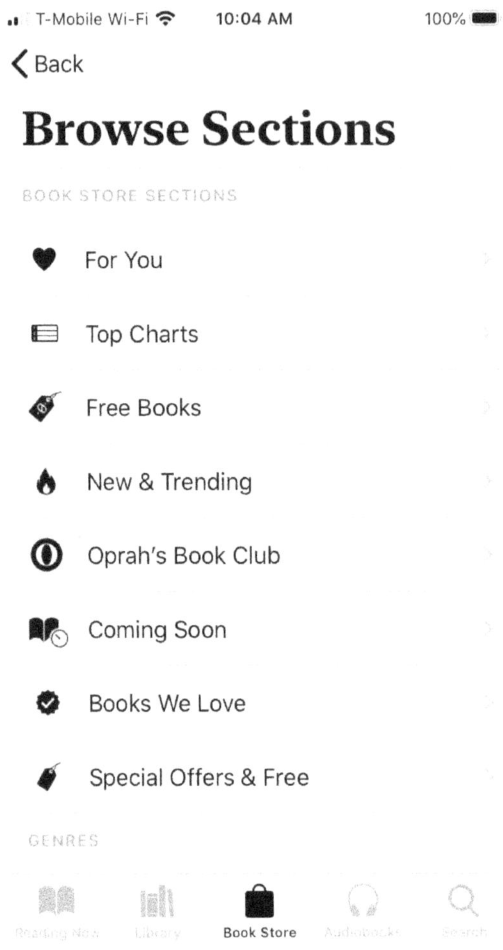

Figure 12.2 – The Book Store screen

4. Tap a category and tap a book that you'd like on your iPhone.

A description of the eBook appears along with a **BUY** button (that lists the price), a **WANT TO READ** button, and a **SAMPLE** button that lets you read a part of the book, as shown in *Figure 12.3*. If an eBook is free, a **GET** button will appear instead of a **BUY** button:

Figure 12.3 – Viewing a single book

5. Tap the **BUY** button to purchase the eBook or tap the **Sample** button to read part of the book.
6. Tap the close (**x**) icon in the upper-right corner of the screen to return to the list of books. You may need to repetitively tap the **Back** button in the upper-left corner of the screen to see previous screens.

When browsing eBooks, you have the option of tapping a **WANT TO READ** button (see *Figure 12.3*). This lets you save a list of eBooks you're interested in so that you don't have to search for it again later.

Once you tap the **WANT TO READ** button, your selected eBook gets stored in the **WANT TO READ** collection. To browse through this list of eBooks that you selected by tapping the **WANT TO READ** button, follow these steps:

1. Tap the **Books** app on the Home Screen. The **Books** screen appears.
2. Tap the **Library** icon at the bottom of the screen. The **Library** screen appears, which shows a list of eBooks stored in your collections, as shown in *Figure 12.4*:

Figure 12.4 – The Library screen

3. Tap **Collections** to view all the different categories available, as shown in *Figure 12.5*:

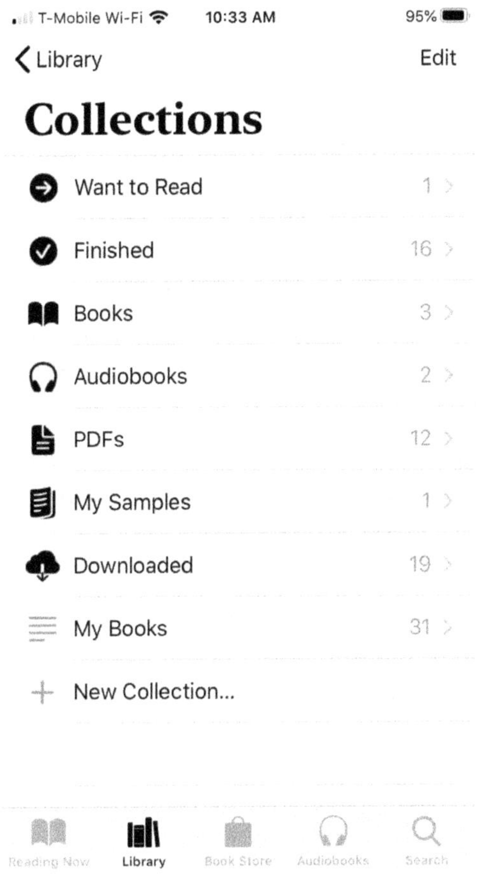

Figure 12.5 – The Collections screen

4. Tap **Want to Read.** A list of eBook samples appears.
5. Tap on the eBook you want to examine.
6. Tap **Edit** in the upper-right corner of the screen when you want to remove an eBook from your **Want to Read** collection.

7. Tap the circle that appears to the left of each eBook you want to remove from your **Want to Read** collection.
8. Tap the Trash icon in the bottom-left corner of the screen. A list of options appears at the bottom of the screen.
9. Tap **Remove from Want to Read**.

Going through Apple's bookstore is the easiest and most convenient way to find eBooks. However, you can find and buy eBooks from third parties on the internet.

Adding eBooks to the Books app

Many companies offer eBooks stored as PDF files that you can download off websites or receive when you sign up for a mailing list. Other eBook sellers may sell eBooks stored in PDF or ePub format.

If you have existing eBooks, you may want to read them on your iPhone using the Books app. That means you'll need to add the eBook to the Books app. If you have an eBook on a Macintosh or iPhone/iPad, you can send that eBook to your iPhone using AirDrop.

Adding eBooks from a Macintosh

AirDrop works between an iPhone and another Apple product such as another iPhone, iPad, or Macintosh computer. The basic step is to send an eBook file to your iPhone and then load that eBook file into the Books app.

To send an eBook by AirDrop from a Macintosh, follow these steps:

1. Unlock your iPhone and place it near the Macintosh that contains the eBook file you want to send.
2. Click the Finder icon on the Macintosh and then choose **Go | AirDrop**. The **AirDrop** window appears and displays your iPhone's icon, as shown in *Figure 12.6*:

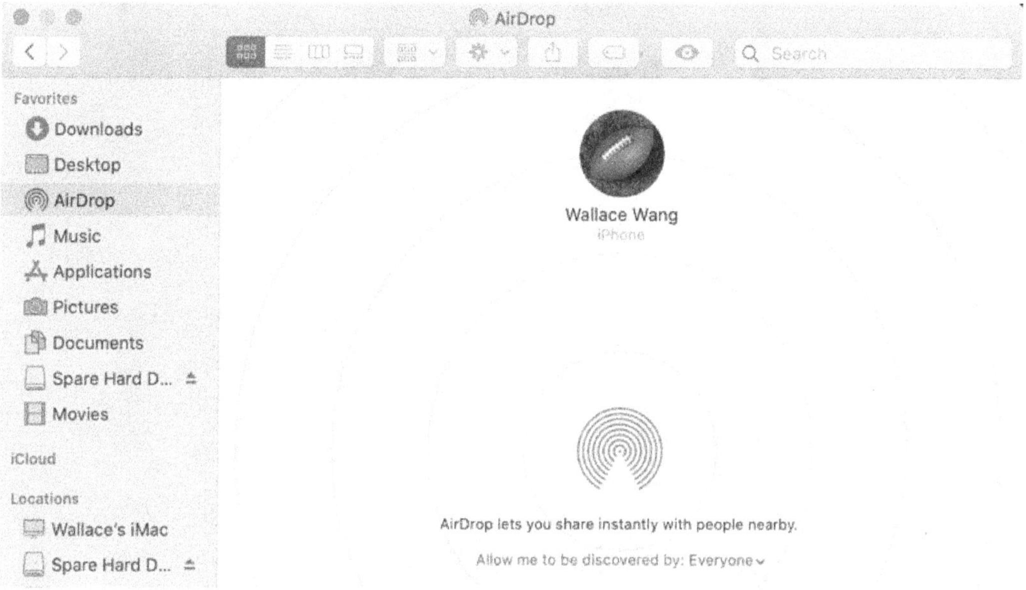

Figure 12.6 – The AirDrop window on a Macintosh

3. Choose **File** | **New Finder Window** from the **Finder** menu and drag the eBook file over the iPhone icon in the AirDrop window. A dialog appears on the iPhone, as shown in *Figure 12.7*:

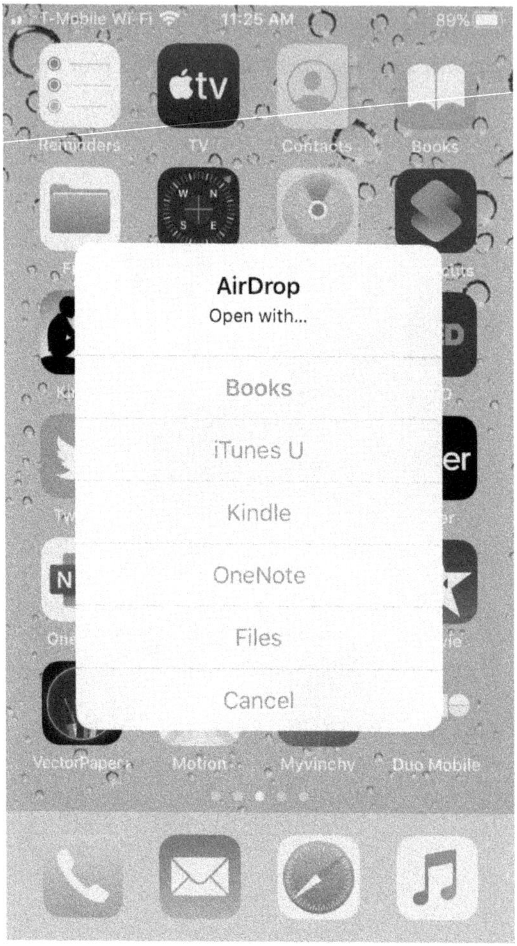

Figure 12.7 – Choosing how to load an eBook file on an iPhone

4. Tap **Books**. Your iPhone loads the sent eBook file into the **Books** app.

If you have an eBook stored on an iPhone or iPad, you can also send it to your iPhone. The only limitation is that this eBook must not be a paid eBook, but an eBook file from a third party such as a PDF or ePub file.

Adding eBooks from an iPhone/iPad

Oftentimes, a person might have a free eBook on their iPhone/iPad that they want to share with you using AirDrop. To send an eBook by AirDrop from another iPhone or iPad, follow these steps:

1. Unlock your iPhone and place it near the iPhone or iPad that contains the eBook file you want to send.
2. Open the **Books** app on the iPhone or iPad that contains the eBook you want to share.
3. Tap the Share icon. A menu will appear.
4. Tap **AirDrop**. When a window appears, listing all devices available to accept AirDrop items, tap your iPhone's icon, as shown in *Figure 12.8*. A dialog appears on the iPhone (see *Figure 12.7*):

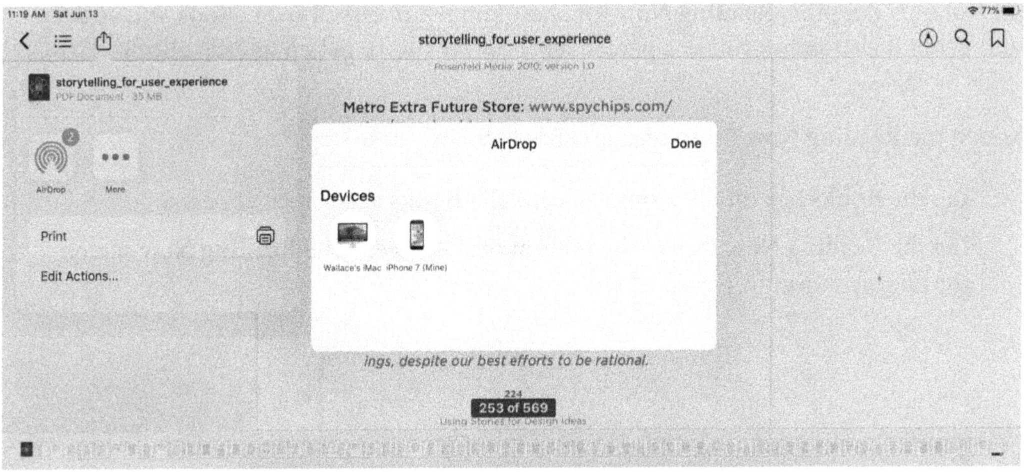

Figure 12.8 – Sending an eBook from an iPad

5. Tap **Books**. Your iPhone loads the sent eBook file into the **Books** app.

Once you've loaded an eBook into the **Books** app, whether through the Apple bookstore or sent from another device, you need to know how to read that eBook.

Opening an eBook

Once you've stored an eBook in the **Books** app on your iPhone, you can open those eBooks at any time. The **Books** app provides three ways to find an eBook to open:

- **Reading Now**: Displays the most recent eBooks you've read
- **Library**: Lets you access all eBooks stored in the **Books** app
- **Search**: Lets you search for a specific eBook title stored in the **Books** app

Choosing from the Reading Now list

Many people may have several eBooks stored in the **Books** app and switch between two or more eBooks. Because of this, the **Reading Now** list displays the most recent eBooks you've opened since it's likely you'll want to return to them later.

So, any time you want to read an eBook you've read recently, check the **Reading Now** list first. Not only does this **Reading Now** list show you the covers of each eBook you've been reading, but it also shows you as a percentage how far you've gotten in each eBook, such as 83% or 45%.

To open the **Reading Now** list to read an eBook, follow these steps:

1. Tap the **Books** app on the Home Screen. The **Books** app screen appears.
2. Tap the **Reading Now** icon at the bottom of the screen. The **Reading Now** screen appears, as shown in *Figure 12.9*:

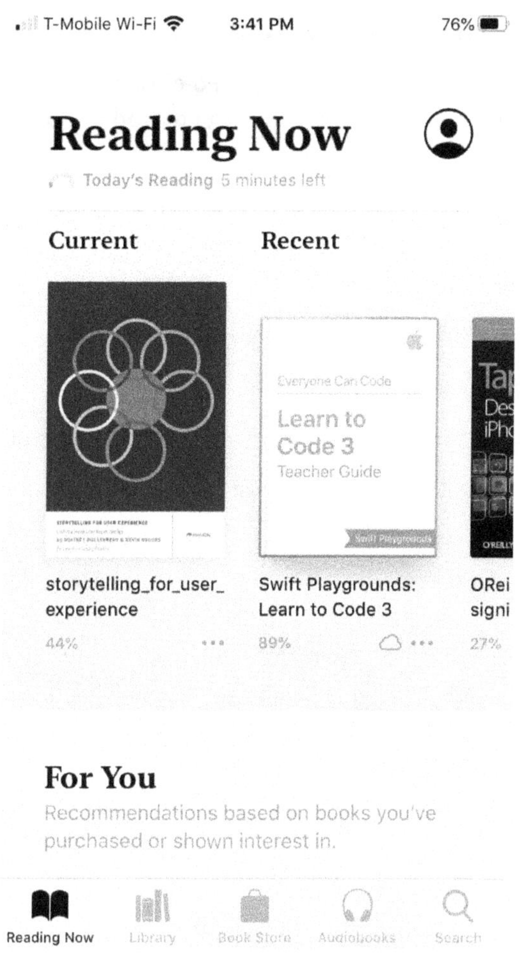

Figure 12.9 – The Reading Now list

3. Scroll left and right to view all your most recently opened eBooks.
4. Tap the eBook you want to read.

The **Reading Now** list shows you the most recently opened eBooks you've opened, but if you want to open a new eBook or an eBook you haven't read in a long time, you need to browse your entire eBook library instead.

Choosing from your eBook library

The **Reading Now** list only shows all recently opened eBooks. However, you may also want to browse through your entire eBook collection to find eBooks you haven't yet started, or haven't opened in a long time.

The **Books** app divides your eBook library into separate categories called **Collections**, as shown in *Figure 12.10*. Each collection contains a different subset of your entire eBook library, including the following:

- **Finished**: eBooks you've read all the way through
- **PDFs**: eBooks stored only in PDF file format
- **My Samples**: Reading samples retrieved from Apple's bookstore
- The remainder of the collections are shown in *Figure 12.10*:

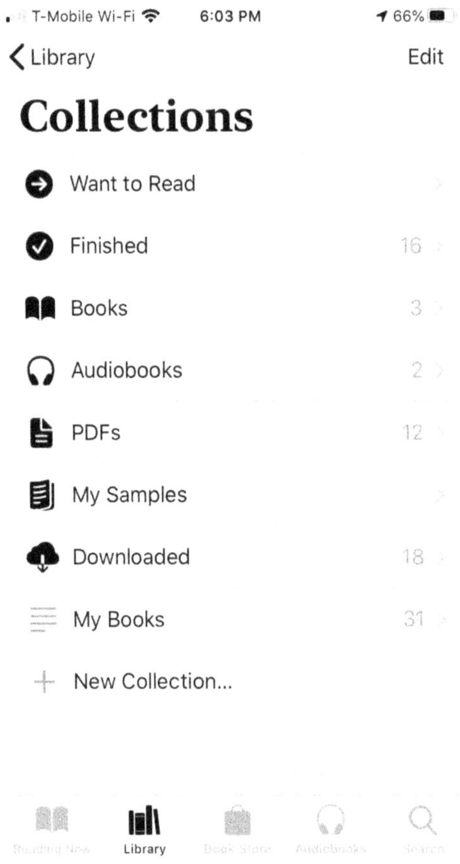

Figure 12.10 – An eBook library consists of multiple collections

To choose an eBook from your entire collection of eBooks, follow these steps:

1. Tap the **Books** app on the Home Screen. The **Books** app screen appears.
2. Tap the **Library** icon. The **Collections** screen will appear (see *Figure 12.10*).
3. Tap on a collection category such as **PDFs** or **Finished**.
4. Tap on the eBook you want to read.

The library lets you browse through your entire eBook list, but if you have many eBooks, this can be cumbersome. For a faster alternative, try searching for a specific eBook title.

Searching for an eBook title

Browsing through a long list of eBooks can be fine when you aren't sure what you want to read and just want to browse to find something interesting. However, if you know what you want, then browsing through a long list of eBooks can be tedious.

To find a specific eBook faster, search for its title instead. By searching, you can find exactly what you want without wasting a lot of time.

To search for an eBook, follow these steps:

1. Tap the **Books** app on the Home Screen. The **Books** app screen appears.
2. Tap on the **Search** icon at the bottom of the screen.

3. Type all or part of a word or phrase that you want to find. As you type, a list of possible matches appears, as shown in *Figure 12.11*:

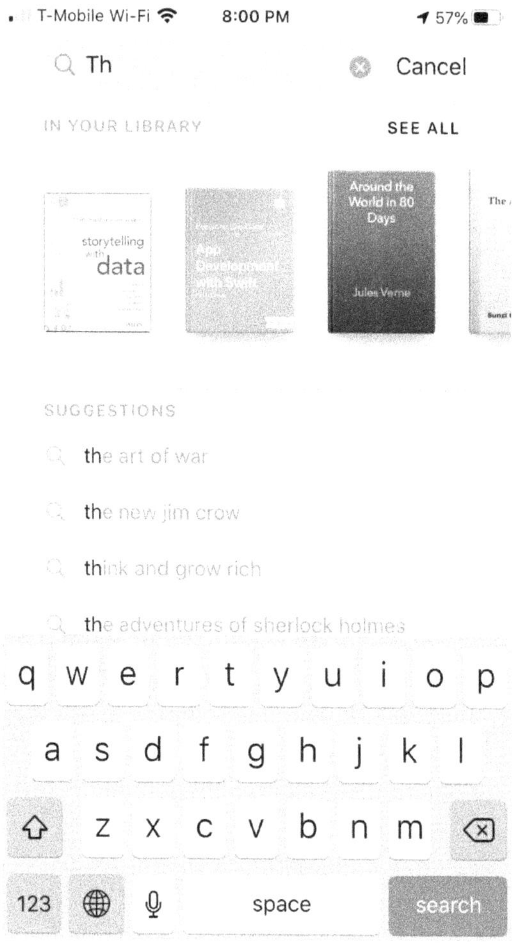

Figure 12.11 – Searching for an eBook

4. Tap the eBook you want to read.

No matter how you choose to select and open an eBook, eventually you'll need to know how to read it. Reading an eBook is similar to reading a printed book, but there are some unique navigation controls you need to know in order to take full advantage of the iPhone's touchscreen for turning the pages of an eBook.

Reading an eBook

With a printed book, it's easy to turn pages individually or jump to another part of the book by just opening it up to another page. With an eBook, navigating from one part to another is different because an eBook displays pages that fill the entire screen. While you can see an entire page, it's much harder to see different parts of an eBook without a little bit of practice.

The **Books** app can store and display two kinds of eBooks: PDFs and ePub. Depending on which format your eBook is stored in, navigating between pages is slightly different.

Regardless of which file format your eBook might be in, the four basic icons available in both ePub and PDF files are shown in *Figure 12.12*:

- **Close**: Closes the book and takes you back to your eBook library
- **Table of contents**: Displays a table of contents for the entire eBook
- **Search**: Lets you type a word or phrase to find in the eBook
- **Bookmark**: Lets you mark a page to make it easy to return to later:

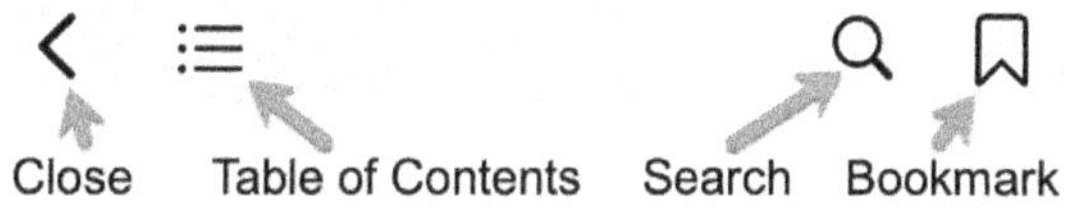

Figure 12.12 – Common eBook navigation controls

By learning to navigate through an eBook, you can jump to the part you want to read without scrolling through multiple pages.

Closing an eBook

You can only view one eBook at a time, although you can have several eBooks open at once. When you're done with one eBook, you need to close it so you can open another eBook. To see how to close an eBook, follow these steps:

1. Tap the **Books** app on the Home Screen.
2. Tap an eBook to open it. You may need to tap a page to view the Close icon in the upper-left corner of the screen.
3. Tap on the Close icon. Your chosen eBook closes and takes you back to the **Reading Now** list of eBooks.

Closing an eBook simply lets you open another one. You do not need to close an eBook if you just want to switch to another app.

Viewing a table of contents

The table of contents lets you view all the chapter headings in an eBook so you can jump to a specific chapter. Depending on whether you're reading an ePub or PDF file, the table of contents looks different.

To use the table of contents, follow these steps:

1. Open an eBook. You may need to tap the screen to make the Table of Contents icon appear at the top of the screen.
2. Tap the Table of Contents icon (see *Figure 12.12*). In an ePub file, the table of contents lists the eBook chapter headings, as shown in *Figure 12.13*:

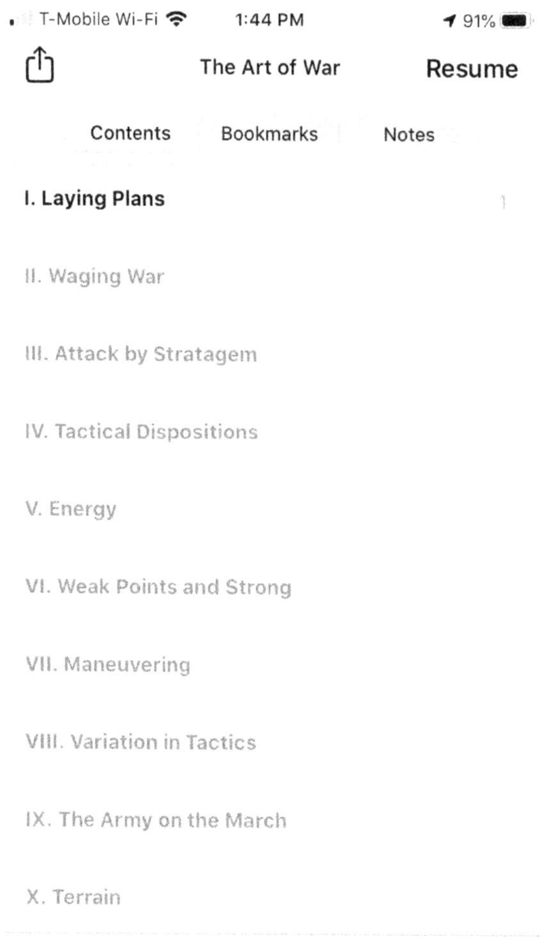

Figure 12.13 – The table of contents in an ePub file

3. In a PDF file, the table of contents displays individual pages, as shown in *Figure 12.14*:

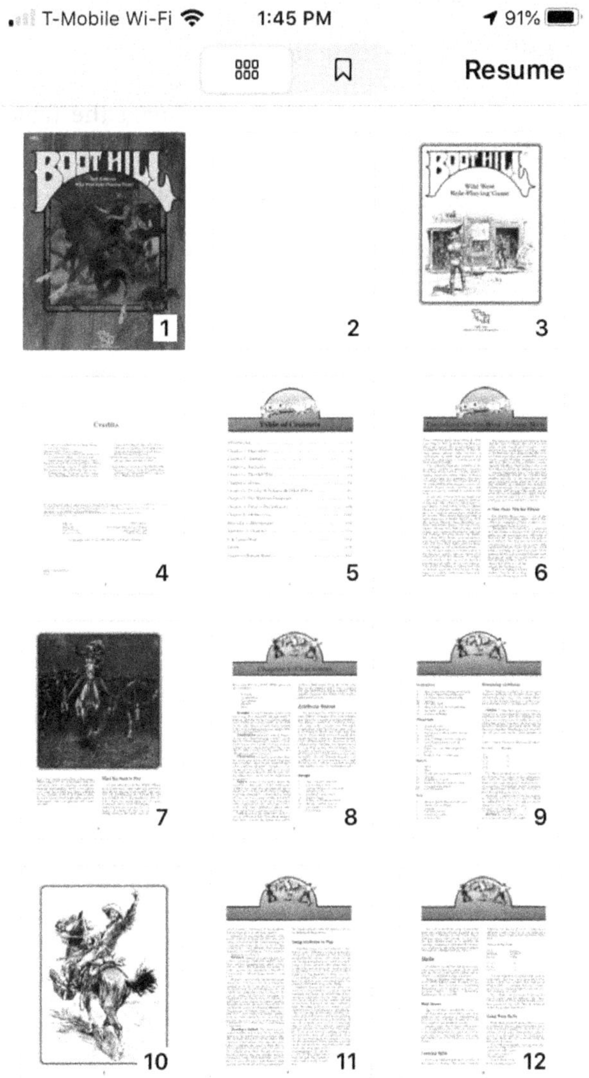

Figure 12.14 – The table of contents in a PDF file

4. Tap **Resume** to return to the page you were reading or tap on a chapter heading (ePub) or page (PDF) to open that new page.

The table of contents can help you jump from one part of an eBook to another, but it can be cumbersome. As a faster alternative, consider searching for specific text instead.

Searching an eBook

Searching lets you look for a word or phrase in an eBook. This way, you can find text without taking time to search for it yourself.

To search for a text in an eBook, follow these steps:

1. Open an eBook. You may need to tap the screen to make the Table of Contents icon appear at the top of the screen.
2. Tap the Search icon (see *Figure 12.12*). A text field will appear at the top of the screen.
3. Type a word or phrase. As you type, a list of matches appears, as shown in *Figure 12.15*:

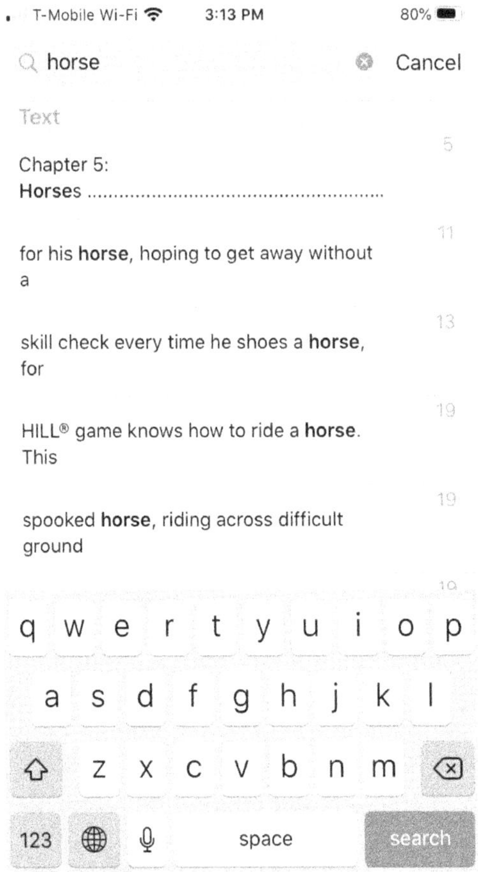

Figure 12.15 – Matching pages appear as you type

4. Tap on a page to jump to that page.

Searching can be fine when you want to find specific text, but what if you just want to find a certain page? In this case, it's easier to use a bookmark.

Bookmarking a page

You'll rarely read an entire eBook from start to finish in one sitting. Instead, you'll likely read some pages, stop, and then come back to read where you left off. To help you mark where you left off, you can place a bookmark.

You can place multiple bookmarks in an eBook and then choose which bookmark to jump to when you want to read that particular page.

To bookmark a page in an eBook, follow these steps:

1. Open an eBook and navigate to the page you want to bookmark.
2. Tap the Bookmark icon (see *Figure 12.12*). (You may need to tap the page first to make the Bookmark icon appear.) The Bookmark icon turns red to let you know you've placed a bookmark.

After you've placed a bookmark, you can look for that bookmark later. The procedure for looking for bookmarks differs depending on whether you're using an ePub file or a PDF file.

To look for bookmarks in an ePub file, follow these steps:

1. Open an ePub eBook and tap the Table of Contents icon.
2. Tap the **Bookmarks** tab. A list of bookmarks appears, as shown in *Figure 12.16*. If you swipe left on any bookmark, you can open a **Delete** button, allowing you to delete that bookmark:

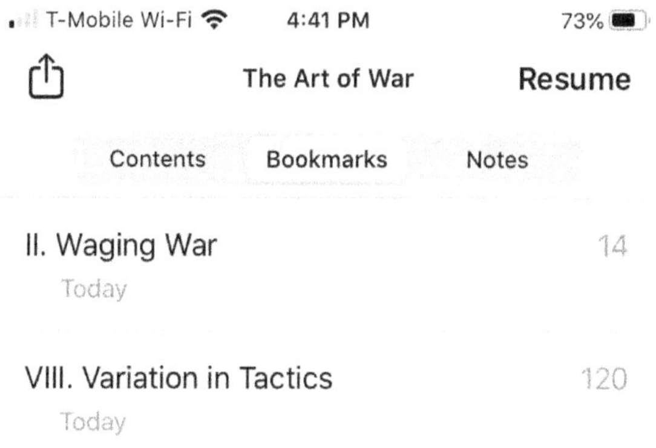

Figure 12.16 – Viewing bookmarks in an ePub file

3. Tap a bookmarked page to jump to that page. The red bookmark icon appears in the upper-right corner of the screen.
4. (Optional) Tap the red bookmark icon to remove the bookmark. The Bookmark icon should now appear white.

If you created a bookmark in a PDF file, follow these steps to view bookmarks:

1. Open a PDF eBook and tap the Table of Contents icon.
2. Tap on the **Bookmarks** tab. All bookmarked pages will appear, as shown in *Figure 12.17*:

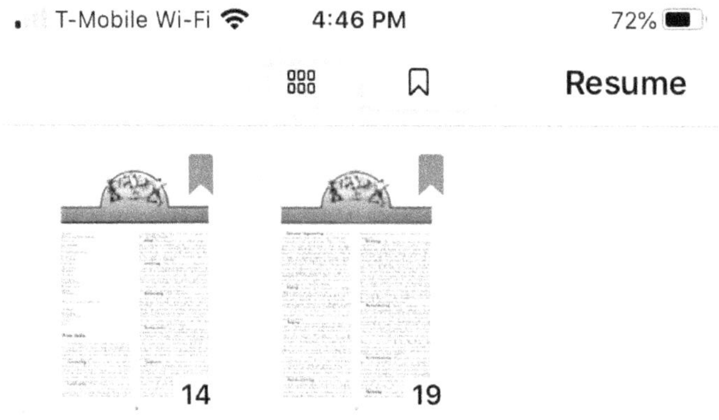

Figure 12.17 – Viewing bookmarks in a PDF file

3. Tap the bookmarked page you want to read. Your chosen page appears on the screen.
4. (Optional) Tap the red bookmark icon to remove the bookmark. The Bookmark icon should now appear white.

Depending on whether you open an ePub or PDF eBook, you'll have different options for reading. An ePub eBook lets you increase and decrease the text size to make it easier to read. A PDF eBook lets you mark up an eBook with color, such as highlighting text.

Changing text size in an ePub eBook

When you're reading an ePub eBook, you have the option of changing the size of text so that you can read easily or to display more text on the screen. Some of the options you can change to make reading easier include the following:

- Screen brightness
- Font size
- Font
- Background color
- How the eBook scrolls pages horizontally (default) or vertically

To change the text size of an ePub eBook, follow these steps:

1. Open an ePub eBook and navigate to any page.
2. Tap the Text Size icon (see *Figure 12.12*). A menu of options appears, as shown in *Figure 12.18*:

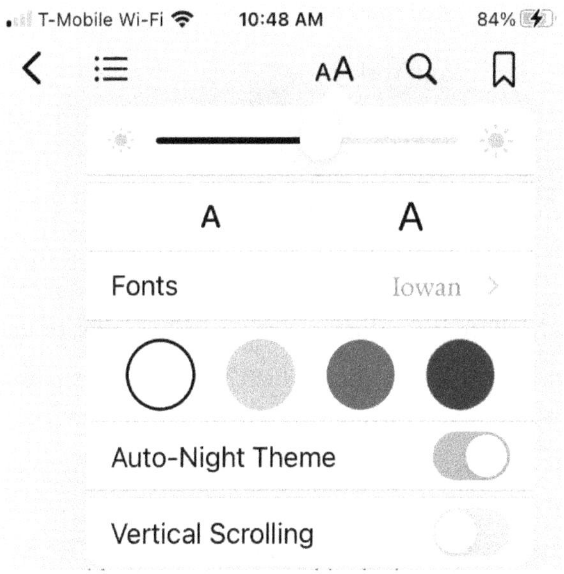

Figure 12.18 – Modifying text in an ePub eBook

3. (Optional) Drag the screen brightness slider left or right.
4. (Optional) Tap on the small or large **A** icons that decrease or increase the font size.
5. (Optional) Tap on **Fonts**. A list of available fonts appears, as shown in *Figure 12.19*. Choose a font and then tap the **Back** button in the upper-left corner of the screen:

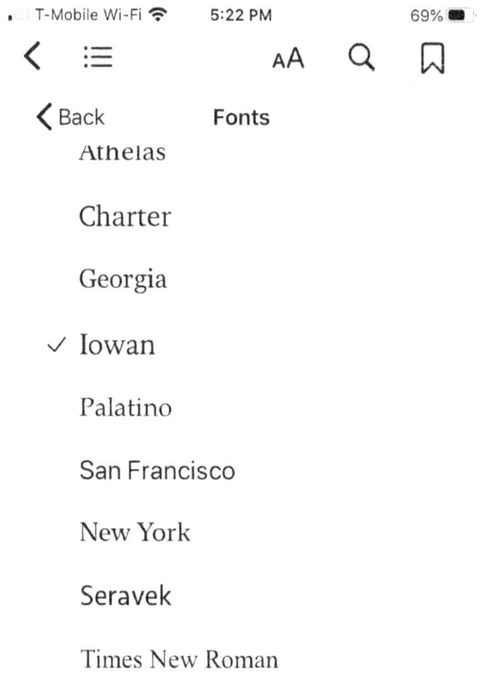

Figure 12.19 – Choosing a new font

6. (Optional) Tap a background color such as white, tan, gray, or black.
7. (Optional) Tap the **Auto-Night Theme** switch if you want the **Books** app to change the background automatically depending on the time of day.
8. (Optional) Tap the **Vertical Scrolling** switch to toggle between scrolling texts horizontally or vertically.
9. Tap away from the menu to make it go away.

Reading an ePub eBook gives you options for making text easier to read. If you want to read an eBook in low lighting, the **Auto-Night Theme** switch can make text easier to read without a bright screen that might distract others, such as someone sleeping next to you.

Besides making eBooks easier to read, you might also want to take notes that you can save and share with others.

Taking notes in an ePub eBook

Oftentimes, when you're reading, you may want to jot down notes or save passages of text. With a paper book, you can scribble in the margins or photocopy a page. With an ePub eBook, you can also take notes.

To take notes in an ePub eBook, follow these steps:

1. Open an ePub eBook and navigate to any page.
2. Tap and press a word to select it and then drag the start and end markers to select more or less text.
3. Tap your selected text to display a menu, as shown in *Figure 12.20*:

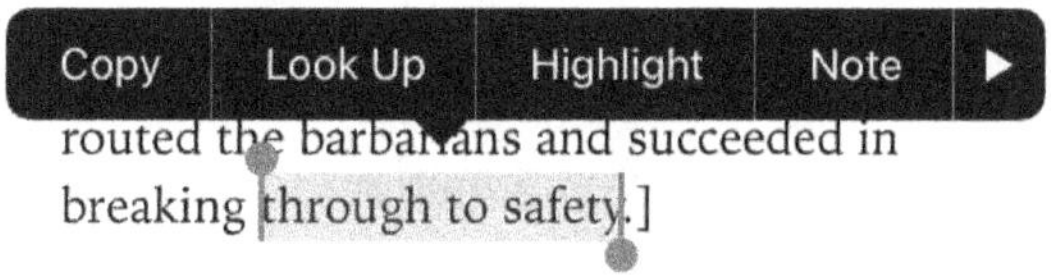

Figure 12.20 – Tapping selected text displays a menu

4. Tap **Note**. The Notes screen appears, as shown in *Figure 12.21*:

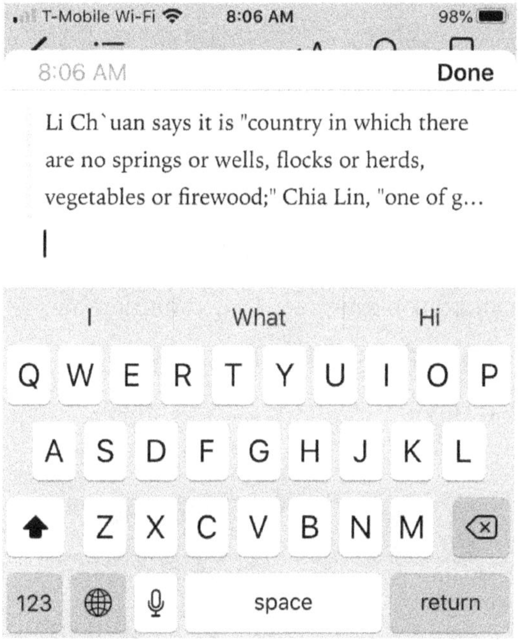

Figure 12.21 – The Notes screen

5. Type some text for your note and tap **Done** in the upper-right corner of the screen.

Once you've saved a note, you can always view or delete that note later. To open a note, follow these steps:

1. Open an ePub eBook, navigate to any page, and tap the page to display the Table of Contents icon at the top of the screen.
2. Tap the Table of Contents icon and then tap **Notes**. A list of notes will appear.
3. Tap the note to jump to that note in the eBook. If you swipe on a note, you will see a Delete icon, allowing you to delete that note if you wish.

Jotting down notes about text can be handy, but sometimes you may just want to highlight passages in an eBook to emphasize what's important to you.

Highlighting in an ePub eBook

Many people like highlighting text with colored markers to signify important text. In an ePub eBook, you can mimic this using a red underline or different colors.

To highlight text in an ePub eBook, follow these steps:

1. Open an ePub eBook and navigate to any page.
2. Tap and press a word to select it and then drag the start and end markers to select more or less text.
3. Tap your selected text to display a menu (see *Figure 12.20*).
4. Tap **Highlight**. A menu of icons appears, as shown in *Figure 12.22*:

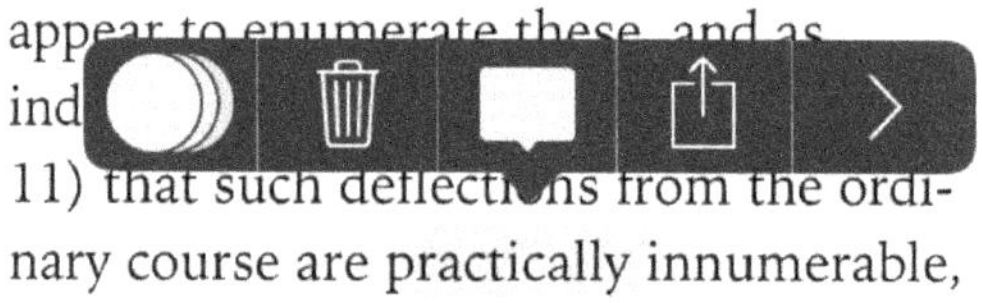

Figure 12.22 – A menu of highlight options

5. Tap the colored circles on the far left. A menu of highlight colors appears, as shown in *Figure 12.23*:

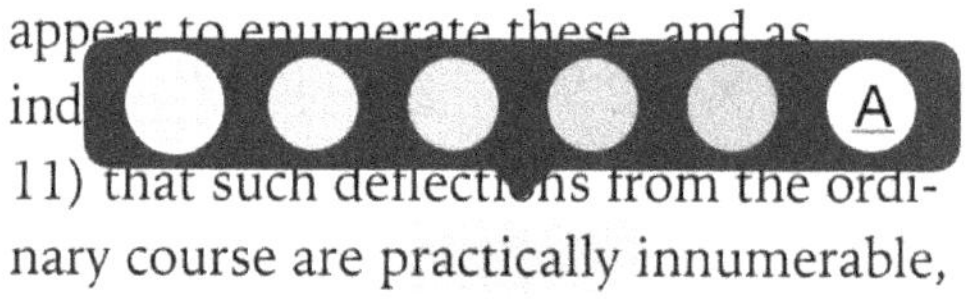

Figure 12.23 – A menu of highlight colors

6. Tap a color to highlight your selected text.

Once you've highlighted text, you can always change the color or remove the highlighting altogether. To delete or change the highlighted text, follow these steps:

1. Open an ePub eBook and navigate to any page.
2. Tap the highlighted text. A menu will appear (see *Figure 12.22*).
3. Tap the Trash icon to remove highlighting or tap the colored circles on the far left and then tap a different highlighting color.

One huge advantage of ePub eBooks is that you can highlight text and take notes. With a PDF eBook, your options are much more limited, but you can still highlight passages.

Reading a PDF eBook

When you're reading a PDF eBook, you have the option of changing the size of the page or marking up pages with a virtual pen. This lets you highlight or mark up text.

To read a PDF eBook, follow these steps:

1. Open a PDF eBook, navigate to any page, and tap the page to display icons at the top of the screen, as shown in *Figure 12.24*:

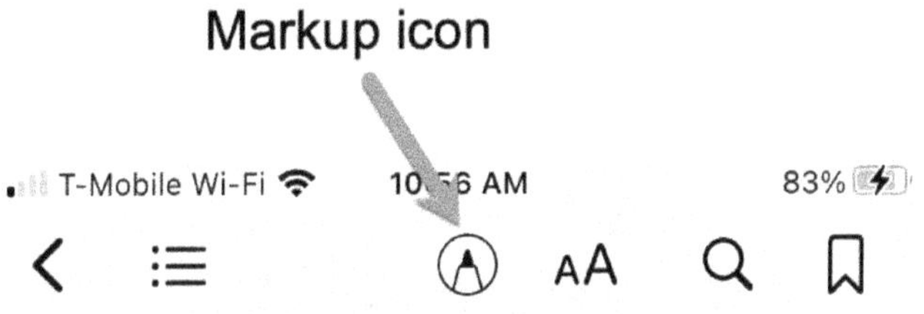

Figure 12.24 – Icons at the top of a PDF eBook

2. Tap on the Markup icon. Menus appear at the top and bottom of the screen, as shown in *Figure 12.25*:

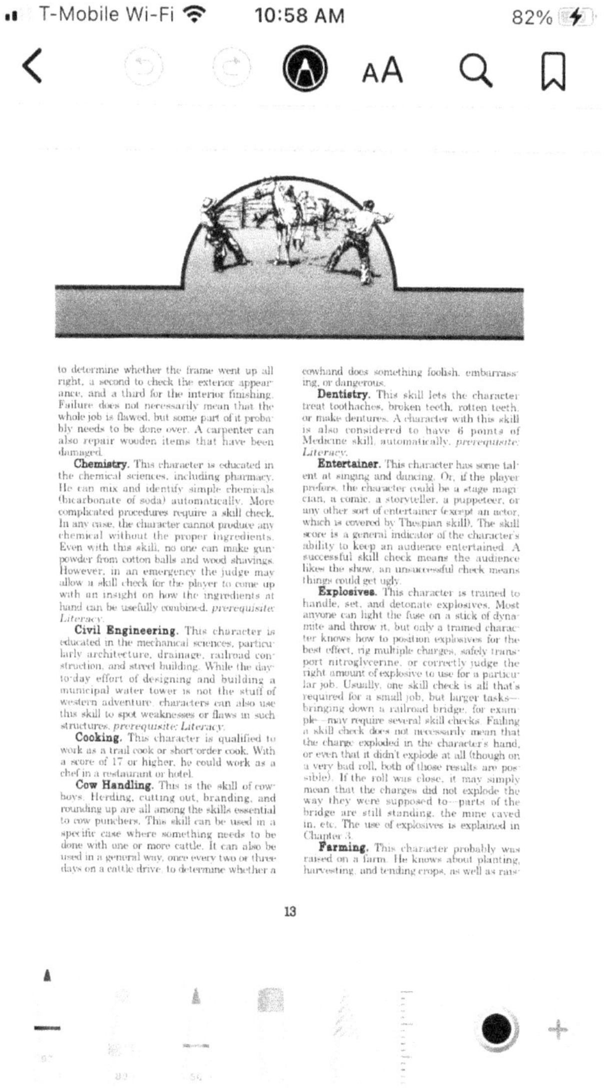

Figure 12.25 – Top and bottom markup menus in a PDF eBook

3. Tap a pen type at the bottom of the screen and slide your finger across the screen to mark up any text.
4. Tap the undo/redo icons at the top of the screen if you made a mistake.
5. Tap the Markup icon at the top of the screen when you're done.

Marking up a PDF eBook is one way to highlight important passages that you'll want to preserve. To make text easier to read, use a pinch gesture to shrink or expand text.

Summary

The Books app ensures that no matter where you go with your iPhone, you'll always have something to read. While the Books app can display both ePub and PDF files, ePub files offer more flexibility in helping you read and jot down notes.

Take time to load some eBooks on your iPhone so you'll never be caught without something to read. Although reading printed books may feel more natural, the more you read eBooks, the easier it will get. Over time, you'll appreciate the advantage of having available dozens or even hundreds of eBooks without carrying bulky books that you might lose.

In the next chapter, you'll learn about storing important contacts. That way, you'll always be able to contact the people you need to reach at any given time.

13
Storing Contact Information

Whether you're at work, in school, or just enjoying your life, you'll likely run into people you'll want to contact in the future. In the old days, you might exchange business cards or phone numbers on a piece of paper, but it's far simpler and more accurate to store someone's name and contact information in your iPhone instead.

Not only can your iPhone keep track of all the important names, phone numbers, and email addresses you need, but your iPhone will also let you call, text, FaceTime, or email someone as well. With your iPhone, you can store information about friends, relatives, and co-workers that you can easily share with others as well.

The topics covered in this chapter are as follows:

- Storing contact information
- Searching for a name
- Communicating through the **Contacts** app
- Combining duplicate contacts
- Identifying special people
- Sharing contacts

- Deleting contacts
- Creating emergency contacts

Storing contact information

The **Contacts** app is a simple database where you can store as much information as you need about each person. At the very least, you need to store someone's first and last name, along with one way to contact that person, such as a mailing address, phone number, or email address.

Once you store a person's name and contact information, you can optionally store any additional information you wish, such as the company where they work, their birthday, their favorite foods, the names of their children, or notes about their personality, which might come in handy when dealing with co-workers or clients.

Unlike collecting business cards that you might lose, you'll always have your contact information as long as you have your iPhone. To protect your contact information, you can copy it to your Macintosh so you'll always have a copy, even if you lose your iPhone.

First, let's take a look at how to store your own contact information. You'll want to keep your own contact information up to date to share with others.

To create your own contact information, follow these steps:

1. Tap the **Contacts** app on the Home Screen.
2. Tap your name at the top of the screen, as shown in *Figure 13.1*:

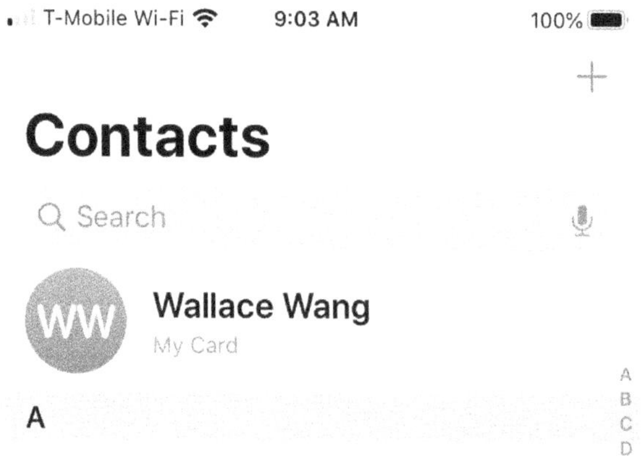

Figure 13.1 – The **Contacts** screen

3. Tap **Edit** (the + icon) in the upper-right corner of the screen. Add your name, phone number, and any other information you want, such as an email address, mailing address, and any other information you want to save and share with others.
4. Tap **Done**.

Once you have stored your own contact information, you can start adding other people's names and contact information as well. To add a new contact, follow these steps:

1. Tap the **Contacts** app on the Home Screen. The **Contacts** screen appears.
2. Tap the + icon in the upper-right corner of the screen. A **New Contact** screen appears, enabling you to add contact information about a person, as shown in *Figure 13.2*:

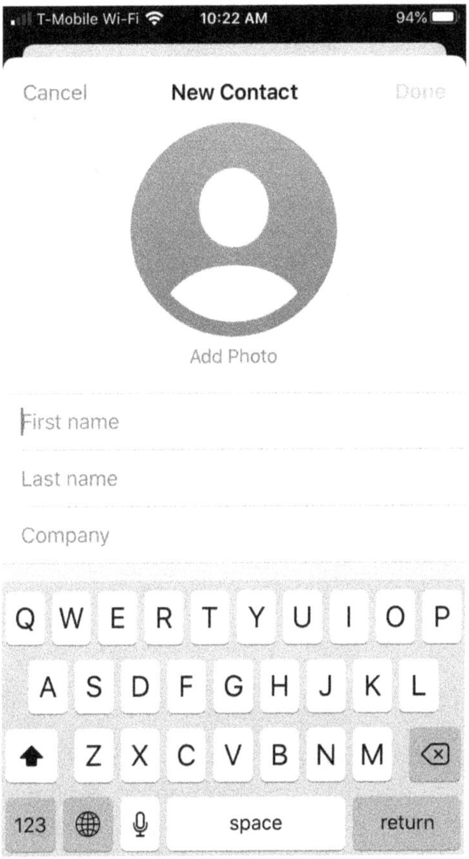

Figure 13.2 – The New Contact screen

3. Type in any information, such as a person's name and phone number.
4. (Optional) Tap **Add Photo**. This lets you use a memoji to represent a person or use your iPhone camera to take a picture of someone, as shown in *Figure 13.3*:

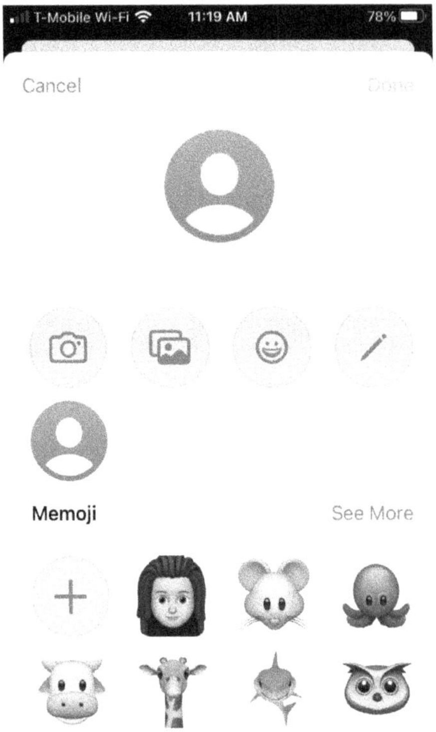

Figure 13.3 – Adding a picture to contact information

5. Tap **Done**. The **Contacts** app now stores your data.

Once you store one or more names and contact information, you'll likely want to find that information again. That means knowing all the different ways to search for information stored in the **Contacts** app.

Searching for a name

The simplest way to look for a particular name in the **Contacts** app is to scroll down the entire list of contacts until you find the name you want. A second way is to tap a letter on the right side of the **Contacts** screen to jump to people whose last name begins with a certain letter, such as R or W.

Yet an even faster method is to search for a name. That way, you can type just part of a name and see all possible matches. Searching can be particularly useful if you only know a person's first name or aren't sure of the complete spelling of someone's name.

To search for a name in the **Contacts** app, follow these steps:

1. Tap in the **Search** text field at the top of the screen.
2. Type a few letters. Each time you type a letter, the **Contacts** app narrows down the list of possible matches, as shown in *Figure 13.4*:

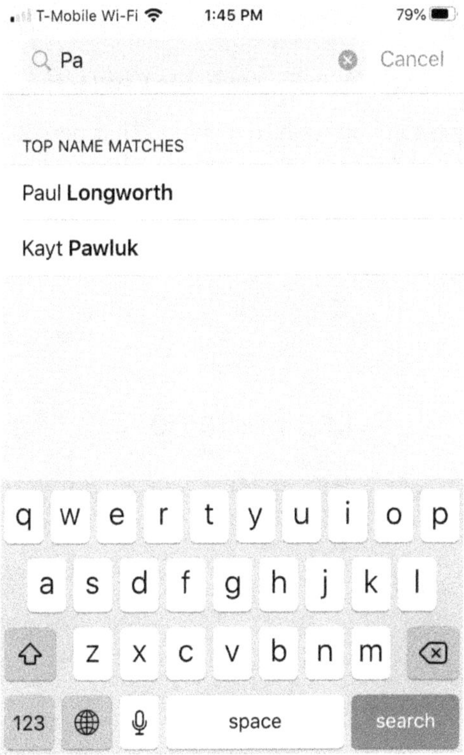

Figure 13.4 – Searching for a name

3. Tap a name to display more information about that person.

The more text you search for, the narrower the list of matches. However, if you aren't sure about the spelling of someone's name, type fewer characters and scroll through the list of matches.

Communicating through the Contacts app

The **Contacts** app does more than just store names and contact information. You can also use the **Contacts** app as a way to communicate with others. Normally, if you want to send an email, make a phone call, or send a text message, you'd have to type in that person's contact information.

Since the **Contacts** app already contains a person's contact information, all you need to do is open the **Contacts** app, find the person you want to reach, and then choose the best method to reach that person, such as by email, FaceTime, phone call, or text message.

To see how to use the **Contacts** app to contact someone, follow these steps:

1. Tap the **Contacts** app on the Home Screen. The **Contacts** app screen appears.
2. Tap the name of the person you wish to contact. That person's contact information appears on the screen, as shown in *Figure 13.5*:

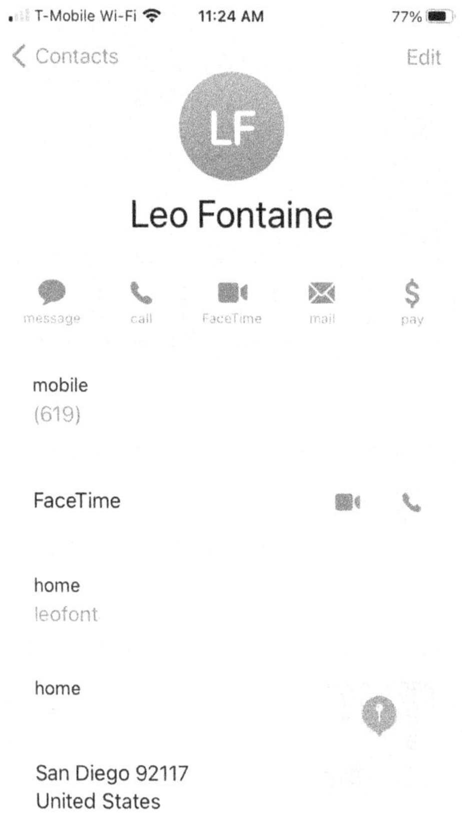

Figure 13.5 – Viewing a person's contact information

3. Tap a phone number or email address to make a phone call, send an email message, or make a FaceTime call. Tap the **message** icon to send a text message.

By opening the **Contacts** app first, you can choose who you want to contact without the hassle of typing in that person's phone number or email address. As long as you typed in a person's phone number or email address correctly, your iPhone can use that correct contact information to make a call or send an email message to others.

The key to using the **Contacts** app is to add in as much contact information about a person as possible because you never know how you may want to reach that person in the future.

Combining duplicate contacts

On many an occasion, you may add information about a person and then suddenly realize that you have already added information about that person before, so you wind up with duplicate names but with different contact information.

For example, imagine you meet someone at a party and get their name and email address. Later, you get in touch with that person to do business, so you enter that person's name, company, and phone number. At this point, you would have the same person stored twice.

Creating duplicate information for a single person might be handy if you want to clearly separate someone's personal information from their business contact information. However in most cases, you might want to keep all contact information for a person under a single name.

Fortunately if you find yourself with duplicate contact information for the same person, you can merge or link the two contact information screens into one.

To see how to combine duplicate contacts, you'll first need to store a name in the **Contacts** app. Then, you'll need to create a duplicate name to combine it with the existing contact information stored under the same name.

To see how to combine contacts, follow these steps:

1. Tap the **Contacts** app on the Home Screen. The **Contacts** app screen appears.
2. Tap the + icon. A **New Contact** screen appears (see *Figure 13.2*).
3. Type a name (such as `John Doe`) and contact information (such as a phone number), tap **Done**, and then tap the **Back** button to return to the list of all names stored in the **Contacts** app. At this point, you have a single John Doe stored in the **Contacts** app.

4. Tap the + icon. A **New Contact** screen appears (see *Figure 13.2*).
5. Type the same name (such as `John Doe`) but different contact information (such as a different phone number).
6. Scroll to the bottom of the **New Contact** screen to view the **link contacts…** button, as shown in *Figure 13.6*:

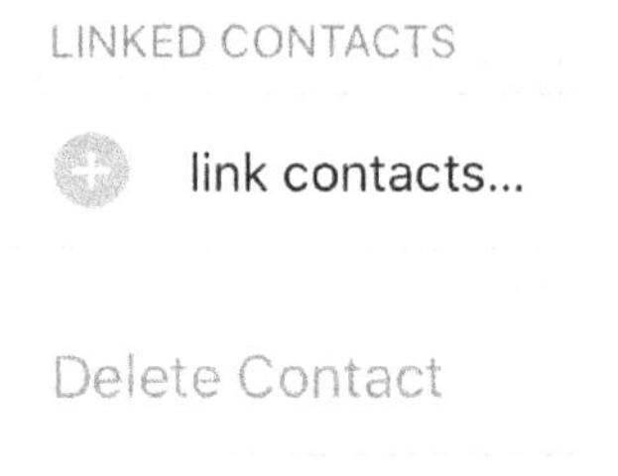

Figure 13.6 – The link contacts button appears at the bottom of the New Contact screen

7. Tap **link contacts…**. The **Contacts** app screen appears again. However, the name you're currently editing will appear dimmed, as shown in *Figure 13.7*:

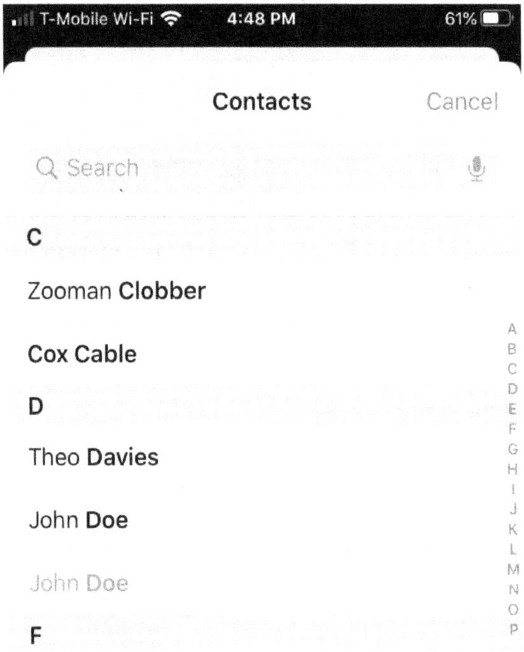

Figure 13.7 – A dimmed name identifies the contact information you're currently editing

8. Tap on the non-dimmed duplicate name that you want to merge with the dimmed name. The non-dimmed name's contact information appears along with a **Link** button in the upper-right corner of the screen, as shown in *Figure 13.8*:

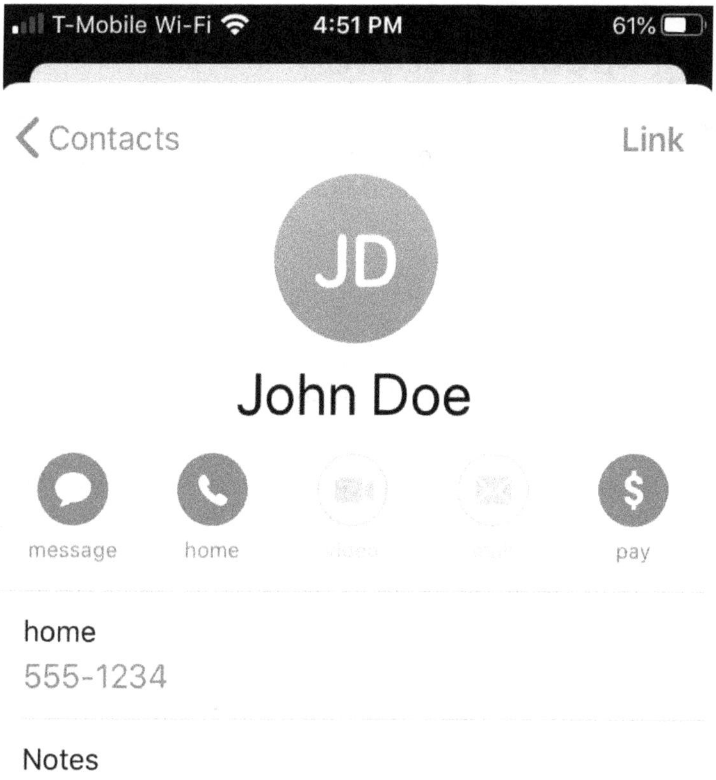

Figure 13.8 – A Link button appears in the upper-right corner

9. Tap **Link** and then tap **Done**. The duplicate contact information now appears merged in a single name.

Eliminating duplicate names can streamline your contacts list. As you add more contacts, you'll likely have some people who are more important to you than others. To identify those special people, take some extra time to mark the names in your contacts list as extra special to you.

Identifying special people

Your contacts list will likely contain names of people you need to know and people you want to know. For those special people you care about the most, take a moment to identify those important people in your life in one of the following ways:

- Birthdays
- Favorites

By adding someone's birthday, you can see that person's birthday on the **Calendar** app. If you regularly view the **Calendar** app to see any appointments you might have for that day, you'll also see anyone's birthday as well.

By designating someone as a favorite, you can create a favorite list in the **Phone** app so you can quickly find your favorite people and send them a text message or call them without the hassle of digging through your entire contact list.

Displaying birthdays

To make the **Calendar** app display somebody's birthday, you must define that person's birthday first. To define a birthday, follow these steps:

1. Tap the **Contacts** app on the Home Screen. The **Contacts** app screen appears.
2. Tap on a name you want to modify.
3. Tap **Edit** in the upper-right corner of the screen.

4. Scroll down until you find the **add birthday** button, as shown in *Figure 13.9*:

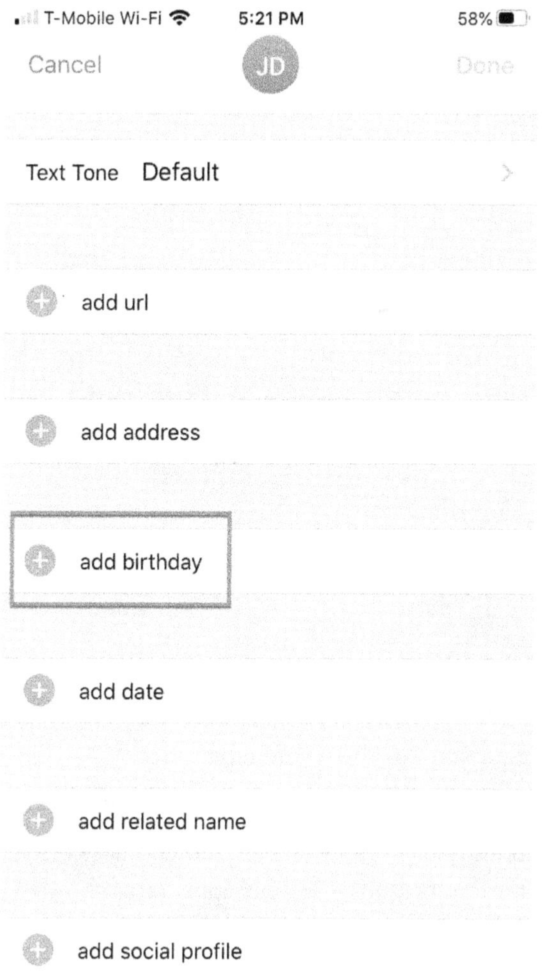

Figure 13.9 – The add birthday button

5. Tap **add birthday**. A date picker appears, as shown in *Figure 13.10*:

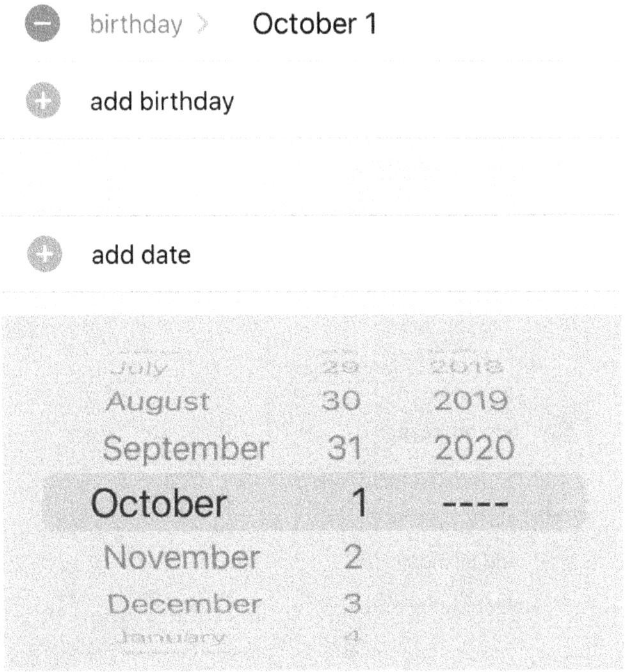

Figure 13.10 – A date picker for defining a birthday

6. Pick a date for that person's birthday and tap **Done**.
7. Tap the **Calendar** app on the Home Screen. The **Calendar** screen appears.
8. Navigate to the month that contains one of your contact's birthdays and tap on that date. A reminder for that person's birthday appears, as shown in *Figure 13.11*:

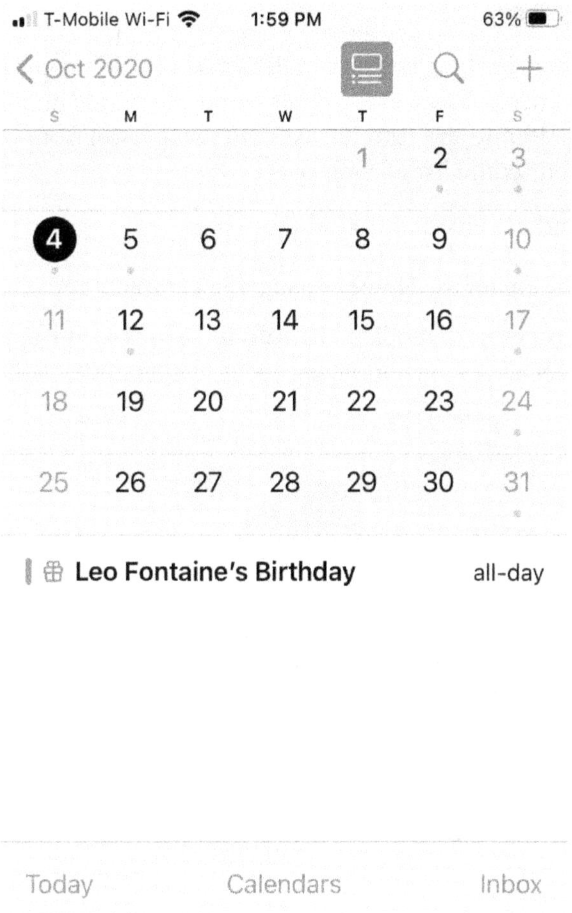

Figure 13.11 – A birthday reminder on the Calendar app

9. Tap the person's birthday reminder near the bottom of the Calendar screen. That person's contact information appears, allowing you to contact them by phone, FaceTime, email, or text message.

If someone is important to you, you can designate them as a favorite. That way, you can get one-tap access to them when you want to call them using the **Phone** app.

Defining favorites

Everyone has people they like best, so you can designate certain people as favorites. When you designate someone as a favorite, their name and phone number appear in the **Favorites** list in the **Phone** app. This lets you call that person from your short list of favorites rather than your entire list of contacts.

To see how to define and use favorites, follow these steps:

1. Tap the **Contacts** app on the Home Screen. The **Contacts** app screen appears.
2. Tap on a name you want to modify. The **Add to Favorites** link appears near the bottom of the screen, as shown in *Figure 13.12*:

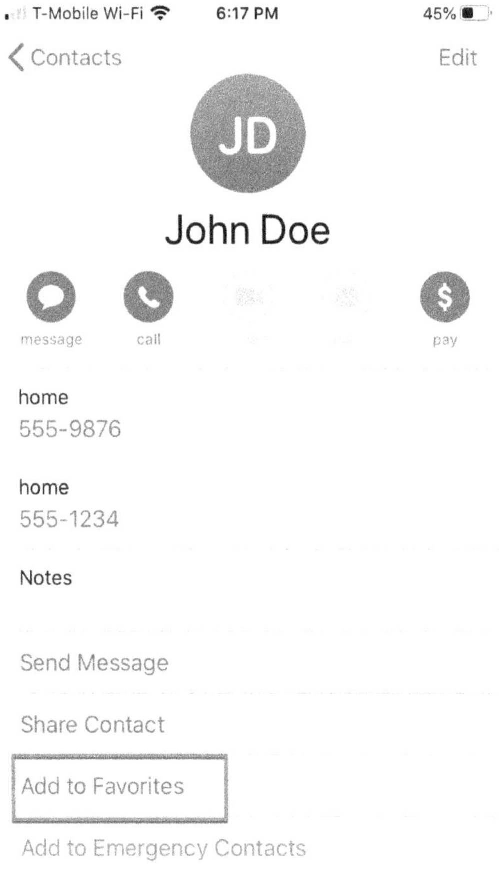

Figure 13.12 – The Add to Favorites link

3. Tap **Add to Favorites**. A menu appears letting you store someone's phone number for text messaging or phone calls, as shown in *Figure 13.13*:

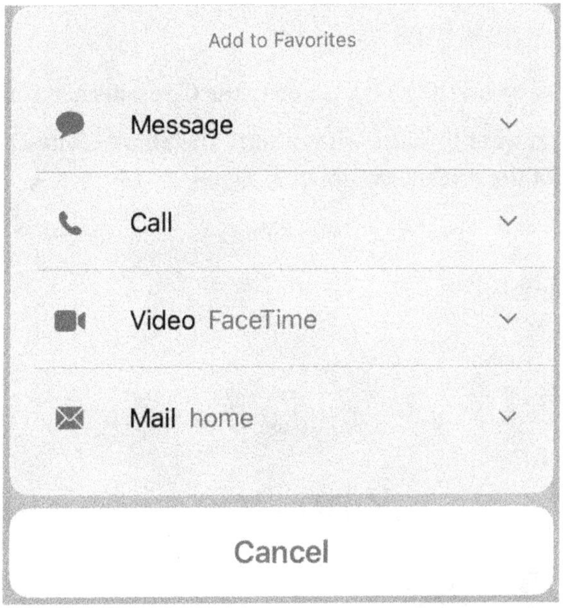

Figure 13.13 – Choosing a favorite way to contact someone

4. Tap **Message**, **Call**, **Video**, or **Mail** and then choose a phone number to use for text messaging or phone calls (if there is more than one phone number stored).
5. Tap the **Phone** app and tap the **Favorites** icon at the bottom of the screen. A list of your favorite people appears. Now you can just tap on a name to send that person a text message or call them.
6. (Optional) To remove a name from this **Favorites** list, swipe left and tap the **Delete** icon when it appears.

As you collect more names and contact information, you may have valuable information that you may want to share with others. If you want to share your contact information with others, you can do so quickly and easily.

Sharing contacts

When you have someone's contact information, you may want to share it with others. While you could exhaustively read off someone's email address and phone number along with their social media contact information, it's much easier to simply send all this information to someone so they can load it into their own **Contacts** database.

To share a contact, follow these steps:

1. Tap the **Contacts** app on the Home Screen. The **Contacts** app screen appears.
2. Tap on a name you want to share with others. The **Share Contact** button appears near the bottom of the screen, as shown in *Figure 13.14*:

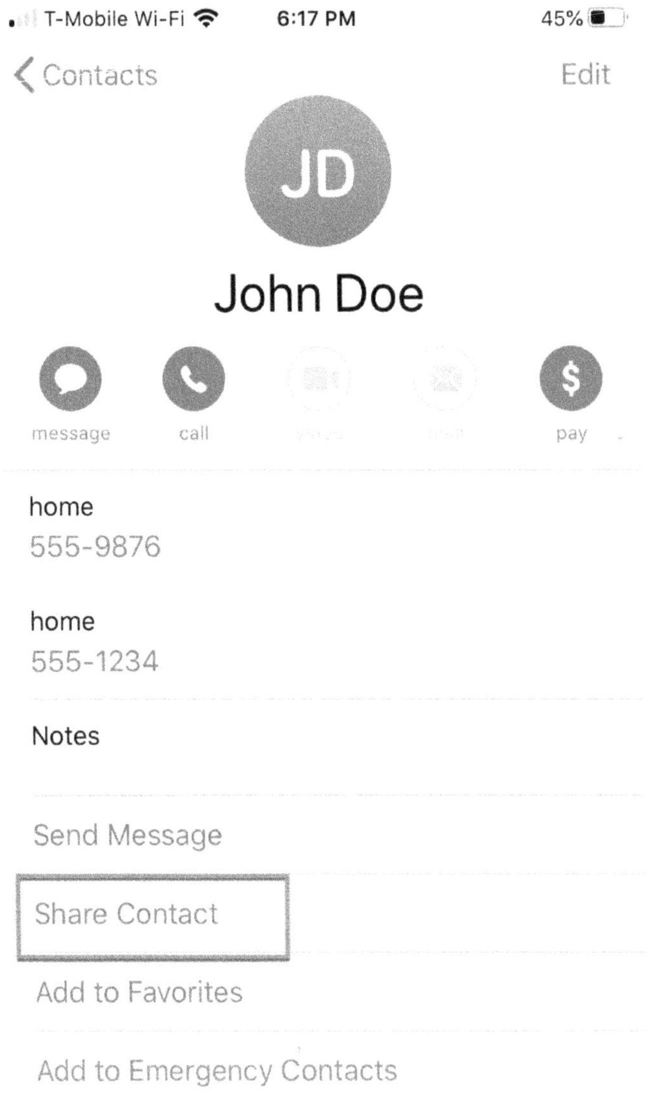

Figure 13.14 – The Share Contact button

3. Tap **Share Contact**. A list of people and ways in which to send contact information to them appears, as shown in *Figure 13.15*:

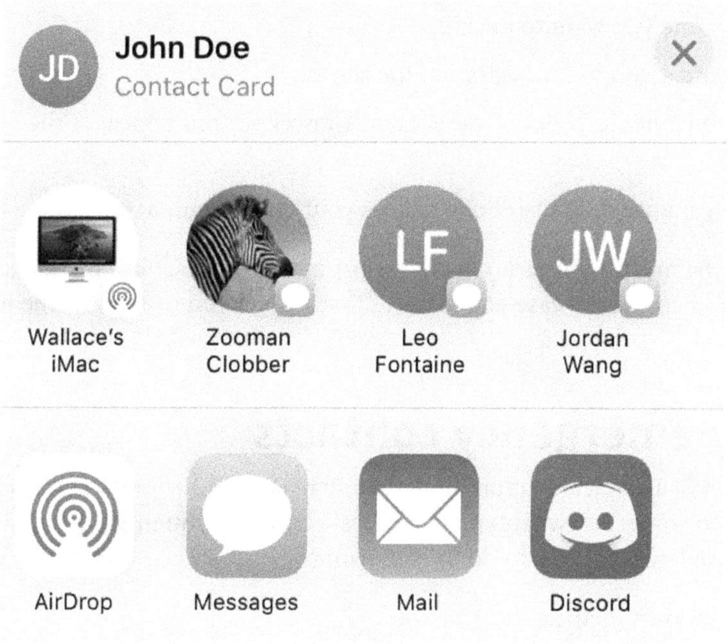

Figure 13.15 – Choosing how to share contact information

4. Tap a person or a method to send contact information, such as **Messages** or **Mail**.

Sharing important contacts can be crucial in business, but eventually you may find you no longer need certain names any more for both work and personal use. That's when you need to trim your contact list.

Deleting contacts

No matter how valuable someone's contact information might be, eventually you may want to delete it because the person moves away or has changed jobs. When that occurs, you can delete a contact.

In fact, you should periodically review your contact list to remove any names you no longer need to save. That way, you can keep a list of only the most important people in your life.

To delete a contact, follow these steps:

1. Tap the **Contacts** app on the Home Screen. The **Contacts** app screen appears.
2. Tap on a name you want to delete.
3. Tap **Edit** and scroll to the bottom of the screen.
4. Tap **Delete Contact**. **Delete Contact** and **Cancel** buttons appear at the bottom of the screen.
5. Tap **Delete Contact**. Your iPhone deletes your chosen contact.

Perhaps one of the most important type of people in your contact list are those people authorities should contact in case you're hurt. That's when you need to define emergency contacts.

Creating emergency contacts

If you should get in a car accident or fall ill for any reason and you're by yourself, nobody will know who to contact or what type of medical condition you might be in. That's why you should take a few moments to do the following:

- Define your own medical information
- List your emergency contacts

When you define your own medical history and define a list of emergency contacts, anyone will be able to retrieve this crucial information from your iPhone's lock screen. That way, they don't need to talk to you or wait for you to unlock your iPhone.

The first step is to define your own medical history, such as what type of medication you might be currently taking or what you might be allergic to, such as certain drugs or food. You can also define anything else you think might help first responders, such as your blood type.

The second step is to define any people in your **Contacts** app whom first responders should contact, such as your spouse or parent.

To define medical information for yourself, follow these steps:

1. Tap the **Contacts** app on the Home Screen. The **Contacts** app screen appears.
2. Tap your own name at the top of the screen.
3. Tap **Edit** in the upper-right corner of the screen.

4. Scroll down and tap **Create or Edit Medical ID**. A **Medical ID** screen appears where you can enter your medical background, such as medication you're using or conditions you have, as shown in *Figure 13.16*:

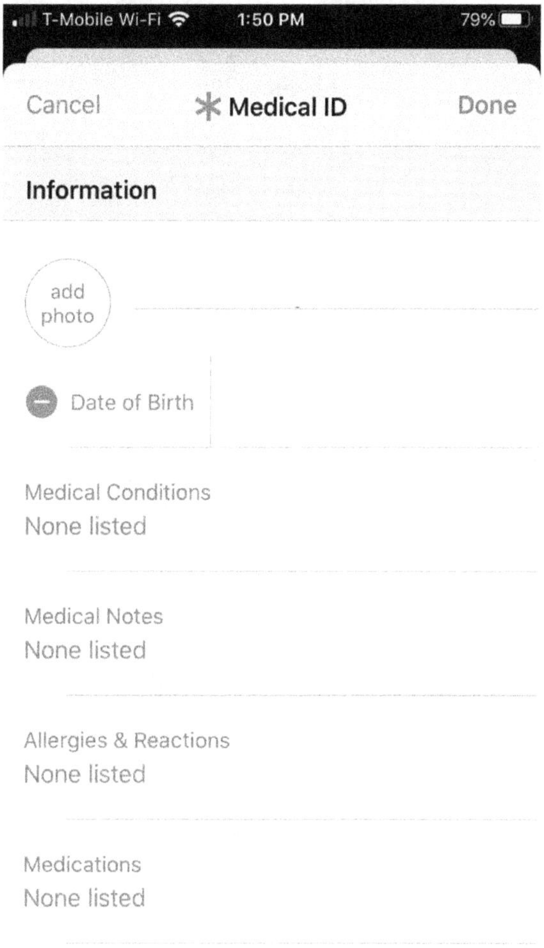

Figure 13.16 – The Medical ID screen

This information can then be accessed from the locked screen of your iPhone. That way, if you're in an emergency, a first responder can tap the **Medical ID** button on your iPhone's lock screen to view any medical information you may have saved.

5. Scroll down until you see the **Emergency Contacts** category, as shown in *Figure 13.17*:

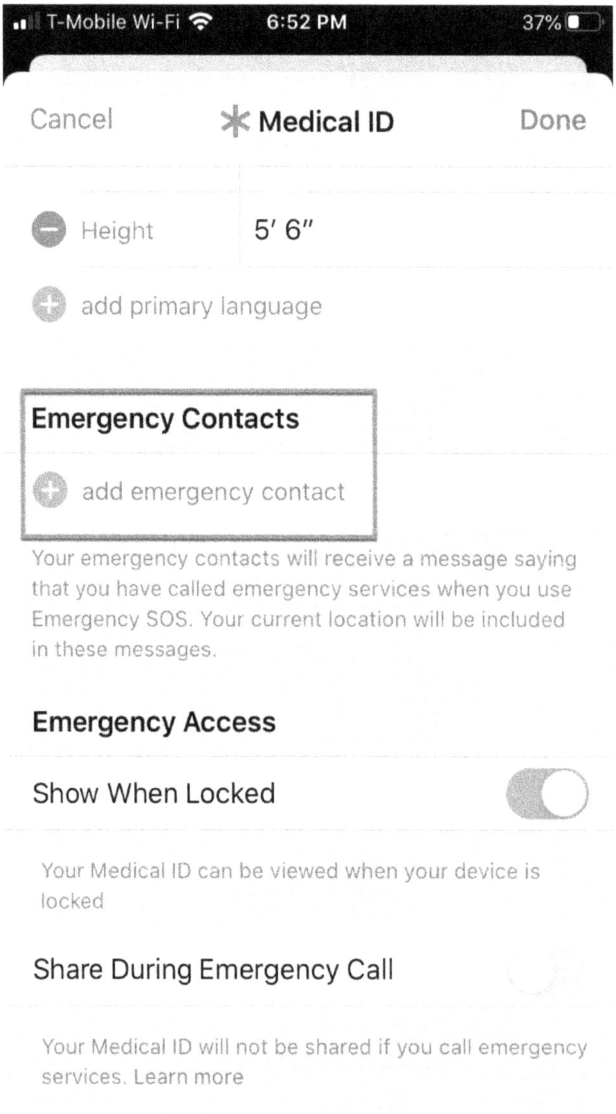

Figure 13.17 – The Emergency **Contacts** category

6. Tap **add emergency contact**. A **Contacts** screen appears.
7. Tap on a name. A **Relationship** screen appears, as shown in *Figure 13.18*:

Figure 13.18 – The Relationship screen

8. Tap a relationship, such as **parent** or **spouse**. Repeat *Steps 7 and 8* as often as necessary.
9. Tap **Done**.

Nobody may ever need your medical information and emergency contacts, but it's better to be safe now just in case an emergency occurs.

Summary

At its simplest level, the **Contacts** app can store names and contact information that you can retrieve at any time. With one tap, you can send an email message, make a phone or FaceTime call, or send a text message. If someone gives you their website or social media contact, you can reach that person that way as well.

Besides storing names and contact information, you can also directly contact people from the **Contacts** app. This saves you time typing an email address or phone number over and over again.

Most importantly, store your own medical information along with emergency contacts. That way, if you're ever in an accident, authorities will be able to contact your loved ones and access your medical history.

Storing names and contact information is important, but often you need this information when you need to call or meet certain people. So, in the next chapter, you'll learn about setting appointments and reminders. That way, you'll never be late or miss an appointment again.

14 Setting Appointments and Reminders

Most people need to be somewhere at a certain time and a certain date. This might be a doctor's appointment, a job interview, a train or plane trip, or just meeting a friend for drinks or lunch. Since nearly everyone needs to keep track of their schedule, you might as well use your iPhone to help you keep track of various appointments you need to keep at certain times and dates in the future.

By storing all your appointments on your iPhone, you won't risk forgetting something important. Even better, you can set reminders so your iPhone can beep to let you know in advance when an appointment is coming up. That way you can prepare in advance.

The topics this chapter covers are as follows:

- Setting appointments
- Editing and deleting an appointment
- Setting reminders and travel time
- Defining recurring appointments

- Adding meeting locations
- Inviting others to an appointment
- Adding notes to an appointment
- Deleting an appointment

Setting appointments

The **Calendar** app is where you can store your appointments and view them again. With each appointment, you need to define a date, a time, and a brief description of that appointment such as "Dentist appointment" or "Lunch with Joan." Optionally, you can also define a location, any additional people you want to invite, reminder alerts, notes, or files related to the appointment.

Once you set an appointment, you can view it on the **Calendar** app. That way, each morning, you can check the **Calendar** app for your appointments that day.

To set an appointment, follow these steps:

1. Tap the **Calendar** app on the Home screen.
2. Tap a date for your appointment, such as June 24 or December 5.
3. Tap the + icon in the upper-right corner of the screen. A **New Event** screen appears as shown in *Figure 14.1*:

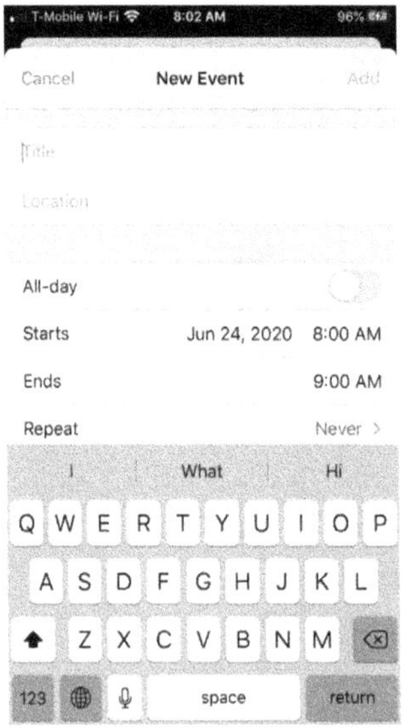

Figure 14.1 – The New Event screen

4. Click in the **Title** text field and type a description of your appointment such as "Pick up Fred from airport" or "Meet Sally for lunch."
5. Tap the **Starts** button. A date and time picker appears as shown in *Figure 14.2*:

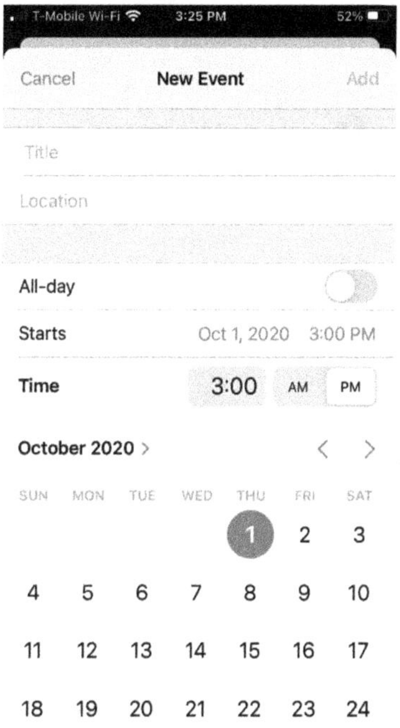

Figure 14.2 – The New Event screen

6. Set a time. You can also change the date if you wish. Scroll down and make sure the **Time Zone** option is correct for your part of the world.
7. Tap **Ends**. Another date and time picker appears, letting you set the estimated ending time.
8. Set an ending time.
9. Tap **Add** in the upper-right corner of the screen.

Once you have added an appointment, you can tap on the date of that appointment in the **Calendar** app to view all appointments for that day as shown in *Figure 14.3*:

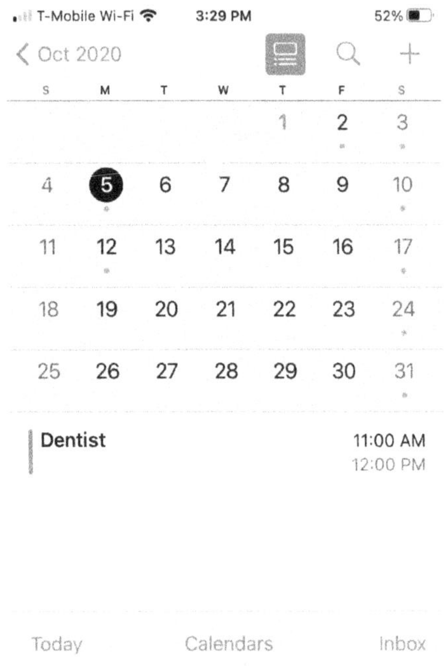

Figure 14.3 – Viewing all appointments for a particular day

After you have set an appointment, you may later want to modify it if you need to change its time or date, or delete the appointment altogether.

Editing and deleting an appointment

Appointments can always change so you need to modify them if necessary. That could mean changing the time, date, or even deleting it altogether. Fortunately, you can edit any appointment just as easily as you created it in the first place.

To edit an existing appointment, follow these steps:

1. Tap the **Calendar** app on the Home screen.
2. Tap a date that contains the appointment you want to edit. A list of appointments for that day appears under the calendar (see *Figure 14.3*).

3. Tap the appointment you want to edit. An **Event Details** screen appears as shown in *Figure 14.4*:

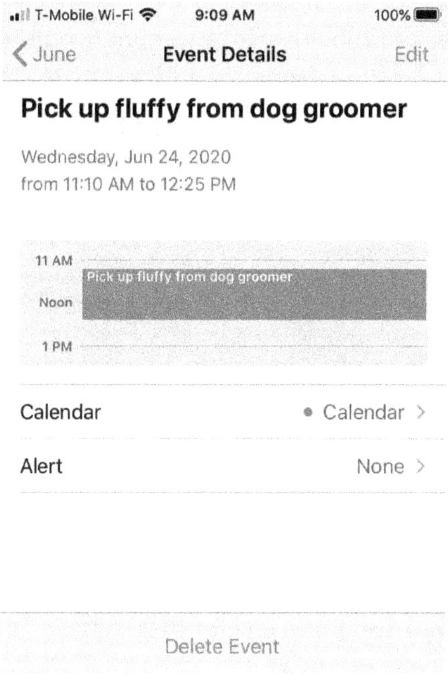

Figure 14.4 – An Event Details screen for viewing an appointment

4. Tap **Edit** in the upper-right corner of the screen. An **Edit Event** screen appears where you can edit all details about the appointment.
5. Change any details you wish, such as the starting time, ending time, description, or date.
6. Tap **Done**. The **Event Details** screen appears again so you can verify all the details of your appointment are correct.
7. Tap the **Back** button in the upper-left corner to return to the calendar.

Editing an appointment can be useful when you need to change details, but you may need to delete an appointment altogether once you no longer need it.

To delete an appointment, follow these steps:

1. Tap the **Calendar** app on the Home screen.
2. Tap a date that contains the appointment you want to edit. A list of appointments for that day appears under the calendar (see *Figure 14.3*).
3. Tap the appointment you want to edit. An **Event Details** screen appears (see *Figure 14.4*).
4. Tap **Delete Event** at the bottom of the screen. A **Delete Event** and **Cancel** button appear at the bottom of the screen.
5. Tap **Delete Event**. Your chosen appointment disappears.

Setting, editing, and deleting appointments are the basics for helping you keep track of where you need to be at any given time on any given day. For more flexibility, you may want to look at some additional features for setting appointments.

Setting reminders and travel time

Setting an appointment won't do you any good if you forget about it. Even if you look at the **Calendar** app to see your appointments for the day, you still might forget about it when the appointment time comes.

For that reason, you might want to set reminders. A reminder lets your iPhone alert you before your appointment occurs. That way you can have enough time to travel and prepare for any upcoming appointments.

You can set reminders when you create an appointment, or you can add a reminder to an existing appointment. In either case, reminders help ensure you don't forget your appointment as long as you have your iPhone nearby.

Another feature you may want to add to an appointment is travel time. Just because an appointment starts at 11:00 a.m. doesn't help you if it will take you 20 minutes to get there and you don't realize this until it's 10:50 a.m.

To set travel time, follow these steps:

1. Tap the **Calendar** app on the Home screen.
2. Either create a new appointment or edit an existing one.
3. Tap **Travel Time**. A **Travel Time** screen appears.
4. Tap the **Travel Time** switch to on so a list of times appears as shown in *Figure 14.5*:

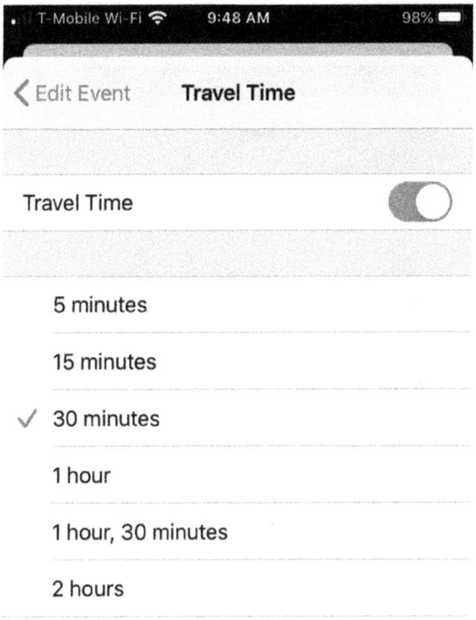

Figure 14.5 – The Travel Time screen

5. Tap a length of time such as **15 minutes** or **30 minutes**.
6. Tap the **Edit Event** back button in the upper-left corner of the screen. Your chosen travel time now appears on the **Travel Time** row.
7. Tap **Done**.

After defining a travel time, you'll see that the travel time is displayed in your appointment on the **Calendar** app as shown in *Figure 14.6*:

Figure 14.6 – Travel time appearing in an appointment

Setting travel time can be handy to let you know what time you need to leave to get to your appointment. However, you may still also want to set a reminder, otherwise you risk forgetting about the travel time and your appointment.

To set a reminder, follow these steps:

1. Tap the **Calendar** app on the Home screen.
2. Either create a new appointment or edit an existing one.

3. Tap **Alert**. An **Alert** screen appears as shown in *Figure 14.7*:

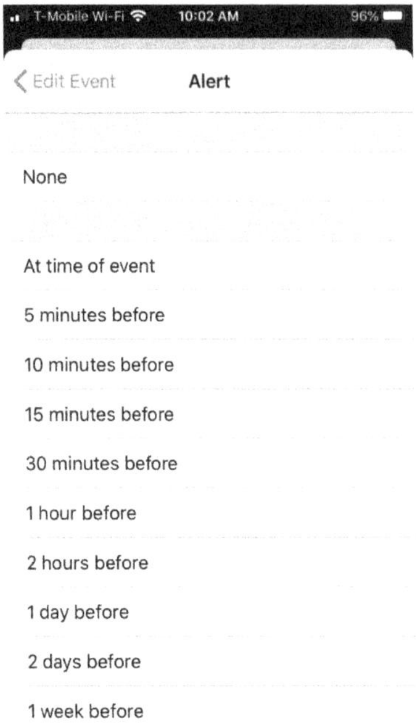

Figure 14.7 – An Alert screen

4. Tap a time when you want to be informed before your appointment. If you defined a travel time, your alert will remind you before the start of the travel time you defined.
5. Tap **Done**.

At the time of your reminder, you'll hear an audio alert along with a notification either at the top of the screen (if your iPhone is unlocked) or in the middle of the screen (if your iPhone is locked) as shown in *Figure 14.8*:

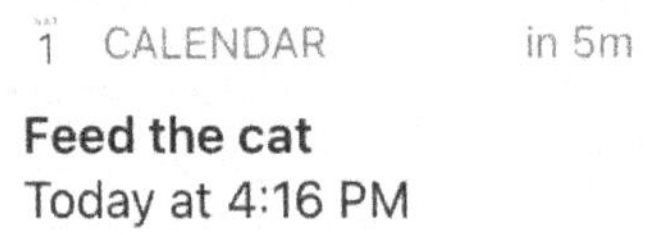

Figure 14.8 – A reminder for an upcoming appointment

Reminders can make sure you don't miss an appointment or start traveling there too late to make it on time. While most appointments occur once, such as a doctor's appointment, others may occur regularly, such as a weekly meeting at work, so you need to know how to define those types of appointments as well.

Defining recurring appointments

If you need to schedule an appointment that occurs regularly, such as every Friday afternoon, you could set that appointment once and then keep editing it to change its date to the next Friday. However, if you forget to do this, you'll risk not posting your appointment on the next date and could miss it.

A far better solution is to define a recurring appointment. Just tell the **Calendar** app how often you want an appointment to occur, such as every week or every month, and then you'll just need to set this appointment once. The **Calendar** app will then automatically keep posting new times for your appointment until you either edit or delete this appointment.

To create a recurring appointment, follow these steps:

1. Tap the **Calendar** app on the Home screen.
2. Either create a new appointment or edit an existing one.
3. Tap **Repeat**. A **Repeat** screen appears as shown in *Figure 14.9*:

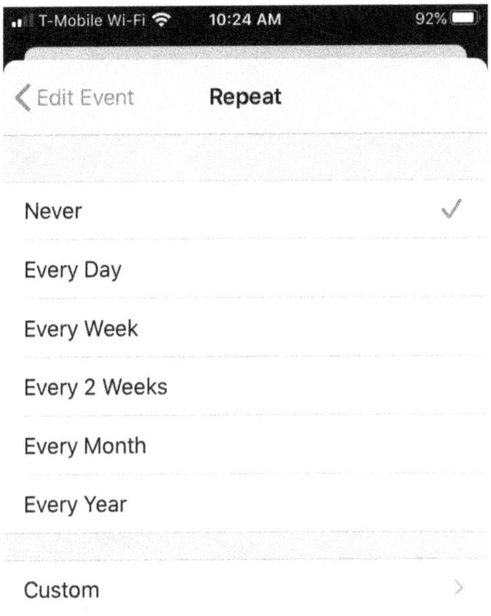

Figure 14.9 – The Repeat screen lets you define a recurring appointment

4. Tap a time interval for your appointment to repeat, such as every week or every month.
5. Tap **Done**. Now your appointment will automatically occur on the time intervals you specified.

Besides setting a time and date for a meeting, you may also want to specify a location. That way you'll know where to go when the meeting occurs.

Adding meeting locations

Many meetings occur in familiar locations such as a conference room or a favorite coffee house. However, sometimes you may need to schedule an appointment at an unfamiliar place. In that case, you may want to define a meeting location with your appointment as well. That way you'll know where to go for your appointment.

To define a location for an appointment, follow these steps:

1. Tap the **Calendar** app on the Home screen.
2. Either create a new appointment or edit an existing one.
3. Tap in the **Location** text field at the top of the screen. A **Location** screen appears as shown in *Figure 14.10*, listing the most recent locations you searched for in the **Maps** app:

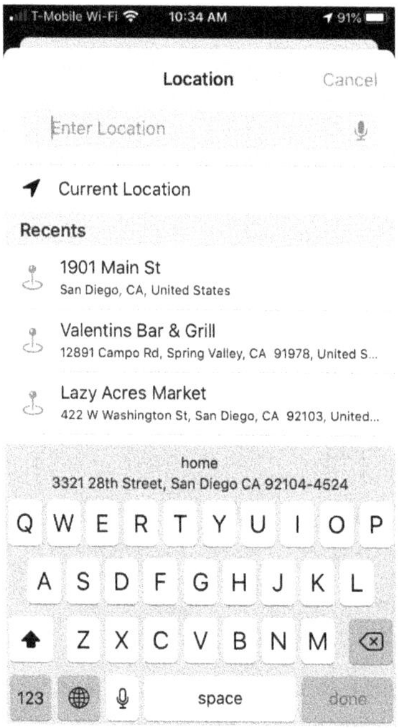

Figure 14.10 – The Location screen

4. Tap a location or type a description or address in the **Enter Location** text field at the top of the screen.

5. Tap **Done**. If you are setting a location for a recurring appointment, you'll see additional options for setting a location for the current appointment or all future events as shown in *Figure 14.11*. Tap the **Save for future events** option:

Figure 14.11 – Verifying whether you want to set a location for a recurring appointment

Many appointments involve several people, so you may want to notify those people that you expect them at an upcoming appointment as well.

Inviting others to an appointment

Oftentimes, an appointment may need other people to attend. So when creating or editing an appointment, you can add a list of people who should be at your meeting and then contact them to verify that they'll be there as well.

To invite others to an appointment, follow these steps:

1. Tap the **Calendar** app on the Home screen.
2. Either create a new appointment or edit an existing one.
3. Tap **Invitees**. An **Add Invitees** screen appears as shown in *Figure 14.12*:

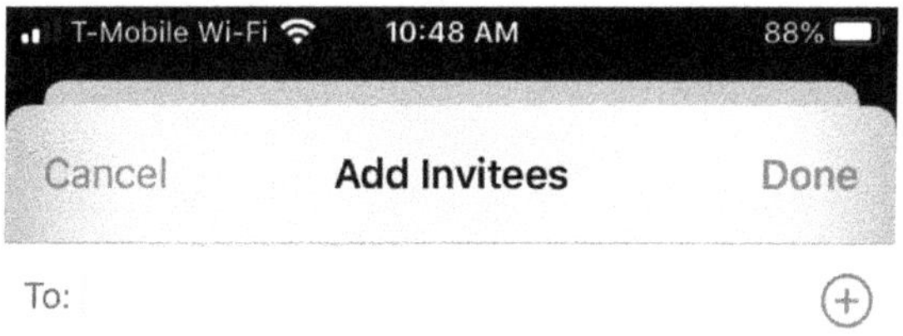

Figure 14.12 – The Add Invitees screen

4. Tap the + icon. The **Contacts** screen appears.
5. Tap on a name to invite them to attend your meeting.
6. Repeat *Steps 4* and *5* for each additional person you want to invite to the meeting.

7. Tap **Done**. The **Invitees** screen now lists all the people you invited to the meeting as shown in *Figure 14.13*:

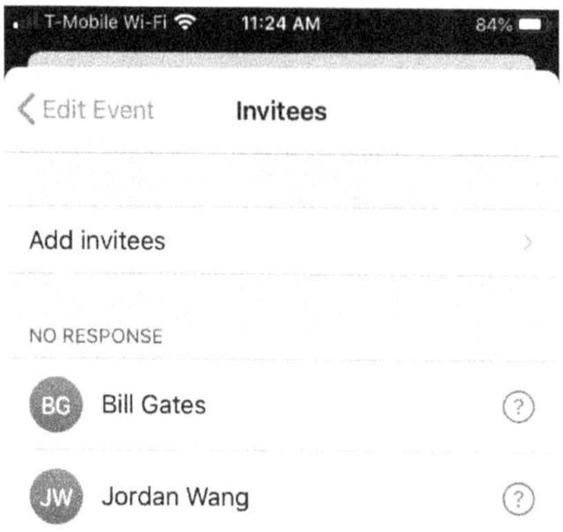

Figure 14.13 – The Invitees screen listing people you want to attend an appointment

> **Note**
> With Microsoft Exchange and other servers, you can send someone an invitation to a meeting even if you didn't originally schedule that appointment.

If you want to remove someone from an appointment, follow these steps:

1. Tap the **Calendar** app on the Home screen.
2. Tap the meeting that you want to remove some invited people from.
3. Tap **Invitees**. The **Invitees** screen appears listing all the people you've invited.
4. Swipe left on the name of the person you want to remove from the meeting. A **Remove** button appears on the right as shown in *Figure 14.14* (A **Make Optional** button also appears if you want to identify someone's attendance as optional for a meeting):

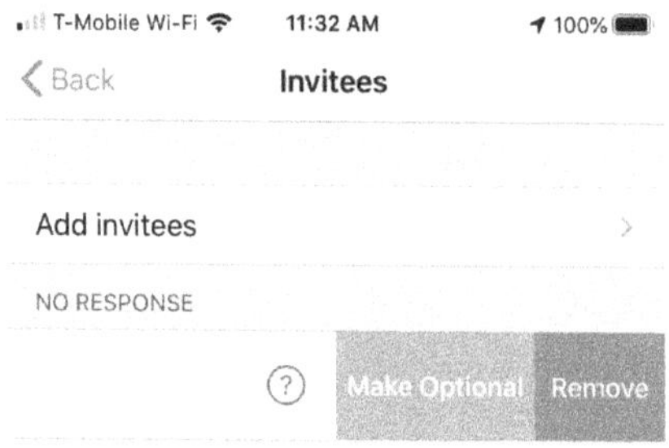

Figure 14.14 – Deleting a person from an appointment

5. Tap the **Remove** button.
6. Tap **Done**.

When you set an appointment, you may want to include notes or other reference materials. That way you'll know what you should review or have with you for an appointment.

Adding notes to an appointment

If you have a doctor's appointment, you might want to bring a list of concerns you have about certain symptoms or drugs. If you have a business appointment, you might want to review notes about what you want to accomplish and information about the person or people you'll be meeting.

In many cases, an appointment may require notes for you to review ahead of time or to take with you to use during the appointment. You may want to use one or more of the following ways to attach notes to an appointment:

- Type text.
- Attach a file.
- Add a URL (website address).

Typing additional text can remind you of things to bring to an appointment that you don't want to forget, or provide you with information you'll need during the appointment.

Attaching a file lets you include a document you may have created using a word processor such as Pages or a spreadsheet such as Numbers. This lets you review the file before or during the appointment.

Adding a URL lets you reference information stored on a website such as useful information that you may need to achieve the goals of your appointment. For example, a sales appointment might link to a company website so you can review or show information during a sales presentation.

Typing text on an appointment

Every appointment provides a **Notes** text field where you can type any information you wish regarding an upcoming appointment. For example, if you're going to a job interview, you might want to jot down notes to remind you what to bring or what to review before the interview.

To type text as a note for an appointment, follow these steps:

1. Tap the **Calendar** app on the Home screen.
2. Either create a new appointment or edit an existing one.
3. Scroll down and tap in the **Notes** text field as shown in *Figure 14.15*:

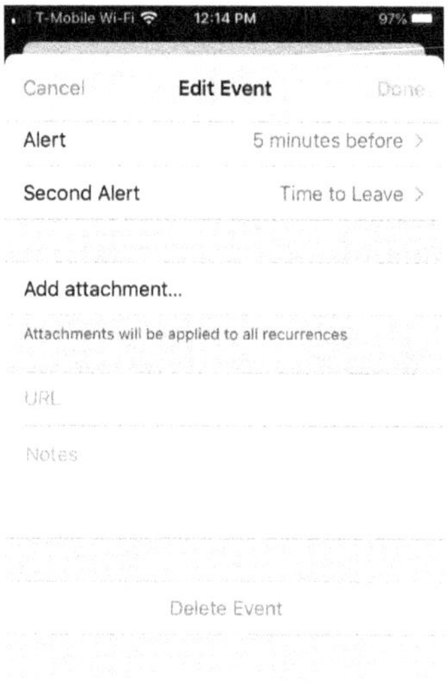

Figure 14.15 – The Notes text field in an appointment

4. Type any information you want to regarding the appointment.
5. Tape **Done**.

The **Notes** text field is handy for typing text, but if you already have information stored in a separate file, it's easier just to attach that file to the appointment instead.

Attaching files to an appointment

You may have several files that you've created using Keynote, Pages, or any app that creates files. If a particular file is important for your appointment, you can attach that file to the appointment.

To attach a file to an appointment, follow these steps:

1. Tap the **Calendar** app on the Home screen.
2. Either create a new appointment or edit an existing one.
3. Scroll down and tap **Add attachment** (see *Figure 14.15*). A **Recents** screen appears, listing all the recent files on your iPhone as shown in *Figure 14.16*:

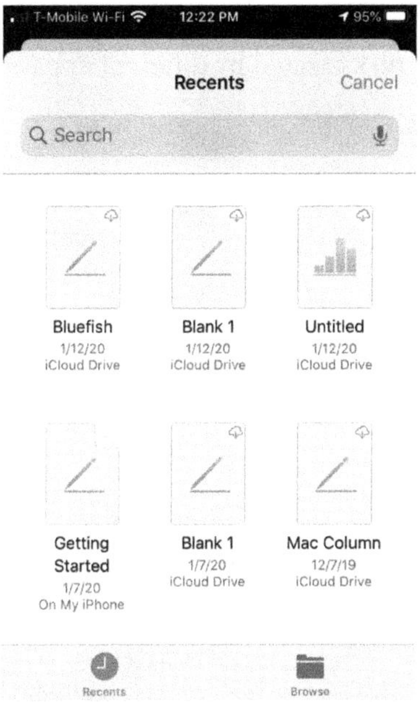

Figure 14.16 – The Recents screen shows recently opened files

4. Tap the **Browse** icon at the bottom of the screen. A **Browse** screen appears, letting you browse for other files to attach to an appointment as shown in *Figure 14.17*:

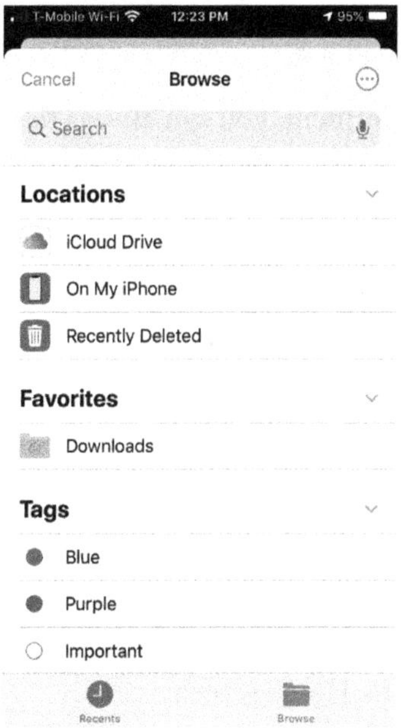

Figure 14.17 – Searching for a location to find a file

5. Tap a location such as **iCloud Drive** or **On My iPhone**. An additional screen appears, listing folders of files created by different apps as shown in *Figure 14.18*:

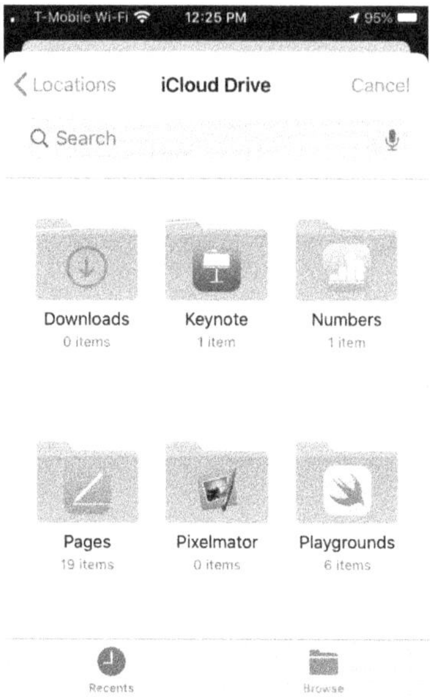

Figure 14.18 – Browsing files to attach to an appointment

6. Tap on a file that you want to attach to an appointment.
7. Tap **Done**.

Once you attach a file to an appointment, you can always remove that file from the appointment by left swiping on the file to display a **Remove** button. Then tap **Remove**.

An attached file can remind you of a file to open (using the app that created it) before or during an appointment. A third way to reference information in an appointment is by storing a URL address.

Attaching URLs to an appointment

A **URL** (**Uniform Resource Locator**) commonly identifies a website address. By linking a website address to an appointment, you can have a reference to review before or during an appointment.

To attach a URL to an appointment, follow these steps:

1. Tap the **Calendar** app on the Home screen.
2. Either create a new appointment or edit an existing one.

3. Scroll down and tap in the **URL** text field (see *Figure 14.15*).
4. Type a website address such as `www.apple.com`.
5. Tap **Done**.

Once you add a website address to an appointment, you can tap on that website address to open it in the Safari browser. Of course, after you create an appointment, you'll probably want to delete it eventually after it's done.

Deleting an appointment

When you're finished with an appointment, you can delete it to keep your calendar uncluttered. To delete an appointment, follow these steps:

1. Tap the **Calendar** app on the Home screen.
2. Tap the appointment you want to delete.
3. Tap **Delete Event** at the bottom of the screen. An action sheet appears at the bottom of the screen, giving you a choice of deleting the appointment or not. If you are deleting a recurring appointment, you'll have the option of deleting just that one occurrence of the appointment or all recurring instances of that appointment as shown in *Figure 14.19*:

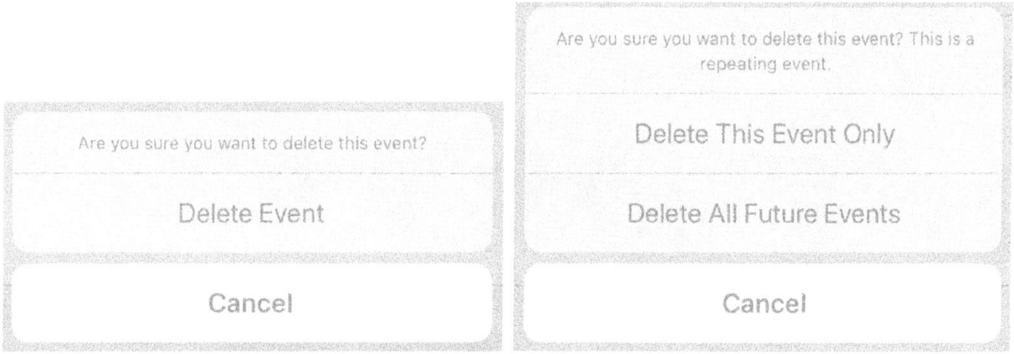

Figure 14.19 – Verifying that you want to delete an appointment

4. Tap the relevant **Delete** button to delete the appointment.

The **Calendar** app asks for verification before deleting an appointment just to make sure you really want to do it so delete an appointment once you're sure you no longer need it.

Summary

Everyone needs to keep track of times and dates when they need to be somewhere or do something. Rather than rely on your memory or a paper calendar or meeting planner, it's far easier to rely on your iPhone instead.

Any time you have an appointment, put it in your calendar so you won't forget it. For an extra reminder, set an alert to remind you about the appointment ahead of time so you won't be late.

To help you during an appointment, consider typing notes, attaching files, or including website addresses that you can reference before or during an appointment. The more prepared you are for an appointment, the more likely it will achieve the results you want.

In addition to setting appointments with others, be sure to set aside time for yourself to relax or pursue your own projects. By defining time for you to achieve projects you want to do, you can increase the chances that you'll have time to do them.

Appointments can be useful when meeting with others. When you're alone, you may come up with ideas and that's when you need to know how to store your ideas as both text and audio recordings, so you don't forget them.

In the next chapter, we will learn how iPhone helps us to write notes and record voice memos.

15 Writing Notes and Recording Voice Memos

When you're away from your desk, it's easy to get a sudden inspiration and need to capture your idea. Far too often, people forget their ideas completely. Other times, you may need to jot your ideas down on any scrap of paper you can find, such as a paper napkin or the back of an envelope. Ideally, you should carry a notepad and pen or pencil at all times since you never know when a good idea might hit you and you'll need to write it down.

Fortunately, with your iPhone, you'll always have a way to record your ideas at any time in one of two ways. First, you can type ideas using the **Notes** app, which acts like a simple word processor for capturing small amounts of text. Second, you can dictate your ideas to the Voice Memos app so you can capture an audio file of your spoken thoughts.

No matter where inspiration strikes you, you'll be able to record your thoughts as written text or spoken audio by using your iPhone. Now you just have to remember to keep your iPhone with you at all times.

The topics covered in this chapter are as follows:

- Creating notes and editing text
- Adding pictures and drawings to notes
- Recording voice memos

Taking notes

The **Notes** app mimics a paper notepad. While a paper notepad has a limited number of pages and each page has a limited amount of space, the **Notes** app lets you create an unlimited number of pages of unlimited size.

Once you capture your ideas in the **Notes** app, you can share them with others or simply copy and paste text from the **Notes** app into another app, such as the Pages word processor.

Understanding folders

To help you keep your notes organized, the **Notes** app can store them in folders, much like folders on a computer. The idea is to create separate folders for storing related notes, such as a folder for work projects and another folder for personal information. By creating and using folders, you can better organize your notes to help you find them again.

To see how to create a folder, follow these steps:

1. Tap the **Notes app** on the Home screen.
2. Tap the Back button in the upper-left corner of the screen until the **Folders** screen appears. The **Folders** screen shows the location of notes in both the iCloud (at the top) and your iPhone, as shown in *Figure 15.1*:

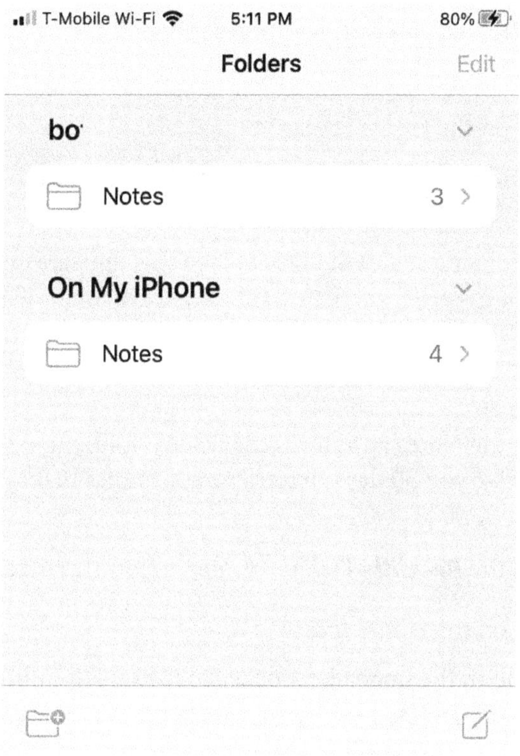

Figure 15.1 – The Folders screen

3. Tap **New Folder** in the bottom-left corner of the screen. A **New Folder** dialog appears, as shown in *Figure 15.2*:

Figure 15.2 – The New Folder screen

4. Type a descriptive name for your folder and tap **Save**. Your new folder appears under the **On My iPhone** category.

Once you have created a folder, you can store notes in that folder. To delete a folder, follow these steps:

1. Tap the **Notes** app on the Home Screen.
2. Tap the Back button in the upper-left corner of the screen until the **Folders** screen appears.
3. Swipe left on that folder and tap the Delete icon that appears on the right. A dialog appears, asking you to verify that you want to delete a folder with any notes and subfolders inside.
4. Tap **OK**.

After you delete a folder, the **Notes** app stores the deleted folder in a special **Recently Deleted** folder that will give you 30 days to retrieve your notes before your iPhone erases them for good.

To retrieve a folder from the **Recently Deleted** folder, follow these steps:

1. Tap the **Notes** app on the Home screen.
2. Tap the Back button in the upper-left corner of the screen until the **Folders** screen appears. The **Recently Deleted** folder appears, as shown in *Figure 15.3*:

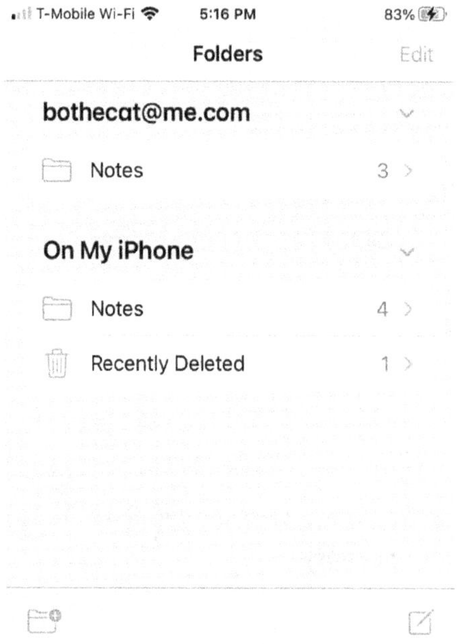

Figure 15.3 – The Recently Deleted folder appears when you delete at least one folder

3. Tap the **Recently Deleted** folder. The **Recently Deleted** screen appears, listing all notes you have deleted.
4. Swipe left on a note to display a folder and a Delete icon, as shown in *Figure 15.4*:

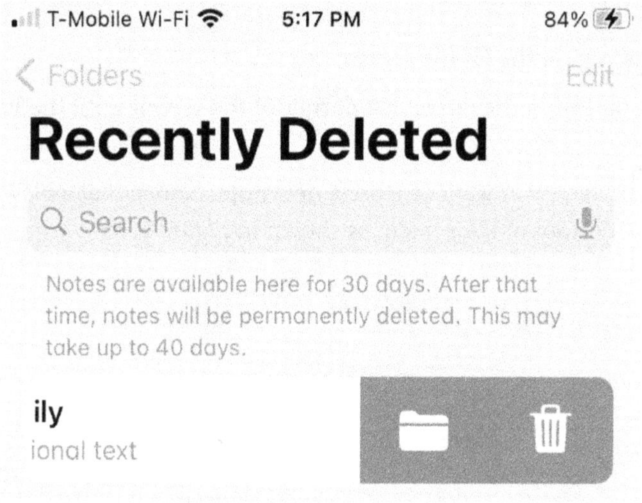

Figure 15.4 – The Recently Deleted screen displays previously deleted notes

5. Tap the **Folder** icon. A **Select a folder** screen appears, letting you choose a folder where you can put the note, as shown in *Figure 15.5*:

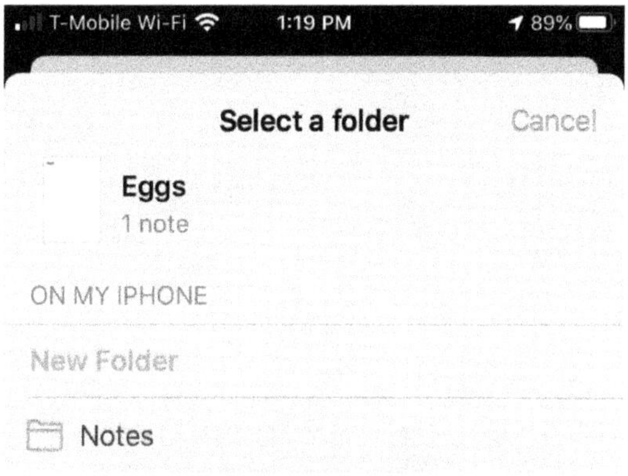

Figure 15.5 – The Select a folder screen

6. Tap a folder or tap **New Folder** to store your note in a new folder.

Once you understand how folders let you organize notes on your iPhone, the next step is to start creating notes so that you can capture your ideas.

Creating a new note

When you create a new note, you must define the folder where you want to store that note. Of course, you can always move that note to a different folder later.

To create a new note, follow these steps:

1. Tap the **Notes** app on the Home screen.
2. Tap the Back button in the upper-left corner of the screen until the **Folders** screen appears.
3. Tap the folder where you want to store a new note. Notice that a New Note icon appears in the bottom of the screen, as shown in *Figure 15.6*:

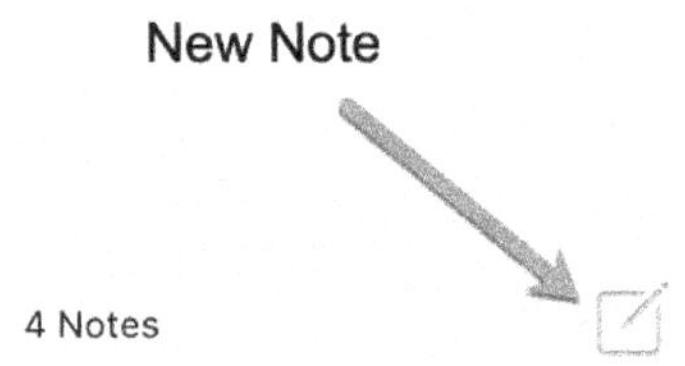

Figure 15.6 – The New Note icon

4. Tap the New Note icon. A blank note screen appears, as shown in *Figure 15.7*:

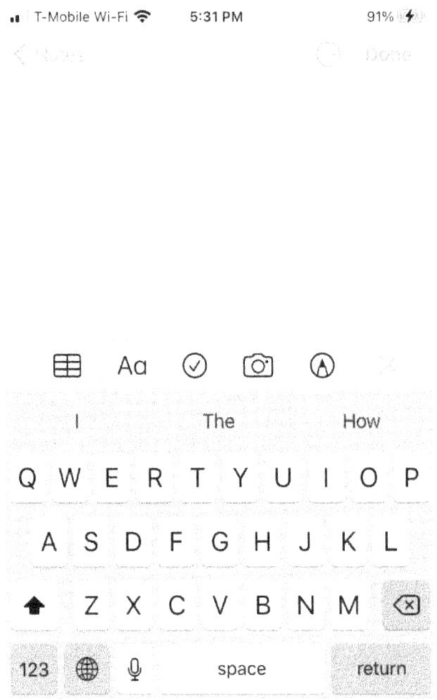

Figure 15.7 – A new note

Once you create a new note, you have several options:

- Type text.
- Create a table.
- Create a checklist.
- Add a picture from the photo library or the camera.
- Draw.

Typing and editing text

The most common use for a note is to type and edit text. To type text in a note, simply tap where you want to insert text and type using the virtual keyboard that appears at the bottom of the screen.

To select a single word, you have two options:

- Press and hold a fingertip over the word.
- Double-tap the word.

To select an entire paragraph, triple-tap any word in that paragraph. As soon as you select any text, a beginning and ending vertical line appears, as shown in *Figure 15.8*:

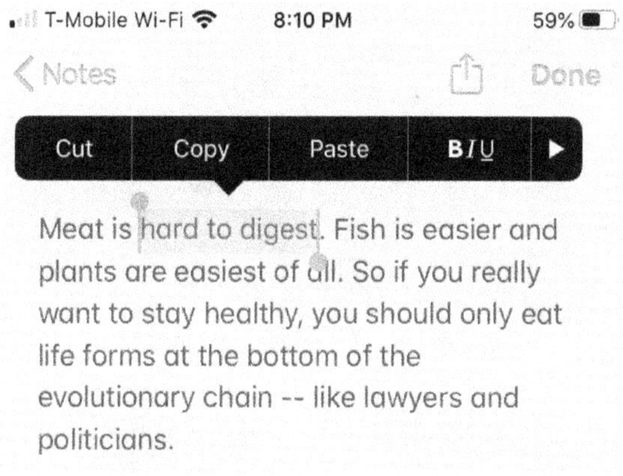

Figure 15.8 – Two vertical lines define the beginning and end of selected text

To select more or less text, drag these two vertical lines in any direction. Tap the selected text and a pop-up menu appears letting you choose the **Cut**, **Copy**, and **Paste** commands.

Cut removes selected text. **Copy** duplicates selected text. **Paste** inserts previously cut or copied text. If you have not cut or copied any text, the paste command won't do anything.

By using the **Cut** and **Paste** commands, you can move text from one location to another. By using the **Copy** and **Paste** commands, you can duplicate text to place in a second location.

Formatting text

Once you've typed text, you have the option of formatting that text to choose a different appearance or style (bold, italics, or underline), along with indenting text or creating numbered or bullet lists. Formatting gives you a way to emphasize some or all of your text stored in a note.

To format text in a note, follow these steps:

1. Tap the **Notes** app on the Home screen.
2. Tap on the note that contains the text you want to format.
3. Select the text you want to format (double-tap a word and/or modify the selection). Notice a + icon that appears above the virtual keyboard, as shown in *Figure 15.9*:

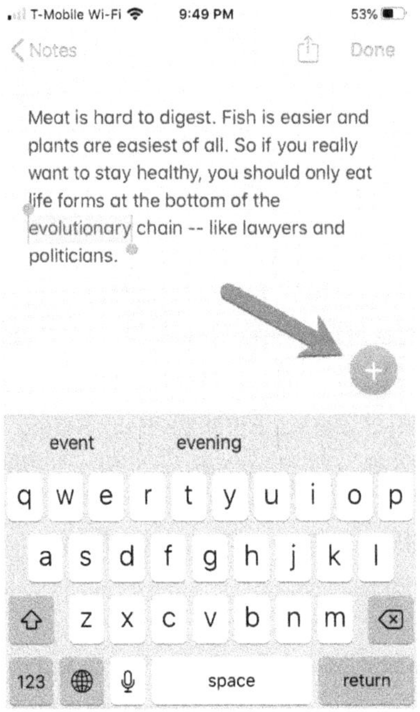

Figure 15.9 – The + icon above the virtual keyboard

4. Tap the + icon. A list of icons appears above the virtual keyboard, as shown in *Figure 15.10*:

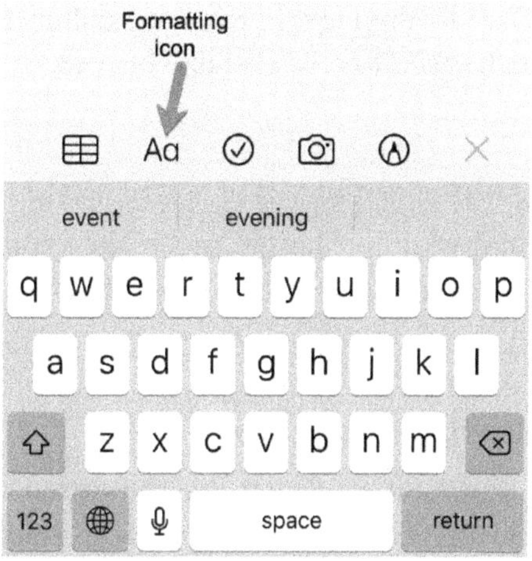

Figure 15.10 – Icons above the virtual keyboard

5. Tap the Formatting icon. A list of formatting options appears at the bottom of the screen, as shown in *Figure 15.11*:

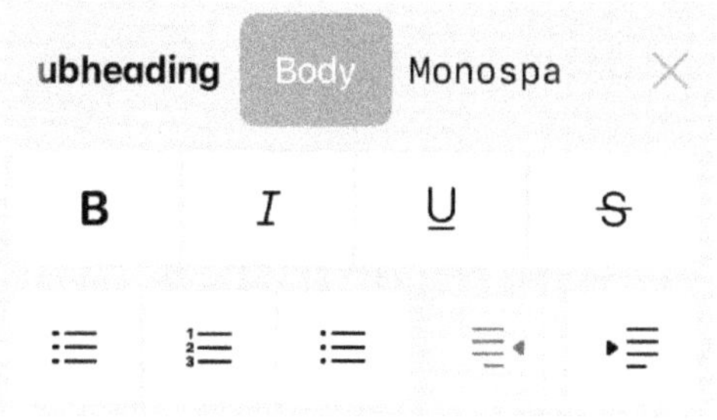

Figure 15.11 – Formatting options

6. Slide your finger left and right over the highlighted **Body** and you'll see other options, such as **Title** and **Subheading**. By tapping one of these other options, you can alter the appearance of the selected text.
7. Tap the Bold, Italics, Underline, or Strikethrough icons to change the selected text.
8. Tap the three different list icons, in the bottom-left corner, to create dashed, numbered, or bullet lists.
9. Tap **Body** again to convert a list back into text.
10. Tap the right and left indent icons in the bottom-right corner.
11. Tap the close (**X**) icon in the upper-right corner of these formatting options to make them go away. The virtual keyboard appears again.

When typing text, you may want to align text in rows and columns. Rather than trying to align text manually, it's much easier to create a table instead.

Using tables

Tables let you organize data in rows and columns, much like a spreadsheet. By using tables, you can align text in ways not possible through ordinary indentation.

To see how to create and use tables, follow these steps:

1. Tap the **Notes** app on the Home screen.
2. Tap on the note where you want to add a table. The virtual keyboard and row of icons appears. The Table icon appears on the far left, as shown in *Figure 15.12*:

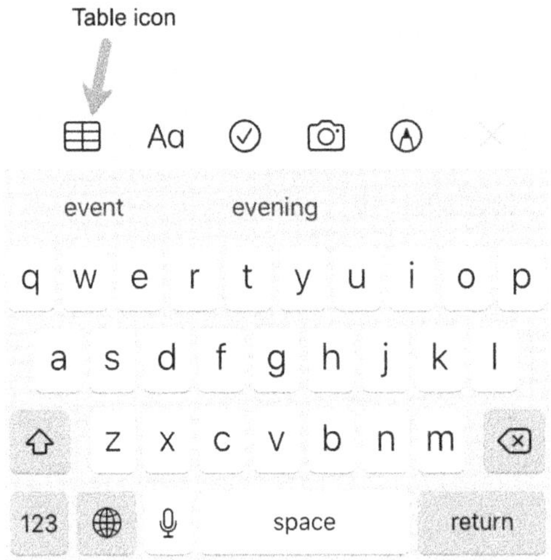

Figure 15.12 – The Table icon

3. Tap the **Table** icon. A table appears, as shown in *Figure 15.13*:

Figure 15.13 – A table in a note

4. Tap in a cell and type text.

Each time you create a table, the **Notes** app creates a 2 x 2 table. If you need to, you can add or delete rows and columns.

Modifying table rows and columns

When you create a table, you may need additional rows or columns. Likewise, a table may have too many rows and columns. At any time, you can adjust the size of a table.

To modify rows or columns in a table, follow these steps:

1. Tap the **Notes** app on the Home screen.
2. Tap inside the table you want to modify. A three dot icon appears above a column and to the left of the rows (see *Figure 15.13*).
3. Tap this three dot icon to display a menu to add or delete a row or column, as shown in *Figure 15.14*:

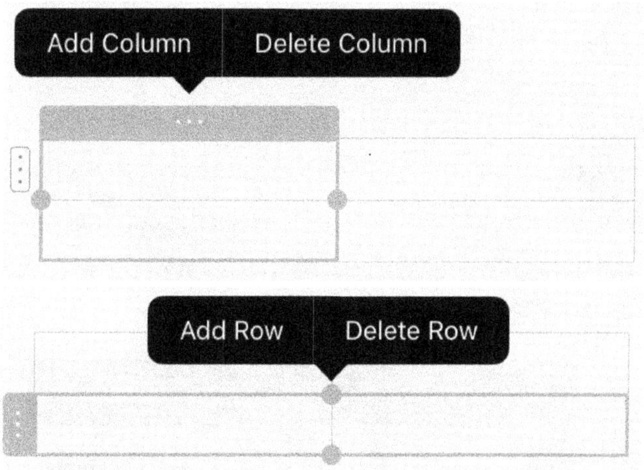

Figure 15.14 – Adding or deleting rows and columns

4. (Optional:) Drag the size of the row or column to select multiple rows or columns you wish to delete.
5. Tap an option such as **Add Row** or **Delete Column** to modify the size of your table.

Remember that if you delete a row or column, you also delete any text stored in that row or column.

Moving and copying rows and columns

Oftentimes, you may have text in a row or column and then decide it should appear somewhere else in that table. You can use the cut, copy, and paste commands on entire rows or columns that contain text.

To move or copy text stored in rows or columns in a table, follow these steps:

1. Tap the **Notes** app on the Home screen.
2. Tap the three dot icon above the column or to the left of the row you want to cut or copy. A menu appears, as shown in *Figure 15.15*:

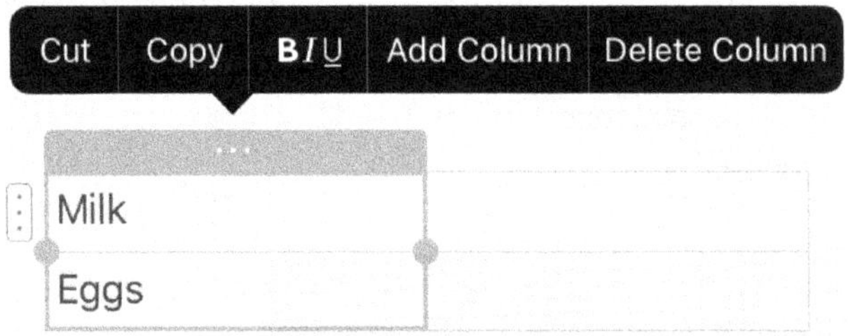

Figure 15.15 – Cutting or copying a row or column

3. Tap **Cut** or **Copy**. (The **Cut** command only cuts text, not the actual row or column.)
4. Tap in the row or column where you want to paste the cut or copied text.
5. Tap the three dot icon above the column or to the left of the row. A menu appears, as shown in *Figure 15.16*:

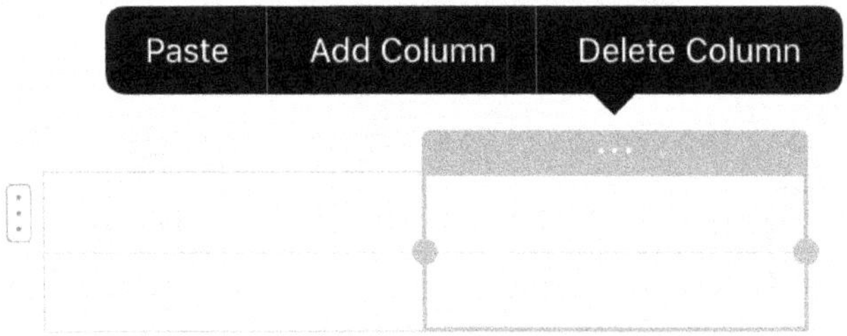

Figure 15.16 – Pasting cut or copied text

6. Tap **Paste**. Your cut or copied text appears in the row or column.

Moving or copying text around a table lets you modify a table, but sometimes you may want to copy a complete table so you can paste it in another note.

Copying a table

Rather than copy text stored in rows or columns, you can copy an entire table along with any text stored inside.

To copy a table, follow these steps:

1. Tap the **Notes** app on the Home screen.
2. Tap inside the table you want to copy. Notice that the Table icon above the virtual keyboard now displays a black dot in the lower-left corner, as shown in *Figure 15.17*:

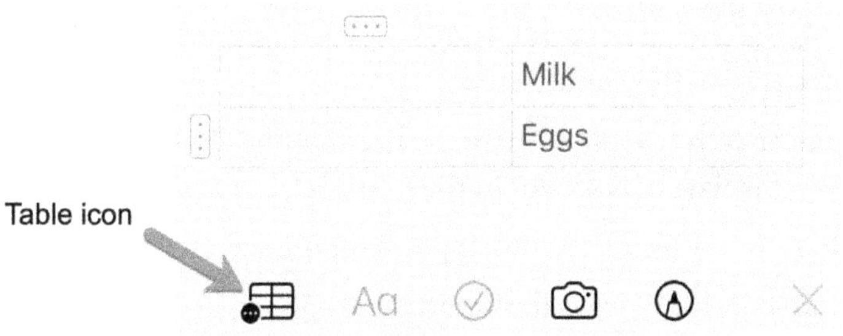

Figure 15.17 – The Table icon when the cursor appears inside a table

3. Tap the Table icon. A list of options appears on the screen, as shown in *Figure 15.18*:

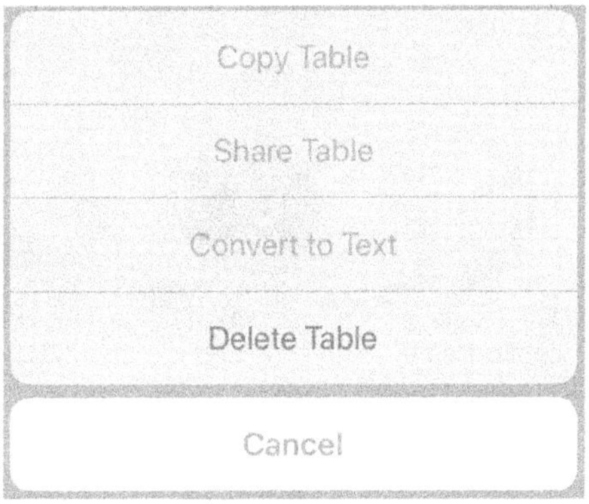

Figure 15.18 – Options for manipulating an entire table

4. Tap **Copy Table**.
5. Press and hold a fingertip at a new location where you want to paste the copied table. A menu appears.
6. Tap **Paste**. Your copied table now appears.

Copying a table can be handy, but if you notice the list of options in *Figure 15.18*, several other options are also available, such as sharing a table.

Sharing a table

If you create a table with text, you may want to share this information with others through AirDrop, **Messages**, Mail, or another app installed on your iPhone. By using AirDrop, you can send a table as a text file to another Apple product such as a Mac. By using **Messages** or Mail, you can send a copy of your table to friends or co-workers.

To share a table, follow these steps:

1. Tap the **Notes** app on the Home screen.
2. Tap inside the table you want to share. Notice that the Table icon above the virtual keyboard now displays a black dot in the lower-left corner (see *Figure 15.17*).
3. Tap the **Table** icon. A list of options appears on the screen (see *Figure 15.18*).
4. Tap **Share Table**. A list of ways to share a table appears at the bottom of the screen, as shown in *Figure 15.19*:

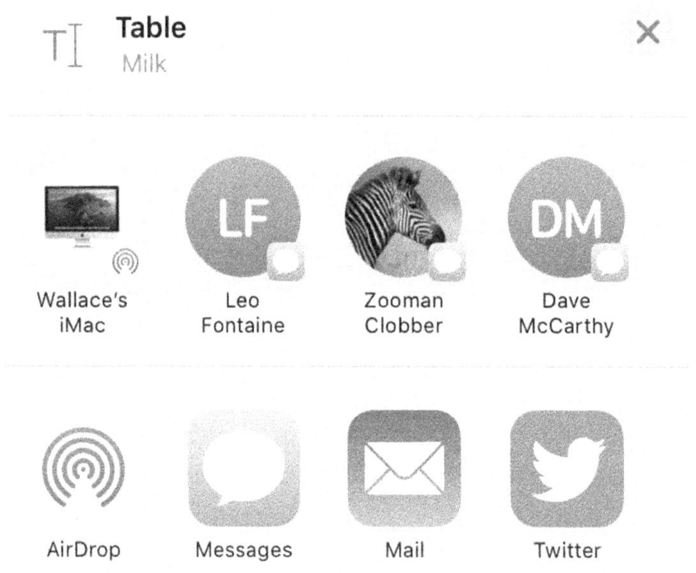

Figure 15.19 – Options for sharing a table

5. Tap a person's name or method to share your table, such as tapping **AirDrop**, **Messages**, or **Mail**.

Tables contain text, but you can convert a table into plain text if you no longer want to align text in rows and columns.

Converting tables to text

Tables can be useful for aligning text, but the lines that make up a table can be distracting. For that reason, you might want to convert a table to text. *Figure 15.20* shows a table and then how text appears after converting the table to text:

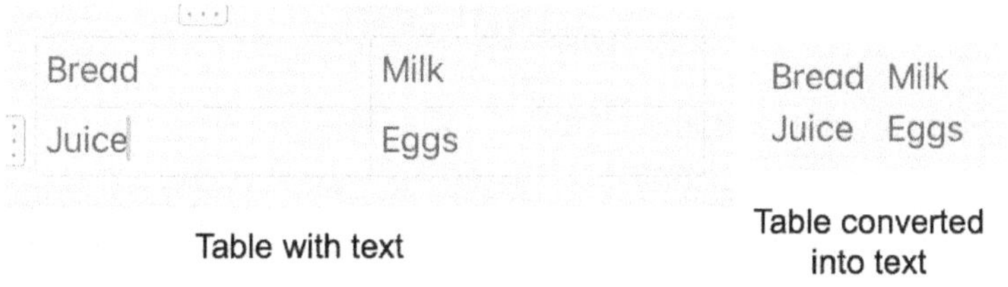

Figure 15.20 – Converting a table to text

To convert a table to text, follow these steps:

1. Tap the **Notes** app on the Home screen.
2. Tap inside the table you want to convert. Notice that the Table icon above the virtual keyboard now displays a black dot in the lower-left corner (see *Figure 15.17*).
3. Tap the Table icon. A list of options appears on the screen (see *Figure 15.18*).
4. Tap **Convert Table**. The text now appears without a table.

Converting a table to text gets rid of a table but preserves its text. However, you may eventually want to delete a table and all the text inside.

Deleting a table

When you no longer need a table, you can delete the entire table, including any text stored inside that table.

To delete a table, follow these steps:

1. Tap the **Notes** app on the Home screen.
2. Tap inside the table you want to delete. Notice that the Table icon above the virtual keyboard now displays a black dot in the lower-left corner (see *Figure 15.17*).
3. Tap the Table icon. A list of options appears on the screen (see *Figure 15.18*).
4. Tap **Delete Table**. The text now appears without a table.

Tables can help organize text, but for another way to organize text, consider using checklists.

Creating checklists

Many people take notes to create to-do lists and checklists of tasks they need to get done. Checklists let you create a list of items with the ability to tap on a circle to the left of each item to mark it as done.

To see how to create a checklist, follow these steps:

1. Tap the **Notes** app on the Home screen.
2. Tap in the location where you want to create a checklist. Notice a + icon that appears above the virtual keyboard (see *Figure 15.9*). (If you already see icons above the virtual keyboard, skip this step.)
3. Tap the + icon to display icons above the virtual keyboard.
4. As shown in *Figure 15.21*:

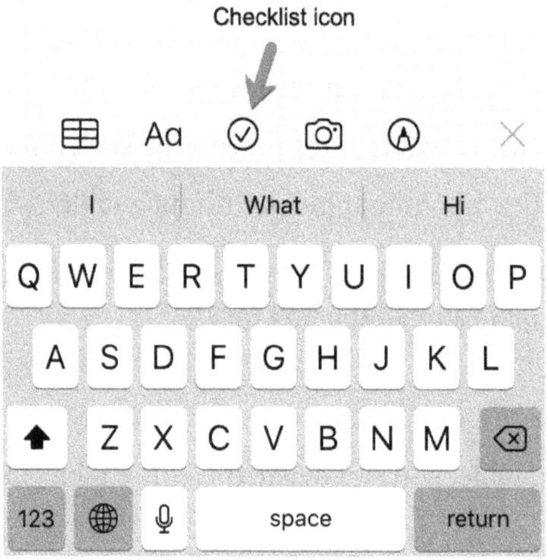

Figure 15.21 – The Checklist icon

5. Tap the **Checklist** icon. An empty circle appears in the note,
6. Type some text and tap the **Return** key on the virtual keyboard to create another checklist item.
7. Tap the **Checklist** icon again to stop creating empty circles.

Once you've created a checklist, you can always mark off items by tapping in the empty circle that appears to the left of each item, as shown in *Figure 15.22*:

Figure 15.22 – Check marks marking off items in a checklist

Tapping this circle toggles between showing an empty circle and a checkmark in it.

Adding pictures to a note

The whole purpose of notes is to capture your ideas and information. Sometimes, typing text is fine, but other times, you may want to capture a picture either from the iPhone's camera or using a picture stored in your photo library.

The **Notes** app offers three ways to add a picture to a note, as shown in *Figure 15.23*:

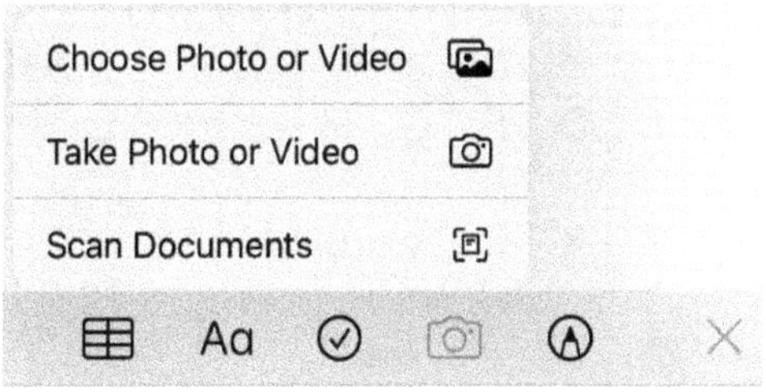

Figure 15.23 – Three options for adding pictures to notes

The options are as follows:

- **Scan Documents** – Lets you crop an image taken with a camera, but does not save it in the Photo Library
- **Take Photo or Video** – Captures a photo or video from the iPhone camera, but does not save it in the Photo Library
- **Choose Photo or Video** – Retrieves an image or video stored in the Photo Library

Cropping images into a note

The **Scan Documents** option is meant to capture images of important papers and let you crop them, but you can use this option to capture any image with the iPhone camera and crop it before inserting it in a note.

To capture and crop a picture for a note, follow these steps:

1. Tap the **Notes** app on the Home screen.
2. Tap in the location where you want to add a picture. Notice a + icon that appears above the virtual keyboard (see *Figure 15.9*). (If you already see icons above the virtual keyboard, skip this step.)
3. Tap the + icon to display icons above the virtual keyboard, as shown in *Figure 15.24*:

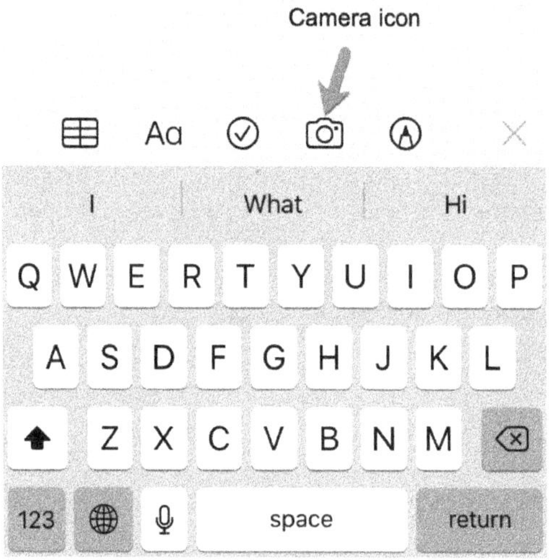

Figure 15.24 – The Camera icon

4. Tap the Camera icon. A list of options appears (see *Figure 15.23*).
5. Tap **Scan Documents**. Aim your iPhone camera at the object you want to capture, as shown in *Figure 15.25*:

Figure 15.25 – Capturing an image

6. Tap the white button to capture an image. Cropping circles appear around the image.

7. Drag these cropping circles to define the image you want to keep, as shown in *Figure 15.26*:

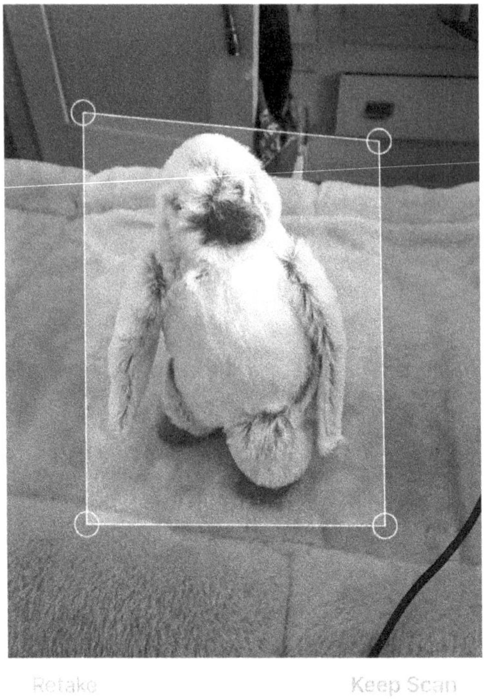

Figure 15.26 – Cropping an image

8. Tap **Keep Scan**. Your cropped image appears in the note.
9. Tap on the cropped image in your note. A list of icons appears at the bottom of the screen, which allows you to modify the image further, as shown in *Figure 15.27*:

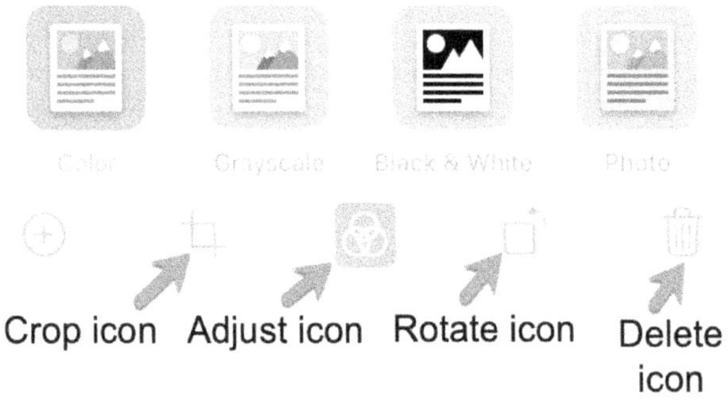

Figure 15.27 – Modifying a cropped image

10. Tap the Crop icon and crop the image if necessary.
11. Tap the Adjust icon and choose from a variety of ways to adjust the appearance of the image, such as **Grayscale** or **Black & White**.
12. Tap the Rotate icon to rotate the image to the left.
13. Tap the Delete icon if you want to remove the cropped image from the note.

Cropping an image can be fine, but sometimes you just want to capture an entire picture or video and insert it into a note.

Adding images and videos to a note

By using the iPhone camera, you can capture a still image or a video to add to a note. When you capture an image or video within a note, that image or video will not be saved to the Photo Library.

To capture a picture or video for a note, follow these steps:

1. Tap the **Notes** app on the Home screen.
2. Tap in the location where you want to add a picture. Notice a + icon that appears above the virtual keyboard (see *Figure 15.9*).
3. Tap the + icon to display icons above the virtual keyboard (see *Figure 15.24*).
4. Tap the Camera icon. A list of options appears (see *Figure 15.23*).
5. Tap **Take a Photo or Video**.
6. Choose **Video** or **Photo** and tap the white (or red if recording video) button.
7. Tap the **Use Photo** or **Use Video** button.

Rather than capture a picture through the iPhone camera, you might have the perfect picture already stored in your Photo Library.

Adding a picture from the Photo Library to a note

Rather than take a picture, you could have the perfect picture or video already stored in the Photo Library. In that case, you can insert that picture or video into a note.

To browse the Photo Library in order to insert a picture or video into a note, follow these steps:

1. Tap the **Notes** app on the Home screen.
2. Tap in the location where you want to add a picture. Notice a + icon that appears above the virtual keyboard (see *Figure 15.9*).
3. Tap the + icon to display icons above the virtual keyboard (see *Figure 15.24*).
4. Tap the Camera icon. A list of options appears (see *Figure 15.23*).
5. Tap **Choose Photo or Video**. The **Photos** screen appears.
6. Tap a category and tap a picture or video to insert into a note.
7. Tap **Done** in the upper-right corner of the screen to insert your selected picture or video into the note.

While inserting a picture into a note may capture your ideas, sometimes you may want to draw something that doesn't exist. In that case, you can scribble ideas and insert them in a note.

Drawing in a note

With a pencil or pen, you can write text, draw pictures, or add ideas to existing text. In many ways, drawing pictures can be faster and more descriptive so the **Notes** app lets you draw images in a note as well.

> **Note**
>
> You may find it easier to create a drawing in a separate note and then cut and paste that drawing to paste into a note with existing text.

To draw in a note, follow these steps:

1. Tap the **Notes** app on the Home screen.
2. Choose a folder.
3. Tap the New Note icon to create a new note.
4. Tap in the location where you want to add a drawing. Notice a + icon that appears above the virtual keyboard (see *Figure 15.9*).
5. Tap the + icon to display icons above the virtual keyboard, as shown in *Figure 15.28*:

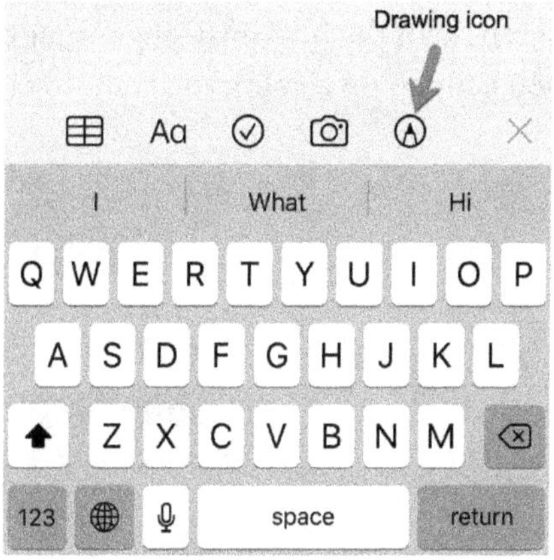

Figure 15.28 – The Drawing icon

6. Tap the Drawing icon. Icons representing different drawing tools appear at the bottom of the screen, as shown in *Figure 15.29*:

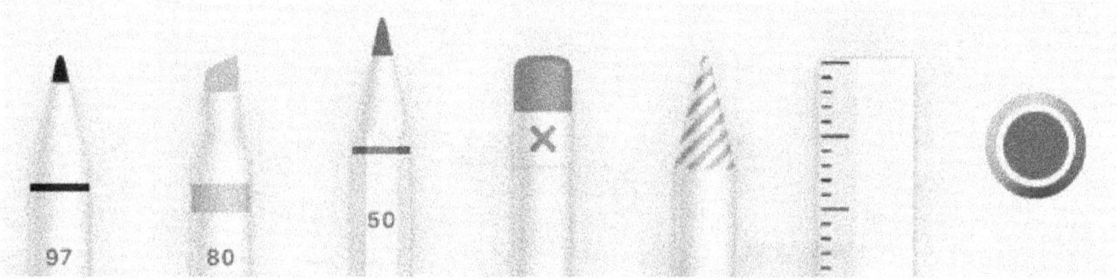

Figure 15.29 – Drawing tools

7. Tap on a drawing tool and drag your fingertip across the screen to create a drawing.
8. (Optional:) Tap a drawing tool to display a drawing thickness, as shown in *Figure 15.30*:

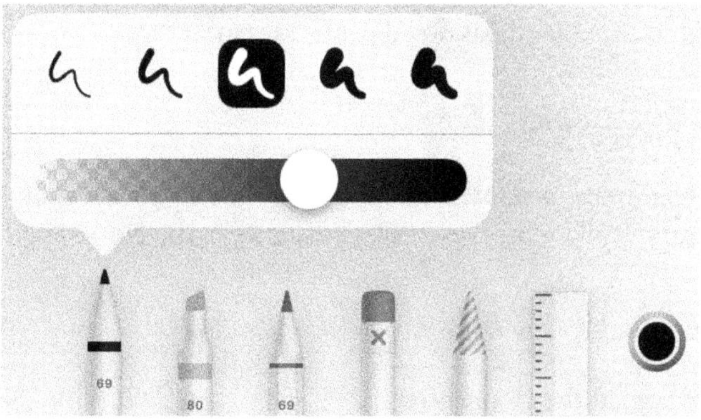

Figure 15.30 – Choosing a drawing tool modification

9. (Optional) Tap the color circle in the bottom-right corner of the screen to display a color palette so that you can tap on a color you want to choose, as shown in *Figure 15.31*:

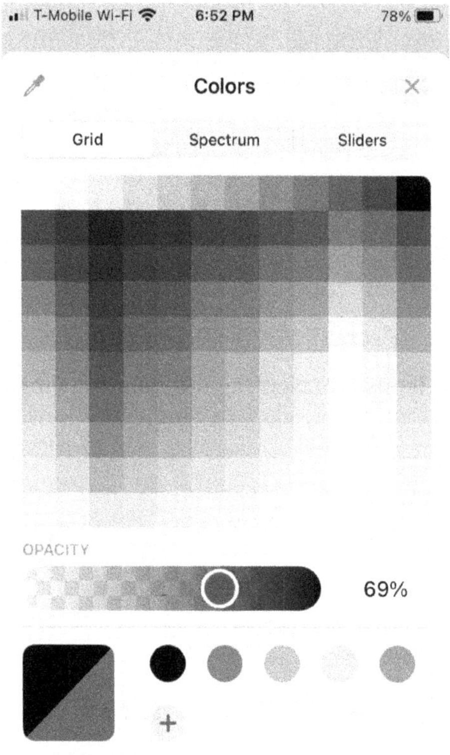

Figure 15.31 – Displaying a color palette

By adding drawings to a note, you can also capture your ideas in whatever form is easiest and fastest for you, whether it be text, pictures, or drawings. Once you create one or more notes, you may need to search and password protect them.

Searching notes

Once you've typed text in one or more notes, you may want to find it again. Rather than manually browse through all your notes, it's far easier to let the **Notes** app search through your text in your notes.

To search for text in a note, follow these steps:

1. Tap the **Notes** app on the Home screen.
2. Tap on a folder that contains the notes you want to search.

3. Tap in the **Search** text field at the top of the screen, as shown in *Figure 15.32*:

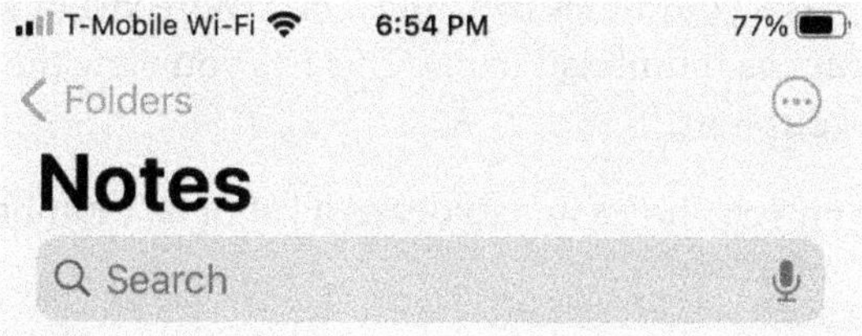

Figure 15.32 – The Search text field

4. Tap in the **Search** text field and type part or all of a word or phrase you want to find. The **Notes** app displays all matches, as shown in *Figure 15.33*:

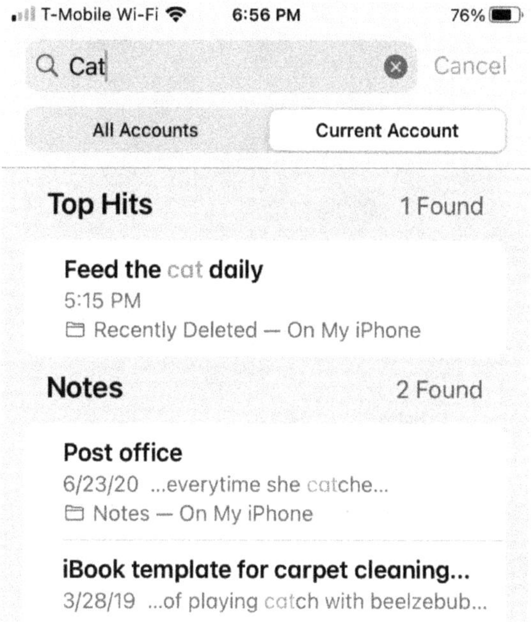

Figure 15.33 – Matching search results

5. Tap the note that contains the search result you want.

Searching notes for text can help you pinpoint the exact note you want. However, in case you just want to browse through your notes, there's another way to display your notes beyond just a list of note names.

Viewing notes as thumbnails

By default, the **Notes** app lists your notes by name. For a more visual way to display your notes, you can display notes as thumbnail icons. This lets you view the text in each note to help you find the one you want.

To toggle between showing your notes in a folder as a list or as thumbnails, follow these steps:

1. Tap the **Notes** app on the Home screen.
2. Tap on a folder to show a list of all notes stored in that folder.
3. Tap on the three dot icon in the upper-right corner of the screen to display a menu, as shown in *Figure 15.34*:

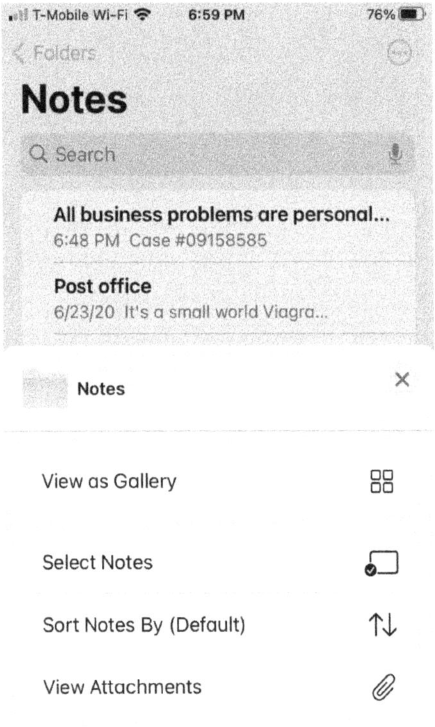

Figure 15.34 – Switching to Gallery view to show notes as thumbnail images

4. Tap **View as Gallery** to toggle between showing your notes as a list or as thumbnail images.

No matter how you view or search your notes, you may have some notes that are more important than others. To protect your privacy, consider password protecting a note.

Password protecting notes

If anyone gets a hold of your iPhone and unlocks it, they can read all your notes. In case you have some important notes that you don't want others to read, you can password protect them.

To password protect a note, follow these steps:

1. Tap the **Notes** app on the Home screen.
2. Tap on a folder that contains the note you want to password protect.
3. Tap on the note you want to password protect.
4. Tap the three dot icon in the upper-right corner of the screen. A menu appears, as shown in *Figure 15.35*:

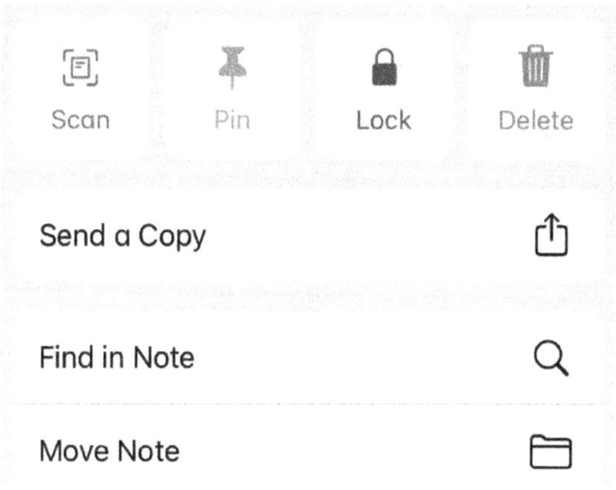

Figure 15.35 – The Lock icon

5. Tap the **Lock** icon. A Set Password screen appears, which either asks for Face ID or Touch ID.
6. Tap **Done**.

Once you have set a password for a note, you can lock and unlock it by repeating the preceding steps. A lock icon appears to let you know which notes are locked, as shown in *Figure 15.36*:

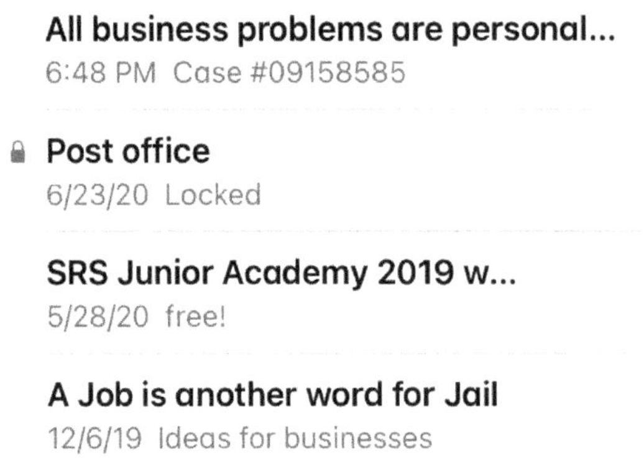

Figure 15.36 – A locked icon on a note

To unlock or lock a note, follow these steps:

1. Tap the **Notes** app on the Home screen.
2. Tap on a folder that contains the note you want to open.
3. Tap on a locked note. A screen appears, letting you know that the note is locked, as shown in *Figure 15.37*:

Figure 15.37 – A locked note

4. Tap **View Note**. A dialog appears.
5. Use Touch ID or Face ID to unlock the note.
6. (Optional:) Tap the unlock icon in the upper-right corner to lock the note when you're done editing or viewing it, as shown in *Figure 15.38*:

Figure 15.38 – The Unlock icon

By locking your notes, you can help protect your privacy even if someone manages to unlock your iPhone.

> **Note**
> To delete a locked note, you must use Touch ID or Face ID.

Capturing audio with Voice Memos

Some people prefer talking rather than writing their thoughts down. As an alternative, you can capture your spoken thoughts using the Voice Memos app.

To capture an audio recording, follow these steps:

1. Tap the **Voice Memos** app on the Home screen.
2. Tap the red Record button and start talking.
3. Tap the red Stop button when you're done talking.
4. The Voice Memos screen displays your audio memo with the time, as shown in *Figure 15.39*:

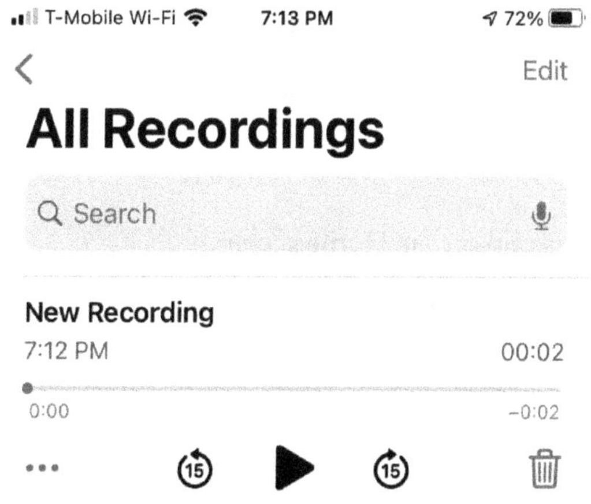

Figure 15.39 – The Voice Memos screen listing an audio recording

After you have recorded a voice memo, you can tap the Play button to listen to it, or drag the slider to move to different parts of the audio file. You can also tap in the location text of your audio memo if you want to type something more descriptive.

To share an audio file, follow these steps:

1. Tap the **Voice Memos** app on the Home screen.
2. Tap the three dots icon (see *Figure 15.39*). A menu appears, as shown in *Figure 15.40*:

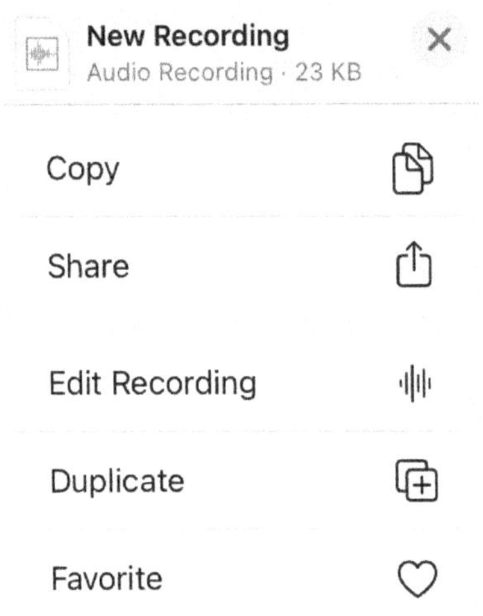

Figure 15.40 – Tapping the three dots icon displays a menu

3. Tap **Share**. A list of different devices and methods for sharing appears.
4. Tap a device name or method, such as **Messages** or Mail, to share your voice memo.

Once you record a voice memo, you can go back and overwrite part of that voice memo or add new audio to that voice memo. To see how to modify an existing voice memo, follow these steps:

1. Tap the **Voice Memos** app on the Home screen.
2. Tap the three dots icon (see *Figure 15.39*). A menu appears (see *Figure 15.40*).
3. Tap **Edit Recording**. An edit voice memo screen appears showing the existing audio file, as shown in *Figure 15.41*:

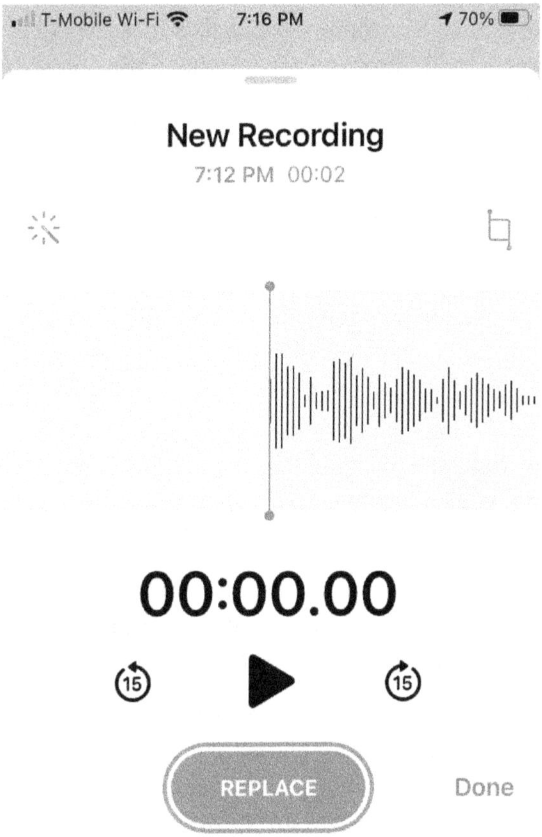

Figure 15.41 – The edit voice memo screen

4. Swipe the audio file left or right. When the blue vertical line appears over existing audio, a **REPLACE** button appears at the bottom of the screen. When the blue vertical line appears at the end of the audio, a Resume button appears at the bottom of the screen.
5. Tap the **REPLACE** or Resume button and record more audio.
6. Tap the Pause button when you're done.
7. Tap **Done**.

While you might want to edit a voice memo to add new ideas, you'll eventually want to get rid of a voice memo altogether. To delete a voice memo, follow these steps:

1. Tap the **Voice Memos** app on the Home screen.
2. Tap the voice memo you want to delete.
3. Tap the **Delete** icon.

Voice memos can be handy for capturing ideas in case you can't or don't like to type in the **Notes** app. By using voice memos, you can capture your thoughts as fast as you can talk.

Summary

The **Notes** app can be the best way to capture your thoughts wherever you take your iPhone. Not only can you type and format text, but you can also capture pictures or video to insert in a note as well.

To help you stay organized, consider creating separate folders to store related notes such as notes for work and notes for personal use. You can use notes to create daily to-do lists or just thoughts you have during the day that you won't want to forget.

You might also use the **Notes** app as a fast way to store useful information, such as website addresses or pictures of interesting places. The **Notes** app can help you save any information you think is worth keeping. If you prefer not to write anything down, consider using the Voice Memo app instead to capture your spoken thoughts.

Since most people take their iPhone everywhere they go, one useful feature is the Maps app, which can not only show you where you are, but also give you directions to get to wherever you want to go, which is the topic of the next chapter.

16
Getting Directions with Maps

When you're in an unfamiliar neighborhood, you may not know where you are or how to get to where you want to go. Even if you're in a familiar part of town, you may not know how to get to certain places, such as stores, parks, or buildings. To help you get around, you need a map.

Of course, paper maps quickly go out of date, so a far better solution is to use the Maps app on your iPhone. Not only can the Maps app accurately map your location as long as you have a cellular phone or Wi-Fi connection, but it can provide directions in major cities around the world.

With your iPhone and the Maps app, you'll never risk getting lost again, whether you're looking for a new place near your home or trying to navigate an unfamiliar part of the world.

The topics covered in this chapter are as follows:

- Customizing the Maps app
- Getting directions
- Searching around you
- Creating favorite locations

- Placing markers on a map
- Using the compass
- Changing the appearance of a map

Customizing the Maps app

Before you start using the **Maps** app, you might want to customize it, such as changing whether it displays distances in miles or kilometers, and whether to make driving or transit the default transportation type displayed.

To customize the **Maps** app, follow these steps:

1. Tap the **Settings** app on the Home Screen. The **Settings** screen appears.
2. Scroll down and tap **Maps**. The **Maps** screen displays various settings you can select, as shown in *Figure 16.1*:

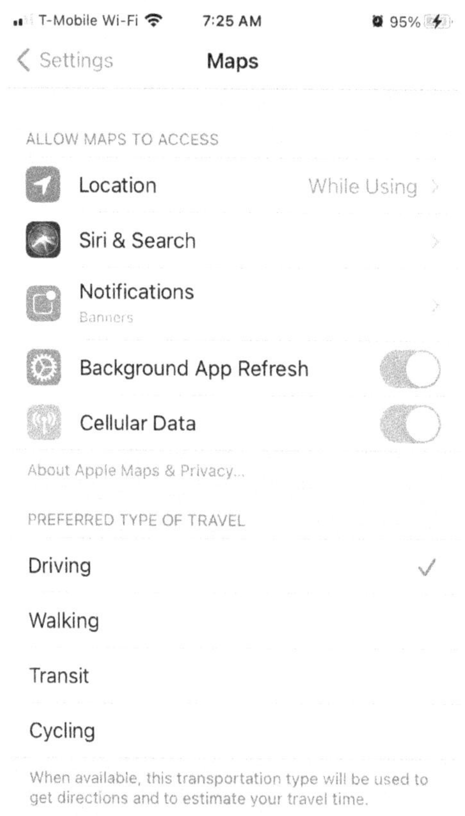

Figure 16.1 – Settings to customize the Maps app

3. Scroll down and choose any options you wish, such as setting distances to miles or kilometers, or changing the default transportation type from driving to transit.
4. Tap **Navigation & Guidance**. A **Navigation & Guidance** screen appears, as shown in *Figure 16.2*:

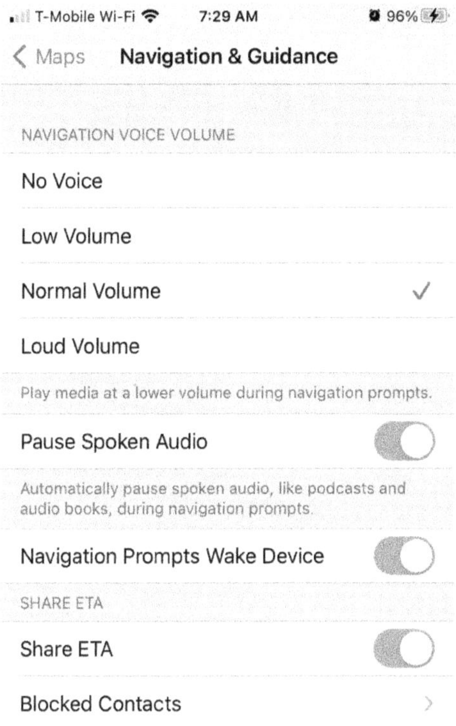

Figure 16.2 – Settings to customize the Maps app

5. Tap any further options, such as adjusting the volume for hearing directions.
6. Tap the **Back** button in the upper-left corner of the screen to return to the **Maps** screen.

Once you've customized the **Maps** app with the options you like, you can start using **Maps** to get directions to where you want to go.

Getting directions

No matter where you are, you can't get to a new location until you know where you're at right now. To get acquainted with the **Maps** app, follow these steps:

1. Tap the **Maps** app on the Home Screen. A blue dot will highlight your current location, as shown in *Figure 16.3*:

Figure 16.3 – A blue dot highlights your current location

2. Pinch two fingers closer together on the screen to see more details, as shown in *Figure 16.4*:

Figure 16.4 – Pinching two fingers together zooms in

3. Pinch two fingers further apart on the screen to zoom out and see a larger-scale map, as shown in *Figure 16.5*:

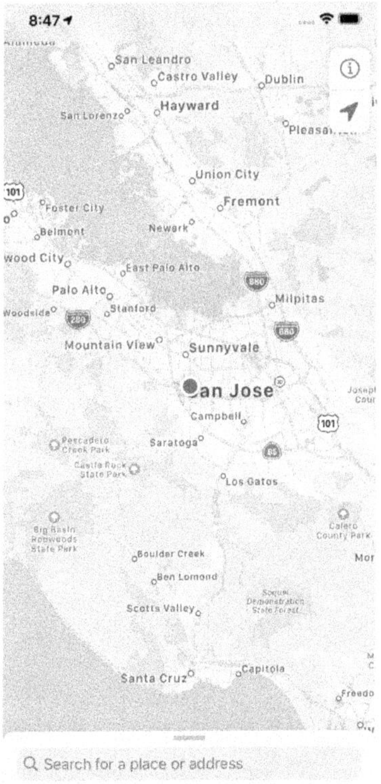

Figure 16.5 – Pinching two fingers apart zooms out

4. Tap in the **Search** text field at the bottom of the screen. A virtual keyboard appears and lists recent searches along with common places to search for, such as restaurants, as shown in *Figure 16.6*:

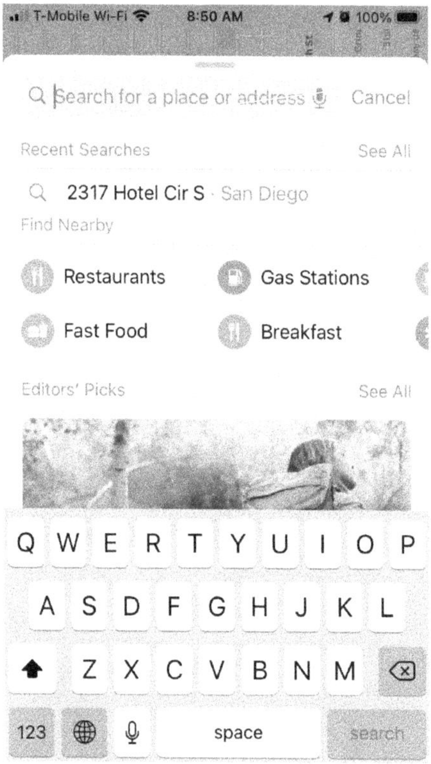

Figure 16.6 – Using the Search text field

5. Type a place or street address and tap the **Search** button in the bottom-right corner of the virtual keyboard. Your search result appears, as shown in *Figure 16.7*:

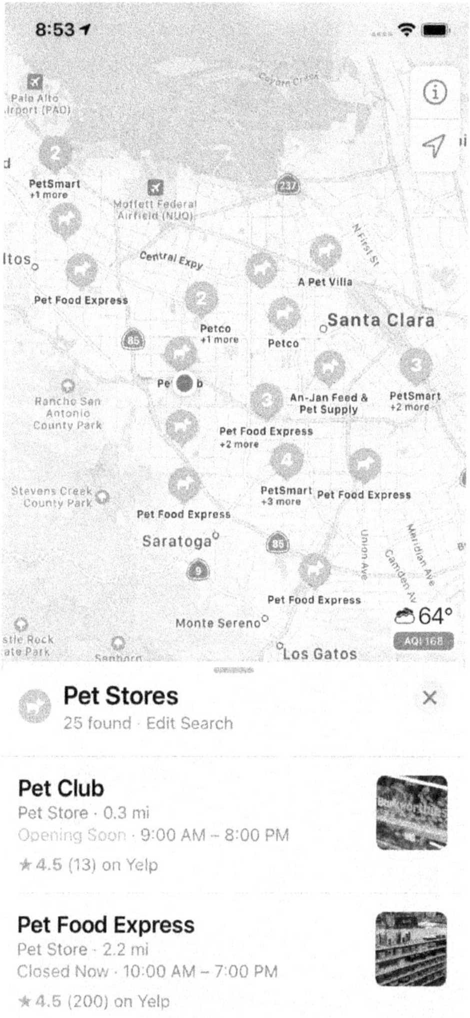

Figure 16.7 – Viewing search results

6. (Optional:) Tap a location (if you searched for a type of place, such as a gas station or restaurant). The **Maps** app displays your chosen location in more detail with a **Directions** button, as shown in *Figure 16.8*:

Figure 16.8 – The Directions button

7. Tap the **Directions** button. The **Maps** app displays different routes and options, such as driving, walking, or mass transit, as shown in *Figure 16.9*:

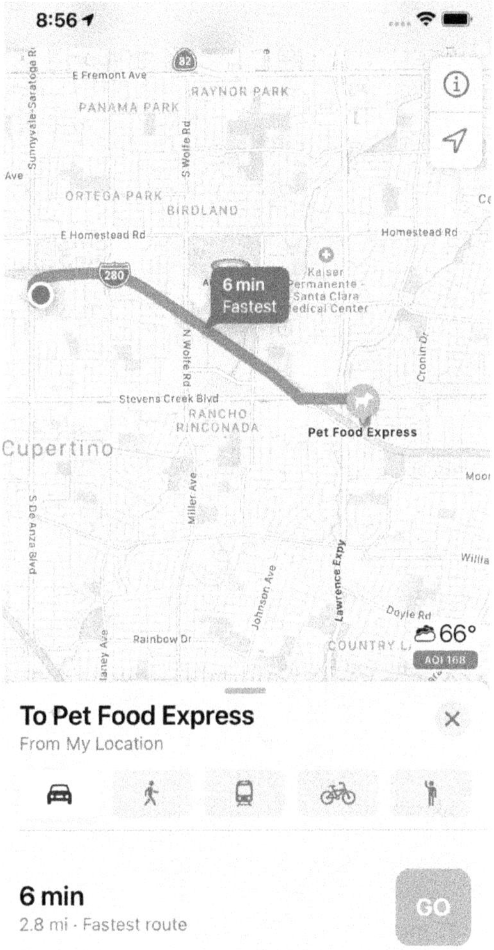

Figure 16.9 – Displaying a route

8. (Optional:) Tap a different icon at the bottom of the screen, such as Walk or Transit, to see different options for getting to where you want to go, as shown in *Figure 16.10*:

Figure 16.10 – Displaying an alternative way to travel

9. Tap the **Go** button to get directions. The **Maps** app displays directions as you travel, as shown in *Figure 16.11*:

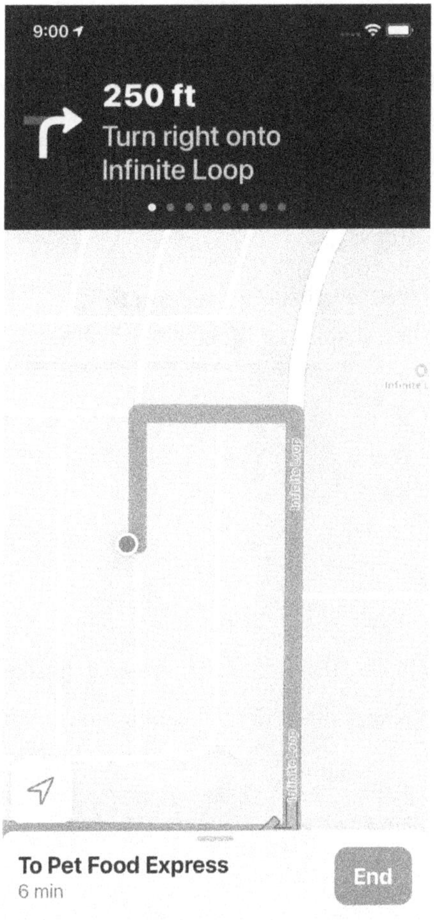

Figure 16.11 – Directions appear as you travel to your destination

Sometimes you may want to go somewhere but stop at places along the way to pick up food or buy gas for your car. Rather than create two separate destinations, you can simply create a detour while heading toward your final destination.

Adding a detour

When you're traveling toward your destination, you might want to stop along the way to get gas (if you're driving) or get something to eat. The **Maps** app will then show you the nearest options so you can pick one and get directions to that destination before heading on to your final destination.

To add a detour, follow these steps:

1. Follow the steps in the *Getting directions* section to start traveling toward a chosen destination. The **Maps** app displays a sheet at the bottom of the screen, as shown in *Figure 16.12*:

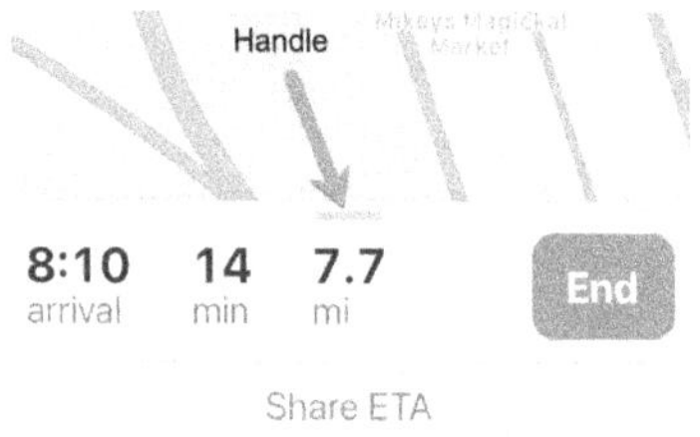

Figure 16.12 – The sheet at the bottom of the screen

2. Swipe the handle up to reveal more details, as shown in *Figure 16.13*:

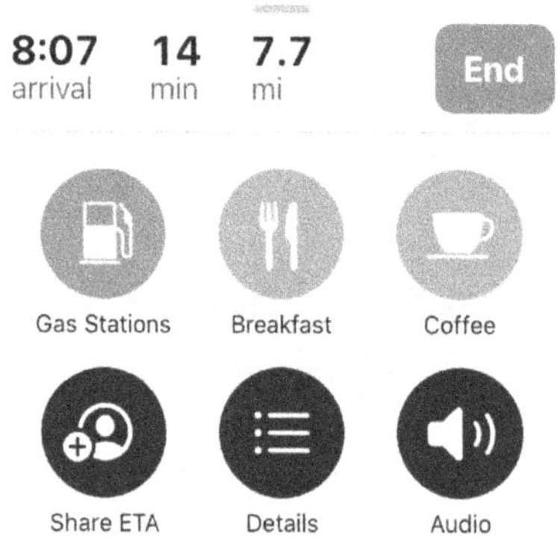

Figure 16.13 – The fully revealed sheet at the bottom of the screen

3. Tap a detour destination, such as **Gas Stations** or **Coffee**. The **Maps** app displays a list of options.
4. Tap an option. The **Maps** app will now give directions to your detour.

The **Maps** app gives you directions as you arrive at intersections or places where there are multiple directions in which you can go. Fortunately, you can see a complete list of instructions, so you know in advance where you need to go.

Viewing a list of instructions

As you travel, the **Maps** app will show and tell you where to go next. However, you may want to view a list of all the instructions. To view a list of instructions, follow these steps:

1. Follow the steps in the *Getting directions* section to start traveling toward a chosen destination.
2. Swipe up the handle to reveal the entire sheet at the bottom of the screen (see *Figure 16.13*).
3. Tap the **Details** icon. A list of instructions appears, as shown in *Figure 16.14*:

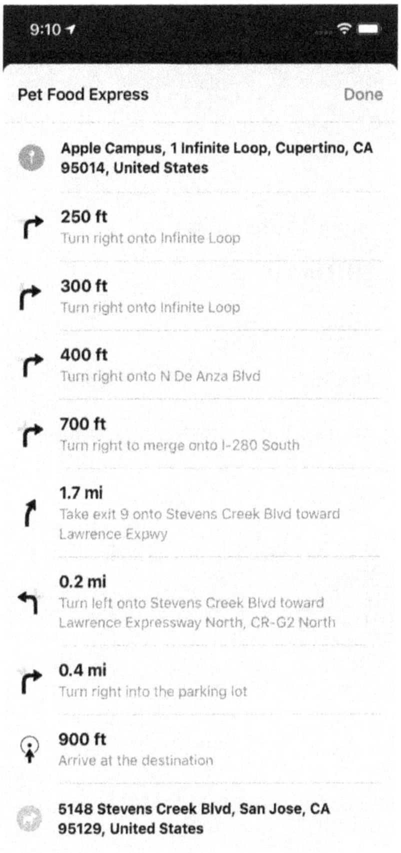

Figure 16.14 – A list of traveling directions

4. Tap **Done** when you're finished viewing the list of instructions.

Sometimes, you might be in a part of town and just want to know what's around you so you can decide which direction you want to go in. In that case, the **Maps** app can show you what's around you, so you can choose from those nearby options which way to go.

Searching around you

If you're in an unfamiliar area, you may not know where you want to go, but you may know you want to go to a restaurant, coffeehouse, or a supermarket. Rather than search for a specific location, you can ask the **Maps** app to show you what's around you.

To find what's around you, follow these steps:

1. Tap the **Maps** app on the Home Screen.
2. Tap in the **Search** text field. A list of recent searches along with a list of nearby places appears, as shown in *Figure 16.15*:

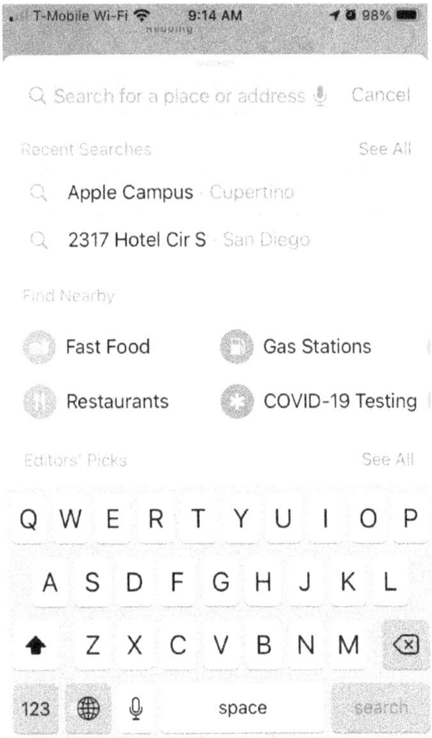

Figure 16.15 – A list of nearby places

3. Tap the type of place you want to find, such as **Groceries or Fast Food**. The **Maps** app displays a list of options, as shown in *Figure 16.16*:

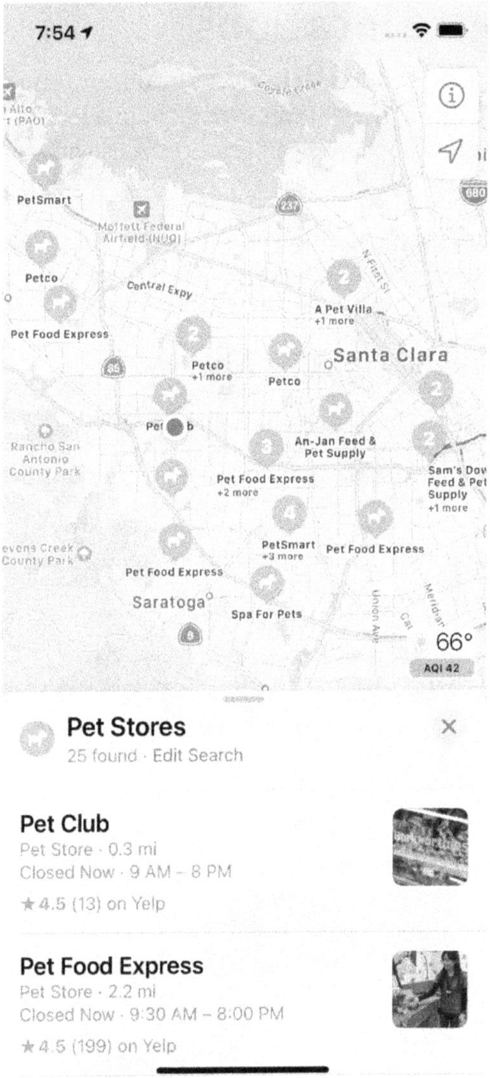

Figure 16.16 – Displaying a list of options for the category you chose

4. Tap on a specific place. The **Maps** app displays a **Directions** button.
5. Tap this **Directions** button and choose a travel option, such as **Driving** or **Transit**, to see your route.

In many cases, you'll tend to visit the same places over and over again. Rather than keep searching for them, you might prefer to store your favorite places in a list that you can then access quickly without searching for it again.

Creating favorite locations

You likely have a favorite restaurant, nightclub, gas station, and supermarket. To make it easy to find your favorite locations, you can save them in a list. That way, when you want to visit one of your favorite locations, you can get directions with a minimal amount of searching.

The first step is to find your favorite location and then save it in your favorites list. Once you've done that, you can then open this favorites list and get directions to a specific location with one tap.

To save a location in your favorite list, follow these steps:

1. Tap the **Maps** app on the Home Screen.
2. Search for a location that you want to save as a favorite until you see a blue **Directions** button.
3. Swipe up on the handle near the bottom of the screen to reveal the entire list of options, as shown in *Figure 16.17*:

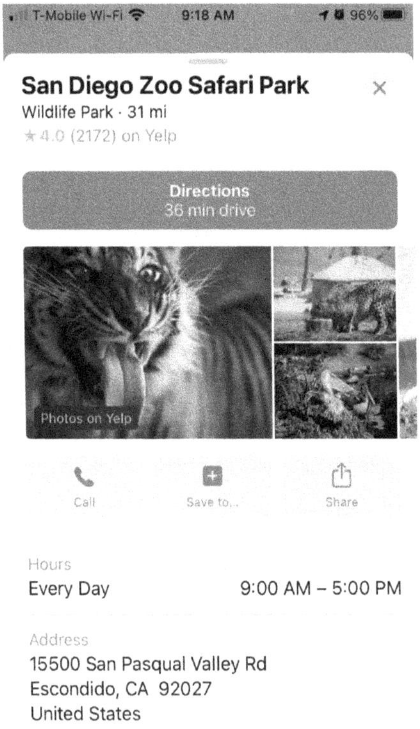

Figure 16.17 – Revealing the Save to... button

4. Tap the **Save to...** button. A list of collections appears. If you have not created a guide yet, a **New Guide...** button appears, as shown in *Figure 16.18*:

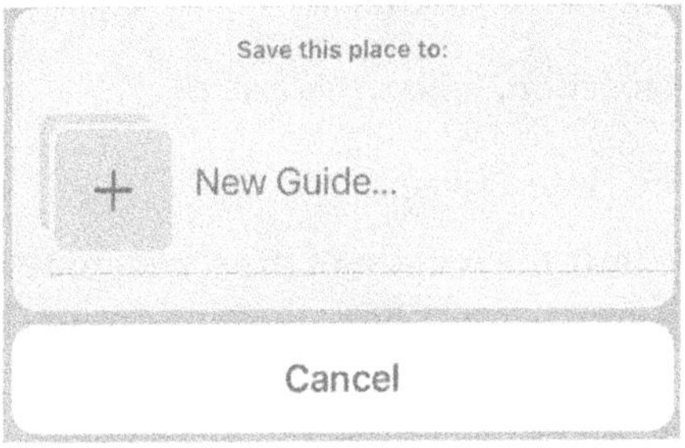

Figure 16.18 – Adding a location to a collection

5. Tap the **New Guide** button. A **New Guide** screen appears, as shown in *Figure 16.19*:

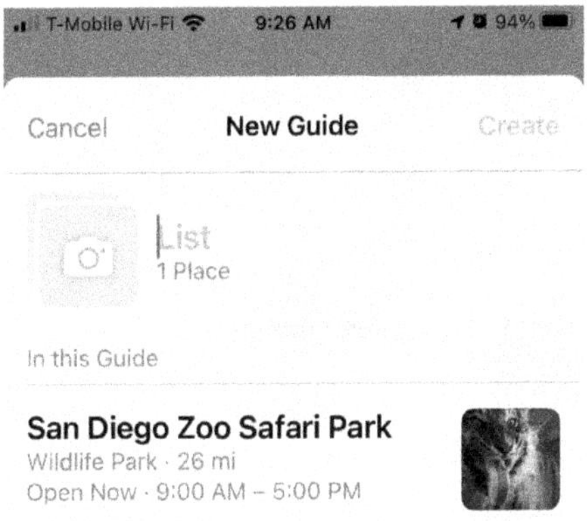

Figure 16.19 – The New Guide screen

6. Type a descriptive name for your guide and then tap **Create**.

Once you've created a guide and added at least one item to that guide, you can access that favorite location at any time.

Using a guide

Once you've stored one or more locations in a collection, you can open that collection at any time to access your list of stored locations.

To get directions to a favorite location, follow these steps:

1. Tap the **Maps** app on the Home Screen.
2. Swipe up on the handle near the bottom of the screen to reveal a complete list of options. The **Guide** category lists all the named guides you have created, as shown in *Figure 16.20*:

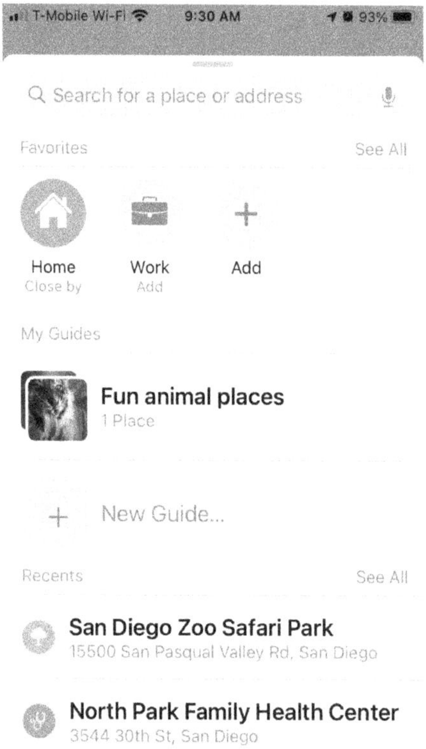

Figure 16.20 – A list of saved collections

3. Tap on the guide name you want to open. A list of saved locations appears inside that collection.
4. Tap on a location to display the blue **Directions** button.
5. Tap the **Directions** button to get directions to your favorite location.

No matter how much you like a location, eventually you may want to delete either that single location or an entire collection storing your favorite locations.

Deleting a location in a guide

You can delete an entire guide (along with any locations stored inside that guide), or just delete an individual location within a guide.

To delete an entire guide or just one location in a guide, follow these steps:

1. Tap the **Maps** app on the Home Screen.
2. Swipe up on the handle near the bottom of the screen to reveal a complete list of options. The Guide category lists all the named collections you have created (see *Figure 16.20*).
3. Tap a guide. A list of favorite locations stored in that guide appears.
4. Swipe left on any stored location. A **Remove** button appears, as shown in *Figure 16.21*:

Figure 16.21 – The Remove button

5. Tap **Remove**. (If you tap the **Share** button, you'll be able to send that location information to someone by email, text messaging, or AirDrop.)

In case you want to delete an entire guide instead of a single location, follow these steps:

1. Tap the **Maps** app on the Home Screen.
2. Swipe up on the handle near the bottom of the screen to reveal a complete list of options. The Guide category lists all the named guides you have created (see *Figure 16.20*).
3. Swipe left on a collection name to display the **Remove** button.
4. Tap **Remove**. A message appears at the bottom of the screen, asking for you to verify that you want to delete an entire collection.
5. Tap **Delete**.

To help you navigate around, you might also want to add markers on a map to identify specific areas of interest.

Placing markers on a map

On a paper map, you might scribble some notes to highlight an area of particular importance, such as someone's house or a favorite area to go hiking. With the **Maps** app, you can also add markers to highlight any area you wish.

By creating a marker, you can identify a place and either save that location so you can find it easily again, or share that location with others so they can find it as well.

To place a marker on a map, follow these steps:

1. Tap the **Maps** app on the Home Screen.
2. Press and hold a fingertip on the screen where you want to place a marker. A marker appears, as shown in *Figure 16.22*:

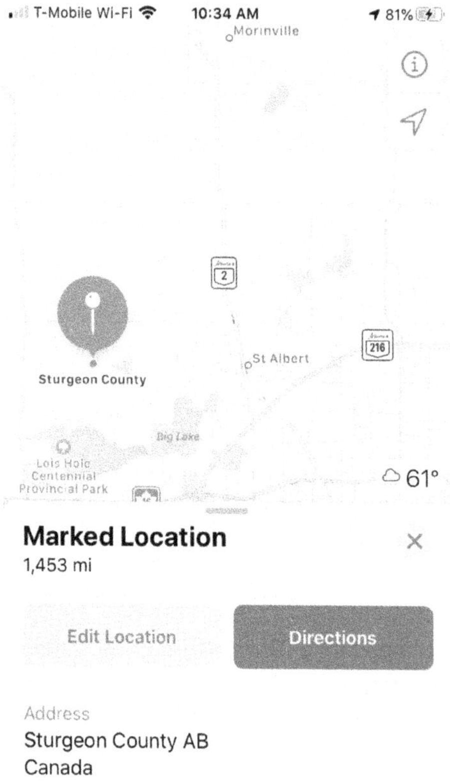

Figure 16.22 – Placing a marker

3. Tap the **Edit Location** button. An **Edit Location** screen appears, letting you place your marker more precisely, as shown in *Figure 16.23*:

Figure 16.23 – Placing a marker

4. Slide and pinch the screen to precisely place the marker over a specific area and then tap **Done**.

5. Slide the handle up to display a **Marked Location** screen, as shown in *Figure 16.24*. At this point, you can tap the **Save** button to store this in a guide or tap the **Share** button to share this location with another person. You can also tap **Remove** to remove the marker from the map:

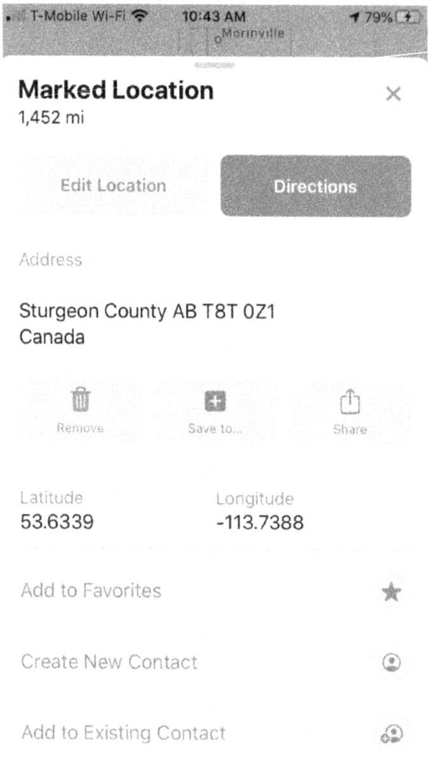

Figure 16.24 – The Marked Location screen

Markers can help you customize a map, but sometimes you may not care about finding a specific location, but about traveling in a specific direction using a compass.

Using the compass

If you're ever lost and need to travel in a specific direction, you can turn your iPhone into a compass. That way, you can see where you want to go and use the **Maps** app to show you how to keep heading in the direction you want to go.

To see how to use a compass in the **Maps** app, follow these steps:

1. Tap the **Maps** app on the Home Screen.
2. Press two fingers on the screen and rotate the screen to show the compass in the upper-right corner of the screen, as shown in *Figure 16.25*:

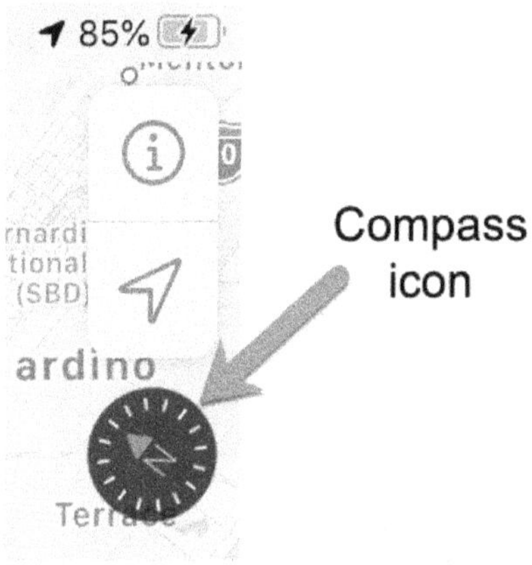

Figure 16.25 – The compass in the Map app

3. Tap the Compass icon to make it go away.

The compass can help you navigate in a particular direction. By default, the **Maps** app displays a cartoon version of an area, but you can switch this appearance to a more realistic satellite image instead.

Changing the appearance of a map

To make it easy to see a map, the **Maps** app displays a cartoon representation of an area. However, you can also switch to a photo-realistic satellite view.

To change the appearance of the map, follow these steps:

1. Tap the **Maps** app on the Home Screen.
2. Tap the **I** icon in the upper-right corner of the screen. A **Maps Settings** sheet appears, as shown in *Figure 16.26*:

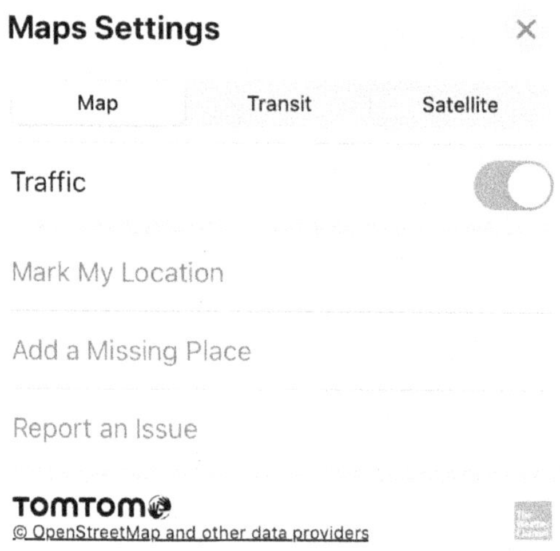

Figure 16.26 – The Maps Setting screen

3. Tap the **Transit** tab to view the map, highlighting mass transit routes, or tap the **Satellite** tab to view a photo-realistic version of the map, as shown in *Figure 16.27*:

Figure 16.27 – The satellite view of a map

4. Tap the close (**X**) icon in the upper-right corner of the sheet to make it go away.

At any time, you can repeat the aforementioned steps to switch back to another version of the map, depending on what you prefer.

Summary

The Maps app can be useful, whether you're traveling in an unfamiliar area or even in your own neighborhood, because it can show you the fastest route to a specific destination. Even if car accidents or detours appear, the Maps app will give you the fastest route, along with alternate routes if you prefer taking a different road.

Besides using the Maps app for directions, you can also use the Maps app to locate favorite spots or places and share those locations with others. If those people also have an iPhone, they can then get directions to that location by driving, walking, or taking mass transit.

The Maps app is handy any time you need to go anywhere. As you travel, you might also want to know the weather conditions in the direction you're heading, or keep track of time or your stock portfolio if you wish.

In the next chapter, we will look at how we can change time and weather settings as well as get stock information.

17

Getting Time, Weather, and Stock Information

One reason why the iPhone has proven so popular is that it can be almost anything you want it to be. Besides letting you make phone calls and send text messages, an iPhone can also be a timepiece and a source for news. Two common types of news that people often want are weather forecasts and stock quote information.

An iPhone comes with the Clock app for not only helping you keep track of time in other parts of the world, but also to serve as a timer and stopwatch so that you can keep track of minutes or seconds to time yourself for exercising, cooking, or any other activity that involves keeping track of time.

The Weather app lets you get the forecast not just for your own area but for any city around the world. This way, you can know the temperatures and climate in another part of the world that you may be traveling to soon so that you can dress appropriately.

Finally, the iPhone includes the Stocks app to let you watch stock quotes. This way, you can keep track of your portfolio and follow your favorite stocks to see how they're doing during the day.

The topics this chapter covers are as follows:

- Using the Clock app
- Getting weather forecasts
- Viewing stock quotes

Using the Clock app

The Clock app can show you the current time. When you open the Home screen on your iPhone, you can view the current time either at the top of the screen (which displays the time in digital format, such as 8:43 AM) or in the Clock app itself (which displays time in analog format, showing an hour and minute hand on a clock face).

The Clock app can do more than just display the current time. Its five features include the following:

- **World Clock**: Tracks time in different time zones
- **Alarm**: Sets one or more alarms so that your iPhone can alert you at a specific time
- **Bedtime**: Defines a time to sleep and wake up
- **Stopwatch**: Tracks the amount of time that has elapsed
- **Timer**: Defines a time interval to count down from, such as 5 minutes

You may not need all of these features, but chances are good that you'll likely want to use one or more of these features when carrying your iPhone one day.

Using the world clock

If you need to make phone calls to people who live in different time zones, you probably don't want to call when someone's likely to be asleep. Likewise, you probably don't want to schedule a phone call when you might be asleep.

To help you keep track of time zones around the world, use the **World Clock** feature to track time in common regions around the world, such as Berlin, Tokyo, or New York. By seeing the current time in another time zone, you'll know the time of the day in another part of the world.

To add a time zone to the **World Clock** feature, follow these steps:

1. Tap the **Clock** app on the Home screen.
2. Tap the **World Clock** icon at the bottom of the screen.

3. Tap the + icon in the upper-right corner of the screen. A **Choose a City** screen appears, as shown in *Figure 17.1*:

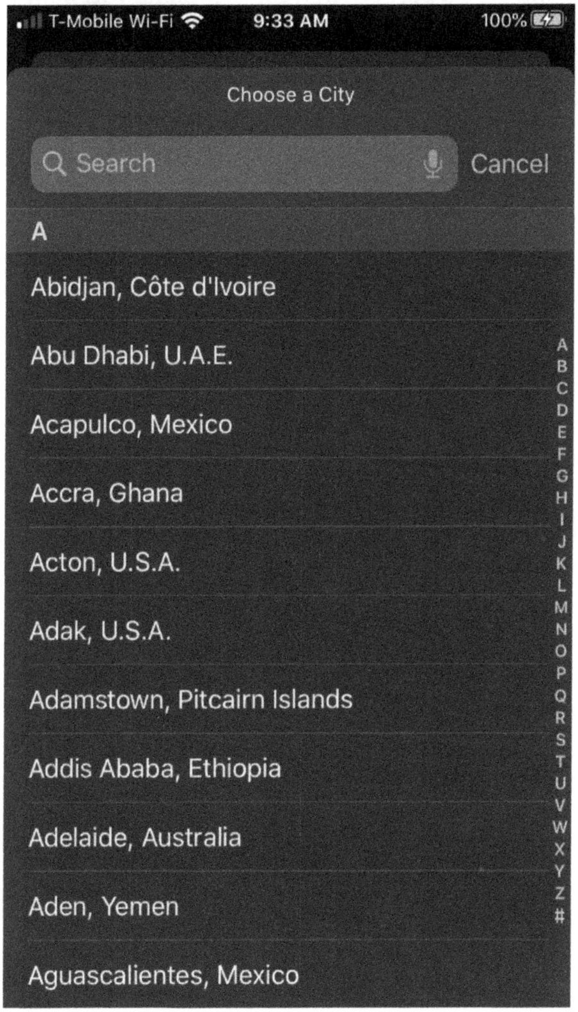

Figure 17.1 – Choosing a city to add to the world clock

4. Scroll through this list and tap a letter on the right side of the screen (such as **T** to jump to cities starting with T, such as Trinidad), or tap in the **Search** field at the top of the screen and type a part or all of the city name you want to use. A list of matching cities appears as you type, as shown in *Figure 17.2*:

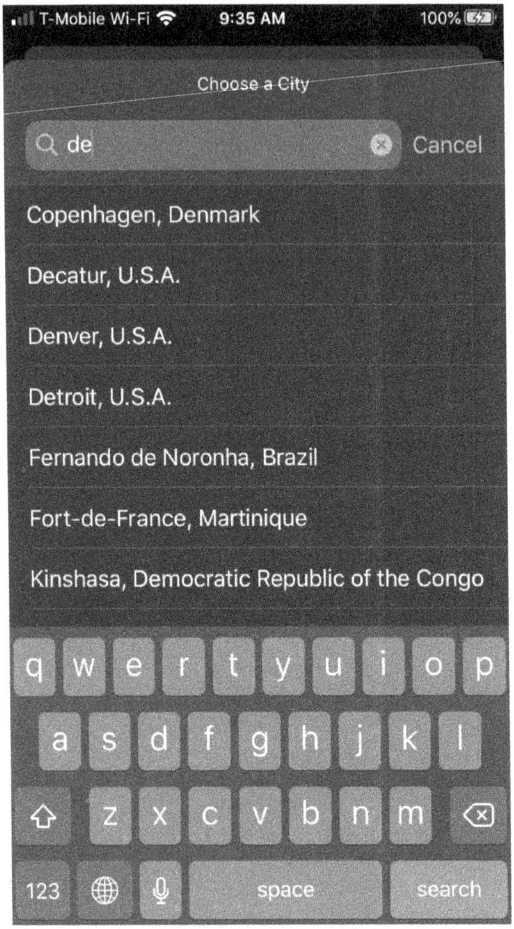

Figure 17.2 – Searching for a city

5. Tap on the city name.
6. Repeat *Steps 3–5* for each additional city you want to add to the world clock to create a list of different cities and their current times, as shown in *Figure 17.3*:

Figure 17.3 – A list of cities in different time zones

The Clock app organizes cities in the order you add them. If you want to rearrange the cities in the world clock list or remove a city from the list, follow these steps:

1. Tap the **Clock** app on the Home screen.
2. Tap the **World Clock** icon at the bottom of the screen.

3. Tap **Edit** in the upper-left corner of the screen. Notice that a three horizontal-line icon appears at the far right of each city, as shown in *Figure 17.4*:

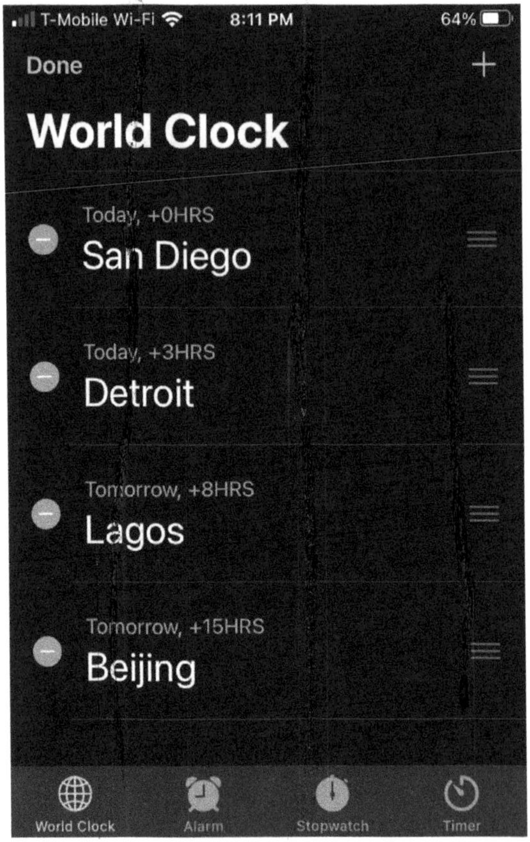

Figure 17.4 – The three horizontal-line icon lets you drag city names up or down

4. Slide the horizontal icon of the city you want to move up or down to rearrange your list.
5. Tap the white - symbol inside the red circle on the left of a city you want to remove, or swipe left. A red **Delete** button appears, as shown in *Figure 17.5*:

Figure 17.5 – Removing a city from the world clock list

6. Tap **Delete** to remove a city from the list.
7. Tap **Done**.

Of course, not everyone needs to know the time zone in another part of the world. For many people, it's far more important to wake up on time or set an alarm to remind them of an upcoming appointment.

Setting alarms

Alarms can be handy to wake up on time (such as catching a flight) or simply to remind you of an upcoming appointment. You can set as many alarms as you wish, but the basic idea is to define a time for the alarm to go off.

Once an alarm goes off, you can save that alarm to use in the future, or simply delete the alarm.

To set an alarm, follow these steps:

1. Tap the **Clock** app on the Home screen.
2. Tap the **Alarm** icon at the bottom of the screen. The **Alarm** screen appears.

3. Tap the + icon in the upper-right corner of the screen. An **Add Alarm** screen appears, as shown in *Figure 17.6*:

Figure 17.6 – The Add Alarm screen

4. Choose a time. You can either scroll up or down on the currently displayed time or type a time using the numerical keypad.
5. (Optional) tap **Repeat** and choose a day you want the alarm to repeat, such as **Every Monday** or **Every Thursday**.
6. (Optional) tap **Label** and type a descriptive name for your alarm.
7. (Optional) tap **Sound** and choose a sound for your alarm.
8. (Optional) tap the **Snooze** switch if you want to allow the snooze feature to temporarily shut off the alarm.

9. Tap **Save** in the upper-right corner of the screen. Your alarm now appears on the **Alarm** screen, as shown in *Figure 17.7*:

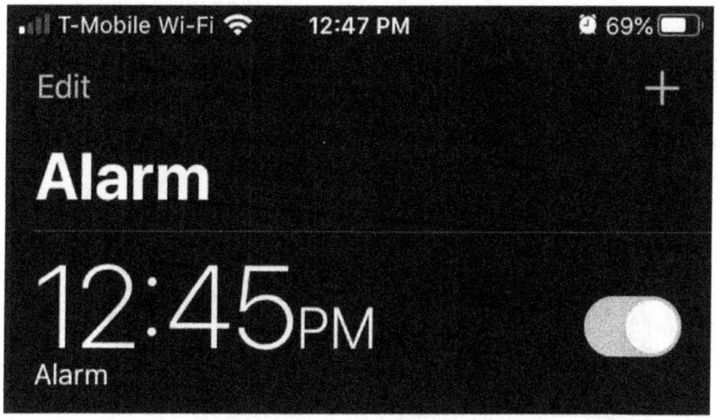

Figure 17.7 – An alarm set and ready to go

10. (Optional) tap the switch to the right of your alarm to toggle it off or on.

Once you set an alarm, you may want to modify it, such as changing its time or its label. To edit an existing alarm, follow these steps:

1. Tap the **Clock** app on the Home screen.
2. Tap the **Alarm** icon at the bottom of the screen. The **Alarm** screen appears.
3. Tap **Edit** in the upper-left corner of the screen.
4. Tap the alarm you want to modify. An **Edit Alarm** screen appears that looks nearly identical to the **Add Alarm** screen (see *Figure 17.6*).
5. Make any changes and tap **Save**. To delete an alarm, swipe left on that alarm and then tap the **Delete** button.

Alarms can be handy for making sure you wake up on time, but if you regularly need an alarm, you should use the **Bedtime** settings instead. Next, let's look at the stopwatch settings.

Using a stopwatch

A stopwatch is commonly used in time events such as a race. To use the stopwatch, follow these steps:

1. Tap the **Clock** app on the Home screen.
2. Tap the **Stopwatch** icon at the bottom of the screen. The stopwatch screen appears, as shown in *Figure 17.8*:

Figure 17.8 – The stopwatch screen

3. Tap the **Start** button to start tracking the time. When the stopwatch starts tracking the time, the **Start** button turns into a **Stop** button.
4. (Optional) tap the **Lap** button each time you want to record a separate time, as shown in *Figure 17.9*:

Figure 17.9 – Timing multiple laps

5. Tap **Reset** to clear the times and start at 0 again.

A stopwatch lets you track time, but sometimes you may want to count down from a certain time interval so that way you know when to take something out of the oven or when to stop exercising after a fixed time interval.

Setting a timer

When cooking, you may need to put something in the oven for 30 minutes or mix something for 10 minutes. That's when you need to set a timer and define a time interval to count down.

To set a timer, follow these steps:

1. Tap the **Clock** app on the Home screen.
2. Tap the **Timer** icon at the bottom of the screen. The timer screen appears, as shown in *Figure 17.10*:

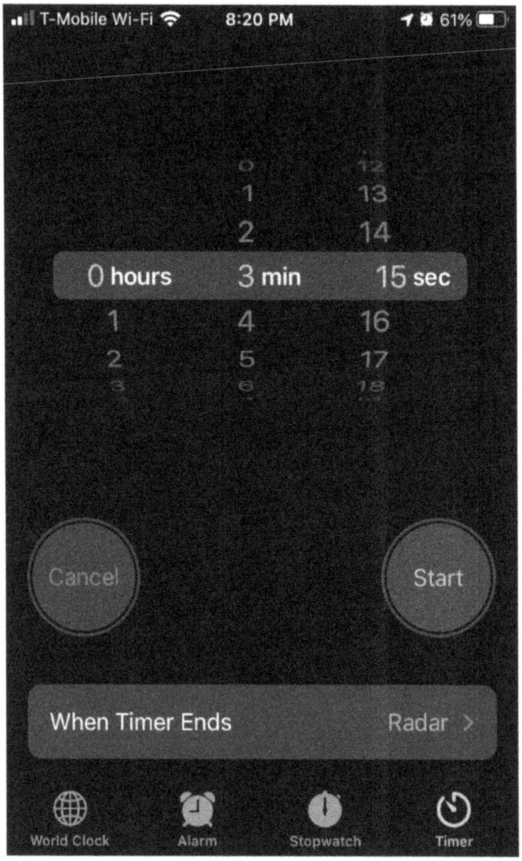

Figure 17.10 – The timer screen

3. Set a time interval to start counting down from, such as 3 minutes or 1 hour and 13 minutes.
4. (Optional) tap **When Timer Ends** and select a sound to use for when the timer reaches zero.
5. Tap the **Start** button.

Time is important, but when you're going outside, you may also want to know about the weather conditions so that you'll know to dress accordingly.

Getting weather forecasts

Knowing how to dress and what to wear can be important in your own city, along with any cities you may plan on visiting in the immediate future. By examining the weather forecast, you can plan for events, travel, and the clothing you'll need.

To use the weather forecast app, follow these steps:

1. Tap the **Weather** app on the Home screen.
2. Tap the three horizontal-line icon in the bottom-right corner of the screen. A list of different cities and their current temperatures appears, as shown in *Figure 17.11*:

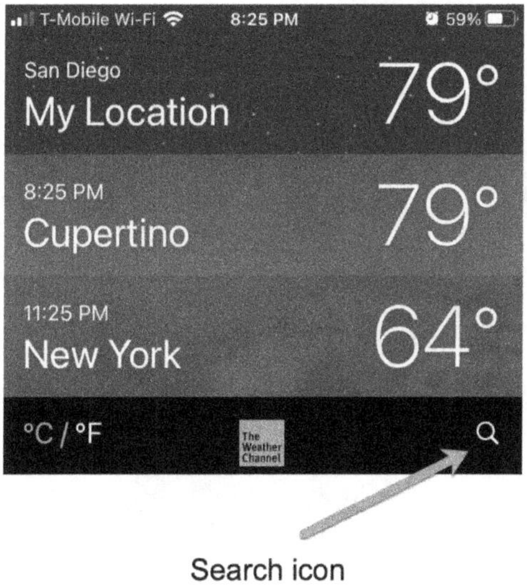

Figure 17.11 – The search icon

3. Tap the search icon. A **Search** text field appears at the top of the screen.

4. Type a part of or the entire city name. A list of the matching city names appears, as shown in *Figure 17.12*:

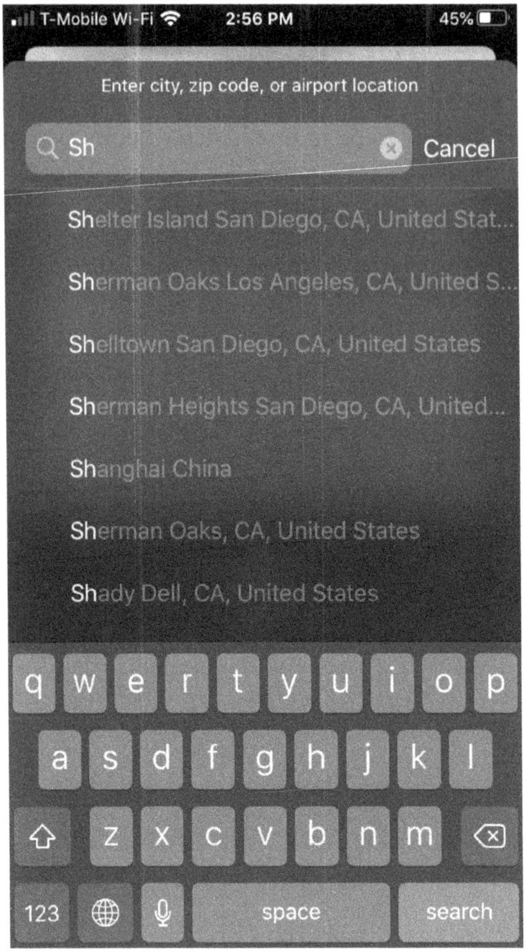

Figure 17.12 – Searching for city names

5. Tap a city name. That city's weather forecast appears.
6. Tap **Add** in the upper-right corner to add this city to your list of weather forecasts, and the result is as shown in *Figure 17.13*:

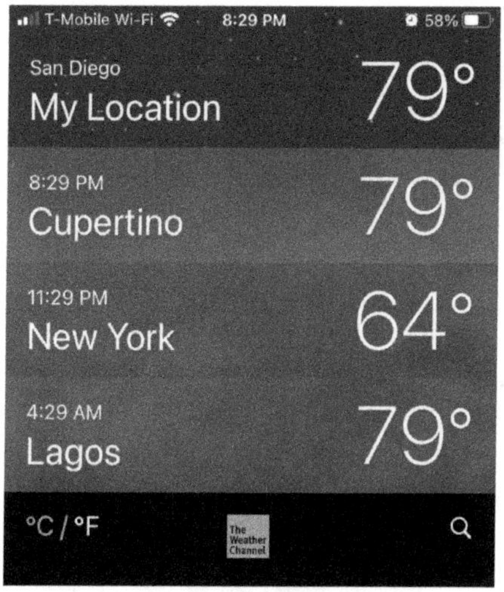

Figure 17.13 – A list of cities

7. Tap the **°C** or **°F** icon to view temperatures in Celsius or Fahrenheit.
8. Tap a city to view more detailed weather forecasts, as shown in *Figure 17.14*:

Figure 17.14 – A weather forecast for the next few days

9. Scroll down to see more weather information, as shown in *Figure 7.15*:

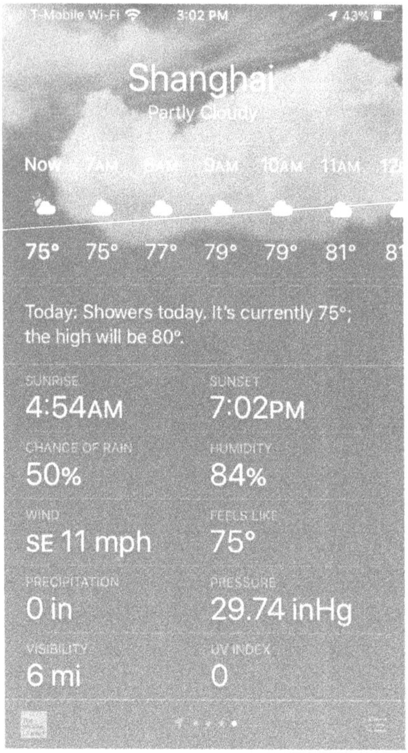

Figure 17.15 – Scrolling down displays additional weather information

10. Swipe left or right to view forecasts for other cities on your list.

Once you've defined a city to display weather forecasts, you can always remove a city if you no longer want to see forecasts for that city. To remove a city from the weather forecast list, follow these steps:

1. Tap the **Weather** app on the Home screen.
2. If a single city's weather forecast appears, tap the list icon in the bottom-right corner of the screen, as shown in *Figure 17.16*. A list of cities appears:

Figure 17.16 – The list icon

3. Swipe left on a city name you want to remove. A **Delete** button appears on the right.
4. Tap the **Delete** button to remove your chosen city from the list of weather forecasts.

Combined with the Clock app, which lets you see the current time in other parts of the world, the Weather app lets you view the weather conditions in those same areas of the world.

Although everyone needs to know the time and weather, not everyone may need to know about the stock market. But even if you don't have any money invested in specific stocks, you may find it interesting to track stocks and business news at the same time.

Viewing stock quotes

The Stocks app lets you view stock quotes and business news. To use the Stocks app, you'll need to add companies you want to follow and remove them when you no longer want to follow them.

To view stock quotes, follow these steps:

1. Tap the **Stocks** app on the Home screen.
2. Tap in the **Search** text field at the top of the screen.
3. Type a part of or the entire company's stock quote symbol, such as AAPL for Apple. A list of possible stock quote matches appears, as shown in *Figure 17.17*:

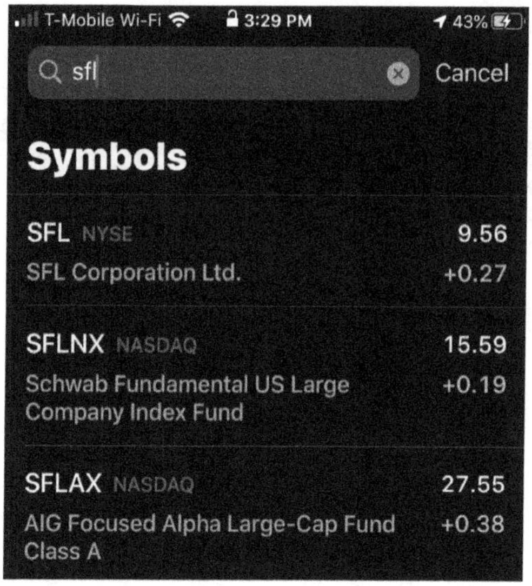

Figure 17.17 – Searching for a specific stock quote

4. Tap on the stock quote you want. The latest financial news for that company appears, as shown in *Figure 17.18*:

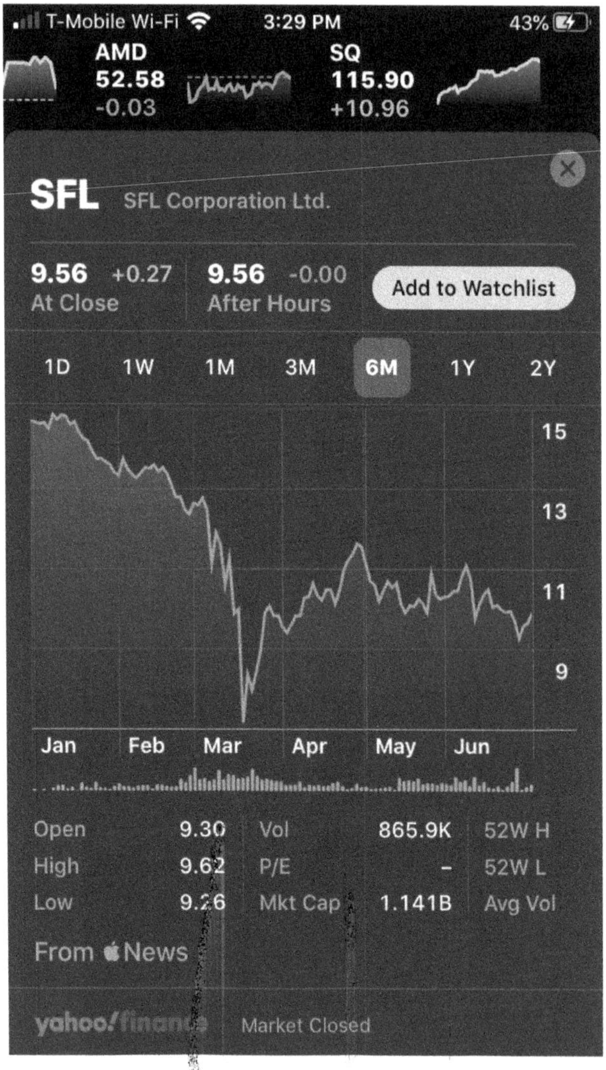

Figure 17.18 – Financial news about a particular company

5. Tap **Add to Watchlist** to save this company's stock quote in the Stocks app.
6. Tap the close (**x**) icon in the upper-right corner of the financial news to make it go away. At any time, you can tap on a stock quote to see more detailed information.

Once you've created a watchlist of stocks, you can always remove a company from your watchlist at any time by swiping left on that stock quote and tapping the **Remove** button.

Summary

The Clock app can be useful for setting alarms to wake up or go to bed, or to alert you of an upcoming appointment or meeting. You can also use the Clock app to turn your iPhone into a stopwatch or a timer.

The Weather app can be handy to give you forecasts for the next few days in your own city or a city you're planning to visit soon. Besides viewing a forecast, you can also view the current weather conditions in different parts of the world.

The Stocks app can help you keep track of your stock portfolio so that you can see how much money you've made or lost.

Since tracking money can be handy, you might also want to learn how to make contactless payments through Apple Pay, which is the topic of the next chapter.

18
Using Apple Pay

Many people still carry cash, but cash can be lost or stolen, and carrying a lot of cash can be cumbersome. Thus, many people rely on credit and debit cards instead.

Although credit and debit cards can be lost or stolen too, they're so much easier to carry than large amounts of cash. However, one huge problem with credit and debit cards is that their numbers can be stolen and used by thieves.

To protect your credit and debit card numbers from thieves, Apple introduced Apple Pay. The main idea behind Apple Pay is that you use an existing credit or debit card, but instead of giving out that credit or debit card to merchants, you use Apple Pay instead, which hides your credit or debit card number. By protecting your credit or debit card number from merchants, Apple Pay reduces the threat of others stealing your crucial credit or debit card numbers by hacking into a merchant's network.

Since Apple Pay is linked to your iPhone, it requires Touch ID (your fingerprint) or Face ID (your face) to authorize payment either in person or online. So, not only does Apple Pay protect your credit or debit card numbers, but it also prevents anyone from getting access to your credit or debit card numbers stored on your iPhone. Apple Pay offers a safe and secure way to make purchases.

> **Important note:**
> Apple Pay may not be available in all areas of the world.

The topics this chapter covers are as follows:

- Setting up Apple Pay
- Defining a shipping address
- Paying with Apple Pay
- Getting an Apple Card

Setting up Apple Pay

Before you can use Apple Pay, you must already have a valid credit or debit card. Once you have a valid credit or debit card, or if you apply for an **Apple Card**, then you can set up Apple Pay by following these steps:

1. Tap the **Wallet** app on the Home Screen. The **Wallet** screen appears.
2. Tap the + icon in the upper-right corner of the screen. A **Card Type** screen appears, as shown in *Figure 18.1*:

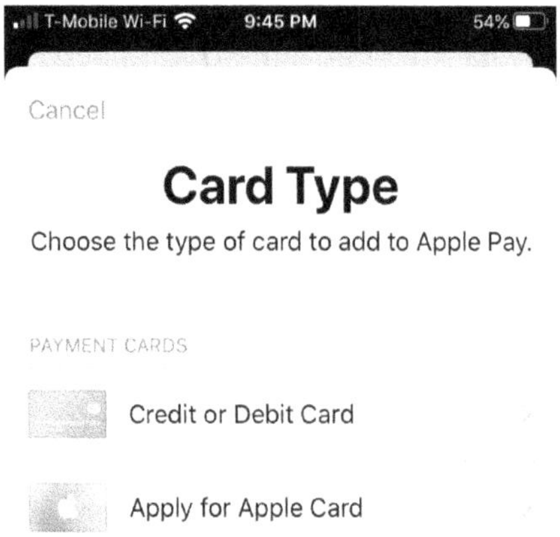

Figure 18.1 – The Card Type screen

3. Tap **Credit or Debit Card**. An **Apple Pay** screen appears.
4. Tap **Continue**. An **Add Card** screen appears that lets you either manually enter credit card numbers or scan an image using the iPhone camera.
5. Scan your credit or debit card with the iPhone camera and tap **Next**. A **Card Details** screen appears.

> **Important note:**
>
> Apple Pay's photo-detection method only works with embossed numbers. If your credit or debit card has flat numbers, you will have to enter the numbers manually.

6. Type the expiration date and security code for the credit or debit card and tap **Next**.
7. Follow the remaining on-screen instructions. You will need to choose a verification method such as receiving an email, text, or phone call to receive a verification code that you will need to enter on the screen to complete the process.

Depending on your bank, you may need to go through another step to authorize your credit or debit card for Apple Pay. Once you go through this additional authentication process, you'll be ready to start using Apple Pay with your chosen credit or debit card.

Adding multiple cards to your Apple Pay account

You can actually assign multiple credit or debit cards to your Apple Pay account. Then, you can choose which card to use when you use Apple Pay by defining a default card to use.

To change the default card to use if you have assigned multiple cards to an Apple Pay account, follow these steps:

1. Tap the **Settings** app on the Home Screen. The **Settings** screen appears.
2. Tap **Wallet & Apple Pay**. The **Wallet & Apple Pay** screen appears, as shown in *Figure 18.2*:

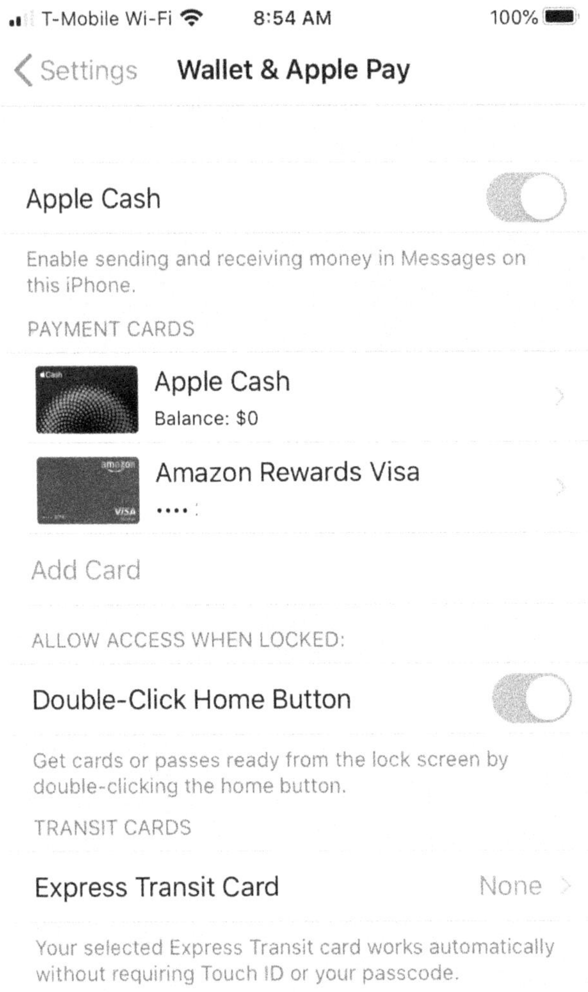

Figure 18.2 – The Wallet & Apple Pay screen

3. Scroll down and tap **Default Card**. A **Default Card** screen appears, listing all the credit and debit cards stored in your Apple Pay account.
4. Tap the card you want to use.

Removing cards from your Apple Pay account

If you have added a credit or debit card to Apple Pay and later want to remove it, follow these steps:

1. Tap the **Settings** app on the Home Screen. The **Settings** screen appears.
2. Tap **Wallet & Apple Pay**. The **Wallet & Apple Pay** screen appears (see *Figure 18.2*).
3. Tap the credit or debit card you want to remove. More detailed information about that card appears.
4. Scroll all the way down and tap **Remove This Card**.

Once you've defined a credit or debit card to use with Apple Pay, you should also define a shipping address. This way, if you purchase items online using Apple Pay, your iPhone can send your shipping address to the merchant automatically so that you won't have to type in your address yourself.

Defining a shipping address

A shipping address defines where you want goods to be sent when you purchase them online. If you move or simply want to ship items to another address other than a home address, you should define a shipping address for Apple Pay to use.

To define a shipping address for Apple Pay, follow these steps:

1. Tap the **Settings** app on the Home Screen.
2. Tap **Wallet & Apple Pay**. The **Wallet & Apple Pay** screen appears (see *Figure 18.2*).
3. Tap **Shipping Address**. A **Shipping Address** screen appears.
4. If multiple addresses appear, tap on the address you want to use by default. If you want to add a new address, tap **Enter New Shipping Address**.

Any time you change addresses, make sure you update your shipping address to ensure that any packages you order get sent to your current location.

Paying with Apple Pay

When you're in a store that accepts Apple Pay, you can use your iPhone to pay for merchandise. Even if you have the credit card itself with you, it's safer to use Apple Pay because it won't let a merchant store your credit or debit card numbers, which an unauthorized person could steal off that merchant's network.

You can use Apple Pay whenever you see one of the following two symbols, as shown in *Figure 18.3*:

Figure 18.3 – The Wallet & Apple Pay screen

To use Apple Pay with Face ID, follow these steps:

1. Double-tap the side button and glance at your phone to authorize Apple Pay.
2. Hold your iPhone near the contactless reader until a checkmark appears on your screen.

To use Apple Pay with Touch ID, follow these steps:

1. Rest your finger on the Home button, which contains the fingerprint recognizer.
2. Hold your iPhone near the contactless reader until a checkmark appears on your screen.

As you use Apple Pay, you may want to review your recent transactions to help you track your spending habits.

Viewing past transactions

When you make purchases with Apple Pay, some banks (but not all) will store your recent transactions so that you can view them again in two different ways. To view Apple Pay transactions through the Wallet app, follow these steps:

1. Tap the **Wallet** app on the Home Screen. Your default Apple Pay credit or debit card appears.
2. Tap **Credit or Debit Card**. A list of transactions appears, as shown in *Figure 18.4*:

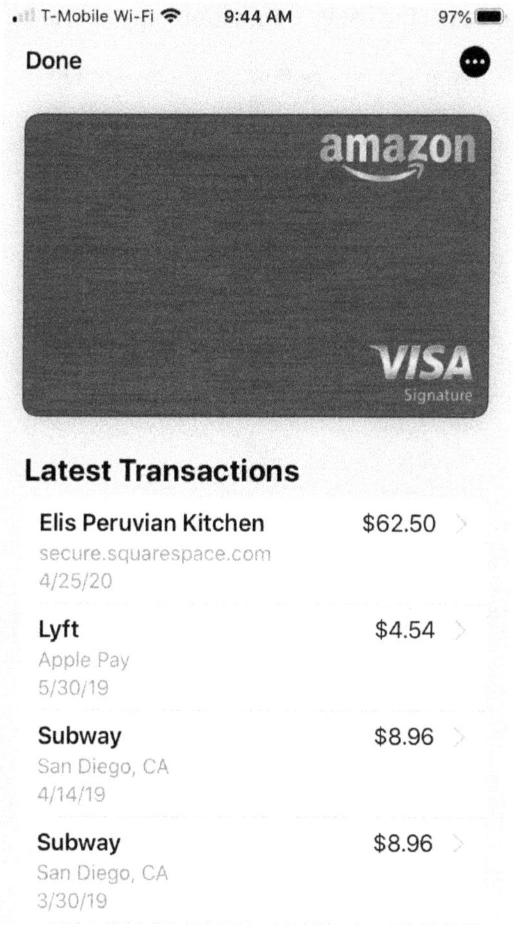

Figure 18.4 – Viewing Apple Pay transactions from the Wallet app

Another way to view recent Apple Pay transactions is through the Settings app, which you can view by following these steps:

1. Tap the **Settings** app on the Home Screen.
2. Tap **Wallet & Apple Pay**. The **Wallet & Apple Pay** screen appears (see *Figure 18.2*).
3. Tap a payment card.

4. Tap the **Transactions** tab. The list of transactions appears, as shown in *Figure 18.5*:

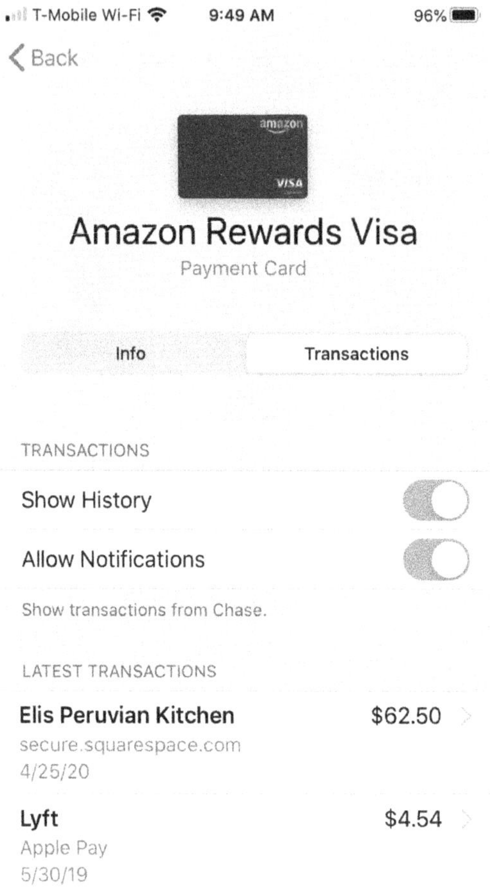

Figure 18.5 – Viewing Apple Pay transactions from the Settings app

Apple Pay is meant to provide a secure form of payment using an existing credit card. Since Apple Pay is meant to provide contactless payments, you might prefer to dedicate a credit card just for Apple Pay. For many people, such a dedicated Apple Pay credit card could be Apple's own credit card, known as **Apple Card**.

Getting an Apple Card

An Apple Card is a credit card created by Apple but issued by **Goldman Sachs**. Although the Apple Card's primary purpose is to link with Apple Pay, Apple will send you a physical Apple credit card to use in places that accept credit cards but do not accept Apple Pay.

To apply for an Apple Card through your iPhone, follow these steps:

1. Tap the **Wallet** app on the Home Screen. The **Wallet** screen appears.
2. Tap the + icon in the upper-right corner of the screen. A **Card Type** screen appears (see *Figure 18.1*).
3. Tap **Apply for Apple Card**. An Apple Card application screen appears, as shown in *Figure 18.6*:

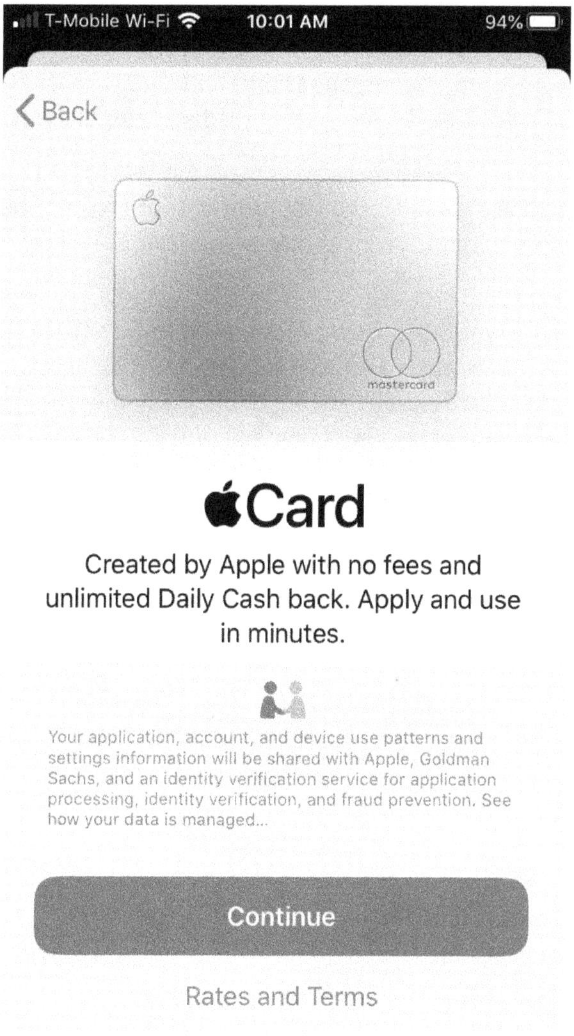

Figure 18.6 – Applying for an Apple Card

4. Tap **Continue** and follow the instructions.

Remember, just because you apply for an Apple Card, does not mean you will automatically get one. To better understand the approval process for an Apple Card and the various features available with the Apple Card, visit Apple's website (`https://www.apple.com/apple-card/financial-health`).

Summary

Every few years, the news releases a story about how hackers have broken into the computer network of a major corporation and stolen all the credit card numbers that the company stored from their customers. Since you can't protect your credit or debit card number once it's stored on another company's computers, you can do the next best thing and protect your credit or debit card from getting read and stored by merchants in the first place.

By using Apple Pay whenever possible, you can protect your credit or debit card numbers because that information will never be given to any merchants, whether you shop online or in-person.

Since Apple Pay is linked to your fingerprint (Touch ID) or face (Face ID), it's extremely difficult for anyone to use your Apple Pay account without your permission. So, Apple Pay protects your credit or debit card numbers from thieves, whether they try to steal your credit or debit card numbers from another company or try to steal your iPhone.

Apple Pay can turn your iPhone into a secure, contactless payment system. With Apple Pay, the risk of hackers or thieves stealing your credit or debit card numbers drops dramatically.

Other Books You May Enjoy

If you enjoyed this book, you may be interested in these other books by Packt:

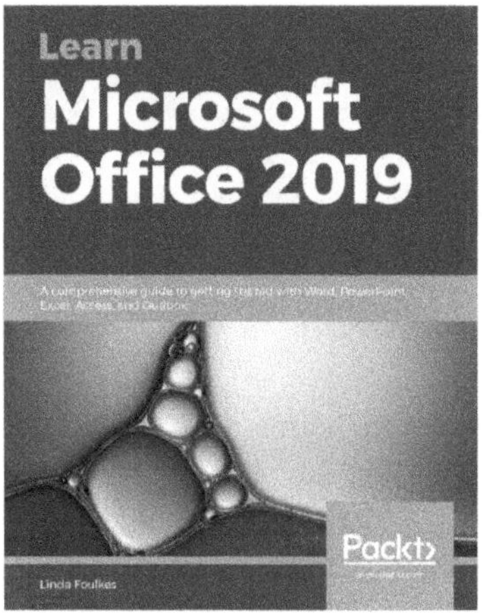

Learn Microsoft Office 2019
Linda Foulkes

ISBN: 978-1-83921-725-8

- Use PowerPoint 2019 effectively to create engaging presentations
- Gain working knowledge of Excel formulas and functions
- Collaborate using Word 2019 tools, and create and format tables and professional documents
- Organize emails, calendars, meetings, contacts, and tasks with Outlook 2019
- Store information for reference, reporting, and analysis using Access 2019
- Discover new functionalities such as Translator, Read Aloud, Scalable Vector Graphics (SVG), and data analysis tools that are useful for working professionals

Hands-On Microsoft Teams
João Ferreira

ISBN: 978-1-83921-398-4

- Create teams, channels, and tabs in Microsoft Teams
- Explore the Teams architecture and various Office 365 components included in Teams
- Perform scheduling, and managing meetings and live events in Teams
- Configure and manage apps in Teams
- Design automated scripts for managing a Teams environment using PowerShell
- Build your own Microsoft Teams app without writing code

Leave a review - let other readers know what you think

Please share your thoughts on this book with others by leaving a review on the site that you bought it from. If you purchased the book from Amazon, please leave us an honest review on this book's Amazon page. This is vital so that other potential readers can see and use your unbiased opinion to make purchasing decisions, we can understand what our customers think about our products, and our authors can see your feedback on the title that they have worked with Packt to create. It will only take a few minutes of your time, but is valuable to other potential customers, our authors, and Packt. Thank you!

Index

A

B

C

D

E

F

G

H

I

J

L

M

N

O

T

U

V

W

www.ingramcontent.com/pod-product-compliance
Lightning Source LLC
Chambersburg PA
CBHW081455050326
40690CB00015B/2807
* 9 7 8 1 8 3 8 6 4 1 0 1 6 *